Sales

CAROLINA ACADEMIC PRESS
Context and Practice Series
Michael Hunter Schwartz
Series Editor

Civil Procedure for All States
Benjamin V. Madison, III

Contracts
Michael Hunter Schwartz and Denise Riebe

Current Issues in Constitutional Litigation
Sarah E. Ricks, with contributions by Evelyn M. Tenenbaum

Employment Discrimination
Susan Grover, Sandra F. Sperino, and Jarod S. Gonzalez

Sales
Edith R. Warkentine

The Lawyer's Practice
Kris Franklin

Sales

A Context and Practice Casebook

Edith R. Warkentine

WESTERN STATE UNIVERSITY COLLEGE OF LAW

Carolina Academic Press

Durham, North Carolina

ISBN 978-1-59460-950-3
LCCN 2011931455

Carolina Academic Press
700 Kent Street
Durham, NC 27701
Telephone (919) 489-7486
Fax (919) 493-5668
www.cap-press.com

Printed in the United States of America

To my parents, Albert and Ruth Resnick, who showed me how to be a good person and how to live a good life; they lived long lives, but not long enough for those of us who knew and loved them.

Contents

Table of Principal Cases

Series Editor's Preface

Welcome to a new type of law text. Designed by leading experts in law school teaching and learning, Context and Practice casebooks assist law professors and their students to work together to learn, minimize stress, and prepare for the rigors and joys of practicing law. **Student learning and preparation for law practice are the guiding ethics of these books.**

Why would we depart from the tried and true? Why have we abandoned the legal education model by which we were trained? Because legal education can and must improve.

In Spring 2007, the Carnegie Foundation published *Educating Lawyers: Preparation for the Practice of Law* and the Clinical Legal Education Association published *Best Practices for Legal Education*. Both works reflect in-depth efforts to assess the effectiveness of modern legal education, and both conclude that legal education, as presently practiced, falls quite short of what it can and should be. Both works criticize law professors' rigid adherence to a single teaching technique, the inadequacies of law school assessment mechanisms, and the dearth of law school instruction aimed at teaching law practice skills and inculcating professional values. Finally, the authors of both books express concern that legal education may be harming law students. Recent studies show that law students, in comparison to all other graduate students, have the highest levels of depression, anxiety and substance abuse.

The problems with traditional law school instruction begin with the textbooks law teachers use. Law professors cannot implement *Educating Lawyers* and *Best Practices* using texts designed for the traditional model of legal education. Moreover, even though our understanding of how people learn has grown exponentially in the past 100 years, no law school text to date even purports to have been designed with educational research in mind.

The Context and Practice Series is an effort to offer a genuine alternative. Grounded in learning theory and instructional design and written with *Educating Lawyers* and *Best Practices* in mind, Context and Practice casebooks make it easy for law professors to change.

I welcome reactions, criticisms, and suggestions; my e-mail address is michael. schwartz@washburn.edu. Knowing the author(s) of these books, I know they, too, would appreciate your input; we share a common commitment to student learning. In fact, students, if your professor cares enough about your learning to have adopted this book, I bet s/he would welcome your input, too!

Professor Michael Hunter Schwartz, Series Designer and Editor
Co-Director, Institute for Law Teaching and Learning
Associate Dean for Faculty and Academic Development
Washburn University School of Law

Preface

This student-centered book draws on a wide variety of teaching materials that I developed over a twenty-year teaching career. I am indebted to generations of law students who challenged me to find effective ways to introduce difficult and often obtuse material. My two primary objectives are:

- To help law students further develop analytical skills, with a particular emphasis on statutory interpretation; and

- To provide students with an opportunity to master the substantive law of Article 2 of the Uniform Commercial Code.

Book Organization and Coverage

This book begins with a quick overview of the entire U.C.C. Because statutory analysis is at the core of the course, the book then discusses how to read and apply a statute. Thereafter, Sales doctrine is introduced in the order that students should follow when analyzing a sales problem. The material on contract formation is found in Chapter 4, but more advanced formation issues are reserved for special treatment at the end of the book. Your professor may wish to address all of that material at the same time. After all of the doctrinal material has been covered, the final book chapter presents a series of comprehensive problems that will help students to review and "put it all together."

Each chapter follows the same organizational approach. Beginning in Chapter 3, each chapter begins with a Sales Graphic Organizer, followed by a Chapter Problem, depicting the overall coverage of Article 2. The organizer is highlighted to identify the subject studied in that chapter, and to help you remember where that subject fits in the "big picture." Next, a table summarizes the code sections to be studied in that chapter, and highlights key phrases, terms or concepts whose definitions must be learned. Each chapter includes descriptive text, one or two cases or excerpts from cases, and several smaller exercises that draw on the material studied in that chapter and require students to select and apply the applicable code sections to solve the problems. At the end of the chapter is a list of additional resources, including ALR annotations, law review articles, and cases.

Professor Douglas Whaley, a renowned professor and himself the author of seven textbooks on contracts and commercial law, suggested that when writing a textbook, the author follow this basic guideline: "give the students enough understanding that they know the basics and can avoid malpractice by looking up the subtleties when they arise later in life. If you teach too many details, the students end up overloaded and top heavy, so that the basics elude them."[1] I have followed that guideline in this book; as a result,

---

1. Douglas J. Whaley, Commentary: Teaching Law: Thoughts on Retirement, 68 Ohio St. L.J. 1387, 1400 (2007).

not every section of Article 2 is discussed, nor is there an exercise or problem illustrating all of the legal issues raised in Article 2. However, the book teaches you all of the tools you will need successfully to attack an Article 2 problem.

How To Use This Book

This book is **deceptively** short. The "star" of the book is the text of the Uniform Commercial Code, and its Official Comments. You must purchase and use a complete version of the text of the Code and the Comments. You will need to spend a significant amount of time reading the statute and the official comments. For emphasis, I have included excerpts of text and comments in the book.[2]

The book does include cases, but only a limited number of cases, and the cases have not been heavily edited. I have, however, omitted many footnotes. When footnotes are included, I have placed them in brackets [ ] within the text. The purpose of including cases in this format is to prepare you to read cases as lawyers read cases—unedited—and to prepare you to use the cases as lawyers use cases—to solve problems.

To get the most out of this book, read the Chapter Problem as you begin each new chapter. You will not be prepared to analyze the problem fully until you have completed the entire chapter, but reviewing the Chapter Problem initially will help to provide context for the material you will be studying. Next, read each of the code sections indicated in the table of code sections for that chapter, along with the Official Comments. Read difficult sections *aloud*. Deconstruct each section. **Do not skip this step!** Students who have been successful in my Sales classes all emphasize that they spent a lot of time reading the statute and the official comments. In addition, be sure that you have your Code open and that you refer to it frequently, as you read the text that explains each code section.

After you complete the assigned reading, including the Code, you are ready to read and prepare your answers to the chapter exercises. I purposely do not indicate what code sections you will have to consult to work through the exercises—learning how to find the appropriate code sections is an essential part of what this course is about. In class, be prepared to discuss how you selected the applicable code sections, and how you applied them to reach a conclusion. Work on the shorter exercises first. When you think you have mastered the material in the chapter, return to the Chapter Problem and try to **write** out a complete analysis.

The book uses visual aids extensively, to help students picture how the individual code sections fit together to reach a conclusion. It has been my experience that students who do not customarily use visual aids such as those contained in this book find them to be extremely helpful. Students who customarily prepare their own flowcharts continue to prepare their own material, but they tell me that they nevertheless use the figures in the book to help them refine their own work. **All students should always keep in mind that the original sources, the statute and the Official Comments, are the primary authority on which they should rely for analysis.** Everything else can be used, if helpful, but never to the exclusion of the statute itself.

---

2. Uniform Commercial Code, copyright by The American Law Institute and the National Conference of Commissioners on Uniform State Laws. Reproduced with the permission of the Permanent Editorial Board for the Uniform Commercial Code. All rights reserved.

Finally, I have included a list of "additional resources" at the end of each chapter, for the students who always come up after class and request some additional reading. If you are not one of those students, you can easily be successful in this course without ever consulting any of the cited material.

Acknowledgments

I would never have written this book but for the encouragement and support of many people. The initial impetus came from Ryan Bay, Western State University College of Law (WSU) Class of 2010, who first told me what he would like to see in a text book, and then told me he had time in his final semester of law school to help me get started. Next, my dad, who had no legal training, but had a great brain and good writing skills, read every word I wrote (and critiqued everything). We decided if he could understand what I wrote, then so would my students. Professor Patricia Leary, my colleague from Whittier Law School, who is primarily a torts, criminal law and constitutional law expert, read the early chapters of the book and her help was astounding. As I worked on the first version of the book, Ashley Crowder and Cindy Hackler, also WSU Class of 2010, helped tremendously. Not only did they give me feedback on every chapter, but they are also largely responsible for all of the tables and flowcharts in the book. Heather Antonie, also WSU Class of 2010, our former law review editor, went over everything with a fine tooth comb. Pam Halverson did all of the typing of the original chapters—she kept her cool as I would hand her a chapter just in time for it to be finalized and distributed to the students for the next class! Then, ALL of my students in the Fall Sales classes evaluated each chapter. Their comments were invaluable. I asked for thoughtful evaluations and they took the time to give very specific, very meaningful feedback. I have incorporated many of their suggestions into this revised version of the book. Michael Deal, Kaleen Harris, and Guillermo Tello, WSU Class of 2011, sat down and went over the revisions with me, chapter-by-chapter. Finally, Kaleen and Heather helped edit the manuscript that went off to the publisher.

I also want to thank Associate Dean Susan Keller, who first suggested that I talk to Michael Schwartz about publishing my book in this Context and Practice series, Mike for his support and help and editorial feedback, and Western State University College of Law for the sabbatical and research assistants that gave me the time and help I needed to get this book finished.

I am indebted to Professor Sidney De Long, Seattle University School of Law, who graciously shared with me the materials he created and uses in his own Sales class. I have always thought his discussion of how to analyze a statute is one of the best I've seen, and he has been kind enough to permit me to adapt and use that discussion in Chapter 2 of this book.

My goal was to produce a very student-friendly book that would help students learn how to do statutory analysis while learning the law of Sales under U.C.C. Article 2. If I have succeeded, it is only because of the support and encouragement of all of these folks. Any defects and flaws that remain in the book are my own.

I lost my dad in January 2011, just as I began the task of finalizing the next version of this book for publication. He was to have helped me on this project as well. With a heavy heart, I am completing it in his honor.

Edith R. Warkentine
Spring 2011

Sales

Chapter 1

The Uniform Commercial Code ("U.C.C.")

1. Uniform Commercial Code Overview

The focus of this course is U.C.C. Article 2. However, before we focus on Article 2, you must first be introduced to the entire U.C.C.[1] Most law students are somewhat familiar with the U.C.C. because they studied portions of Article 2 in their Contracts classes. Therefore, this chapter presents only a quick overview of the U.C.C. It next emphasizes important parts of Article 1, which you will need to learn and use whenever you solve a sales problem, and then introduces Article 2.

Figure 1-1 on the next page gives you a quick glimpse at the basic coverage of the U.C.C. What else do you need to know? Does the title accurately describe the statute? Critics suggest that the U.C.C. is not really "uniform." No state has adopted the U.C.C. verbatim; moreover, there are conflicting judicial interpretations of certain code provisions; hence, it is not truly "uniform." The U.C.C. does not apply solely to "commercial" transactions. A common student misconception is that the U.C.C. applies only to transactions involving "merchants." However, except for specific provisions of the U.C.C., it applies equally to transactions when one or both of the parties are not merchants. Hence, it is not truly "commercial." Indeed, it is not really a "code" in the civil law sense of the meaning of the term.[2] However, it is one of the most successful of the uniform laws to be promulgated by its sponsors, the Uniform Law Commission (ULC)[3] and the American Law Institute (ALI).[4] The U.C.C. has been enacted into law, with some variation, in every state in the United States. It addresses almost every aspect of a typical commercial transaction. U.C.C.

---

1. Unless otherwise stated in this book, all references to sections are to U.C.C. sections. The U.C.C. is sometimes referred to as "the Code."

2. Grant Gilmore, one of its drafters, said: "The Uniform Commercial Code, so-called, is not that sort of Code—even in theory.... We shall do better to think of it as a big statute—or a collection of statutes bound together in the same book—which goes as far as it goes but no further. It assumes the continuing existence of a large body of pre-Code and non-Code law on which it rests for support, which it displaces to the least possible extent, and without which it could not survive."Grant Gilmore, *Article 9: What It Does for the Past*, 26 La.L. Rev. 285, 285-86 (1966).

3. The ULC was formerly known as the National Conference of Commissioners on Uniform State Laws. Its website states: "[It] has worked for the uniformity of state laws since 1892. It is a non-profit unincorporated association, comprised of state commissions on uniform laws from each state, the District of Columbia, the Commonwealth of Puerto Rico, and the U.S. Virgin Islands. Each jurisdiction determines the method of appointment and the number of commissioners actually appointed. Most jurisdictions provide for their commission by statute." http://www.nccusl.org/Update/Desktop Default.aspx?tabindex=0&tabid=11 (last visited June 21, 2010).

4. According to its website, the American Law Institute is the leading independent organization in the United States producing scholarly work to clarify, modernize, and otherwise improve the law. http://www.ali.org/ (last visited June 21, 2010).

3

Figure 1-1: Uniform Commercial Code Overview

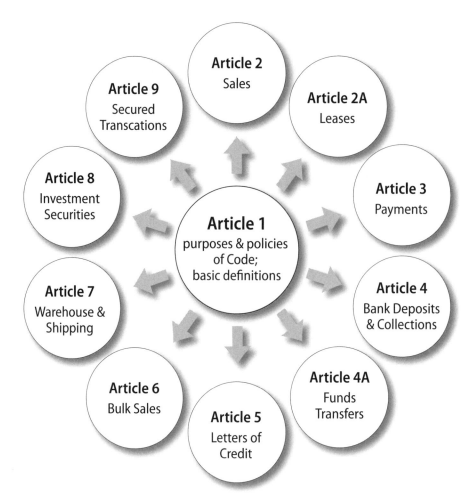

Article 1 is applicable to all of the other U.C.C. articles. It contains basic definitions and some of the most important concepts students need to learn and use whenever they solve a U.C.C. problem. Article 2, Sales, contains the rules applicable to contract formation, performance, breach and remedies when there is a transaction in goods. Article 2A contains similar rules to govern leases of goods. Articles 3, 4, 4A and 5 concern payment. Article 6 governs bulk sales,[5] and Article 7 deals with shipment and storage of goods. Article 8 governs investment securities, and Article 9 addresses secured financing.[6] Articles 10 and 11 contain transition provisions, which determine what version of the U.C.C. applies to a transaction based on the date of the transaction and the effective date of different versions of the Code.

---

5. Bulk sales are defined in section 6-102(c). The U.C.C. sponsors recommend the repeal of this Article, and a majority of states have followed that recommendation.

6. Article 8's coverage appears to be a departure from the U.C.C.'s otherwise consistent coverage, mirroring "standard" commercial transactions; however, it is frequently used in connection with Article 9 financing.

Because the U.C.C. is a statute, students should always begin their analysis of a legal problem by reviewing the applicable part(s) of the statute. Therefore, they should always have a copy of the U.C.C., with its Official Comments, on hand.[7] Students find it helpful to put index tabs in their copy of the U.C.C., so that they quickly can move from article to article, and so that they quickly can find important definitions. Before you read the rest of this chapter, look at your copy of the U.C.C. Start with the Table of Contents, which lists every article by title. Note how code sections are constructed. Each article in the U.C.C. is divided into parts, which are further divided into sections. The sections are sometimes divided into subsections. The U.C.C. sections consist of four-digit numbers, representing the article, part and section number. Thus, in *Figure 1-2*, the code section is in Article 2, Part 2, section 07. You will recognize that section as section 2-207 ("two-two-oh-seven," or "twenty-two-oh-seven.")

Figure 1-2: Construction of a U.C.C. Code Section

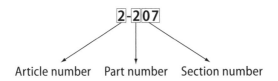

Article number   Part number   Section number

2. Article 1

Next, look at the table of contents to Article 1 that appears at the beginning of that article. It provides a convenient outline of Article 1's contents. Note the scope of Article 1. Section 1-102 states, "This article applies to a transaction to the extent that it is governed by another article of the Uniform Commercial Code." Section 1-102 therefore tells you that when you analyze a problem within the scope of Article 2, you need to incorporate the applicable general provisions of Article 1 in your analysis. Students will find themselves constantly referring to certain sections in Article 1, especially 1-103 (rules of construction; U.C.C. purposes and policies), 1-202 (notice; knowledge), 1-205 (reasonable time; seasonableness), 1-302 (variation by agreement), 1-303 (course of performance, course of dealing and usage of trade), 1-304 (good faith) and 1-305 (remedies to be liberally administered).

The concepts of course of performance, course of dealing and usage of trade are so important throughout the Sales course that we introduce them now. The basic notion is that when parties have been performing a specific contract in a particular way (*course of performance*), it makes sense that their performance reflects their understanding of the contract. Accordingly, if a dispute arises over a specific term, and the parties have previously acted in a way that sheds light on the meaning of that term, their course of performance is important to explain what the parties intended that specific term to mean. For example, if an installment contract provides for payment "within five days" of an event and the parties have always made and accepted payment within five *business* days of that event, their *course of performance* shows that they must have meant that five business days rather than five calendar days would be used to calculate the time for

---

7. For convenience, most law professors teach from the uniform version of the U.C.C., rather than the version enacted in a particular state. Of course, practitioners must consult the version of the Code that is the law of their state.

payment. Similarly, if parties had several contracts in the past for the same goods as are the subject of a new contract, and each of the past contracts contained a particular term, if the parties leave that term out of the new contract, it is likely that they both intended the same term to prevail, but "took it for granted" because of their past history. Thus, their past *course of dealing* is probative to understand their current contract. Finally, where the contract parties both have experience in a particular trade, and in that trade a term has a particular meaning, or most contracts contain that particular term, it is very possible that they assumed that term would be part of their contract, even if they did not express it. Therefore, the *usage of trade* can shed light on the parties' intention with respect to their current contract. *Figure 1-3* suggests an easy way to remember what each of these terms represents.

Figure 1-3: Understanding Course of Performance, Course of Dealing, Usage of Trade

Course of Performance ⟶ Same parties: same contract
Course of Dealing   ⟶ Same parties: different contract
Usage of Trade   ⟶ Different parties: different contract

Exercise 1-1: Course of Performance, Course of Dealing, Usage of Trade

Read the Code's definition of "agreement" and "contract" in section 1-201. What is the relationship between "agreement" and "contract," on the one hand, and course of performance, course of dealing, and usage of trade, on the other hand?

3. The Official Comments

Each Code section is followed by an Official Comment. The drafters wrote the Official Comments to clarify or expand on the statutory text. On occasion, you will see an Official Comment that seems to contradict the statute. Be careful! Remember that although the Comments are sometimes easier to read than the statutory text, they are not part of the statutory text. When state legislatures enact the Code, they do not enact the Official Comments as law. Accordingly, the Official Comments are neither law, nor do they have the force of legislative history. Nevertheless, even if the Comments are neither statutes nor legislative history, they are very persuasive authority. Technically, if a Comment conflicts with the text of the Code, the Code controls. But the vast majority of courts, commentators, and lawyers consider the Comments of virtually equal status with the Code, citing the Comments liberally to construe the Code's meaning.

Exercise 1-2: The Official Comments

Skim the Official Comments to sections 1-201, 1-301, 2-104 and 2-105. You will find that collectively they contain all of the types of information that you can typically expect to find in the Official Comments. List at least eight types of information contained in the Official Comments.

---

4. U.C.C. Amendments

The U.C.C. has been amended several times since its promulgation. In 2003, after many long years of debate and negotiation, the sponsors published a revised Article 2. However, no states ever adopted revised Article 2, and on May 11, 2011, the American Law Institute withdrew the 2003 proposed amendments to Articles 2 and 2A from the Official Text of the UCC.[8] For that reason, this book continues to study the "old" (pre-2003) version of Article 2. However, Article 1 was revised in 2001, and the revised version has now been adopted in more than half of the states in the United States.[9] Therefore, although all references to Article 2 are to the "old" Article 2, all references to Article 1 are to the "new" (post-2001) Article 1. When you read cases, you should keep in mind that Article 1 was recently revised, and citations to Article 1 in many cases are to the "old" Article 1. For convenience, the Appendix contains a table reflecting the differences between the "old" and the "new" Article 1.[10]

5. Relationship of U.C.C. to Other Laws

As you study the U.C.C., you will encounter many familiar concepts. You have studied some of these concepts in your Contracts, Torts, or Property classes. The U.C.C. supersedes some of these areas of common law. However, in many other instances, common law supplements the U.C.C. You will find, therefore, that this course is a helpful review of many common law concepts. Section 1-103 makes the key statement of the relationship between the U.C.C. and common law. It provides both that (1) the U.C.C. may displace other bodies of law (In other words, if there is a conflict between the U.C.C. and common law, the U.C.C. prevails.) and (2) unless displaced by particular provisions of the U.C.C., the principles of law and equity *supplement* the Code.

You will need to refer back to section 1-103 constantly, when Article 2 does not spell out a legal rule necessary for your analysis, so that you can supplement Article 2 with common law rules.

---

8. If you are interested in reading about the reasons why, see William H. Henning, *Amended Article 2: What Went Wrong?* 11 Duq. Bus. L.J. 131 (2009).

9. As of March 1, 2010, Revised Article 1 was in effect in thirty-seven states: Alabama, Alaska, Arizona, Arkansas, California, Colorado, Connecticut, Delaware, Florida, Hawaii, Idaho, Illinois, Indiana, Iowa, Kansas, Kentucky, Louisiana, Maine, Minnesota, Montana, Nebraska, Nevada, New Hampshire, New Mexico, North Carolina, North Dakota, Oklahoma, Oregon, Pennsylvania, Rhode Island, South Dakota, Tennessee, Texas, Utah, Vermont, Virginia, and West Virginia. http://ucclaw.blogspot.com/2010/03/ucc-legislative-update.html (last visited Aug. 12, 2010).

10. *See* Appendix 1, *infra*.

Figure 1-4: Life Cycle of a Sales Transaction

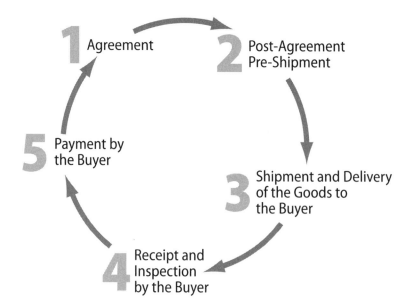

6. Article 2 Overview

Before we study the "trees" (the individual sections and official comments) in Article 2, take a quick look at the entire "forest" (an overview of the contents of Article 2). It is easier to understand the individual code sections by first looking at the entire forest. Also, this section introduces some key concepts that you will continue to encounter as you work with Article 2.

Article 2 is organized chronologically, corresponding to the events in the life of a contract, as shown in *Figure 1-4*. In this text, we study, in depth, several issues that you first encountered in Contracts, such as contract formation and remedies. We also study other issues that you encountered in Torts, i.e., implied warranties. Finally, you encounter new concepts, such as shipping terms and risk of loss.

Some legal scholars suggest that the easiest way to understand Article 2 is to recognize that its organizational framework follows the life cycle of a sales transaction through five stages shown in *Figure 1-4*.[11] If a contract is performed as the parties intended at the time of contracting, after the contract is performed successfully, the parties are likely to enter into subsequent agreements, and the cycle repeats itself.

Students with a business background often find this analytic approach to be very meaningful. However, most students are more comfortable with an approach that poses a series of questions relating to the chronology of contract formation and performance, which

---

11. Richard E. Speidel, Robert S. Summers & James J. White, *Commercial Law Teaching Materials* 404-411 (4th Edition 1987).

is the order that this book follows. *Figure 1-5* is a list of the questions we will address, with an indication of where this book discusses those questions. You can use this series of questions as your basic outline for analyzing a Code problem.

Figure 1-5: A Question/Checklist Approach to Article 2

Is the transaction within the SCOPE of Article 2? (*Chapter 3*)
Is there a CONTRACT? (*Chapter 4*)
Are there any DEFENSES to formation? (*Chapter 5*)
What are the TERMS of the contract? (*Chapters 6, 7 and 8*)
What are the respective PERFORMANCE obligations of the parties? (*Chapter 9*)
Is there any legal EXCUSE for non-performance? (*Chapter 10*)
Has either party failed to perform? (BREACH) (*Chapter 11*)
What are appropriate REMEDIES for breach? (*Chapter 12*)

Exercise 1-3: Article 2 Overview

Figure 1-5 suggests a checklist approach to Article 2, and indicates where this book addresses each topic. Fill in the following table to indicate what Part of Article 2 addresses each topic.

Topic	Article 2, Part _____
Is the transaction within the SCOPE of Article 2?	
Is there a CONTRACT?	
Are there any DEFENSES to formation?	
What are the TERMS of the contract?	
What are the respective PERFORMANCE obligations of the parties?	
Is there any legal EXCUSE for non-performance?	
Has either party failed to perform? (BREACH)	
What are appropriate REMEDIES for breach?	

This chapter was designed to lay a foundation for the remainder of the course. Now, you are almost ready to begin an intensive study of U.C.C. Article 2. Before going directly to the substantive law, however, Chapter 2 is designed to prepare you for learning from statutes.

Chapter 2

Statutory Analysis

This course is based on a statute; therefore, Chapter 2 teaches how to analyze a statute and apply it to solve a legal problem. Not only is this an important skill for you to learn for this course, but it is also a critically important skill for lawyers in practice. You may have already been introduced to the skill of statutory analysis in other law school classes. If so, some of the material in this chapter will appear to be somewhat basic. However, many students have never had an opportunity to focus on reading and applying statutes before. Therefore, this chapter gives all students the opportunity to gain or refine their statutory analysis skills.

This chapter uses U.C.C. Article 2 as an exemplar statute to teach the process of statutory analysis.[1] This analytical approach will accelerate your ability to read and understand Article 2.

1. The Anatomy of a Modern Statute

New law students learn that most appellate opinions contain the same parts in more or less the same order: facts, procedural history, issue, etc. Students look for these parts when they read cases and organize their case briefs around them.

Similarly, most modern statutes and regulations exhibit a uniform structure. Like cases, statutes contain basically the same parts in basically the same order. Using the parts, students can "brief" or "deconstruct" a statute just as they brief a case. Occasionally, a statute may lack one of these parts, but you can usually find its function being fulfilled by other parts. These parts usually appear in the order shown in *Figure 2-1*, on the next page.

Figure 2-1 describes the parts you may expect to find in a modern statute. Not every statute, however, has exactly one of each of these parts. For example, sometimes there is no specific "scope" provision. Or, there may be more than one section that state rules. Sometimes the same section that states a rule also states the consequences for following (or not following) the stated rule. Sometimes the consequences are stated separately.

Furthermore, most statutes contain other, less important parts: The *title* names the statute. The *effective date* tells when the statute goes into effect and what events it applies to. *Repealer* provisions eliminate inconsistent legislation. *Transition provisions* explain how to transition from a previous law to the current statute. Some statutes contain explicit instructions on

---

1. This chapter is based on materials authored by Professor Sidney DeLong, Seattle University School of Law. Reproduced with permission.

Figure 2-1: Parts of a Modern Statute

Purpose: Why was the statute enacted? This part states the legislators' purpose in enacting the statute and is intended as an aid to interpretation and application. It may include legislative findings about the problems the statute was intended to solve. A statute that is the result of political compromise may assert several inconsistent purposes.

Some statutes omit a purpose provision, necessitating recourse to legislative history. Others simply recite whatever legislative purpose is necessary to the statute's constitutionality.

Scope: a.k.a. "Applicability." What kinds of events or persons does the statute apply to? Some statutes omit the scope provision and the scope must be deduced from the next three parts.

Exclusions: What things that would otherwise be in the scope of the statute are excluded from its coverage? Exclusions often reflect either the existence of conflicting regulations or the political victory of some special interest. Sometimes exclusions are combined with the scope section and sometimes they are hidden in, or inferable from, the definitions.

Definitions: What do the words of the statute mean? Defined words are the terms of art the statute uses. The more modern the statute, the more terms it will define. A defined term is like an algebraic sign whose definition should be plugged into the statutory formula wherever the defined term appears. The more modern the statute, the more technical and less intuitive will be the definitions and the more you will have to be careful to keep them in mind in applying the statute.

Operative Provisions: What does the statute do? This part of the statute is the motor that drives the statute. It usually takes one of three main forms: (1) It prohibits or requires certain acts: "Thou shalt not kill," "All contracts by minors are voidable," (2) It states requirements: "A lender must file a financing statement to perfect a security interest," (3) It states the consequences of the action or omission: "Any lender who omits to state the rate shall forfeit its claim to interest." You can think of the operative provisions as containing the elements of the rule that, if satisfied, lead to a legal consequence.

Consequences: What happens if the statute is complied with or violated? The consequences include private remedies for violating the statute, public penalties for violation, and the legal effect of the actions and omissions that the operative provisions describe.

how to interpret or construe them. A *severability* clause preserves the rest of the statute if part of it is declared to be invalid. Remedies may be made subject to *statutes of limitations*. Certain courts may be given *subject matter jurisdiction* of enforcement actions.

Exercise 2-1: Identifying the Parts of a Statute

This exercise is designed to help you apply what you have learned about a statute to an actual statute that you will be referring to repeatedly throughout this course.

Read U.C.C. Article 1. How many of the parts of a statute listed in *Figure 2-1* can you find? Try to complete the following chart, to show which section of Article 1 corresponds to the identified parts of a statute.

Part of Statute	Article 1 Section Number
Purpose	
Scope	
Exclusions	
Definitions	
Operative Provisions	
Consequences	

Exercise 2-2: Identifying the Parts of a Statute

This exercise gives you an opportunity to reinforce what you learned from Exercise 2-1, while introducing you to a statute that you will often need to consult in connection with a sales transaction.

Repeat Exercise 2-1, using the Uniform Electronic Transactions Act ("UETA").

Part of Statute	UETA Section Number
Purpose	
Scope	
Exclusions	
Definitions	
Operative Provisions	
Consequences	

2. Statutory Language: Rules v. Standards

As you work with statutes, keep in mind the difference between statutory "rules" and statutory "standards."[2] Statutory rules attempt to describe with precision the type of permitted or prohibited activity. Statutory standards, on the other hand, are vaguer. Each has its own advantages and disadvantages. Rules give greater certainty and predictability, but have little flexibility and are often arbitrary. Standards are more flexible but give less certainty. People are encouraged to behave "right up to the edge" of a rule, *e.g.*, if a statute permits driving up to 55 mph, they will drive at 54.5 mph. Standards may have more deterrent power "at the edge" precisely because they are more vague, *e.g.*, if a statute

---

2. This important distinction was explained by Professor Duncan Kennedy in Duncan Kennedy, *Form and Substance in Private Law Adjudication*, 89 Harv. L. Rev. 1685 (1976).

Figure 2-2: Table of Examples of Rules and Standards

Goal	Rule	Standard
Regulate driving behavior	All motor vehicles traveling on a class two highway must not exceed 50 miles per hour.	All motor vehicles traveling on a class two highway must travel at a reasonable rate of speed in light of road conditions.
Impose a notice requirement	"[Notice] satisfies the requirements of subsection (1) against such party *unless written notice of objection to its contents is given within ten days after it is received.*" U.C.C. § 2-201(2) (emphasis added).	"Where the resale is at private sale the seller must give the buyer *reasonable notification* of his intention to resell." U.C.C. § 2-706(3) (emphasis added).

provides for driving at a rate of speed "reasonable under the circumstances," drivers may drive slower in appropriate weather conditions.

Figure 2-2 gives examples of common statutory rules and standards with which you may already be familiar, and adds some examples of each taken from U.C.C. Article 2.

The U.C.C. is replete with the most common legal standard, reasonableness. Sometimes it appears three or four times in the same sentence. The problem is the lack of predictability that this standard creates.

3. Taxonomy of Statutory Disputes

The six general types of disputes that involve statutes are shown in *Figure 2-3*.

Figure 2-3: General Types of Statutory Disputes

(1) Disputes about the **facts** (what happened?)

(2) Disputes over the **validity** of the statute: *e.g.*, is it constitutional? Was it implicitly repealed? Is it preempted by federal law?

(3) Disputes over the **choice of law** to be applied to the dispute: *e.g.*, Does California's tort law apply to a plane crash in Oregon?

(4) Disputes about **classifying** real world events in the terms used by the statute: *e.g*, Is a mobile home a "motor vehicle"? Was the defendant's reliance "reasonable"?

(5) Disputes about statutory **interpretation**: *e.g.*, Does sub-section (b) create an exception to the general rule in part II? Are these requirements to be read in the disjunctive or conjunctive?

(6) Disputes about whether a court should recognize a **non-statutory exception** to the literal application of a valid statute; *e.g.*, Should a murderer be permitted to inherit from the estate of his victim under the inheritance statutes? Should the court recognize an equitable defense to liability under the Sherman Act?

The types of statutory disputes described in *Figure 2-3* are not conceptually watertight. For example, most disputes about classification can be re-cast as disputes about interpretation and vice versa. And an argument about an exception to the statute might be recast as one about classification or interpretation. But most arguments still seem to take one of these forms and some disputes will involve more than one of the forms.

The different parts of a statute come into play in the typical statutory dispute. Thus, in deciding what the meaning of a term is in a classification dispute, you can often get guidance from the purpose clause or the definitions. To decide whether to create an exception to the statute, you might be able to make arguments from the purpose clause or the exclusions.

4. Statutory Analysis, Generally

Statutory analysis can be divided into the basic steps shown in *Figure 2-4*.

Figure 2-4: Basic Steps of Statutory Analysis

Step 1: Scope. Determine whether the statute applies to the problem at hand. Most statutes contain provisions that define their applicability.

Step 2: Deconstruct the statute. The process of deconstructing a statute is the same as the process of identifying the elements of any rule of law. Every law student develops his/her own way of effectually deconstructing or elementizing a rule. I suggest that you always read a statute *aloud* and use punctuation as a key to help identify the parts or elements of the statutory rule.

Step 3: Define Terms. Many statutes contain definitions of key terms. The definitions of some terms may refer to other defined terms. The definitions may conflict with ordinary usage; indeed, in some statutes the definitions may change from part to part. Some key terms may not be defined at all. Definitions should be treated like any other rule statements. Statutory legal analysis should quote and apply definitions to the facts of the issue to reach a conclusion.

Step 4: Apply the statute to your facts. Once you have elementized the rule (Step 2), simply discuss each element in order.

Step 5: Linking Up. Generally, when students have done legal analysis of a common law problem, they work with only one legal rule and maybe an exception to it. But many statutes will require reference to more than one section. Several provisions may apply to the analysis of one problem, and students will need to go through Step 4 for several different sections. They will then have to link one provision to another to another until they construct a logical chain leading to their conclusion.

Step 6: Consult secondary sources. Just as in any legal analysis, secondary sources may be extremely helpful in statutory analysis.

5. Statutory Analysis Under the U.C.C.

5.1 Types of Disputes

Disputes under the U.C.C. can be of any of the six types suggested in *Figure 2-3*. Disputes over **validity** can occur when the Code, as state law, is preempted by federal legislation or when a party challenges the constitutionality of Code provisions, such as those relating to self-help repossession.[3]

Most Code disputes are of the four other types: **factual, classification, interpretation, and exceptions.** In real life litigation, factual disputes usually predominate: If you can prove what happened, you win. Most problems presented in law school eliminate factual disputes by requiring that you assume an agreed upon statement of facts. Thus, most issues you will encounter in this course are one of the three remaining types.

To successfully analyze a U.C.C. problem, your ability to read statutory language closely and carefully in light of terms of art defined in the statute is very important. Discovery of the appropriate language in the statute and application of appropriate facts lead to a solution. This analytical process resembles the common law reasoning that you learned in your Legal Writing course and in doctrinal courses, such as Contracts. This reasoning will be bolstered by the special policies of the U.C.C. that become apparent from the Official Comments, case law and legislative history.

5.2 Code Methodology

U.C.C. statutory analysis follows the basic steps outlined in *Figure 2-4*. The following discussion emphasizes particular provisions of the U.C.C. that assist in analysis, and gives an example using U.C.C. 2-102.

Step 1: Scope.

Article 2's scope is defined in section 2-102, which contains both inclusionary and exclusionary provisions.

Step 2: Deconstruct the statute.

I recommend that whenever you want to apply the U.C.C. to solve a legal problem, you identify the applicable code section(s) and begin to read *aloud*, pausing at every punctuation mark and coordinating conjunction.[4] This is the first step in "deconstructing" the statute; that is, breaking it down into understandable parts. After you deconstruct the statute, you can then begin to apply the statute to the facts of your problem. Take U.C.C. section 2-102, which follows, as your example:

---

3. For the most part, choice of law disputes have been eliminated because the U.C.C. is in effect in all states, but some local variations still exist. The Code permits the parties to select applicable law, within certain limits. *See* U.C.C. § 1-105.

4. The coordinating conjunctions are: and, but, or, yet, for, nor and so.

Unless the context otherwise requires, this Article applies to transactions in goods; it does not apply to any transaction which although in the form of an unconditional contract to sell or present sale is intended to operate only as a security transaction nor does this Article impair or repeal any statute regulating sales to consumers, farmers or other specified classes of buyers.

The preceding simple statute (one overly long sentence) actually contains several very different ideas. Let's break it down to focus on the different ideas:

- The prefatory clause, "unless the context otherwise requires" modifies the entire remaining body of the statute. For now, let's translate it to mean: "After you go through all the work of applying this statute to reach a determination, you may still have to change your mind because of the context of the problem."

- After the first comma and continuing until the semi-colon is the positive rule of the statute — *the operative provision*—this Article applies to transactions in goods. That is the statement of what types of transactions are within the scope of Article 2.

- After the semi-colon, and continuing until the word "nor," is the *exclusionary* rule of the statute — this Article does not apply to transactions "intended to operate only as a security transaction" (even if it looks like something else).

- After the word "nor" the statute changes topics again. Now, it addresses a possible conflict between Article 2 and some other state statute. The rule it provides is that in the event of such a conflict, the *other* statute's rule will apply (because Article 2 does not impair or repeal such statute).[5]

Step 3: Define Terms.

Like other statutes, the U.C.C. has its own terms of art. Words may have meanings that differ from common usage. Furthermore, some frequently used terms, such as "transaction" or "reasonable" are not defined. They mean whatever you can persuade a court that they mean. It is impossible to tell whether a word in Article 2 is a defined term just by looking at it. When in doubt, of course, look for a definition.

The first two places in which to look are Article 1, section 1-201 (the general definitions) and in the table of contents to Article 2. You must also take into account the U.C.C. purposes and policies.[6] In addition, each Code section is followed by an "Official Comment" that also can be helpful. Many Official Comments include examples and cross-references to different parts of the U.C.C. Sometimes, the "Definitional Cross-References" that appear at the end of the Official Comment that follows each section will direct you to appropriate definitions. Unfortunately, although helpful, the definitional cross references are woefully incomplete.[7] If you do not find the necessary definition within the statute, you also can

---

5. The statute is written this way is to facilitate adoption in the various states, which have a wide range of different types of special consumer and farmer protection statutes. State legislatures could adopt the U.C.C. without laboriously cross-referencing all other relevant state law and without explicitly resolving possible conflicts between those other laws and the U.C.C.

6. U.C.C. § 1-103.

7. For example, look at U.C.C. section 2-102, the scope section of Article 2. It says that Article 2 applies to "transactions in goods," but the Definitional Cross-References do not refer to the definition of the most important word, "goods." The definition of "goods" is in U.C.C. section 2-105.

use common law precedent, and even everyday dictionary definitions, to help you understand the statute.

As you work with the U.C.C., you will become more familiar with its terms of art and you will learn which terms are defined and which are not. You also will learn the definitions of frequently used words. In practice, you will need to consult treatises and case law to determine the meaning of undefined terms.

Step 4: Apply the statute to your facts.

After you have deconstructed the statute, you are ready to try to apply it to your legal problem. Take each separate part and try to identify the facts that are affected by that part. Again, read the statute aloud. This time, stop at each separate part indicated above and "fit in" the applicable facts. It is possible that this approach will not always work, especially if one of the elements requires extended analysis. But your initial read-through can settle the clear points and you can reserve the difficult ones for later. I refer to this process as "thinking-aloud," and an example of a problem, and a possible "think-aloud" approach to analyzing it follow:

Facts

[In real life litigation, factual disputes usually predominate. In this course, as in most other law school courses, you will receive a narrative statement of "the facts," and you must decide how to apply the statute to the given facts.]

Alpha is a well digger. In a conversation in Alpha's office, she agreed with Beta that she would dig a water well on Beta's property for $15 per foot including the installation of a well casing and would also sell and install a pump for $450. The parties shook hands on the deal and Alpha promised to begin work the next day. Alpha mailed Beta an unsigned proposal listing these prices. Beta promised to sign and return the proposal but never got around to it. Beta's husband, however, noticed the purchase order on the desk, signed it, and then filed it in the desk. Alpha began work on the well, but after digging for 200 feet without striking water, she abandoned the project, again with Beta's approval. When presented with the bill for $3,450, Beta refused to pay and Alpha sued. Beta raised the defense of the statute of frauds, because Beta never signed a written contract.

The Call of the Question

Before you begin to analyze the problem, be sure you understand the question you are being asked to address. Here, you must analyze the validity of Beta's statute of frauds defense.

The Problem

To determine the validity of the defense, Alpha's lawyer first must decide if the U.C.C. statute of frauds (section 2-201) governs the problem. If Article 2 does not apply, Alpha's lawyer must research and apply some other law that governs the analysis of the parties' transaction. That determination requires the lawyer to read and apply Article 2's scope provision, section 2-102. Using the above deconstruction of the statute, Alpha's lawyer must apply the elements of the statute to the relevant facts.

Think Aloud

[The think aloud approach means "plugging" relevant facts into the deconstructed statute. Based on the statement of facts, a lawyer might do the initial read through of the statute somewhat as follows, with the words of the statute in bold, and the mental processes in italics.]

Unless *the context otherwise requires I'd better remember to consider this possibility, whatever conclusion I reach ...*

[This Article] applies to transactions. *This is one of two elements needed to decide that Article 2 applies to my client's situation—what does it mean? Section 2-101 says Article 2 is referred to as Uniform Commercial Code—Sales—so a sale must be a transaction; the word seems to be broader than that. I will have to check the Code's definitional provisions to see if it is defined anywhere. If not, I will have to see if there are any cases on point. Here, based on the facts given, the contract seems to be for the services of digging and installation, as well as for the sale of a pump.*

in Goods *This is the other element. Again, I need to know what it means. There is no reference in the definitional cross references that immediately follow the text of the statute, but I'd better check section 2-103—definitions and index of definitions. I see a reference there to a definition of goods in section 2-105. Goods are defined in the Code as things that are moveable at the time of identification to the contract. I remember reading that "identification" is discussed in section 2-501.*

does not apply to any transaction *which* **although in the form of an unconditional contract to sell or present sale is intended to operate only as a security transaction** *This is an exclusion—I remember that a security transaction is governed by Article 9 and refers to the giving of a lien on personal property to secure an obligation— that's not what is going on here, so the exclusion does not apply.*

Nor *Here comes another exception—things that are excluded from the scope of Article 2 even if it otherwise seems that they are included.*

does this Article impair or repeal any statute regulating sales to

   consumers

   farmers or

   other specified classes of buyers

   It sounds like I will have to decide if there are any special consumer protection or similar statutes that would apply to my facts and bring about a different result; if so, if there is, for example, an exception to the statute of frauds if a protected class of buyer is involved, that protective statute would apply (because this Article doesn't impair it ...)—in my case, Beta is not a consumer but maybe Beta is a farmer.

[You can see that a number of questions are raised that must be resolved before the lawyer can reach a conclusion.]

Step 5: Linking Up.

The U.C.C. is an integrated Code. Its parts are not freestanding but have meaning only in relation to each other. You will usually have to work through Step 4 for several different Code sections to resolve an issue arising under the Code. Then, you will have to link one provision to another to another until you construct a logical chain that leads to your conclusion. If you fail to link the necessary steps up, you invite confusion and error. At a minimum, you will have to refer to definition sections along with operative sections. (Notice how many other code sections were implicated by section 2-102: sections 2-105, 2-107, 2-501, and the definitions in section 1-201.)

Step 6: Consult secondary sources.

One treatise is uniformly recognized as authoritative on issues involving the Code: James J. White and Robert S. Summers, *The Uniform Commercial Code*.[8] It is clearly written, occasionally entertaining, and highly recommended. Courts often cite it and most commercial lawyers use it. I would not think of concluding an analysis of a U.C.C. problem without checking White & Summers. This is not to say that their analysis is always above reproach. They even disagree with each other on a number of issues, including how to interpret the battle of the forms provision, section 2-207. But even when you disagree with their analysis, you must be prepared to respond to it because you can be sure that your opponent and the judge have consulted it. Other helpful sources are identified at the end of this chapter.[9]

6. Conclusion: Statutory Analysis and the U.C.C.

The preceding brief survey demonstrates that statutory analysis is simply another branch of legal reasoning and analysis that all law students study throughout their law school careers. The main difference is the relatively easy accessibility of the "black letter law" in statutes. With practice, as demonstrated in *Figure 2-4*, students can learn to deconstruct statutes into elements and apply the relevant facts to each element. The U.C.C. is a good statute to use as the basis for improving your statutory analysis skills.

Legal analysis of a sales problem should always begin with a determination of whether the statute is applicable. Thereafter, students should identify the individual code sections that are relevant to an analysis of the problem at hand, and demonstrate how those sections "link up." In some cases, there may be a dispute other than the interpretation of a particular section, or even a question regarding its applicability. Such disputes can be resolved by reference to the Code's underlying purposes and policies, as well as case law and commentaries by learned academics and practitioners.

Finally, in some situations, none of the Code provisions discloses any obvious rule that would apply to your facts. If the issue in question falls within such a gap, you should first say so, then proceed to try to fill the gap from other sources of law. Supplemental principles of law and equity apply under section 1-103. You also might reason by analogy to other Code provisions, or from the general philosophy or articulated policies of the Code.[10]

Exercise 2-3: "Think-Aloud" Statutory Analysis

Now that you have read about how to deconstruct a statute using the "think-aloud" approach, and seen an example based on section 2-102, this exercise gives you an opportunity to try it yourself. Using the set of facts provided below, and sections 2-102, 2-105 and 2-107 (and other sections you decide you need to use)

---

8. James J. White & Robert S. Summers, The Uniform Commercial Code (6th ed.) (hereinafter referred to as "White & Summers").

9. *See* Additional Resources, at the end of this chapter.

10. See Note, *U.C.C. Application by Analogy*, 6 Ind. L. Rev. 108 (1972), Daniel E. Murray, *The Spreading Analogy of Article 2 of the Uniform Commercial Code*, 39 Fordham L. Rev. 447 (1971).

prepare a written response to the problem presented. (I have also provided the "call of the question," and "the problem" portions of the analysis for you.)

Your response should be in the "think-aloud" format illustrated above.

Facts

Alpha manufactures water pumps, which are commonly used to keep ground water from filling basements. Alpha and Beta signed a simple written contract to memorialize Alpha's sale of a water pump to Beta. After Alpha delivered the pump, Beta discovered that the pump could not keep up with the water that filled her basement, and the basement continued to experience standing water. She consults you to see if she has any claim against Alpha under the contract. Your research suggests that if the U.C.C. governs the claim, there may be an implied warranty, upon which she could base her claim.

The Call of the Question

Before you begin to analyze the problem, be sure you understand the question you are being asked to address. Here, the ultimate question is whether there is an implied warranty upon which Beta can base her claim. However, for purposes of this exercise you have been told that your research has already resolved that question affirmatively. *Therefore, the only question you need to address at this point is the applicability of the U.C.C.*

The Problem

To determine whether Beta can rely on an implied warranty claim against Alpha, Alpha's lawyer first must decide if the U.C.C.'s implied warranty provisions (sections 2-314 and 2-315) govern the problem. If Article 2 does not apply, Alpha's lawyer must research and apply some other law that governs the analysis of the parties' transaction. That determination requires the lawyer to read and apply Article 2's scope provision, section 2-102.

Use what you have learned about deconstructing the statute, and apply the elements of the statute to the relevant facts.

Think Aloud

Additional Resources

Kent Greenawalt, *Statutory Interpretation: 20 Questions* (1999).

Linda H. Edwards, *Legal Writing Process, Analysis and Organization*, 128-131 (2010).

William D. Hawkland, *Uniform Commercial Code Series* (1982).

Karl N. Llewellyn, *Remarks on the Theory of Appellate Decision and Rules or Canons About How Statutes Are to be Construed*, 3 Vand. L Rev. 395 (1950).

Thomas M. Quinn, *Quinn's Uniform Commercial Code Commentary & Law Digest* (1991).

Finally, for a quick way to find U.C.C. cases, try the digest for the *Uniform Commercial Code Reporting Service.*

Figure 3-1: Graphic Organizer

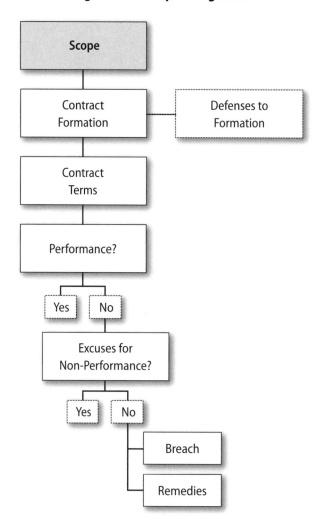

Chapter 3

The Scope of Article 2

Chapter Problem

Here is a memorandum from your supervisor. Read it carefully, and then try to predict how a court would resolve the dispute described in the memorandum, and why. By the end of this chapter, you will be able to fully analyze this problem. *For now, develop a hypothesis you will test as you work your way through the chapter. Then, as you read this chapter, keep this problem in mind and look for hints about how to go about solving it.*

INTRA-OFFICE MEMORANDUM

Date: September 13
To: Ann Associate
From: Ima Partner
Subject: Festival Foods

We represent Sasha Seller, the owner and operator of a business, Festival Foods, which serves concessions to the general public at county fairs and similar events throughout the state of California from late April to late October each year. The assets of the business include a truck and servicing trailer and equipment such as refrigerators and freezers, roasters, chairs and tables, fountain service, and signs and lighting equipment. Sasha estimates that the collective fair market value of these assets is approximately $75,000.

In 2009, Brayden Buyer approached Sasha about purchasing the business. He met several times with Sasha, and observed the business in operation. Sasha states that on August 13, 2009, she and Brayden entered into an oral agreement for her to sell Festival Foods to him for $150,000. For the $150,000, Brayden would receive the business, including all of its assets, existing contracts to operate at designated fairs, and Sasha's services to continue to generate new contracts for Festival Foods to work at additional events.

Brayden paid $10,000 on August 14, 2009. He took possession of Festival Foods the next day and operated Festival Foods for the remainder of the 2009 season. During that time, he received the income from the business, purchased inventory, replaced equipment, and paid employees. Title to the truck and trailer remained in Sasha's name. Sasha explained that she planned to transfer title to Brayden after he paid her the balance of the purchase price, which she claimed was to be paid when he received his loan money from the bank.

Apparently, Brayden's position is that he met with Sasha on August 14, 2009, and paid her $10,000 for the right to continue to purchase the business because Sasha had another interested buyer. He says that he and Sasha agreed that he would run Festival Foods while he continued to pursue buying the business.

In January, 2010, Brayden told Sasha he was no longer interested in purchasing Festival Foods. She wants to sue him for breach of what she believes was an oral contract.
Initially, I need you to determine what body of law governs the analysis of this dispute.

Figure 3-2: Article 2 Scope Analysis

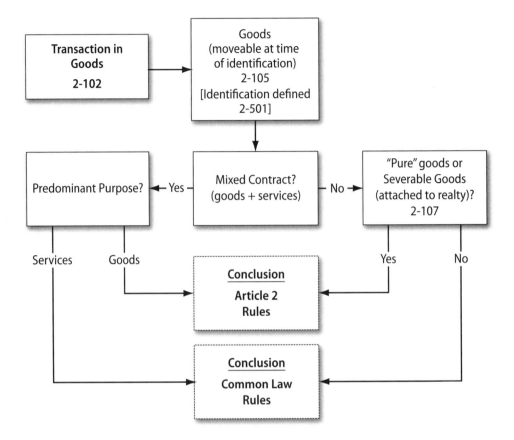

1. The Importance of Analyzing Scope

To analyze a legal problem, the first thing a lawyer should do is determine the body of law that provides the appropriate rules for the analysis. A client does not walk into a lawyer's office and say, "Hello, I have a Sales problem!" Accordingly, this book begins by studying the scope of Article 2; i.e., when does Article 2 govern the legal analysis of a specific problem? As you learned in Chapter 2, many statutes contain a "scope" section that helps a lawyer determine whether the statutes apply to the problem at hand.[1] U.C.C. Article 2 is no exception. Section 2-102 is Article 2's basic scope section. In addition, as *Figure 3-2* illustrates, a full "scope" analysis requires students to "link up" a number of other code sections. Students must also learn the definitions listed in *Figure 3-3*.

---

1. Some statutes will have separate sections, setting forth in detail both included and excluded transactions. *See, e.g.,* U.C.C. Art. 9, §9-109.

Figure 3-3: Scope Sections and Definitions

Section	Definitions
2-102	Transaction
	Goods (See 2-105)
	Predominant Purpose Test
	Gravamen Test
2-104	Merchants
2-105	Goods
	Future Goods
	Identification (See 2-501)
2-106	Contract
	Agreement
	Contract for Sale
	Conforming
	Termination
	Cancellation
2-107	Severance
2-501	Identification
	Fungible

2. The Basic Scope Rule

Section 2-102 both defines the types of transactions that are within Article 2's scope, and identifies excluded transactions. In addition, over time, complex transactions that involve both goods and services led to the development of a body of case law that provides a more sophisticated analysis of such transactions. Legal analysis should dispose of scope and exclusions in one or two sentences unless an issue is presented. (It is surprising that many lawyers and courts still "miss" the fact that Article 2 applies to transactions in which they are involved. A quick "scope" analysis would prevent such an error.) If the issue is presented, it deserves full analysis. Even if a transaction does not fall directly within the scope of Article 2, a court may apply Code principles by analogy. **Be prepared to explain the appropriate analogy if you want to convince a court to so apply the Code.**

Section 2-102 provides the general rule regarding when Article 2 applies: The general rule is that Article 2 applies to "transactions in goods." The rule has two elements: "goods," and "transactions."

2.1 Goods

Article 2 defines goods" as "things that are moveable at the time of identification to the contract for sale." This definition requires an understanding of the concept of identification, which we will study in more detail later in this course.[2] The key to understanding the definition of goods for purposes of a scope analysis is that the emphasis of the inquiry must be on whether the property (the goods) that is the subject of the sale is capable of moving. It does *not* need to be moveable at the time the parties enter into the contract. Indeed, the Code contemplates different types of goods including "future goods," and "specially manufactured goods," which by definition will not even exist at the time of the contract.[3] Real property is not goods because it is not moveable (distinguish "dirt," which may be "goods," because it can be picked up and hauled away.)

Exercise 3-1 illustrates the importance of being able to determine when something is identified, for purposes of a correct scope analysis.

Exercise 3-1: "Moveable at the time of identification"

Buyer and Seller entered into a contract for a modular home, to be manufactured to Buyer's specifications in Seller's plant, and then delivered to Buyer's site and placed on a foundation constructed by Buyer. Is this a transaction in goods?

You know from your previous reading that whether the modular home can be classified as goods depends on whether it was moveable at the time of identification to the contract. Accordingly, in this exercise you must determine when the modular home would be identified.

Hint: Section 2-501 on identification would treat the modular home as "future goods" because it did not exist when the parties entered into the contract.

2.2 Transactions

Article 2 does not define "transactions." It is commonly stated, loosely translating the statute, that Article 2 governs "sales of goods."[4] However, as a matter of statutory interpretation, since the drafters used a word other than "sales" when they clearly knew

---

2. "Identification" is perhaps the most difficult concept you must learn to fully analyze whether a problem is within the scope of Article 2. As you work through the applicable Code sections, you will encounter major difficulties and circular definitions. You may find some small comfort in the following discussion by David Mellinkoff, in a wonderful law review article regarding the language of the U.C.C.:

> Some years ago, a smiling paranoiac offered to prove to our class in abnormal psychology that he was the true Christ and that Jesus was an imposter. "It's simple, he said, I am the Christ because the Christ wouldn't lie to you!" The startling swiftness of that circular explanation is rivaled by the U.C.C. on identification....

Mellinkoff illustrates the circularity of section 2-501 with the following "translation":

> When you make a contract for the sale of existing goods, identification occurs when identification occurs, unless you explicitly agree that identification does not occur when it occurs.

David Mellinkoff, *The Language of the U.C.C.*, 77 Yale L.J. 185, 191 (1967).

The concept of identification will be important in certain other topics we take up later in the course, including casualty losses, and remedies. *See infra* Chapter 8.

3. "Future Goods" are goods that are not both existing and identified. U.C.C. § 2-105(1). "Specially Manufactured Goods" are "specially manufactured for the buyer and are not suitable for sale to others in the ordinary course of the seller's business." U.C.C. § 2-201(3)(a).

4. Professor Bryan Hull explains that U.C.C. section 2-106 limits the scope of Article 2 by defining a contract and an agreement only as a contract or agreement to sell goods. Therefore, he reasons, Article 2 applies only to sales of tangible personal property. Bryan D. Hull, *Inside Sales and Leases: What Matters and Why* 10 (2008).

that word (the title of the article is, after all, "Sales") other commentators maintain that the scope of Article 2 is broader than just sales. Sales are certainly the main type of transaction to which Article 2 will apply. However, the use of the word "transactions" leaves the door open for a talented lawyer and a receptive court to apply Article 2 to non-sales transactions.[5]

2.3 Mixed Transactions: Predominant Purpose Test

Article 2 does not apply to transactions that involve "purely" real estate or services. However, some transactions can involve a combination of goods and services (as in a contract to sell goods and provide maintenance services for a specified period of time), or goods and real property (as in the sale of a business that owns both real and personal property). Such transactions are commonly referred to as "mixed" or "hybrid" transactions, and the general rule based on case law is that you must determine what aspect of the transaction "predominates." Specifically, after you determine that there is a contract involving both goods and services, you must decide whether the contract's predominant factor is (1) the providing of services, with goods incidentally involved (e.g., a contract with an artist for a painting) or (2) to sell goods, with labor incidentally involved (e.g., the sale of a stove, followed by its installation). This test essentially involves consideration of the contract in its entirety, applying the U.C.C. to the entire contract or not at all. In other words, if the predominant purpose of a transaction is to sell goods, Article 2 governs the analysis of all of the legal contract issues with respect to that transaction. If the predominant purpose of a transaction is to provide services, common law governs the analysis of all of the legal contract issues with respect to that transaction.

The difficult issue in these types of scope analyses is determining the predominant purpose of a given transaction. Many courts have addressed the issue in a cursory or conclusory manner.[6] Courts that have given a more thoughtful analysis of the issue generally look to the language and circumstances surrounding the contract, the relationship between the goods and services, the compensation structure and the intrinsic worth of the goods provided.[7] These courts consider the factual circumstances surrounding the negotiation, formation and contemplated performance of contract.[8]

Figure 3-4 on the next page summarizes the variety of factors that courts have considered and weighed to determine whether the thrust or purpose of a particular transaction was more likely goods or non-goods.

---

5. One area where lawyers and courts have taken advantage of this lack of definition is in the application of Article 2 to software licenses. *See* Chapter 13, *infra*.

6. *See, e.g.*, U.S. ex rel. Bartec Indus. v. United Pac. Co., No. 91-15805, 1992 U.S. App. Lexis 38274, at *7 (9th Cir. Oct. 6, 1992); U.S. v. Twin Falls, 806 F.2d 862, 871 (9th Cir. 1986); TK Power v. Textron, 433 F. Supp. 2d 1058, 1061-1062 (N.D. Cal. 2006).

7. Integrity Material Handling Sys., Inc. v. Deluxe Corp., 722 A.2d 552, 555 (N.J. Super. 1999) ("When a contract is a mixed contract for goods and services, a court must determine whether the sales or services aspect predominates." (citing Custom Com. Eng'g, Inc. v. E.F. Johnson Co., 269 N.J.Super. 531, 537, (App.Div.1993))); Huyler Paper Stock Co. v. Info. Supplies Corp., 117 N.J.Super. 353, 360 (Law Div.1971); Quality Guaranteed Roofing, Inc. v. Hoffmann-La Roche, Inc., 302 N.J.Super. 163, 166-67 (App.Div.1997).

8. *See* True North Composites, LLC v. Trinity Indus., Inc., 65 Fed. Appx. 266 (Fed. Cir. 2003) (applying Delaware law), *infra*.

Figure 3-4: Factors Courts Use to Determine Predominant Purpose

	SALE OF GOODS	PROVISION OF SERVICES
Contract Provisions	Describes Goods	Describes Services
Language of Contract	Reflects sale of goods (e.g., "buyer," "seller," "Agreement to Purchase")	Emphasizes services (e.g., "design" "construct," "Contract for Work, Labor, Services and Materials")
Special Skills	Creation of goods did not require special skills/services	Contract required special skills (particularly professionals, such as doctors and dentists)*
Labor	Little labor involved in contract	Significant time spent producing the goods
Business of "Seller"	Involves sale of goods	Involves provision of services
Importance of Who Sells the Goods	Contract reflects that buyer was more concerned with the goods and less concerned with the installation, either who would provide it or the nature of the work (based on recitals and details in the contract)	Contract reflects emphasis on expertise and experience of company who is providing goods, and details of what that company will be doing (based on recitals and details in contract)
Sales Tax	Charged**	Not charged

* *But see* Analysts Intern. Corp. v. Recycled Paper Prods., Inc., 45 U.C.C. Rep. Serv. 746 (N.D. Ill. 1987) (suggesting that if a unique product is involved even if service is substantial, where getting a unique good is the goal, service is only incidental.) Note that under this court's reasoning, in almost any contract a conclusion can be reached that the goods were the predominant purpose of the transaction.

** Meeker v. Hamilton Grain Elevator Co., 110 Ill.App. 3d 668, 671 (1972).

2.4 Mixed Transactions: Gravamen Test

A small minority of U.S. courts has formulated the "gravamen test" as an alternative test for determining the applicability of Article 2. In a mixed contract involving both goods and services, this test seeks to determine whether the aggrieved party is complaining about the quality of the services rendered or the quality of the goods delivered. If the complaint is about the goods, Article 2 will govern the analysis. If the complaint is about the services, the rules of common law contracts will apply instead.

2.5 Other Scope Analyses

In limited circumstances, legal scholars and courts have also applied Article 2 to transactions that do not involve the sale of goods, justifying their application of Article 2 rules on policy grounds. Alternatively, they will use Article 2 rules stating that the transaction before the court is "analogous" to a goods sales transaction, and the Article 2 rules are therefore helpful to apply.[9]

Exercise 3-2: True-North Composites v. Trinity Industries

The following case illustrates a court's application of the predominant purpose test. As you read it, see if the court discusses any of the factors identified in *Figure 4-3*. Does the court give any other reasons for its decision?

True North Composites, LLC v. Trinity Industries, Inc.

65 Fed. Appx. 266 (Fed. Cir. 2003)

LINN, Circuit Judge.

Trinity Industries, Inc. ("Trinity") appeals from a judgment of the United States District Court for the District of Delaware in favor of True North Composites, LLC ("True North") following a jury verdict and award of damages on its complaint for breach of a Carbodies Supply Agreement ("Agreement").... Because the district court erred as a matter of law in interpreting the Agreement as not predominantly a contract for goods subject to the limitations on damages of Delaware's version of the Uniform Commercial Code, 6 Del. C. § 1-101 et seq. (2000) ("U.C.C."), we conclude that True North was not entitled to the diminution of business value and closure cost damages awarded by the jury. We find the remaining damages supported by substantial evidence. Therefore, we *affirm-in-part and reverse-in-part* the district court's denial of Trinity's motion for judgment as a matter of law, *vacate-in-part* the district court's award of damages, and *remand* for proceedings consistent with this opinion.

BACKGROUND

Because our opinion is directed to the parties, and because the facts are already recounted in some detail in the district court's opinion denying Trinity's motion for judgment as a matter of law, *True North Composites, LLC v. Trinity Indus., Inc.,* 191 F.Supp.2d 484, 490-513 (D.Del.2002) (*"Order"*), we discuss only those facts relevant to our decision.

The Agreement was entered into by True North and Trinity for the purpose of co-developing and building composite railcars using a patented manufacturing technique licensed to True North and known as SCRIMP technology.... The Agreement called for True North to produce composite carbodies, the box-like structures of railcars. For its part, Trinity agreed to separately manufacture steel undercarriages, with wheels and a platform. True North was then to mount its carbodies to Trinity's undercarriages to create complete railcars. Following assembly, Trinity was responsible for marketing and selling the railcars ...

The Agreement contemplated the eventual production of 2000 railcars and specified that Trinity would pay a price per carbody for the construction and mounting of the first 500 carbodies. The price of the remaining 1500 carbodies was to be set by taking True North's estimated costs of production, adding a 10% profit, and tacking on an additional payment of $3647.... If Trinity's composite railcar sales showed a profit in excess of 13%, the Agreement called for True North and Trinity to evenly divide the excess profits.... Finally, the Agreement provided that it was to be governed by Delaware law.

---

9. White & Summers, *supra.* n. 20, at 27.

Following cost overruns and difficulties in agreeing on final specifications, including length of the carbodies, True North filed a complaint in the United States District Court for the District of Delaware on November 12, 1999, alleging that Trinity breached the Agreement and its duty of good faith and fair dealing by refusing to negotiate in good faith on the final specifications of the carbodies, by refusing to purchase carbodies on the terms required by the Agreement, and by ordering True North to stop production of the 68-foot carbodies.... True North also sought a declaratory judgment that it did not breach the Agreement ... Trinity answered denying True North's allegations, asserting various affirmative defenses, and counterclaiming that True North breached the Agreement and its duty of good faith and fair dealing, among other things ...

True North's complaint also originally alleged federal patent and antitrust claims. On the eve of trial, the parties resolved the patent claim and True North withdrew its antitrust claim. The district court agreed to the parties' request that the district court retain jurisdiction over the remaining state law claims pursuant to 28 U.S.C. § 1367.... Following the filing of this appeal, we determined that appellate jurisdiction is proper in this court ...

At trial, Trinity argued that Delaware's version of the U.C.C. governed the Agreement because it was a contract predominantly for goods and that the U.C.C. limited the types of damages that True North could be awarded if breach were found. *See* 6 Del.C. § 1-106(1) (limiting remedies to the extent "that the aggrieved party may be put in as good a position as if the other party had fully performed but neither consequential or special nor penal damages may be had"). Trinity suggested a jury instruction and verdict form consistent with its position. The district court rejected Trinity's requested instruction and verdict form, noting that it considered the Agreement to be not predominantly a contract for goods, and thus, not governed by the U.C.C....

Trinity appeals to this court, seeking review of the district court's denial of its motion for judgment as a matter of law as to the issues of whether the Agreement is governed by Delaware's version of the U.C.C.... .

DISCUSSION
III

We begin with the construction of the Agreement and specifically whether the Agreement is governed by Delaware common law or the U.C.C. The distinction has significance on the damages resulting from a breach. On the one hand, damages for breach of contract under Delaware common law typically include both "damages for breach and those consequential damages that were reasonably foreseeable at the time the contract was made."... On the other hand, contractual damages under the U.C.C. are limited and include only that needed to put "the aggrieved party ... in as good a position as if the other party had fully performed but neither consequential or special nor penal damages" may be awarded. 6 Del. C. § 1-106(1) (2000).

The district court determined that common law, rather than the U.C.C., governed the Agreement. The court reasoned that, because the U.C.C. only applies to "transaction[s] in goods," 6 Del. C § 2-102, and because the Agreement was a mixed contract for goods and services, a threshold determination must be made as to "whether the contract is predominantly or primarily a contract for sale of goods or for services."... The court concluded from the terms of the Agreement that the sale of goods was not predominant and gave three reasons for its determination ... First, the court concluded that the contract's requirement to design the new railcars to unsettled and changing specifications demonstrated that the Agreement was a contract for services. Second, the court found persuasive the fact that True North played a direct role in the design and construction of the production tooling and equipment and that Trinity not only reimbursed True North for the tooling and equipment costs, but also agreed to pay a premium above the price of the railcar for learning curve costs. From this, the district court concluded that the design and construction of the production process itself was a significant component of the Agreement and that the contract was not merely for goods ... Third, the court found support for its conclusion that the Agreement was not predominantly for goods in the requirement that True North attach the underframes supplied by Trinity and that True North lease land to Trinity for production of the underframes. The court cited *Glover School and Office Equipment,* 372 A.2d 221, and *Wharton Management Group v. Sigma Consultants, Inc.,* 1990 WL 18360, (Del.Super.Ct. Jan. 29, 1990), in support of its conclusions. It distinguished the cases cited by Trinity, *Micro Data Base Systems, Inc., v. Dharma Systems, Inc.,* 148 F.3d 649, 655 (7th Cir.1998) and *Neilson Business Equipment Center, Inc. v. Monteleone,* 524 A.2d 1172, 1174 (Del.1987), on the ground that, unlike these cases, the Agreement in the present case did not simply require customization of an existing product, but rather, the creation, design, and building of an entirely new product, including the equipment needed to make it....

Before this court, Trinity argues that the U.C.C. governs the Agreement, that the U.C.C. does not permit an award of consequential damages, that diminution of business value and closure costs are consequential damages, and that the jury's award of damages in these two categories must therefore be vacated as a matter of law. In the alternative, Trinity argues that the question of whether the Agreement was predominantly for goods or services was a question for the jury and requests that we vacate the district court's determination and remand the issue for a new trial. True North does not dispute that diminution of business value and closure costs are consequential damages, but asserts that the district court properly concluded that the Agreement was not within the U.C.C..We agree with Trinity that as a matter of law the U.C.C. governed the Agreement.

IV

Under Delaware law, a determination of whether a contract is subject to the U.C.C. requires that a court "review the factual circumstances surrounding the negotiation, formation, and contemplated performance of the contract to determine whether the contract is predominantly or primarily a contract for the sale of goods." ...

Although the district court focused on the performance contemplated by the Agreement, ... Trinity argues that various aspects of both the contemplated performance and the formation of the contract support its assertion that the U.C.C. governs the Agreement. In particular, Trinity argues that the very language of the Agreement demonstrates that the parties intended to enter a contract predominantly for the sale of goods; that the inclusion of provisions excluding warranties demonstrates that the parties intended the U.C.C. to govern; that the specification of payment terms by railcars purchased is indicative of a goods contract; and that the requirement of some design effort does not remove the Agreement from the realm of the U.C.C.

With respect to the language of the Agreement, Trinity notes that the terms used and agreed to in the formation of the Agreement are indicative of a contract for goods, including "purchase," "buyer," and "seller." True North echoes the district court's reasoning for concluding the Agreement to be not predominantly for goods-that the Agreement requires the design of railcars to unspecified specifications, includes compensation for the unreimbursed tooling and equipment costs and learning curve costs, and specifies additional service components, such as leasing and mounting. True North also contends that the Agreement includes other evidence that the contract was predominantly not for goods, such as a required commitment of exclusivity by True North.

We agree with Trinity and conclude that the language of the Agreement fairly attests to the "goods-centric" nature of the contract. The Agreement is entitled "Carbodies Supply Agreement." The "whereas" clauses in the preamble of the contract characterize the Agreement as setting forth the "rights and obligations regarding the production … and sale … of carbodies." The first provision of the Agreement concerns the "Sale and Purchase of the Carbodies." The pricing and invoicing schemes set forth in the Agreement are on a per-carbody basis. The third section of the Agreement is entitled, in part, "Delivery Schedule," and sets forth a release schedule based upon the number of carbodies produced. Overhead costs are also allocated on a carbody basis, and all tooling and production equipment paid for under the Agreement must be turned over at the completion of the contract. There are sections of the Agreement devoted to subsequent carbody orders and excessive production. And finally, the termination provisions of the Agreement are grounded in either the failure of Trinity to deliver carbodies or the failure of True North to pay for carbodies. Even were we to agree with True North that the aspects it cited were probative of a contract not predominantly for goods, those aspects are not outweighed by the clear language and provisions of the Agreement cited above. Thus, the best evidence of the formation and contemplated performance of the contract-the very language of the Agreement itself-establishes that the contract is predominantly concerned with and primarily provides for the sale of goods.

As Trinity next argues, section 8.1 of the Agreement excludes certain warranties as is typical of a contract for the sale of goods. True North, on the other hand, contends that the inclusion of the warranty provisions is probative of the parties' recognition that the U.C.C. did not apply and that the inclusion of the provisions indicates that the parties "endeavored to make explicit that the U.C.C. did not apply to their arrangement." We disagree with this strained assertion. The exclusion of warranties, as well as the wording and format of the exclusion provisions themselves, fit precisely within Delaware's U.C.C. section 2-316(2). 6 Del. C. § 2-316(2) (2000). This is consistent with the conclusion that, at the formation of the contract, the parties intended that the U.C.C. govern the Agreement.

Another factor in determining whether a mixed contract is predominantly for goods or services is the allocation of payment terms. *See, e.g., Glover,* 372 A.2d at 223; *BMC Indus., Inc. v. Barth Indus., Inc.,* 160 F.3d 1322, 1330-32 (11th Cir.1998). In this case, the Agreement clearly allocates price by carbody, that is price per goods delivered. True North argues that the division of profits in excess of 13% is indicative of a contract for services and that Trinity's argument neglects a number of service aspects that are not quantified in the Agreement. The division of excess profits does not change the fact that the main basis for price allocation is on a per-carbody basis. Because the document to be construed is the Agreement, True North's arguments about aspects not quantified, and for which it provides no record citations, are not persuasive. Thus, we agree with Trinity that this factor also supports the conclusion that, at the time of formation as well as by the contemplated performance, the Agreement was predominantly a contract for goods.

Trinity also argues that, even though the contract calls for products to be modified in specified circumstances, that does not necessarily mean that the contract is predominantly one for services, because the U.C.C. includes contracts for "specially manufactured goods."

See Advent Sys. Ltd. v. Unisys Corp., 925 F.2d 670, 675 (3d Cir.1991). The U.C.C. explicitly states that goods include "all things (*including specially manufactured goods*) which are movable at the time of identification to the contract for sale other than the money in which the price is to be paid, investment securities (Article 8) and things in action." 6 Del. C. §2-105(1) (2000) (*emphases added*). Trinity contends that some amount of services are rendered in the performance of specially manufactured products contracts and that such incidental service activity does not remove the agreement from U.C.C. coverage. True North argues that this case instead is similar to those where engineering services predominate. The Agreement, however, does not reflect a contract where special engineering skills and services are predominant; rather, as noted above, the very language of the Agreement indicates that it is a contract predominantly for and primarily concerned with the production of carbodies.

Moreover, we find that the cases cited by the district court, as well as the characterization by the district court of the cases cited by Trinity, do not support True North's position. The district court cited *Glover* and *Wharton Management* in concluding that the Agreement was predominantly for services. *Glover*, 372 A.2d 221; *Wharton Mgmt. Group*, 1990 WL 18360. The facts of these decisions are distinguishable from those of the present case. In *Glover,* the contract was for the provision and installation of school lockers ... The *Glover* court determined that the goods in question, the lockers, were of standard issue and not specially manufactured for the job. *Id.* Thus, the primary focus of the contract, and what the buyer was bargaining to obtain, was the service component, or the installation. In *Wharton Management,* the contract was for the design, development, and installation of a computer system ... The court in that case determined that, although the end result may have been a software product, the contract was primarily to obtain the special skills and abilities provided by the seller's programmers-a service component. *Id.* Here, as noted above, the contract is predominantly for the provision of goods-carbodies. That there are related service components, such as the lease of land or the mounting of the carbodies onto the undercarriages, does not change the fact that what Trinity contracted for under the Agreement was a product, not a service.

We also disagree with the distinctions drawn by the district court over the cases cited by Trinity- *Micro Data Base* and *Neilson*. In *Micro Data Base,* the court found that a contract for the sale of a customized computer program based on a basic program was a contract for goods-notwithstanding the programming effort required ... In *Neilson,* the court similarly found that a contract for a customized computer system was a contract for goods even though some customizing services were required ... The district court distinguished *Micro Data Base* and *Neilson* from the present case based on the fact that each of the prior cases concerned customization of an existing product. That distinction finds no basis in law; the U.C.C. does not distinguish between specially made goods that are customized from existing products and goods that are entirely specially made. Further, there is no indication in either *Micro Data Base* or *Neilson* that the buyer in either case was bargaining for anything except a specially made product; the service component of the contracts in both cases was ancillary to the product actually sought. As noted above, the facts in this case are similar. Trinity was ultimately bargaining to receive specially made goods, and the service components noted by the district court were merely ancillary to those goods.

Finally, True North finds dispositive, or at least persuasive, a comment of the district court at trial, observing "[a] lot of the duties that the plaintiff has identified as having been breached are duties that don't really relate themselves to the good itself, but to duties arising out of a relationship between the parties." True North then cites *Glover,* arguing that if the cause of action arises from exclusively the goods portion or exclusively the services portion of the contract, there is no need to determine whether goods or services are predominant in a hybrid contract and that the determination may rest solely on the portion from which the cause of action lies.......We are not persuaded by this argument. First, the court's observation seems to be little more than a passing comment made in open court and is not reflected in the court's reasoned opinion denying Trinity's motion for judgment as a matter of law. Nor is it supported by any evidence. Further, True North mischaracterizes the comment as meaning that the cause of action relates to the services aspects of the contract. There is a difference between "duties arising out of a relationship between the parties" and duties arising from the services portion of the Agreement. Second, the significance of this comment must be tempered by the court's own characterization of True North's complaint: "True North alleges that Trinity breached the CSA, including the warranty of good faith and fair dealing, by refusing to negotiate in good faith on the final specifications of the carbodies, *refusing to purchase* carbodies on the terms required by the CSA, and ordering True North to *stop production* of the 68-foot carbodies."... (emphasis added). Because the language of the Agreement strongly indicates that the contract is predominantly for the sale of goods and True North's allegations are also related to sale of the goods, not the service components as True North contends, we disagree with True North.

For all of these reasons, we hold that the district court erred as a matter of law in concluding that the Agreement is not predominantly a contract for goods governed under Delaware's U.C.C..Because we hold that the Agreement falls under the U.C.C., the award of consequential damages, namely diminution of business value and closure costs, cannot stand. Those portions of the judgment are hereby vacated ...

CONCLUSION

We hold that the Agreement was predominantly for the sale of goods and is, thus, governed by the Delaware U.C.C..Because the district court erred as a matter of law in concluding that the Agreement was not predominantly for goods, we reverse that part of the district court's denial of Trinity's motion for judgment as a matter of law ...

———————

3. Other Bodies of Law Applicable to Sales Problems

Although this course concentrates on U.C.C. Article 2, sales students should be aware of some of the other bodies of law that may be applicable to transactions in goods. First, as has already been discussed, where Article 2 does not specifically displace common law, principles of law and equity supplement its provisions. Second, some "transactions in goods" are leases, whose analysis is now governed by Uniform Commercial Code Article 2A. Third, because Section 2-102 specifically provides that Article 2 is not intended to impair or repeal any statute regulating sales to consumers, farmers or other specified classes of buyers, students should be aware of the need to determine whether any such laws are applicable to a given situation. For example, in California, the Civil Code contains a wide range of consumer protection law particularly in the area of warranties. A lawyer in California with a consumer client who has a sales warranty issue would therefore have to consult the applicable Civil Code provisions in addition to California's version of the Uniform Commercial Code. Almost every state in the United States has some special protective legislation affecting particular classes of buyers.

Another state law that might apply to supplement the Code's provisions in a transaction in goods is the Uniform Electronic Transactions Act ("UETA"). Since Article 2 was written before the advent of "electronic contracting," this law helps fill gaps that would otherwise make application of some of Article 2's provisions difficult when such transactions are involved. As of January 2011 only three states, Illinois, New York, and Washington have not enacted UETA, and these states have their own statutes governing electronic transactions. For the current status of UETA see http://nccusl.org/Update/uniformact_factsheets/uni-formacts-fs-ueta.asp.

Applicable federal law will also supercede U.C.C. provisions in some instances and supplement the U.C.C. in others. Three examples are the Federal Magnuson-Moss Consumer Warranty Act, which we will study later in this course, the Federal Arbitration Act, 9 U.S.C. section 1 *et. seq.* (2010) which must be consulted if a sales contract has an arbitration provision, and the Electronic Signatures in Global and National Commerce Act ("ESign"), 15 U.S.C. sections 7001 *et. seq.* (2010). Finally, in some cases, if the parties to a sales contract are residents of countries that are signatories to the United Nations Convention on Contracts for the International Sale of Goods (the "CISG"), the rules of the treaty may govern the transaction.

As you can see, in practice a lawyer cannot confine her analysis of a sales problem to the Uniform Commercial Code.

Exercises 3-3 through 3-6 give you an opportunity to apply what you have learned about the U.C.C.'s basic scope provisions. Then return to the Chapter Problem, which gives you a more complex fact pattern, raising the "mixed transaction" issue, and requires a more sophisticated analysis.

Exercise 3-3: Are Crops "Goods"?

John Gable is a farmer. John decides that he wants to sell his entire harvest of wheat this coming fall to Able Pet Food. John and Able entered into a valid contract in April 2010 for the sale of John's entire wheat harvest in the fall. After the price of wheat dropped dramatically, Able unambiguously told John that Able will not buy John's wheat. John has contacted you and seeks your help. Determine whether U.C.C. Article 2 governs the proper legal analysis of John's situation.

Exercise 3-4: Applying Section 2-102

1. Nancy Neighbor enters into a contract with Boy Nextdoor to purchase water from Boy's well. After a few weeks, Boy refuses to let Nancy take any more water. Does Article 2 govern this dispute?

2. While jogging, you stop off at a restaurant and they GIVE you a glass of water—what if you cut your lips? What if the water is poisoned? Does Article 2 govern your dispute?

3. You receive free toothpaste in the mail. It makes you sick. You want to sue for breach of the implied warranty of merchantability under U.C.C. Article 2. Does Article 2 govern your dispute?

4. While in a grocery store, you pick up a six-pack of soda—it explodes. Does Article 2 govern your dispute?

5. You leave your movie film at a retail store to have it transferred to digital format. Does Article 2 govern your dispute if the store destroys your film?

6. A photographer sells her rights to use her photos in a book to a publisher. When the publisher uses the photos and fails to pay as agreed, what law governs the dispute?

7. A sliced meat manufacturer and a food distributor exchange correspondence regarding the sale of meat products. The distributor now claims no contract was formed. What law determines the outcome of this dispute?

8. A service station operator seeks an injunction to stop an oil company from terminating the operator's franchise. What law governs?

9. Mary Marketer enters into a contract with Digital Dan Camera Manufacturing pursuant to which Mary agrees to use her best efforts to establish a market for Digital Dan's cameras. The agreement provides, in pertinent part, that Mary shall cause customers to contract Dan directly with camera orders and that Dan shall pay Mary a commission based on actual orders received. When Dan refuses to pay, what law governs the dispute?

10. Perry President guaranties the obligations of Big Corporation under its contract to purchase goods from Bigger Corporation. If Big defaults, and Bigger wants to sue Perry, what law will govern the dispute?

11. Perry President guaranties the obligations of Big Corporation under its contract to borrow money from Bigger Bank. If Big fails to repay the loan, and Bigger wants to sue Perry, what law will govern the dispute?

Exercise 3-5

Anita wanted a new car. She went to the local car dealer, who talked her into leasing instead of buying. Anita has changed her mind. She believe that the car dealer put undue pressure on her, and she got a bad deal. What law will govern this dispute?

Exercise 3-6

Bert's place of business is New York, U.S.A. Sam's place of business is Barcelona, Spain. Bert entered into a valid contract with Sam for the purchase of 1,000 widgets to be used in his business. When the widgets arrived, they did not conform to the description in the contract.

Assume that the contract has no choice of law provision. What law governs this dispute?

Additional Resources

Foster v. Colorado Radio Corp., 381 F.2d 222, 4 U.C.C. Rep. Serv. 446 (10th Cir. 1967) (Art. 2 applied to goods portion of bulk sale of business, which included real property).

J.P. Ludington, Annotation, *Construction and effect of Article 2, dealing with sales*, 17 A.L.R.3d 1010 (1978).

Sonja A. Soehnel, Annotation, *Applicability of U.C.C. Article 2 to mixed contracts for sale of goods and services*, 5 A.L.R.4th 501 (1991).

Sonja A. Soehnel, Annotation, *What constitutes "goods" within scope of U.C.C. Article 2*, 4 A.L.R.4th 912 (1991).

Figure 4-1: Graphic Organizer

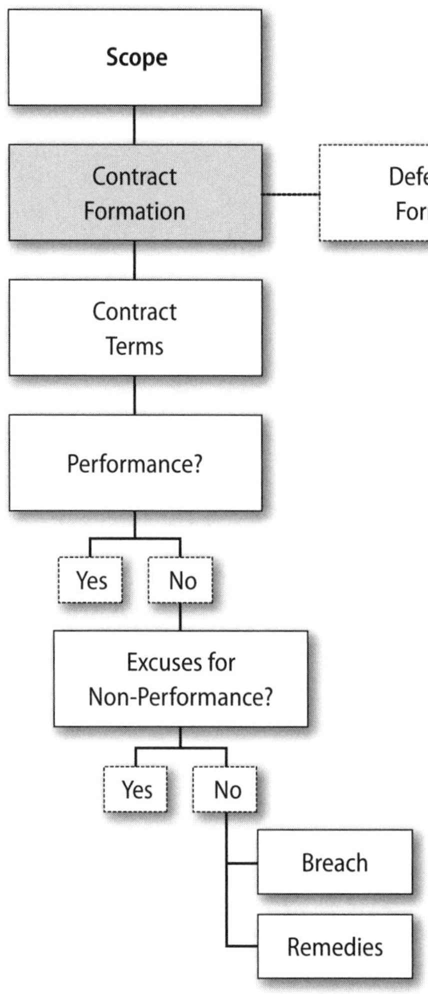

```
┌─────────────────────┐
│       Scope         │
└─────────────────────┘
           │
┌─────────────────────┐       ┌─────────────────────┐
│     Contract        │ ······│    Defenses to      │
│    Formation        │       │     Formation       │
└─────────────────────┘       └─────────────────────┘
           │
┌─────────────────────┐
│     Contract        │
│      Terms          │
└─────────────────────┘
           │
┌─────────────────────┐
│   Performance?      │
└─────────────────────┘
        │    │
      ┌─────┐ ┌─────┐
      │ Yes │ │ No  │
      └─────┘ └─────┘
                 │
      ┌─────────────────────┐
      │    Excuses for      │
      │  Non-Performance?   │
      └─────────────────────┘
            │     │
          ┌─────┐ ┌─────┐
          │ Yes │ │ No  │
          └─────┘ └─────┘
                     │
              ┌─────────────┐
              │   Breach    │
              └─────────────┘
                     │
              ┌─────────────┐
              │  Remedies   │
              └─────────────┘
```

Chapter 4

Contract Formation

Chapter Problem

Barry Beyer owns Barry's Ice Creamery, a neighborhood ice cream parlor. He decided to expand his business to include gelato sales, and found a great gelato freezer advertised on the internet by Delilah Distributor, a wholesale distributor of ice cream and related products. On March 1, Barry called Delilah to discuss the purchase of a Master-Bilt GEL-12 Gelato Merchandiser / Dipping Cabinet— 86. At the end of the conversation, Barry stated, "OK, Delilah, we have a deal— I'll buy the Gelato Cabinet from you for $16,999." "It's a deal," replied Delilah. As soon as Barry hung up the phone, he grabbed a piece of letterhead, and dashed off the following quick note to Delilah:

102 Decadence Dr.
Anytown, CA 90000

Dear Delilah,

This will confirm our phone conversation of March 1. You will ship me a Master-Bilt GEL-12 Gelato Merchandiser / Dipping Cabinet—86. I know we didn't talk about this on the phone, but I'm having some cash flow problems right now, so I will pay within 120 days.

Also, after we hung up, I noticed your sales of ice cream toppings Please ship immediately ten pounds each of (1) chopped M&M's, (2) chopped Cookies & Cream and (3) chopped nuts.

I look forward to a long and fruitful relationship.

When Delilah received Barry's note, she was so angry at his reference to cash flow problems that she threw the note on the floor and went home for the day. Her faithful employee, Rufas, read the note and stated, "What a dope! Everyone in the ice cream industry knows that payment is expected within 30 days of shipment!" Then, trying to be helpful, he packaged and shipped ten pounds each of (1) chopped Reese's pieces, (2) chopped Cookies & Cream and (3) chopped nuts.

Delilah never shipped the Gelato Cabinet. Now Barry is suing Delilah for breach of contract. Delilah consults your firm for advice. Answer the following questions. Do **not** attempt to analyze the possible applicability of the statute of frauds.

1. Does Barry have a valid contract with Delilah for a Master-Bilt GEL-12 Gelato Merchandiser / Dipping Cabinet—86? Why or why not? If so, what are the terms of payment?

2. Does Barry have a valid contract with Delilah for the purchase and sale of thirty pounds of ice cream toppings? Why or why not? If so, what ice cream toppings are the subject of the contract?

---

1. Introduction

This chapter reviews the typical patterns of contract formation that U.C.C. Article 2 addresses. The U.C.C. defines a contract as "the total legal obligation that results from the parties' agreement...."[1] It is necessary to see how a contract was formed, to determine the rights and obligations of the contract parties. Accordingly, after you determine that Article 2 governs the analysis of a particular transaction, it is then necessary to assure that the parties have exchanged legal obligations. *Figure 4-2* links Article 2's basic contract formation provisions.

Figure 4-2: Basic Contract Formation

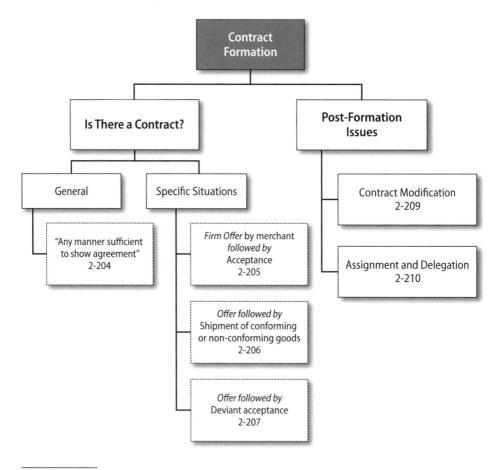

---

1. U.C.C. §1-201(12).

Four code sections contain the basic contract formation rules. Section 2-204 states the general rule, and the three sections that follow state the rules for specific situations. The sections that students need to link up, and definitions students need to understand the material in this chapter are set forth in *Figure 4-3.*

Figure 4-3: Contract Formation Sections and Definitions

Section	Definitions
2-204	Agreement (See 1-102(3))
2-205	Merchant (See 2-104)
	Sign (See 1-201(37))
	Writing (See 1-201)(43))
	Reasonable Time (See 1-205)
	Assurance
2-206	Conforming (See 2-106)
	Non-Conforming
2-207	"Definite and Seasonable Expression of Acceptance"
	"Additional or Different terms"
	"Material Alteration"
	"Undue Surprise or Hardship"
2-208	Course of Performance
	Express Terms
	Implied Terms
2-209	Modification
	Rescission
	Waiver
2-210	Assignment
	Delegation

2. Contract Formation in General

Section 2-204 is a general provision that recognizes that a contract can be formed relatively informally. Section 2-204 applies whether or not one or both of the parties to the alleged contract are merchants. Historically, one of the most common ways of forming a contract was through the process of offer and acceptance. The U.C.C. does not define an "offer." Accordingly, students must analyze whether an offer was made using the common law definition.[2] Under the Restatement (Second) of Contracts section 24, an offer is "the manifestation of willingness to enter into a bargain, so made as to justify another person in understanding that his assent to that bargain is invited and will conclude it."[3] At common law, an acceptance is the manifested willingness to enter into the same bargain.[4] Furthermore, for a contract to be found, definite terms are required. section 2-204 liberalizes the common law's rigid requirements of an acceptance, by providing that

---

2. *See* U.C.C. § 1-103.
3. Restatement (2d) of Contracts § 24 (1981).
4. Restatement (2d) of Contracts § 50 (1981).

a contract can be found even though the time of its making is undetermined and even though some terms are missing.[5]

Exercise 4-1: Corono-Oro, Inc. v. Harry Thompson

The following case illustrates a court's application of section 2-204 to determine whether a contract was formed. As you read the case, consider the following questions:

1. Did the court discuss offer, acceptance and consideration? Why or why not?

2. Do you think the court would have reached a different conclusion regarding contract formation if Article 2 did not govern the analysis of this dispute?

Corono-Oro, Inc. v. Harry Thompson

2002 Cal. App. Unpub. LEXIS 2501

March 28, 2002, Plaintiff Corono Oro, Inc., doing business as Stewart's Office Furniture (reseller), brought this action against defendant Harry Thompson (broker), doing business as Hetson & Associates, for damages arising out of an alleged breach of a contract to sell office work stations or cubicles. After a court trial, the court entered judgment for reseller in the principal amount of $40,500.00 plus $9,087.53 prejudgment interest dating from April 1, 1998. The principal amount consisted of $36,000.00 for the extra cost of cover goods, extra delivery charges of $850.00, additional installation time of $1,000.00, and $2,650.00 for additional work performed by Steven Hollenback, a principal of reseller.

On appeal broker contends that the judgment lacks evidentiary support as to the existence of a contract and the amounts of damages ...

TRIAL EVIDENCE

At the end of February 1998, Steven Hollenback, an owner of reseller, told Mark Dalton, a sales representative of reseller, that reseller had a business customer, Silicon Valley Communications (SVC), that was looking for 76 work stations or cubicles on a budget. Dalton heard that a company named Radius had work stations for sale so he made an appointment to see them. At the company's site Hollenback, Dalton, and an SVC representative viewed the cubicles. They encountered broker and Dave Repco taking inventory. Dalton talked primarily with broker while Hollenback talked with Repco, who was working with broker.

According to Dalton, broker said he had cubicles for sale. They were not his cubicles. He was brokering them for Radius. Dalton assumed from his experience in the office furniture business that broker would not be inventorying the product unless Radius had already agreed he could sell it.

The work stations were in good condition. Dalton and Hollenback told broker they wanted 76 cubicles. Broker said they had enough. Dalton told broker he would give him

---

5. U.C.C. §§ 2-204(2), (3).

a deposit. Dalton thought there might be several offers on such a good product and he wanted to secure the transaction. Hollenback told broker that he would like to be able to pick out the nicest pieces and red tag them. Broker said he would do that. They would be available for pickup within a few days.

According to broker, he told Dalton that he was inventorying the product in order to prepare an estimate to make a bid to Radius.

On Thursday, February 26, 1998, Dalton picked up a check for $38,000.00 from Hollenback. Hollenback told Dalton he wanted the deal carved in stone because he had taken a $60,000.00 deposit from SVC.

Dalton brought the check to broker's office the next day. He asked for a receipt for the deposit and confirmation that they were looking at 76 work stations. Broker had a woman in his office prepare the document. What Dalton received was an invoice form (sometimes "the document") from Hetson & Associates dated February 27, 1998. It described 76 work stations at a price of $1,000 each, 10 eight-by-ten work stations and the rest eight feet by eight feet. It also listed 76 chairs at $75 each. It included a sales tax and a total amount. The document also acknowledged that a $38,000.00 deposit had been received.

The document showed that reseller would be billed. It did not include reseller's address, a shipping address, or a purchase order number.

According to Dalton, he circled the sales tax amount on the document and told broker there should be none, as the product was being resold. Broker agreed. Broker did not say that the document was really a deposit receipt and not an invoice and that they were not selling him the goods. Dalton was relieved to get an invoice because in his experience it meant that reseller had a contract to purchase the work stations. Dalton testified, "An invoice means that it's yours." He did not ask broker why he received an invoice instead of a receipt.

According to broker, when Dalton brought the deposit check in, broker showed him that he was preparing a bid for the workstations. They discussed what Dalton's client wanted if broker got the product. Broker told Dalton that he would simply hold the check. He was uncomfortable taking the check because he did not own the product.

According to broker, Dalton brought in prices for the work stations that Dalton had worked out with Don Brady. Broker had a woman in his office type up a form. She selected the wrong form. Broker did not realize it at the time because he did not look at the form before Dalton took it away.

According to broker, he found out on Monday, March 2, 1998, that Radius had not accepted his bid. He called Dalton and told him so.

According to Dalton, on Tuesday, March 3, 1998, broker called him and said there might be a delay in getting the product. Broker did not elaborate. Dalton stopped by broker's office that afternoon. Broker said he still did not know anything more. He was waiting to hear from Radius. Broker handed back reseller's check, telling Dalton to hold it until they knew for sure.

According to broker, Dalton came by to pick up the check after learning the deal was off. Broker showed him alternative product which Dalton declined.

According to Dalton, broker called the next day, March 4, 1998, to tell Dalton the product was not available. Radius had received a better offer from a sublessee and they wanted to keep the cubicles in place.

Hollenback heard that the deal had collapsed from his customer before he heard it from Dalton. On March 5, 1998, Hollenback told Dalton to find some similar product for his client.

On March 6, 1998, Hollenback's attorney sent a letter to broker demanding performance of the contract....

1. DID THE PARTIES ENTER A CONTRACT TO SELL CUBICLES?

On appeal broker contends "**the parties['] intentions and expectations establish there was no contract to sell Radius' property.**" (Bold in original.)

It is undisputed that the transaction between the parties is governed by California's Uniform Commercial Code — Sales, found in the Uniform Commercial Code section 2101 et seq. The California Uniform Commercial Code has adopted what was called in 1935 the "modern" view of contracts. (*Brant v. California Dairies, Inc.* (1935) 4 Cal.2d 128, 133, 48 P.2d 13.) An objective manifestation of assent is controlling, not the undisclosed intentions of the parties. (*Ibid.*; *Windsor Mills, Inc. v. Collins & Aikman Corp.* (1972) 25 Cal. App. 3d 987, 992, 101 Cal. Rptr. 347.) As *Steiner v. Mobil Oil Corp.* (1977) 20 Cal.3d 90, 141 Cal. Rptr. 157, 569 P.2d 751 (*Steiner*) pointed out, "The California code comment ... explicitly states: '"[A] meeting of the minds on the essential features of the agreement" is not required....')[This is expressed partly in section 2204. "(1) A contract for sale of goods may be made in any manner sufficient to show agreement, including conduct by both parties which recognizes the existence of such a contract.... (3) Even though one or more terms are left open a contract for sale does not fail for indefiniteness if the parties have intended to make a contract and there is a reasonably certain basis for giving an appropriate remedy."]

Steiner explained, "The official comments accompanying section 2204, other provisions of the code, and the case law interpreting section 2204, all support the conclusion that section 2204 does not require mutual assent to all essential terms." (*Steiner, supra*, 20 Cal.3d 90, 103.)

Under section 2204, "a court, if it is to enforce a contract, must first make two findings. Initially, the court must find some basis for concluding that the parties engaged in a process of offer and acceptance, rather than inconclusive negotiations. Second, the court must find that it possesses sufficient information about the parties' incomplete transaction to apply the provisions of the California Uniform Commercial Code which fill in the gaps in parties' contracts...." (*Steiner, supra*, 20 Cal.3d at p. 104, fn. omitted.)

As broker recognizes, "section 2207 inquires as to whether the parties intended to complete an agreement: 'Under this Article a proposed deal which in commercial understanding has in fact been closed is recognized as a contract.'...

In other words, the initial inquiry is whether there was an objective manifestation that the parties intended to make a contract. Whether parties have reached a contractual agreement and on what terms are questions for the fact-finder when conflicting versions of their discussions require a determination of credibility.[citations omitted] Under such circumstances, on appeal we will uphold the trial court's factual findings when they are supported by substantial evidence.[citations omitted] ...

In this case, the trial court was not simply called upon to interpret the document written on an invoice form. The court was required to reconcile conflicting versions of the discussions between broker and Dalton, reseller's agent, leading up to and following the document. Dalton and broker agreed that when Dalton first spoke with broker at the

Radius site, Dalton was aware that broker did not have title to the cubicles. Dalton brought a check to broker about two days later as a deposit to secure the transaction. Dalton and broker disagreed about what occurred at that meeting. According to Dalton, he expected to get a deposit receipt. Instead, he was given an invoice form from Hetson & Associates, broker's firm, showing the cost of 76 work stations. According to Dalton, he pointed out to broker that the document charged sales tax, which did not apply because the transaction was going to be a resale. Broker did not say the document was really a deposit receipt and not an invoice. According to broker, he never saw the document before Dalton left his office. According to broker, he showed Dalton that he was in the process of writing up a bid for the work stations.

Broker contends that he clearly expressed his lack of title to the work stations at all times. As reseller points out, the trial court as the fact-finder was not required to believe broker's testimony, which was contradicted by Dalton.

Contrary to broker's characterization, we do not understand reseller to be arguing that "a bare 'invoice' overrides the parties' actual intentions." Reseller's position was essentially as follows. Reseller presented a check to broker in the hope he could deliver the goods as he had suggested he could. Broker had indicated earlier both that he did not yet have title and that he expected to obtain it. When broker gave reseller an invoice instead of a deposit receipt for the check, as reseller argued to the trial court, broker "prepared a document which on its face is an invoice for the sale of the goods.... He put into the stream of commerce what appears to a reasonable business person to be a sale document." When broker acknowledged to Dalton an error on the completed form regarding the sales tax, he did not say that it was the wrong form and that he was not selling the goods.

Section 2206 states in part: "(1) Unless otherwise unambiguously indicated by the language or circumstances [P] (a) An offer to make a contract shall be construed as inviting acceptance in any manner and by any medium reasonable in the circumstances." Reseller's position is essentially that the document constituted acceptance of its offer to purchase the cubicles.

Broker contends that, in these "doubtful circumstances," it was not reasonable for reseller to silently treat the document as acceptance. *South Hampton Co. v. Stinnes Corp.* (5th Cir. 1984) 733 F.2d 1108, on which broker relies, involved a different situation. In that case, a dispute arose as to whether an oil seller was performing under its contract to sell oil. The buyer asked if the seller was exercising an option to provide an alternate source of supply. The seller did not respond. The appellate court stated, "Silence in response to a direct inquiry, made necessary by doubtful circumstances that [seller] itself created, hardly comports with even a generous reading of the word 'reasonable.'" (*Id.* at p. 1119.) In other words, the seller could not silently exercise its option after performing in a different way.

Broker suggests that the burden was on reseller to clarify whether broker really meant the document to be an invoice. Broker's premises are that the circumstances were doubtful and the document was ambiguous. But reseller had no doubt of the meaning of receiving an invoice in the context it did. Based on Dalton's experience in the furniture business, "an invoice means it's yours." Reseller was entitled to rely on what appeared to be broker's outward manifestation of assent to sell the cubicles.

Broker contends that "**regardless of whether the deposit receipt is treated as an invoice, it is not a sales contract.**" (Bold and emphasis in original.) Broker relies on *India Paint Co. v. United Steel Prod. Corp.* (1954) 123 Cal. App. 2d 597, 267 P.2d 408, which stated in part: "it is pertinent to observe that even if the shipping document is regarded as an invoice, as India contends, this would not *ipso facto* transform it into the contract between the parties, unless so intended by them or unless such effect is given to it by the application or operation of some principle of contract law. The prevailing rule is that an invoice, standing alone, is not a contract [citations]; and a buyer is ordinarily not bound by statements thereon which are not a part of the original agreement." (*Id.* at p. 607.) The court in *India Paint Co.* concluded that a buyer was not bound by disclaimers of previously made warranties in shipping documents when the disclaimers were "finely-printed" and "so located as to easily escape attention." (*Id.* at p. 610.)

We perceive no inconsistency between *India Paint Co.* and the trial court's conclusion in this case. The question for the trial court was not whether the document by itself was a contract, but whether the document in the context of the discussions between the parties amounted to acceptance of reseller's offer to buy the cubicles. Section 2207, subdivision (3), states in part: "Conduct by both parties which recognizes the existence of a contract is sufficient to establish a contract for sale although the writings of the parties do not otherwise establish a contract." Broker's presentation of a document appearing to be an invoice in response to reseller's offer to purchase cubicles can be regarded as conduct recognizing the existence of a contract.

In various Commercial Code cases, an invoice has been found under the circumstances to be either a sufficient confirmation or acceptance of a contract. (E.g., *Transamerica Oil Corp. v. Lynes, Inc.* (10th Cir. 1983) 723 F.2d 758, 765; *Mid-South Packers, Inc. v. Shoney's, Inc.* (5th Cir. 1985) 761 F.2d 1117, 1123; *Alarm Device Mfg. Co. v. Arnold Industries, Inc.* (Ohio Ct.App. 1979) 65 Ohio App.2d 256 [417 N.E.2d 1284, 1288]; cf. *National Controls, Inc. v. Commodore Bus. Machines, Inc.* (1985) 163 Cal. App. 3d 688, 694, 209 Cal. Rptr. 636 — purchase order was confirmation.) The document here contains broker's letterhead. It identifies reseller as the buyer, the items to be sold, and their price. It also describes the receipt of a $38,000 deposit. Under the circumstances, we conclude that there was substantial evidence that this document objectively manifested broker's acceptance of reseller's offer to purchase 76 work stations and chairs.

Howard Construction Co. v. Jeff-Cole Quarries, Inc. (Mo.Ct.App. 1984) 669 S.W.2d 221, on which broker relies, is factually distinguishable. At issue there was whether a purchase order was a writing sufficient to indicate that a contract for sale had been made between the parties. The court explained, "Most courts have required that the writing indicate the consummation of a contract, not mere negotiations. [Citations.] Thus, a writing which contained language indicating a tentative agreement has been found insufficient to indicate that a contract for sale had been made. [Citation.] Writings which do not contain words indicating a binding or complete transaction has occurred have been found insufficient. [Citation.] Some courts have required that the writings completely acknowledge the evidence of an agreement. [Citation.] Even those courts giving a liberal interpretation to the requirement that the writing evidence an agreement have insisted that the terms of the writing at least must allow for the inference that an agreement had been reached between the parties." (*Id.* at p. 227.) The writings in that case did not "allow for the inference that any agreement was reached between the parties." (*Id.* at p. 228.)

In our case, the document prepared on an invoice form can reasonably be understood to reflect an agreement by broker to sell reseller 76 work stations at a price of $1,000 each. Determining the meaning of the document required the trial court to reconcile conflicting versions of the circumstances surrounding its preparation. The testimony by Dalton and Hollenback about their discussions with broker provides substantial evidence supporting the trial court's implicit finding that the parties had reached an agreement.

[The Court's discussion of impracticability has been omitted.]

---

3. The Role of Merchants in Contract Formation and Throughout Article 2

3.1 Who Are Merchants?

One of the most important concepts that Article 2 introduces is the idea that people who are professionals in business should be held to higher (or at least different) standards when they deal in goods than people who are not professionals. The Code names such professionals "merchants" and defines a merchant in section 2-104. Official Comment 2 to section 2-104 explains that "merchant" status embodies the concept of a professional in business, and that the professional status may be based upon:

- Specialized knowledge as to the goods or
- Specialized knowledge as to the business practices involved in the transaction.

Figure 4-4 shows the different ways that people may be classified as merchants.

Students find it easy to recognize a merchant who "deals in goods of the kind." Any seller whose business is selling goods is a merchant who deals in goods of the kind *when that seller is selling the goods he normally deals in.* Thus, an office supply store is a merchant

Figure 4-4: People who are Classified as Merchants under 2-104

Type of Merchant	Definition	Example
"Dealer"	A person who deals in goods of the kind.	A manufacturer of widgets, engaged in the sale of those widgets, is a person who deals in goods of the kind (the widgets).
"Knowledge or skill"	A person who "otherwise" by his occupation holds himself out as having knowledge or skill peculiar to the practices or goods involved in the transaction.	Official Comment 2 to section 2-104 suggests that for purposes of the code sections involving normal business practices which "are or ought to be typical of and familiar to any person in business" almost every person in business would be deemed a merchant under this definition. When acting in a mercantile capacity, the Comment suggests that universities, banks and even lawyers will be "merchants" because of their familiarity with normal business *practices.*
By Attribution	A person to whom such knowledge or skill may be attributed by his employment of an agent or broker or other intermediary who by his occupation holds himself out as having such knowledge or skill.	If a buyer, who lacks any specialized knowledge regarding horses, employs a person who has experience as a horse breeder, to assist the buyer in a purchase of a horse, the special knowledge of the horse breeder would be attributed to the buyer, who would then be a merchant under this definition.

who deals in goods of the kind when it sells any of the office supplies it normally sells. Keep in mind that a seller will *not* be a merchant who deals in goods of the kind when it sells something it does not ordinarily sell. For example, if the office supply store does not normally sell cars, and it decides to sell one used car that it has used in its business, it will not be a merchant who deals in goods of the kind in the used car sales transaction.

The next type of merchant is sometimes harder to recognize. There are actually two ways that someone may be a merchant because he "otherwise" (other than by dealing in goods of the kind) by his occupation holds himself out as having knowledge or skill. Specifically, (1) he may hold himself out as having knowledge or skill *with respect to the goods involved in the transaction* or (2) he may hold himself out as having knowledge or skill *with respect to the business practices involved in the transaction.* Official Comment 2 explains that the type of specialized knowledge that is sufficient to establish the merchant status is indicated by the nature of the code provisions. It explains that for purposes of certain provisions of Article 2 that deal primarily with normal business practices which are or ought to be typical of and familiar to any person in business, for purposes of these sections almost every person in business would therefore be deemed a merchant under the language "who ... by his occupation holds himself out as having knowledge or skill peculiar to the practices ... involved in the transaction."'

The last type of merchant is a person who is treated as a merchant because she employs someone who has the requisite skill or knowledge with respect to a particular transaction. Official Comment 3 gives as an example a university, which may be a merchant by reason of its employment of people in a purchasing department "who are familiar with business practices and who are equipped to take any action required."

3.2 Special Article 2 Rules that Apply Only to Merchants

A significant number of sections of Article 2 contain special rules that apply only to merchants. Some of these sections apply only "between merchants." Official Comment 2 to section 2-104 arranges these code sections into the categories shown in *Figure 4-5.*

Figure 4-5: Types of Provisions with Special Merchant Rules under 2-104

Normal business practices ("paperwork provisions")	Applicable to "practices" merchants sections 2-201(2), 2-205, 2-207, 2-209
"Merchant-plus" requirements (different standards for merchants)	Applicable to "goods" merchants sections 2-312(3), 2-314, 2-402(2), 2-403(2), 2-509(3)
"General goods and practices"	Applicable to both "practices" and "goods" merchants sections 2-327(1)(c), 2-103(1)(b), 2-603, 2-605, 2-509, 2-609

Exercise 4-2: Who Is a Merchant?

In each of the situations described below, deconstruct and apply section 2-104 to determine whether either or both of the parties are merchants in the described transaction. If you decide that a party is a merchant, indicate whether that party is a merchant because (1) it deals in goods of the kind (2) it has specialized knowledge as to the goods or specialized knowledge as to the business practices, or both, (3) it is a merchant by attribution. (There may be more than one reason for deciding that a party is a merchant—list as many as you can identify.)

1. Jay's Jewelry Store sells a diamond necklace to Carl Consumer, who is buying it for his wedding anniversary.

2. Jay's Jewelry Store sells a watch to Larry Lawyer, who is buying it to wear to work.

3. Jay's Jewelry Store remodels, and sells its old display tables and waiting room chairs to a used furniture dealer.

4. Frank Farmer sells corn to Giant Grocery Store.

Exercise 4-3: Merchants Throughout the Code

Review the code sections we have studied **to date**. Which, if any, articulate a special rule that applies only to merchants? As we begin to study new code sections, pay particular attention to rules that have different rules applicable to merchants and non-merchants.

---

4. Contract Formation; Specific Rules

The three sections that follow section 2-204 each address a narrower set of facts under which a contract can be found.

4.1 Contract Formed by Merchant's Firm Offer Followed by Acceptance

Section 2-205 defines a firm offer. One way to attack this section is to try to find the parts of the statute, as we discussed in Chapter 2. *Figure 4-6* on the next page takes this approach.

The section is easily deconstructed into the following elements:

- An offer

- By a merchant

- To buy or sell goods

- In a signed writing

- That by its terms gives assurances that it will be held open

It is easy for someone familiar with section 2-205 to write a firm offer. For example, a merchant may include the following language in an offer letter or purchase order: "This is a firm offer under section 2-205 of the Uniform Commercial Code and will remain open for____ days from _____."

Figure 4-6: Finding the Parts of a Statute
U.C.C. Section 2-205: Firm Offers

Purpose	Official Comment 2: The primary purpose of this section is to give effect to the deliberate intention of a merchant to make a current firm offer binding.
Scope	Statute: Merchants Official Comment 3: Current "firm" offers
Exclusions	Statute: The period of irrevocability may not exceed three months Official Comment 3: Does not apply to long term options.
Definitions	Official Comment 2: "Signed" includes reasonable authentication, with reasonableness of authentication determined in light of the purpose of this section. Definitional Cross References: "Goods," section 2-105; "Merchant," section 2-104; "Signed," section 1-201; "Writing," section 1-201.
Operative Provisions	[A firm offer] is not revocable for lack of consideration
Consequences	The offer is not revocable during the time stated or, if no time is stated, for a reasonable time

To determine whether a particular offer is a firm offer, each element of section 2-205 must be analyzed separately. First, because the U.C.C. does not define an "offer," under section 1-103 you can use the common law definition of "offer" for your analysis.[6] Next, you must apply the Code's definition of "merchant."[7] You will already have analyzed whether "goods" are involved in your scope analysis. The language of section 2-205 seems to limit its applicability to actual sales of goods because it uses the language "to buy or sell goods." If you want to determine that there is a firm offer when a sale is not involved, you will need to argue policy. The next element is the requirement of a "signed writing." Both the terms "signed" and "writing" are defined in Article 1. Look up those definitions now. What if a merchant posts what appears to be a firm offer on its website? Will that format satisfy section 2-205's requirements for a "signed writing"? Will UETA or ESIGN help with your analysis? The final requirement for a firm offer is that the offer itself "gives assurances that it will be held open." The actual language used in the offer must be interpreted to determine whether this element is satisfied.

Section 2-205 "specifically displaces" the common law rule that provides generally that an offer can be revoked at any time before acceptance, unless the offeror receives consideration to hold the offer open for a period of time. If the elements of section 2-205 are satisfied, the result under the statute (the operative provision) is that the offer is not revocable for the time stated or, if no time is stated, for a "reasonable" time. The maximum period of irrevocability is three months.

Section 2-205 contains a special rule for a firm offer when the offer is made on a form supplied by the offeree. In such cases, the term of assurance must be "separately signed by the offeror." Official Comment 4 explains the reason for this special rule. Students can

---

6. Restatement (2d) of Contracts section 24 states: "An offer is the manifestation of willingness to enter into a bargain, so made as to justify another person in understanding that his assent to that bargain is invited and will conclude it."

7. U.C.C. § 2-104.

best understand the rule and its underlying rationale if they picture a purchaser of goods who has significant clout—such as Microsoft, Boeing Aircraft, or other major companies who purchase goods. Such companies often require vendors to present purchase orders using the big company's standard form rather than the vendor's standard form. Thus, when the vendor submits a purchase order using the big company's standard form, the vendor's offer will be on a form supplied by the offeree.

Exercise 4-4: Applying Section 2-205

Now that you have had a chance to work with several more sections of Article 2, this exercise is designed to assess your statutory analysis skills. You have already seen a deconstruction of section 2-205. Now you must apply that rule to the following facts. Note that the call of the question is whether a contract has been formed. As you read the facts you will see that resolution of the contract formation question ultimately depends on whether a firm offer was made. If there was a firm offer, it was not revocable and it was accepted, forming a contract. However, if there was not a firm offer, the offeror revoked the offer before it was accepted and no contract was formed.

Write out your analysis of the following facts.

Facts

S, a retailer, sold personal computers manufactured by M. After preliminary negotiations, B, a corporation, mailed to S a printed form prepared by B inviting S to make an "offer" to sell 10 described personal computers for $25,000. The form contained five paragraphs of printed material, inserted on a single page between blank lines to be filled in at the top and a signature line at the bottom. The third paragraph above the signature line provided: THIS OFFER WILL BE HELD OPEN FOR 30 DAYS AFTER RECEIPT BY THE OFFEREE. S filled in the blanks as requested by B, signed the form, dating it May 30, 2007, and returned it to B, who received it on June 3, 2007. On June 15, 2007, S notified B by telegram that the offer was revoked. A better deal had been worked out with C for the personal computer. On June 16, 2007, B telegraphed to S an acceptance of the offer, which was received the same day. B insists that there was a contract. Is B correct?

The Call of the Question

This question asks whether a contract was formed. For purposes of this exercise, you can *assume* that Article 2 governs your analysis.

The Problem

To determine whether a contract was formed, review sections 2-204, 2-205, 2-206 and 2-207. Which one seems to address the facts in this exercise? You should recognize the pattern of offer, attempted revocation of offer, and purported acceptance. The resolution of the contract formation question will depend on whether S's offer was revocable. If so, S revoked before B purported to accept. If the offer was not revocable, however, B accepted, and a contract was formed. Section 2-205 deals with when an offer is irrevocable. Hence, that is the section you will need to apply. Use what you have learned about deconstructing the statute, and apply the elements of the statute to the relevant facts.

Think Aloud:

(You may want to use the "think-aloud" technique to analyze the problem before you begin to write your answer.)

Your analysis:

4.2 Contract Formed by Shipment of Conforming or Non-conforming Goods in Response to Offer

Recall that at common law, courts construed offers as creating a power of acceptance. As you remember from your Contracts course, distinctions between unilateral and bilateral contracts, requirements of notice of acceptance, and similar issues were often dispositive on an issue of contract formation.[8] The U.C.C. addresses these topics in section 2-206.

Section 2-206 covers a range of topics. First, section 2-206(1)(a) liberalizes the common law "mirror image rule" that requires an offeree to respond in the same manner and medium as required by the offer and provides instead that unless unambiguously indicated in the offer, the offer is construed as inviting acceptance in any manner and by any medium reasonable in the circumstances. Second, section 2-206(2) addresses the common law issue of whether notice of acceptance of an offer to form a unilateral contract is needed. Perhaps its most significant provision, however, is section 2-206(1)(b), which specifically changes common law rules regarding shipment in response to an offer. You may recall that at common law, if a buyer made an offer to buy goods and the seller shipped different goods in response to that offer, a contract was formed on the seller's terms, because the seller's shipment was treated as a counter-offer, which the buyer accepted by accepting the goods. No contract was formed until the buyer accepted the goods. Accordingly, if a seller did not ship goods in response to the buyer's offer, there was no breach of contract because there was no contract.

Under section 2-206(1)(b), the seller can still prevent contract formation if it fails to respond to the buyer's offer at all. However, if the seller ships goods in response to the offer, *whether or not the goods are conforming*, the seller's shipment of goods is treated as the *acceptance* of the *buyer's offer* — so a contract is formed *on the terms of the buyer's offer*. And, because the contract formed is on the terms of the buyer's offer, if the goods fail to conform, the seller is in breach of contract. To avoid this result, section 2-206(1)(b) permits a seller who wants to avoid liability for breach of contract to ship non-conforming goods "as an accommodation," in which case the shipment of goods will be treated as a counter-offer, and not an acceptance. Under those circumstances, if the buyer then accepts the goods, a contract is formed *on the terms of the seller's counter-offer* (the shipment).

Exercise 4-5: *Corinthian Pharmaceutical Systems, Inc.v. Lederele Laboratories*

The following case illustrates an analysis of contract formation under section 2-206. As you read the case, consider the following questions:

---

8. *See, generally*, E. Allen Farnsworth, *Contracts* 140-144 (4th ed. 2004)

1. Why does the court apply the rules of U.C.C. Article 2?

2. How does the court determine that the parties are merchants? Does their status as merchants matter to the outcome of this case?

3. Who made the offer? How?

4. How did the offeree accept the offer (if it did)?

Corinthian Pharmaceutical Systems, Inc. v. Lederele Laboratories

724 F. Supp. 605 (S.D. Ind. 1989)

McKINNEY, District Judge.

This diversity action, which is presently set for trial by jury on December 18, 1989, comes before the Court on the defendant's motion for summary judgment. The issues raised have been fully briefed and the parties have submitted supporting evidence. The issues raised were ripe as of July 21, 1989. For the reasons set forth below, the Court GRANTS the motion.

I. FACTUAL AND PROCEDURAL BACKGROUND

Defendant Lederle Laboratories is a pharmaceutical manufacturer and distributor that makes a number of drugs, including the DTP vaccine. Plaintiff Corinthian Pharmaceutical is a distributor of drugs that purchases supplies from manufacturers such as Lederle Labs and then resells the product to physicians and other providers. One of the products that Corinthian buys and distributes with some regularity is the DTP vaccine.

In 1984, Corinthian and Lederle became entangled in litigation when Corinthian ordered more than 6,000 vials of DTP and Lederle refused to fill the order ... That lawsuit was settled by written agreement whereby Lederle agreed to sell a specified amount of vaccine to Corinthian at specified times. Lederle fully performed under the 1984 settlement agreement, and that prior dispute is not at issue. One of the conditions of the settlement was that Corinthian "may order additional vials of [vaccine] from Lederle at the market price and under the terms and conditions of sale in effect as of the date of the order."

After that litigation was settled Lederle continued to manufacture and sell the vaccine, and Corinthian continued to buy it from Lederle and other sources. Lederle periodically issued a price list to its customers for all of its products. Each price list stated that all orders were subject to acceptance by Lederle at its home office, and indicated that the prices shown "were in effect at the time of publication but are submitted without offer and are subject to change without notice." The price list further stated that changes in price "take immediate effect and unfilled current orders and back orders will be invoiced at the price in effect at the time shipment is made."

From 1985 through early 1986, Corinthian made a number of purchases of the vaccine from Lederle Labs. During this period of time, the largest single order ever placed by Corinthian with Lederle was for 100 vials. When Lederle Labs filled an order it sent an invoice to Corinthian. The one page, double-sided invoice contained the specifics of the transaction on the front, along with form statement at the bottom that the transaction "is governed by seller's standard terms and conditions of sale set forth on back hereof, notwithstanding any provisions submitted by buyer. "Acceptance of the order is expressly conditioned on buyer's assent to seller's terms and conditions."

On the back of the seller's form, the above language was repeated, with the addition that the "[s]eller specifically rejects any different or additional terms and conditions and neither seller's performance nor receipt of payment shall constitute an acceptance of them." The reverse side also stated that prices are subject to change without notice at any time prior to shipment, and that the seller would not be liable for failure to perform the contract if the materials reasonably available to the seller were less than the needs of the buyer. The President of Corinthian admits seeing such conditions before and having knowledge of their presence on the back of the invoices, and Corinthian stipulates that all Lederle's invoices have this same language ...

During this period of time, product liability lawsuits concerning DTP increased, and insurance became more difficult to procure. As a result, Lederle decided in early 1986 to self-insure against such risks. In order to cover the costs of self-insurance, Lederle concluded that a substantial increase in the price of the vaccine would be necessary.

In order to communicate the price change to its own sales people, Lederle's Price Manager prepared "PRICE LETTER NO. E-48." This document was dated May 19, 1986, and indicated that effective May 20, 1986, the price of the DTP vaccine would be raised from $51.00 to $171.00 per vial. Price letters such as these were routinely sent to Lederle's sales force, but did not go to customers. Corinthian Pharmaceutical did not know of the existence of this internal price letter until a Lederle representative presented it to Corinthian several weeks after May 20, 1986.

Additionally, Lederle Labs also wrote a letter dated May 20, 1986, to its customers announcing the price increase and explaining the liability and insurance problems that brought about the change. Corinthian somehow gained knowledge of this letter on May 19, 1986, the date before the price increase was to take effect. In response to the knowledge of the impending price increase, Corinthian immediately ordered 1000 vials of DTP vaccine from Lederle. Corinthian placed its order on May 19, 1986, by calling Lederle's "Telgo" system. The Telgo system is a telephone computer ordering system that allows customers to place orders over the phone by communicating with a computer. After Corinthian placed its order with the Telgo system, the computer gave Corinthian a tracking number for its order. On the same date, Corinthian sent Lederle two written confirmations of its order. On each form Corinthian stated that this "order is to receive the $64.32 per vial price."

On June 3, 1986, Lederle sent invoice 1771 to Corinthian for 50 vials of DTP vaccine priced at $64.32 per vial. The invoice contained the standard Lederle conditions noted above. The 50 vials were sent to Corinthian and were accepted. At the same time, Lederle sent its customers, including Corinthian, a letter regarding DTP vaccine pricing and orders. This letter stated that the "enclosed represents a partial shipment of the order for DTP vaccine, which you placed with Lederle on May 19, 1986." The letter stated that under Lederle's standard terms and conditions of sale the normal policy would be to invoice the order at the price when shipment was made. However, in light of the magnitude of the price increase, Lederle had decided to make an exception to its terms and conditions and ship a portion of the order at the lower price. The letter further stated that the balance would be priced at $171.00, and that shipment would be made during the week of June 16. The letter closed, "If for any reason you wish to cancel the balance of your order, please contact [us] ... on or before June 13."

Based on these facts, plaintiff Corinthian Pharmaceutical brings this action seeking specific performance for the 950 vials of DTP vaccine that Lederle Labs chose not to deliver. In support of its summary judgment motion, Lederle urges a number of alternative grounds for disposing of this claim, including that no contract for the sale of 1000 vials was formed, that if one was formed, it was governed by Lederle's terms and conditions, and that the 50 vials sent to Corinthian were merely an accommodation. Before reaching these issues, the relevant summary judgment standards must be set forth …

[The Court discusses the appropriate standards for review of a motion for summary judgment.] With these standards at hand, the Court will address the substantive questions raised.

III. DISCUSSION

Despite the lengthy recitation of facts and summary judgment standards, this is a straight-forward sale of goods problem resembling those found in a contracts or sales casebook. The fundamental question is whether Lederle Labs agreed to sell Corinthian Pharmaceuticals 1,000 vials of DTP vaccine at $64.32 per vial. As shown below, the undisputed material facts mandate the conclusion as a matter of law that no such agreement was ever formed.

A. Lederle Labs Never Agreed to Sell 1,000 Vials at the Lower Price:

Initially, it should be noted that this is a sale of goods covered by the Uniform Commercial Code, and that both parties are merchants under the Code. The parties do not discuss which state's laws are to apply to action, but because the Code is substantially the same in all states having any connection to this dispute, the Court will, for ease of reference, refer in general to the U.C.C. with relevant interpretations from Indiana and other states …

The starting point in this analysis is where did the first offer originate. An offer is "the manifestation of willingness to enter into a bargain, so made as to justify another person in understanding that his assent to that bargain is invited and will conclude it." H. Greenberg, *Rights and Remedies Under U.C.C. Article 2* § 5.2 at 50 (1987) [*hereinafter* "Greenberg, *U.C.C. Article 2*"], (*quoting* 1 *Restatement (Second), Contracts* § 4 (1981)). The only possible conclusion in this case is that Corinthian's "order" of May 19, 1986, for 1,000 vials at $64.32 was the first offer. Nothing that the seller had done prior to this point can be interpreted as an offer.

First, the price lists distributed by Lederle to its customers did not constitute offers. It is well settled that quotations are mere invitations to make an offer, Greenberg, *U.C.C. Article 2* § 5.2 at 51; *Corbin on Contracts* §§ 26, 28 (1982), particularly where, as here, the price lists specifically stated that prices were subject to change without notice and that all orders were subject to acceptance by Lederle. Greenberg, *U.C.C. Article 2* § 5.2 at 51; *Quaker State Mushroom v. Dominick's Finer Foods,* 635 F.Supp. 1281, 1284 (N.D.Ill.1986) (No offer where price quotation is subject to change and orders are subject to seller's con-firmation); *Interstate Industries, Inc. v. Barclay Industries, Inc.,* 540 F.2d 868, 873 (7th Cir.1976) (price quotation not an offer).

Second, neither Lederle's internal price memorandum nor its letter to customers dated May 20, 1986, can be construed as an offer to sell 1,000 vials at the lower price. There is no evidence that Lederle intended Corinthian to receive the internal price mem-orandum, nor is there anything in the record to support the conclusion that the May 20, 1986, letter was an offer to sell 1,000 vials to Corinthian at the lower price. If anything, the evidence shows that Corinthian was not supposed to receive this letter until after the price increase had taken place. Moreover, the letter, just like the price lists, was a mere quotation (i.e., an invitation to submit an offer) sent to all customers. As such, it did not bestow on Corinthian nor other customers the power to form a binding contract for the sale of one thousand, or, for that matter, one million vials of vaccine ...

Thus, as a matter of law, the first offer was made by Corinthian when it phoned in and subsequently confirmed its order for 1,000 vials at the lower price. The next question, then, is whether Lederle ever accepted that offer.

Under the Code, an acceptance need not be the mirror-image of the offer. U.C.C. § 2-207. However, the offeree must still do some act that manifests the intention to accept the offer and make a contract. Under § 2-206, an offer to make a contract shall be construed as inviting acceptance in any manner and by any medium reasonable in the circumstances. The first question regarding acceptance, therefore, is whether Lederle accepted the offer prior to sending the 50 vials of vaccine.

The record is clear that Lederle did not communicate or do any act prior to shipping the 50 vials that could support the finding of an acceptance. When Corinthian placed its order, it merely received a tracking number from the Telgo computer. Such an automated, ministerial act cannot constitute an acceptance. *See, e.g., Foremost Pro Color, Inc. v. Eastman Kodak Co.*, 703 F.2d 534, 539 (9th Cir.1983) (logging purchase orders as received did not manifest acceptance); *Southern Spindle & Flyer Co. v. Milliken & Co.*, 53 N.C.App. 785, 281 S.E.2d 734, 736 (1981) (seller's acknowledgement of receipt of purchase order did not constitute assent to its terms). Thus, there was no acceptance of Corinthian's offer prior to the deliver of 50 vials.

The next question, then, is what is to be made of the shipment of 50 vials and the accompanying letter. section 2-206(b) of the Code speaks to this issue:

> [A]n order or other offer to buy goods for prompt or current shipment shall be construed as inviting acceptance either by a prompt promise to ship or by the prompt or current shipment of conforming or non-conforming goods, *but such a shipment of non-conforming goods does not constitute an acceptance if the seller seasonably notifies the buyer that the shipment is offered only as an accommodation to the buyer.*

§ 2-206 (emphasis added). Thus, under the Code a seller accepts the offer by shipping goods, whether they are conforming or not, but if the seller ships non-conforming goods *and* seasonably notifies the buyer that the shipment is a mere accommodation, then the seller has not, in fact, accepted the buyer's offer. *See* Greenberg, *U.C.C. Article 2* § 5.5 at 53.

In this case, the offer made by Corinthian was for 1,000 vials at $64.32. In response, Lederle Labs shipped only 50 vials at $64.32 per vial, and wrote Corinthian indicating that the balance of the order would be priced at $171.00 per vial and would be shipped during the week of June 16. The letter further indicated that the buyer could cancel its order by calling Lederle Labs. Clearly, Lederle's shipment was non-conforming, for it was for only 1/20th of the quantity desired by the buyer. *See* § 2-106(2) (goods or conduct are conforming when they are in accordance with the obligations under the contract); *Michiana Mack, Inc. v. Allendale Rural Fire Protection*, 428 N.E.2d 1367, 1370 (Ind.App.1981) (non-conformity describes goods and conduct). The narrow issue, then, is whether Lederle's response to the offer was a shipment of non-conforming goods not constituting an acceptance because it was offered only as an accommodation under § 2-206.

An accommodation is an arrangement or engagement made as a favor to another. *Black's Law Dictionary* (5th ed. 1979). The term implies no consideration. *Id.* In this case, then, even taking all inferences favorably for the buyer, the only possible conclusion is that Lederle Labs' shipment of 50 vials was offered merely as an accommodation; that is to say, Lederle had no obligation to make the partial shipment, and did so only as a favor to the buyer. The accommodation letter, which Corinthian is sure it received, clearly stated that the 50 vials were being sent at the lower price as an exception to Lederle's general policy, and that the balance of the offer would be invoiced at the higher price. The letter further indicated that Lederle's proposal to ship the balance of the order at the higher price could be rejected by the buyer. Moreover, the standard terms of Lederle's invoice stated that acceptance of the order was expressly conditioned upon buyer's assent to the seller's terms.

Under these undisputed facts, §2-206(1)(b) was satisfied. Where, as here, the notification is properly made, the shipment of nonconforming goods is treated as a counteroffer just as at common law, and the buyer may accept or reject the counteroffer under normal contract rules. 2 W. Hawkland, *Uniform Commercial Code Series* §2-206:04 (1987).

Thus, the end result of this analysis is that Lederle Lab's price quotations were mere invitations to make an offer, that by placing its order Corinthian made an offer to buy 1,000 vials at the low price, that by shipping 50 vials at the low price Lederle's response was non-conforming, but the non-conforming response was a mere accommodation and thus constituted a counteroffer. Accordingly, there being no genuine issues of material fact on these issues and the law being in favor of the seller, summary judgment must be granted for Lederle Labs.

B. Any Contract Formed Would Have Been Governed By Lederle's Conditions:

Additionally, assuming arguendo that a contract for the sale of 1,000 vials were somehow formed, it is clear that Lederle Labs would still prevail for two related reasons. First, it is undisputed that as a result of the 1984 litigation between the parties, Corinthian agreed to be bound by the seller's terms and conditions in effect as of the date of any order. Mr. Eaton, as president of Corinthian, signed the written release in that 1984 litigation; thus he and his company are charged with knowledge of its contents. *Walb Construction Co. v. Chipman*, 202 Ind. 434, 175 N.E. 132, 135 (1931) (parties to a contract are deemed to know the contents of the agreement); *National Steel Corp. v. L.G. Wasson Coal Mining Corp.*, 338 F.2d 565, 567-68 (7th Cir.1964) (same under Kentucky law); *Terry Fashions, Ltd. v. Ultracashmere House, Ltd.*, 462 N.E.2d 252, 255 (Ind.App.1984) (same under New York law).

Throughout the parties' relationship, Lederle's terms and conditions, as set forth in its price lists and its invoices, remained the same. The price of all products remained subject to change at any time, and the seller retained the right to allocate its product as it deemed proper without incurring liability for failure to perform any contract. Under a separate contractual agreement compromising a similar dispute, Corinthian agreed to be bound by these conditions. Thus, even if a contract were ever formed in this case, Lederle retained the defenses set forth in its standard conditions.

Second and similarly, the invoice sent by Lederle clearly stated that the transaction would be governed by Lederle's terms and conditions, and that acceptance of the order was expressly made conditional on the buyer's assent thereto. Lederle thus followed the prophylactic language of §2-207 and insulated itself from any other conditions (such as the low price demanded by Corinthian) that a buyer might attempt to impose. Again, even if a contract were formed, it remained bound by Lederle's conditions giving the seller the price and allocation defenses.

For all these reasons, the defendant's motion for summary judgment is granted.

IT IS SO ORDERED.

Exercises 4-6 through 4-9 are designed to help you walk through section 2-206.

Exercise 4-6: Shipment as Acceptance: Non-conforming goods

On March 15, 2010, John sent an order to KAT TRACTORS to have three (3) brand new XLZ tractors delivered to John's property as soon as possible, but in any event no later than April 1, 2010. On March 27, 2010, KAT delivered three (3) BTR tractors (a smaller model than the XLZ model). John doesn't know what to do because the ground must be tilled by April 5, 2010, and John can't have any other tractors delivered until April 30, 2010.

Was a contract formed when KAT shipped the tractors on March 27, 2010? Why or why not? If a contract was formed, what would be a conforming tractor?

Exercise 4-7: Shipment as Acceptance: Conforming goods

BuyCo sent a purchase order to SellCo, its normal distributor of DVD players, which stated, in pertinent part: "Ship 1000 BrandX DVD Players, Model 1234, at $575 per player." SellCo received BuyCo's purchase order within two days after it was mailed. SellCo did not send any kind of writing to BuyCo, but immediately upon receipt of the purchase order, shipped the players as ordered by BuyCo. BuyCo received the players three days after shipment. BuyCo has changed its mind, and seeks your advice. Is there a contract? If so, when was it formed? If a contract was formed, what would be a conforming DVD player?

Exercise 4-8: Shipment as Acceptance: Non-Conforming Goods

BuyCo sent a purchase order to SellCo, its normal distributor of DVD players, which stated, in pertinent part: "Ship 1000 BrandX DVD Players, Model 1234, at $575 per player." SellCo received BuyCo's purchase order within two days after it was mailed. SellCo did not send any kind of writing to BuyCo, but immediately upon receipt of the purchase order, shipped 1000 BrandY DVD Players, Model 1234, at $575 per player. BuyCo does not want BrandY players, and seeks your advice. Is there a contract? If so, when was it formed? If a contract was formed, what would be a conforming DVD player?

Exercise 4-9: Shipment as Acceptance: Accommodation Shipment

BuyCo sent a purchase order to SellCo, its normal distributor of DVD players. The purchase order stated, in pertinent part: "Ship 1000 BrandX DVD Players, Model 1234, at $575 per player." SellCo received BuyCo's purchase order two days after it was mailed. In response, SellCo mailed its acknowledgement form along with the shipment. The form stated "We regret that we do not have BrandX in stock. We are sending BrandY players, instead; we hope they will be satisfactory." BuyCo does not want BrandY players and seeks your advice. Is there a contract?

If so, when was it formed? If a contract was formed, what would be a conforming DVD player?

4.3 Contract Formed by "Deviant" Acceptance of Offer

Section 2-207 is known as the attempted statutory solution to the "battle of the forms." This often-misunderstood section is poorly written. Students should carefully deconstruct the statute, one subsection at a time, before trying to apply it.

Deconstructing section 2-207 is a daunting task. First, it is important to understand what each subsection does and does not do. Following is a brief overview of each subsection, in words and graphics, followed by a more detailed discussion. *Figures 5-4, 5-5, 5-6 and 5-7 depict what the statute is trying to say—not exactly what it says—be sure to read the statute **aloud** as you review the Figures to assist you in translating the statute.*

4.3.1 Section 2-207(1)

Subsection 2-207(1) involves only one question: is there a contract? It deals with two distinct fact patterns. The first situation is one where the parties first form a contract, usually orally, and one or both of the parties follows the contract formation by sending a "written confirmation" to the other "within a reasonable time." If that written confirmation contains "additional or different terms," Section 2-207(1) confirms that section 2-207 governs the analysis of that fact pattern.

Figure 4-7 depicts the legal results of a written confirmation following contract formation, where the written confirmation contains additional or different terms.

Figure 4-7: Section 2-207(1)
Contract followed by written confirmation with additional or different terms

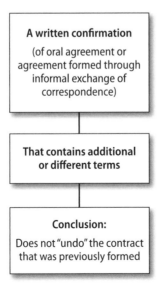

A written confirmation

(of oral agreement or agreement formed through informal exchange of correspondence)

That contains additional or different terms

Conclusion:

Does not "undo" the contract that was previously formed

The second situation is one that involves an offer and a "definite and seasonable expression of acceptance" that states terms additional to or different from the terms of the offer." In such a situation, section 2-207(1) describes two possibilities: (1) that a contract is formed, **even though** the acceptance is not a mirror image of the offer; or (2) that a contract is not formed **if** the offeree's acceptance was "expressly made conditional." The general rule under section 2-207(1) is that a contract is formed even though the acceptance contains additional or different terms. Official Comment 2 explains "Under this Article a proposed deal which in commercial understanding has in fact been closed is recognized as a contract. Therefore any additional matter contained in the confirmation or in the acceptance falls within subsection (2) and must be regarded as a proposal for an additional term."

The exception to this result is where "acceptance is expressly made conditional on assent to the additional or different terms." (This language in section 2-207(1) is sometimes referred to as "the proviso clause.") Most courts have been very strict in construing acceptances. They require more than a "conditional acceptance." Only if the acceptance expressly states that it is conditional on the offeror's assent to the additional or different terms do the courts conclude that the purported acceptance is not an acceptance. Language such as "this acceptance is subject to the following terms and conditions" has been construed as *not* making acceptance "expressly conditional on assent." An example of language that has been construed as falling within the proviso clause is, "This acceptance is expressly made conditional on your assent to the following additional terms and conditions." *Figure 4-8* depicts the legal results of an offer followed by a "definite and seasonable expression of acceptance" that contains additional or different terms.

Figure 4-8: Section 2-207(1)
Offer followed by acceptance that contains "additional or different terms"

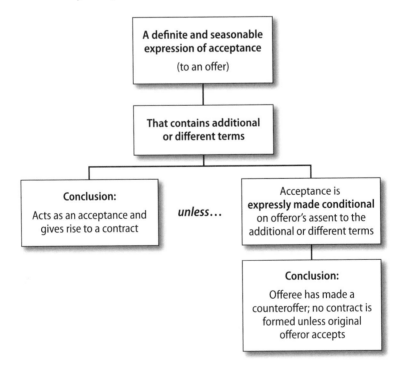

Exercise 4-10: Understanding Section 2-207

Sometimes the best way to understand a complex statute is to try to rewrite it in simple sentences, using your own words. Try that approach now. Rewrite section 2-207(1). Use simple sentences. Be sure to separate the treatment of offer and acceptance from the treatment of written confirmations. If you desire, you may create separate section numbers (For example, sections. 2-207(1.1) and (1.2).

4.3.2 Section 2-207(2): Additional Terms

Subsection (2), diagrammed in *Figure 4-9*, answers the question, if there is a contract under Subsection (1), what are its terms?

Specifically, subsection (2) governs what happens to the additional terms contained in the acceptance—are those terms part of the contract? If you apply section 2-207(1)

Figure 4-9: Section 2-207(2)

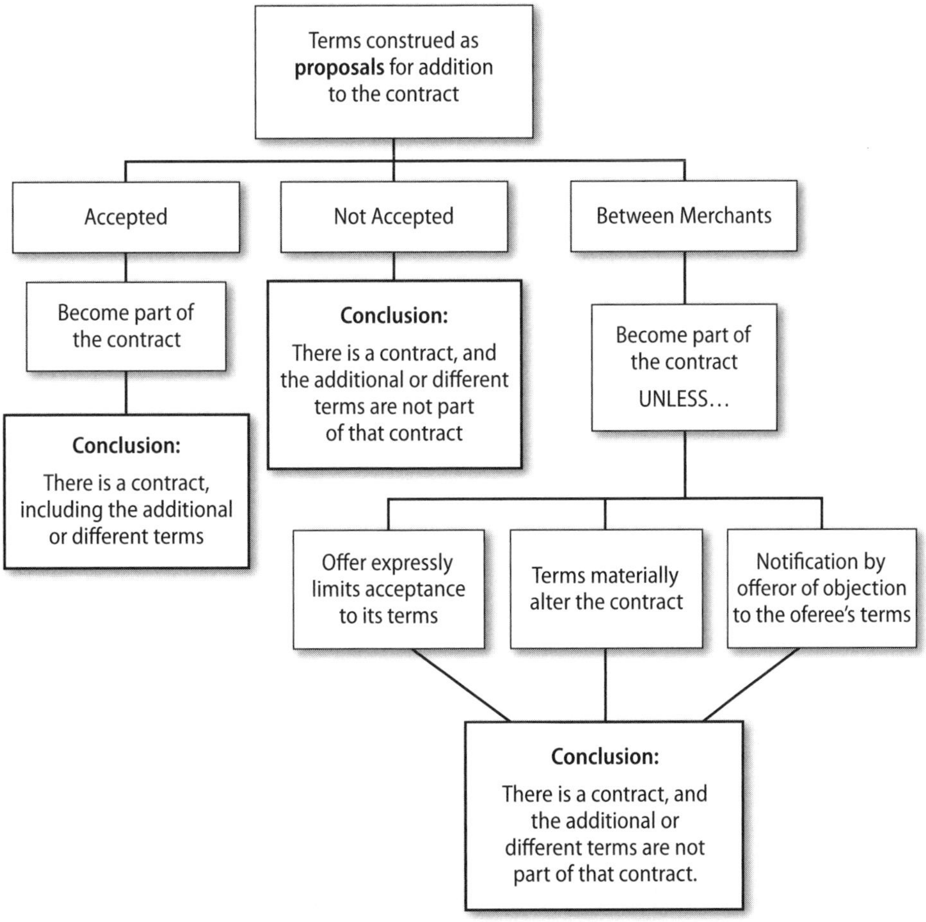

and conclude either (1) a contract was formed through an offer and acceptance OR (2) a contract was formed followed by a written confirmation, then you must apply section 2-207(2) to determine the resulting contract terms. If you apply section 2-207(1) and conclude that there is no contract, then and only then should you proceed to section 2-207(3) to see if the parties acted as if there were a contract. *Because section 2-207(2) does not address contract formation, regardless of your conclusions regarding the additional contract terms under section 2-207(2), you can **never** reach a conclusion regarding contract formation when applying section 2-207(2). That conclusion was reached when you did your analysis under section 2-207(1).*

4.3.3 Section 2-207(2): Different Terms

Subsection (2) is perhaps the most confusing part of the entire statute. Although subsection (1) refers to "additional or different" terms, subsection (2) drops the reference to "different" terms. As a result, conflicting lines of authority have developed with respect to whether section 2-207(2) addresses different terms, or whether its application is limited to additional terms only. The two basic approaches are (1) subsection (2) applies only to additional terms, and (2) subsection (2) applies to both additional and different terms.

The majority of jurisdictions follow the first approach, which says that section 2-207(2) does not apply to "different" terms because the word "different" does not appear in section 2-207(2). The majority of courts to follow this view have adopted the so-called "knock-out" rule, under which different terms in the offer and acceptance "knock each other out." The rationale of this approach is that the acceptance is treated as accepting only the terms in the offeror's form which do not conflict with the terms of the offeree's form. If as a result of the "knock out," a term is missing, Article 2 gap fillers are used to fill in the missing term.

In a minority of jurisdictions, who also conclude that section 2-207(2) does not apply to "different terms," the offeree is treated as having accepted all of the offeror's terms. The "different" terms in the offeree's form disappear, and the offeror's terms control.

The second approach, which is followed in a minority of jurisdictions, treats "different" terms as included under the aegis of "additional" terms in section 2-207(2). Under section 2-207(2)(b), these "different terms" materially alter the contract, so they do not become part of the contract.

4.3.4 Section 2-207(3)

Section 2-207(3), diagrammed in *Figure 4-10*, answers two questions: (1) Is there a contract? AND (2) If so, what are its terms? If your analysis under section 2-207(1) leads to the conclusion that no contract was formed through the exchange of writings, but the parties nevertheless act as if there is a contract, you may find that a contract exists under section 2-207(3). In that case and that case only, section 2-207(3) will also tell you the resulting contract terms.

Some students find that flowcharts or tables assist in the deconstruction process. Figures 4-11, 4-12 and 4-13 are more examples of such study aids.

Figure 4-10: Section 2-207(3)

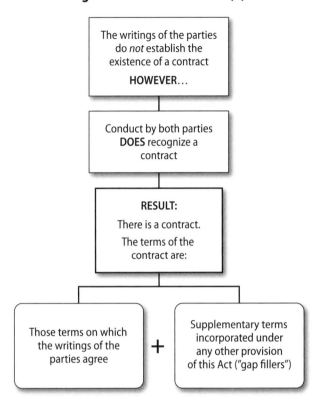

Figure 4-11: Approaches to Analyzing Section 2-207 Problems

Fact Pattern Involves **Written Confirmation of Existing Contract**

(1) Did the parties enter into an oral agreement regarding a transaction in goods?

(2) If yes, did one party then send a written confirmation of the agreement to the other?

(3) If yes, did the written confirmation contain terms different or additional to those previously agreed upon?

(4) If yes, use section 2-207(2) to analyze contract terms.

(5) Were both parties merchants? If not, those additional/different terms are proposals for addition to the contract and should be analyzed under section 2-209 re contract modification—will need to be accepted.

(6) If both parties are merchants analyze under section 2-207(2)—specifically, determine whether proposed terms 'materially alter' oral agreement (Consult OC 3, 4, 5)

(7) If they materially alter, they do NOT become part of the contract. (But there is still a contract!)

(8) If they do not materially alter, they DO become part of the contract.

Figure 4-12: Paths to Contract Formation and Contract Terms Analysis Under U.C.C. § 2-207

	2-207(1)	2-207(1)	2-207(1)	2-207(3)
Statutory Language Applies to:	**Offer** / *followed by* / Definite and seasonable **expression of Acceptance** / "that contains additional or different terms"	**Oral or Informal Agreement (Contract is formed at this stage under section 2-204)** / *followed by* / **Written Confirmation** / "that contains additional or different terms"	**Offer** / *followed by* / Definite and seasonable **expression of acceptance** that contains additional or different terms **that makes acceptance expressly conditional on the original offeror's assent to the offeree's additional or different terms**	**Offer** / *is **not** followed by acceptance,* **either** because / (a) there is no response, / (b) the response is not a "definite and seasonable expression of acceptance," / **or** / (c) the acceptance is "expressly conditional" **and** it is **not** followed by "express assent."
Result:	A contract is formed; to determine the terms of the contract, see section 2-207(2).	Section 2-207(2) applies to determine the terms of the contract.	When an "expressly conditional" acceptance is sent in response to an offer **there is no contract yet.** The "expressly conditional" acceptance is a counter-offer, which the original offeror must accept for a contract to be formed. **If** the offeror expressly assents, the terms of the contract are those of the *counter-offer* (Sections 2-207(2) and 2-207(3) will not apply to the analysis).	There is no contract formed under section 2-207(1). You will *never* refer to section 2-207(2) in such a fact pattern. However, if the parties' **conduct** forms a contract, even though the writings do not, section 2-207(3) finds a contract. The terms are those on which the parties' **writings agree** plus the Code "gap fillers."

Figure 4-13: Approaches to Analyzing Section 2-207 Problems

Fact Pattern Involves **Contract Formation Through Exchange of Forms**

(1) Did one party transmit an offer to enter into a contract, to which the offeree responded in writing?

(2) If yes, was the response a "definite" and "seasonable" expression of acceptance?

(3) If not, there is no contract under section 2-207(1).

(4) If YES, did the definite and seasonable expression of acceptance contain additional or different terms?

(5) If YES, did it make acceptance "expressly conditional on assent to the additional or different terms?"

(6) If YES, there is NO CONTRACT under section 2-207(1) (the proviso clause)—the 'acceptance' is treated like a counter-offer and the original offeror must expressly assent to the additional/different terms. If the offeror DOES so assent, there is a contract under section 2-207(1) and the terms are the terms of the original offer AS MODIFIED BY the ones the offeror expressly assented to.

(7) If NO to question 5 (meaning acceptance is NOT 'expressly conditional') there IS a contract under section 2-207(1) and the issue is what are the terms of the contract—go to section 2-207(2).

(8) Are the parties merchants? If NO, did they assent to the additional/different terms? If NO, there IS STILL a contract under section 2-207(1)—additional/different terms are NOT included.

(9) If YES, the parties ARE merchants, need to determine whether the additional/different terms become part of the contract. Apply section 2-207(2)(a)(b)(c).

(10) IF YOU DETERMINE THAT NO CONTRACT IS FORMED UNDER section 2-207(1), DID THE PARTIES NEVERTHELESS ACT AS IF THEY HAD A CONTRACT? (usually this means someone shipped goods and someone else kept them/paid for them)

(11) If YES, there is a contract under section 2-207(3) and the terms are those on which the writings agree PLUS the code 'gap fillers.'

Exercise 4-11: Applying Section 2-207: Representative Fact Patterns

White and Summers identified a variety of fact patterns that raise section 2-207 issues.[9] For each fact pattern described below, determine (a) whether a contract was formed and (b) if so, what the terms of the contract would be. In each case, make the determination twice: once, assuming the parties are not merchants; a second time, assuming that the parties are merchants.

1. Cases in which the parties send printed forms to one another, and an express term in the second form is different from an express term in the first. (Assume, for example, that buyer's form (the "offer") states that disputes must be arbitrated, whereas the seller's form (the "acceptance") says "no arbitration.")

---

9. White & Summers, *supra* n.20, at 38-39.

2. Cases in which an express term is found in the first form sent (the offer), but no term on that question appears in the second. (Assume, for example, that the offer states that disputes must be arbitrated, and the second form is silent on that matter.)

3. Case in which an express term is found in the second form (the acceptance), but there is no consistent or conflicting term in the first. (Assume, for example, that the offer is silent with respect to arbitration, and the second form states that disputes must be arbitrated.)

4. Cases in which an express term is found in the second form but not in the first, and the second form is a counter-offer (because "expressly conditional"). (Assume the facts as set forth in #3, but that in addition, the second form states "Our acceptance of your offer is expressly conditioned on your agreement to the arbitration provision.")

5. Cases in which the offeror's form contains a term that provides that no contract will be formed unless the offeree accepts all of the terms on the form and suggests no others. (For example, the offer may read: This offer can only be accepted by agreement to each and every term set forth herein and no additional or different terms.)

6. Cases in which there is a prior oral agreement or other agreement, followed by a written confirmation. (In cases (1) through (5) White and Summers assumed that there may be prior oral negotiations but that no oral agreement was reached before parties sent their forms.) (Assume, for example, that buyer and seller speak over the phone and agree to buy and sell 1000 XYZ widgets at $1 per widget. The parties do not discuss arbitration. Thereafter, seller mails buyer a "sales confirmation" that states that disputes must be arbitrated.)

7. Cases in which the parties do not use forms but send a variety of messages and letters, and conduct intermittent oral negotiations that ultimately produce an agreement.

8. Cases in which the second form differs so radically from the first that it does not constitute an "acceptance." (Assume, for example, the offer states "Buyer will buy 1000 red XYZ benches at $15/bench" and Seller's reply states: "Seller will sell 50 blue ABC chairs at $10/chair.")

9. Cases in which the conduct of the parties indicates that there is a contract.

Exercise 4-12: Applying Section 2-207: Is there "a definite and seasonable expression of acceptance?"

Buyco sent Selco a signed writing, offering to buy 100 Apple 4-G iPods for $150 each, delivery date to be October 15th.[10] Selco responded, agreeing to sell

---

10. You should assume that Buyco made an offer.

the iPods to Buyco, in a signed writing that mirrored all of the terms of Buyco's offer, except that it changed the delivery date to December 15.

Did the parties form a contract through the exchange of writings described above? Explain why or why not. If a contract was formed, what is the delivery date?

Exercise 4-13: Applying Section 2-207:
Is Acceptance "expressly made conditional" on assent to additional or different terms?

Bertha Businesswoman needed a new copy machine for her office. She surfed the internet and saw Kopy King's advertisement for a new Kopy King Model 12345 copier for $1,500. The ad stated: "Quantities limited. Call now to order." She faxed the following message to Kopy King: "I saw your advertisement on the net. Please ship me immediately one Kopy King Model 12345 copier for $1,500." Kopy King responded with the following fax: "Thank you for your offer to buy a Kopy King Model 12345 for $1,500. We are pleased to accept your offer. Any disputes regarding the performance of the copier must be decided through binding arbitration. We will ship the copier within three days, however, we must first receive your written assent to arbitrate any disputes. We look forward to hearing from you."

As soon as Bertha receives Kopy King's fax, she calls her lawyer and asks: "What is going on? Do I have a contract to buy a copier? Why or why not? If so, do I have to arbitrate any disputes?" Please respond to Bertha's questions.

Exercise 4-14: Applying Section 2-207:
Merchants and Non-Merchants; Material Alterations

After a series of communications, on January 1, 2007 Serena Seller, *who was engaged in the business of selling fax machines*, signed and mailed the following written **offer** to Paula Purchaser, *a consumer*.

I **offer** to sell you a model F-120 fax machine for $750 cash, payment due within ten days of delivery. You have until January 20, 2007, to accept this offer. Serena Seller

Paula responded to Serena's **offer** by depositing the following response in the mail at noon on January 15, 2007: Paula's response reached Serena before January 20.

I assent to your offer and will take the fax machine for $750, payment due within ten days of delivery. I reserve the right to return the machine before the expiration of that ten day period if it is not satisfactory. Paula Purchaser

Serena did not respond, and did not ship the fax machine to Paula.

1. If Paula sues Serena for breach of contract, who will win? Why? Discuss fully.

2. **Regardless** of your answer to the previous question, **assume** that a contract was formed between Serena and Paula. Is the right to return the machine a term of that contract?

3. **Now, regardless of your answers to the previous questions, assume** that a contract was formed between Serena and Paula. **Also assume** that both Serena and Paula are merchants. Is the right to return the machine a term of that contract?

4.4 Contract Modifications

Students sometimes wonder why the topic of contract modifications is included in this chapter on contract formation. The short answer is that Part 2 of Article 2 is entitled "Form, Formation and Readjustment of Contract," and this book follows the order of the Code. However, if you reflect on the question, you will realize that many of the same issues that arise in connection with contract formation arise in connection with attempted contract modification. For example, at common law, a basic rule is that consideration is required to make a contract enforceable.[11] Common law also requires consideration to make a modification enforceable.[12] Contracts are generally formed through the process of offer and acceptance.[13] Similarly, parties often arrive at contract modifications through the process of offer and acceptance. Accordingly, it makes sense to study the topic of contract modifications in connection with our study of contract formation.

Section 2-209 is the Code's black letter law on contract modifications. It is relatively straightforward. Subsection (1) specifically displaces the common law rule that requires consideration. It states "an agreement modifying a contract within this Article needs no consideration to be binding." Subsection (2) validates a contract clause commonly known as a "no oral modification clause." At common law, even when parties' contracts provided that the contract could only be modified in writing, courts uniformly held that an oral modification could be enforced so long as there was consideration for the change.[14] Subsection (2) provides that such a provision will be enforced, with one exception. In an exception that parallels the exception in the merchant firm offer provision, Subsection (2) requires that a "no oral modification" clause in a form prepared by a merchant and signed by a non-merchant must be "separately signed" by the non-merchant to be enforceable.[15]

Subsection (3) requires compliance with the statute of frauds for a contract modification to be enforceable.[16]

---

11. E. Allen Farnsworth, *Contracts* 18 (4th ed. 2004).
12. *Id* at 267.
13. *Id* at 110.
14. *Id* at 570-571.
15. See discussion of U.C.C.section 2-205 in Section 3.1 of this book, supra. regarding "separately signed."
16. There is an interpretive issue regarding the application of section 2-209(3): Specifically, if the original contract fell within the statute of frauds and the statute of frauds was satisfied, must the modification nevertheless also satisfy the statute of frauds? Or, alternatively, does it only mean that if the original contract did not fall within the statute of frauds and the contract as modified DOES fall within the statute of frauds, the *modification* must satisfy the statute of frauds?

Finally, Subsections (4) and (5) codify common law rules regarding rescission, waiver, and retraction.

Because the most common issues raised by contract modifications are issues of good faith and issues of compliance with the statute of frauds, problems involving contract modifications are included in Chapter 5 on contract defenses, rather than in this chapter.

4.5 Third Parties, Assignment and Delegation

4.5.1 Basic Terminology

Section 2-210 states the basic rules for assignment and delegation. To understand the rules, it is important to understand the context in which the rules apply. Both assignments and delegations involve a party who was not a party to the original contract. This party becomes involved sometime after the original contract is formed. The original contract does not contemplate performance by (or to) that party. Subsequently, one of the original contract parties seeks to transfer his rights and/or duties under the contract to a third party. This third party is known as an assignee or delegate. The terminology used to discuss this topic is explained in *Figures 4-14* and *4-15*.

Figure 4-14: Assignment Parties

Assignor	The one who makes the assignment
Assignee	The one who receives the assignment
Obligor	The one who will be rendering the performance that is the subject matter of the contract (the party who is obligated to perform)
Obligee	The one who is to receive the performance that is the subject matter of the contract (At the time of contract formation, the obligee is the party who is the assignor in the assignment; after the assignment, the obligee is the assignee)

Figure 4-15: Delegation parties

Obligor	The one who is obligated to perform
Delegator	The one who delegates the duty to perform (same person as obligor)
Obligee	The one who is to receive the performance that is the subject matter of the contract
Delegatee	The one who receives the delegation and is now obligated to both the delegator and the obligee to perform

Figures 4-16 and *4-17* on the next page clarify the relationship(s) of parties to assignments and delegations. These figures may assist you in your analysis of these issues. Always try to "picture" the cast of players from the case you are currently reading or the problem you are trying to analyze, to see which of the following roles they play.

Figure 4-16: Parties to an Assignment (Assignment of Rights)

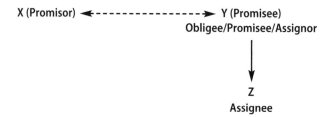

Figure 4-17: Parties to a Delegation: (Delegation of Duties)

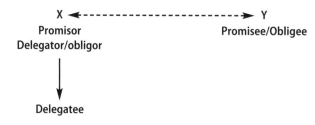

4.5.2 Basic Rules

Now that you understand who the parties are, read section 2-210 and its Official Comments. As you can see, most of the rules that you learned in common law contracts remain the same under the Code. Official Comment 7 emphasizes that the section is not intended as a complete statement of the law of delegation and assignment, but is limited to "clarifying a few points" doubtful under the case law.

The general rule is that contract rights are assignable, and duties are delegable. The exception to this general rule is that rights cannot be assigned where the assignment would materially change the duty of the other party or increase materially the burden or risk imposed on him by contract or impair materially his chance of obtaining return performance. Such situations are relatively rare. Similarly, the general rule is that duties may be delegated unless otherwise agreed or unless the other party has a substantial interest in having his original promisor perform.

Because the Code favors free assignability, clients are well advised to respond to an attempted assignment or delegation with a demand for adequate assurances of performance as stated in section 2-210(6) (discussed in Chapter11, *supra.*) rather than treating the attempt as a breach of contract.

Additional Resources

C. Itoh & Co. v. The Jordan Int'l Co. 552 F.2d 1228 (7th Cir 1977).

Con. Aggregates Corp. v. Hewitt-Robins Inc., 404 F.2d 505 (7th Cir 1968).

Dorton & Collins v. Aikman Corp., 453 F.2d 1161 (6th Cir 1972).

David Harrison, Annotation, *Farmers as "merchants" within provisions of U.C.C. article 2, dealing with sales,* 95 A.L.R.3d 484 (2008).

David Harrison, Annotation, *Who is "merchant" under U.C.C. § 2-314(1) dealing with implied warranties of merchantability,* 91 A.L.R.3d 876 (2008).

Thomas McCarthy, "*Ending the 'Battle of the Forms': A Symposium on the Revision of Section 2-207 of the Uniform Commercial Code,*" The Bus. Law. 1019, 1053 (May 1994).

Figure 5-1: Graphic Organizer

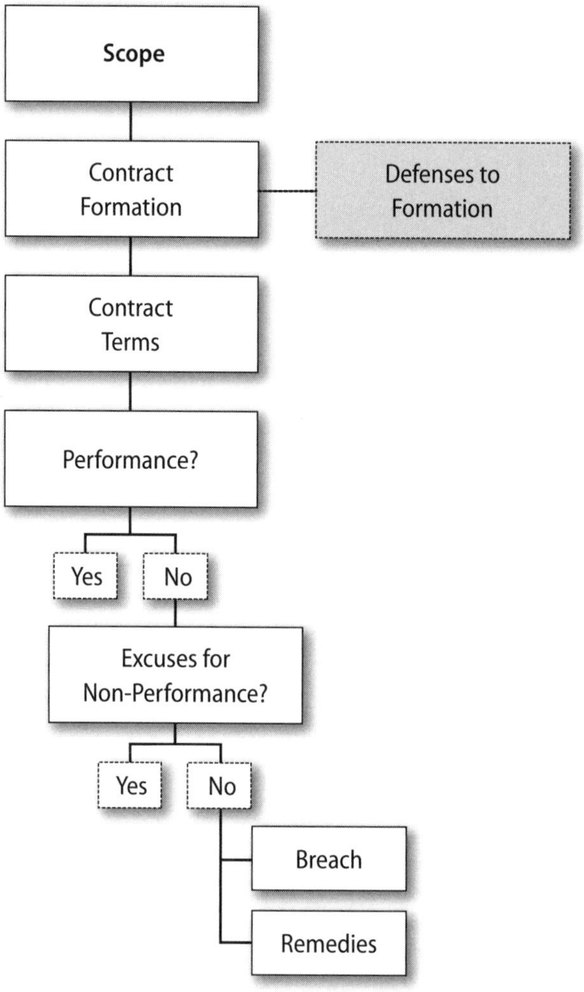

Chapter 5

Defenses

Chapter Problem

On Tuesday, November 13, 2005, Bobby Z, a well known Hip Hop artist, telephoned Snoop Dog, the manufacturer and distributor of Snoop's Super Snack Barz. "Hey, Snoop," Bobby greeted, "I heard your snack barz aren't selling too well and thought you might have some overstock. I'm sponsoring a Twenty Cent Basketball Camp in Long Beach for young kids over the Christmas Break. You know how hungry kids get. Is there any chance you could make me a good deal?" "Yeah," Snoop responded. "I got overstock of 20,000 cases; I'd be willing to let you have all you can use to feed those little players at the reduced price of $5.00 per case." "That's cool, man," Bobby replied. "Since Long Beach is your old neighborhood, you ought to be willing to help out the kids."

The next day, Bobby sent the following brief note to Snoop:

"This is to confirm our agreement entered into yesterday for the purchase and sale of 20,000 cases of Snoop's Super Snack Barz for immediate delivery at $5.00 per case. Any disputes arising out of this order shall be arbitrated under the laws of the State of Western. We appreciate your help in sponsoring the Twenty Cent Basketball Camp."

/s/ Bobby Z

The note arrived at Snoop's business offices and was promptly filed. No one responded to Bobby's note. The Snack Barz were not shipped. Because of Snoop's promise, Bobby Z made no other arrangements to provide food for the campers. He was unable to make last minute arrangements and as a result, several campers suffered severe hunger pangs and collapsed from weakness. Their parents are suing Bobby.

Bobby begins arbitration proceedings against Snoop for breach of contract in the State of Western. **Assume that a contract was formed during the phone conversation between Bobby and Snoop, and answer the following question ONLY:**

Can Snoop defend the action based on the fact that he never signed anything relating to the sale?

In this chapter, we study Article 2's defense provisions. As *Figure 5-2* illustrates, the effect of contract defenses is to render a contract unenforceable. Article 2 has not codified all of the defenses that historically were raised to prevent enforcement of certain contracts; however, under section 1-103 the common law defenses are applicable to sales contracts. The common law defenses include fraud, mistake, undue influence, duress, lack of capacity, and unconscionability. Also, courts historically have refused to enforce some contracts on public policy grounds (sometimes courts refer to those contract defenses as

Figure 5-2: Effect of Contract Defenses

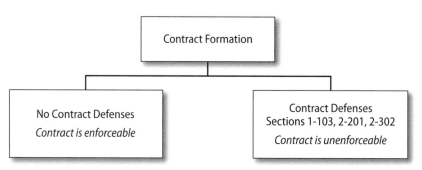

"illegality.") Unconscionability and the statute of frauds are the only defenses to formation that are explicitly codified in Article 2.[1]

The Code sections and definitions that you need to know for this chapter are summarized in *Figure 5-3*.

Figure 5-3: Contract Defenses Sections and Definitions

Section	Definitions
1-103	Fraud, Mistake, Undue Influence, Duress, Capacity, Unconscionability, Public Policy
2-201	Merchant (2-104) Writing (1-201)
2-302	Unconscionable

1. The Statute of Frauds

You will recall that under common law, several types of contracts usually were subject to the applicable statute of frauds. These types of contracts included contracts for the sale of goods above a certain price. Although the elimination of the statute of frauds was considered and hotly debated during the recent U.C.C. Article 2 revision process, the U.C.C. continues to retain a statute of frauds.

To deconstruct section 2-201, first determine whether the statute applies at all. A contract to which the statute of frauds applies is commonly said to be "within" the statute of frauds. See *Figure 5-4*.

Next, if you determine that the contract is "within" the statute of frauds, you must see whether the statutory requirements are met. If not, the contract will not be enforceable. *Figure 5-5* illustrates the questions that must be resolved to decide if the requirements of section 2-201(1) are met, and the statute of frauds is "satisfied."

---

1. Article 2 also contains a statute of limitations provision, U.C.C. section 2-725, which we study in connection with warranties.

Figure 5-4: Is a Contract Within the Statute of Frauds?

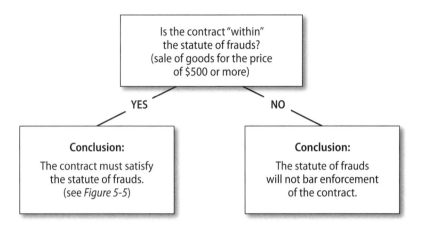

Figure 5-5: Statute of Frauds Analysis under § 2-201(1)

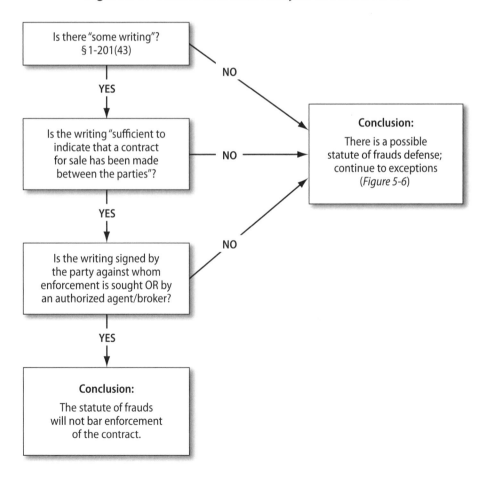

Figure 5-6: Exceptions for Contracts That Fail to Comply with § 2-201(1)

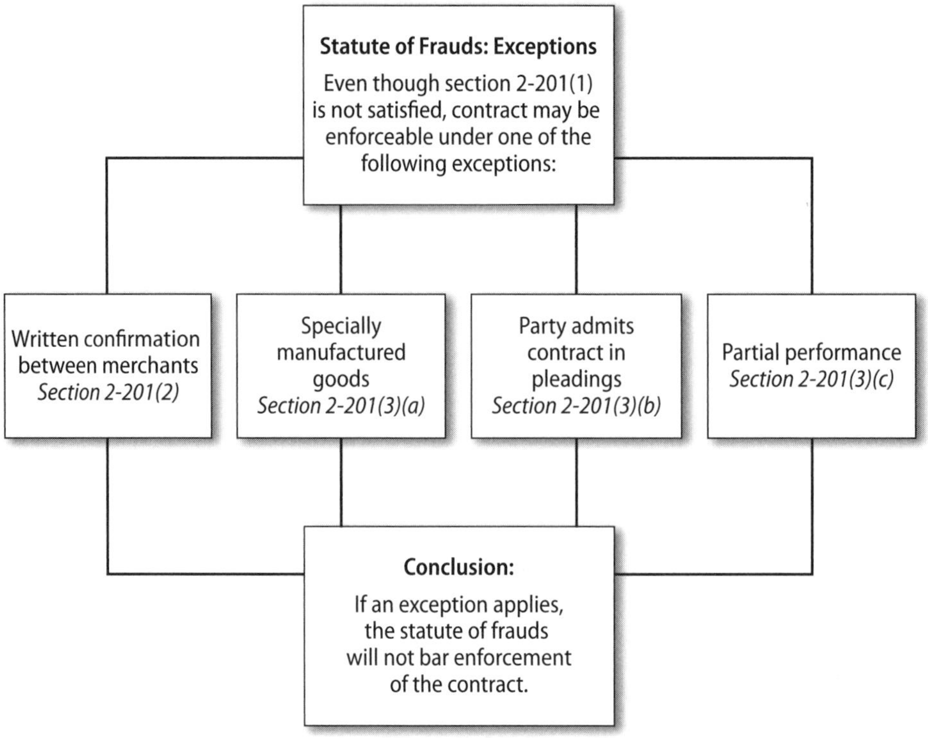

Figure 5-5 indicates that if a contract fails to satisfy the requirements of section 2-201(1) it is premature to reach a conclusion regarding unenforceability. Instead, as shown in *Figure 5-6*, you must first analyze each of the exceptions in sections 2-201(2) and 2-201(3) to see if they apply.

Note that sections 2-201(2) and 2-201(3) must be deconstructed for proper analysis. Section 2-201(2) is particularly complex.

Exercise 5-1: Deconstructing Sections 2-201(2) and 2-201(3)

Use the statutory analysis skills you have developed in this course, and create a diagram, table or other method to deconstruct sections 2-201(2) and 2-201(3).

Exercise 5-2: Contract Modifications and the Statute of Frauds

Sal decided to sell his used car. On Sunday morning, he parked the car on a vacant lot, and placed a "for sale" sign in the window. On Monday, Bea saw the "for sale" sign and called Sal to inquire about the car. Sal told her that the car needed a paint job, but was otherwise in good condition. After further discussion, Bea agreed to buy the car for $3500 and to pay Sal by Friday, June 1.

On Tuesday, Sal's wife, who was unaware of the agreement between Sal and Bea, had the car repainted. When Sal came home from work and saw what his wife had done, he called Bea to inform her that the car had been repainted and asked for $3990 instead, to account for the paint job.

Assume that an oral contract was formed.

1. Does Bea have an enforceable contract to buy the car for $3500? Why or why not?

2. If Bea tells Sal she will pay $3990 and changes her mind, does Sal have an enforceable contract to sell the car to Bea for $3990? Why or why not?

Now assume the same facts except that the car was a toy car, the original price agreed upon was $450, and after the paint job, Bea agreed to pay $550.

1. Does Bea have an enforceable contract to buy the toy car for $450? Why or why not?

2. If Bea tells Sal she will pay $550 and changes her mind, does Sal have an enforceable contract to sell the car to Bea for $550? Why or why not?

---

2. Unconscionability[2]

The doctrine of unconscionability focuses on the formation stage of the contract. Unlike an assent analysis, however, an unconscionability analysis does not examine whether the parties agreed to the disputed terms. An unconscionability analysis focuses on (1) the bargaining process leading to purported agreement to the terms (sometimes referred to as "procedural unconscionability"), and (2) the substantive "fairness" of the disputed terms ("substantive unconscionability"). If a court deems a term unconscionable, it will strike the term from the contract. When the contract as a whole is unconscionable, the court may refuse to enforce the entire contract.

The unconscionability defense developed in the equity courts, where chancellors used the analysis to police bargains which appeared to be unfair, but which resisted attack under traditional contract defenses. Although the defense long predates legislative enactment, its use became increasingly widespread after its incorporation into U.C.C. Article 2 and the Restatement (Second) of Contracts. Most jurisdictions have applied the doctrine not only to transactions governed by Article 2, but also to contracts outside its scope.

The most common approach to an unconscionability analysis follows the framework first outlined by Arthur Leff in his seminal article that critiqued section 2-302 for its failure to include a definition of the term.[3] However, although section 2-302 is itself silent on how to determine unconscionability, the Official Comments give some guidance. Specifically, it can be inferred from the Official Comments that "[t]he basic test of unconscionability

---

2. The unconscionability discussion is taken from Edith R. Warkentine, *Beyond Unconscionability: The Case for Using "Knowing Assent" as the basis for Analyzing Unbargained-for Terms in Standard Form Contracts*, 31 Seattle U. L. Rev. 469 (2008).

3. Arthur A. Leff, *Unconscionability and the Code — The Emperor's New Clause*, 115 U .Pa. L .Rev. 485 (1967).

is whether, in the light of the general commercial background and the commercial needs of the particular trade or case, the clauses involved are so one-sided as to be unconscionable under the circumstances existing at the time of the making of the contract.... The principle is one of the prevention of oppression and unfair surprise (citation omitted) and not of disturbance of allocation of risks because of superior bargaining power."

The Official Comments reflect Leff's proposed analytic framework. He advanced a two-prong analysis where a court will not enforce the term if it finds both procedural and substantive unconscionability. Procedural unconscionability typically rests on defects in the bargaining process, such as clauses that are "buried" in fine print, or lack of negotiations over terms. On the other hand, terms are substantively unconscionable when they are unduly "harsh," or "one-sided." Although most courts follow Leff's view that elements of both procedural and substantive unconscionability must be present before a term is un-enforceable, many have adopted the viewpoint that a "sliding scale" is appropriate; that is, the more egregious the procedural unconscionability, the less substantive unconscionability need be present, and vice versa. In a minority of jurisdictions, terms may be excised upon proof of either procedural or substantive unconscionability; both are not required.

Immediately after states began adopting Article 2, parties rarely raised unconscionability defenses, and those who did had little success. Gradually, however, the number of reported cases involving an unconscionability defense swelled. These cases usually involve the enforceability of particular standard form contract terms. If a court deems a clause uncon-scionable, the court will not enforce it. Sometimes the behavior complained of is so severe that a court will refuse to enforce the entire contract. What most of the successful cases tend to have in common is a consumer defendant who signed a standard form contract. Cases involving sophisticated business people who have successfully asserted an unconscionability argument are almost nonexistent. However, courts have been willing to rule in favor of non-consumers who raise the defense that they lack business sophistication and legal rep-resentation, because they more closely resemble a consumer than a business person.

Decisions based on unconscionability are fact sensitive and, to a great extent, reflect trial judges' subjective determinations. As a result, although there are now many cases that address unconscionability, they have little value as precedents. One can make predictions as to the outcome of a particular case based on how closely the facts resemble a reported decision, but ultimately it will always be necessary to await the decision of the court.

Exercise 5-3: Applying Section 2-302

In the Chapter Problem, assume that Snoop is located in Boston, Massachusetts, and Bobby is located in Long Beach, California. Now assume that instead of as stated in the Chapter Problem, Snoop followed up the telephone conversation with the following note to Bobby:

"This is to confirm our agreement entered into yesterday for the purchase and sale of 20,000 cases of Snoop's Super Snack Barz for immediate delivery at $5.00 per case. Any controversy related to our agreement, or any breach thereof, including without limitation any claim that the agreement or any portion of it is invalid, illegal or otherwise voidable or void shall be submitted to binding arbitration in Boston Massachusetts; provided, however, I reserve the absolute right to obtain a provisional remedy including without limitation injunctive relief from any court of competent jurisdiction as may be necessary in my sole subjective judgment to protect my proprietary information including, without limitation, my recipe for the Snack Barz. The Arbitrator, and not any federal, state or local court or agency, shall have exclusive authority to resolve any dispute relating to the interpretation, applicability, enforceability or formation of our agreement including, but not limited to any claim that all or any part of our agreement is void or voidable. All costs of arbitration shall be divided equally between the parties."

Also assume that Bobby read the note and called Snoop to discuss it, and Snoop replied "Take it or leave it. I don't sell to you without your signature on that agreement." Anxious to conclude the deal and worried about his ability to buy the necessary snacks in time for his event, Bobby signed the note.

Now, when the campers' parents sue Bobby he tries to sue Snoop for breach of contract in California. Snoop moves for an order staying the action and compelling Bobby to submit his claims to arbitration and Bobby argues that the arbitration agreement is unconscionable.

How should the trial court rule on Snoop's motion?

Additional Resources

Arthur Allen Leff, *Unconscionability and the Crowd—Consumers and the Common Law Tradition*, 31 U. Pitt L. Rev. 349 (1970).

M.P. Ellinghaus, *In Defense of Unconscionability*, 78 Yale L.J. 757 (1969).

Robert A. Hillman, *Debunking Some Myths About Unconscionability: A New Framework for U.C.C. Section 2-302*, 67 Cornell L. Rev. 1 (1981).

Randy Koeners, Annotation, *Sales: construction of statute of frauds exception under U.C.C. § 2-201(2) for confirmatory writing between merchants*, 82 A.L.R.4th 709 (2009).

Thomas Malia, Annotation, *Sales: "specially manufactured goods" statute of frauds exception in U.C.C. § 2-201(3)(a)*, 45 A.L.R.4th 1126 (2009).

John E. Murray Jr., *Unconscionability: Unconscionability*, 31 U. Pitt L. Rev. 1 (1969).

Susan Randall, *Judicial Attitudes Toward Arbitration and the Resurgence of Unconscionability*, 52 Buff. L. Rev. 185 (2004).

Martin B. Shulkin, *Unconscionability—The Code, the Court and the Consumer*, 9 B.C Indus. & Com. L. Rev. 367 (1968) (reviewing early cases decided under U.C.C. § 2-302).

John A. Spanogle Jr., *Analyzing Unconscionability Problems*, 117 U. Pa. L. Rev. 931 (1969).

Richard E. Speidel, *Unconscionability, Assent and Consumer Protection*, 31 U. Pitt. L. Rev. 359 (1970).

Timothy Travers, *Three annotations regarding the statute of frauds*, 88 A.L.R.3d 416 (2008), 97 A.L.R.3d 908 (2008), 40 A.L.R.2d 760 (2009).

Figure 6-1: Graphic Organizer

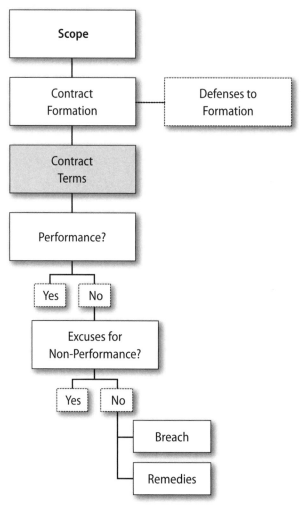

Chapter 6

Contract Terms: Warranties, Warranty Disclaimers, and Remedy Limitations

Chapter Problem

Bruce Byer was interested in buying a yacht. He visited the YachtCo showroom and spoke with a YachtCo salesperson, who gave him a copy of YachtCo's sales brochure for the 3375 Espirit model yacht, manufactured by YachtCo. Byer read and reviewed this brochure, paying particular attention to a page that contained a photograph of YachtCo's 3375 Espirit model apparently moving through water at a high rate of speed. Accompanying the photograph was a caption that read as follows:

"Offering the best performance and cruising accommodations in its class, the 3375 Espirit offers a choice of stern drive or inboard power, superb handling and sleeping accommodations for six."

Byer paid somewhat less attention to the following two paragraphs, which appeared on the last page of the 25-page brochure, in the same size font as all of the other information in the brochure:

1. Any YachtCo yacht found by the factory to be defective in materials or workmanship within 10 years from the date of purchase will be repaired or replaced at the option of the manufacturer.

2. This warranty is expressly in lieu of all other warranties, and any implied warranties of merchantability or fitness for a particular purpose created hereby are limited in duration to the same duration as the express warranty herein.

Due in part to the depictions in the brochure, Byer bought a 3375 Espirit model yacht for over $150,000.

Discuss the following issues ONLY:

1. Did any express warranties arise by virtue of the sales brochure given by the YachtCo salesperson to Byer? If so, be very specific with respect to what each express warranty would be.

2. Did any other warranties arise by virtue of the sale from YachtCo to Byer?

3. What is the legal significance of the two paragraphs from the brochure reproduced above?

1. Introduction to the Study of Contract Terms

Once you have determined that the parties have formed an enforceable contract and that there are no applicable defenses, the question becomes: what has each of the parties agreed to do? To answer that question, we now begin our study of contract terms. This chapter is the first of three chapters that explain how to determine the terms of the contract. The contract terms determine the parties' rights and obligations. A thorough understanding of contract terms, then, enables the student to analyze performance by comparing what was promised to what was actually received.

Contract terms can be express (stated by the parties, either orally or in writing) or implied (in fact or by law). In addition, because Article 2 makes it relatively easy to form contracts and the parties may well not have negotiated each and every term of the contract, Article 2 contains many "default" terms, often referred to as "gap fillers," that become part of the parties' agreement unless the parties expressly negate those terms. Warranties are some of the most important contract terms in sales contracts, so we begin our study of contract terms with warranties. (Note that warranties can be express or implied.)

2. Introduction to Warranties

The subject of warranties is very complex. I have learned from past students that it is helpful to first overview all of the material to be covered, and then return to each topic separately. Therefore, what follows is a short synopsis to make it easier for you to grasp the technical nuances involved in understanding warranties, warranty disclaimers, and remedy limitations.

First, we explore how warranties are created. Under appropriate circumstances, the warranty of title is automatically part of a sales contract. Express warranties arise because of affirmative acts or statements made by the seller of goods. Unless properly disclaimed, the implied warranty of merchantability arises when goods are sold by certain types of merchants and the implied warranty of fitness for a particular purpose arises when specified conditions are met.

Next, we focus on warranty disclaimers. Even though the Code provides for all of the warranties described above, it also permits a seller to sell goods without warranties and to exclude or modify warranties. A contract clause that modifies or excludes warranties is referred to as a warranty *disclaimer*. An effective warranty disclaimer deprives the buyer of a cause of action against the seller when the goods would otherwise be warranted. Therefore, it is important to study how warranties can be disclaimed.

Buyers normally do not like to buy goods without warranties; therefore, many sellers avoid warranty disclaimers. Instead, these sellers take advantage of the Code provisions that permit a seller to limit a buyer's remedies. In many cases, remedy limitations deprive the buyer of more redress than do warranty disclaimers. Accordingly, this chapter looks in depth at remedy limitations.

Next, we look at the warranty material from the perspective of a litigant, and examine a cause of action for breach of warranty and the typical defenses raised in warranty actions. We also compare and contrast a warranty action to a products liability suit.

Finally, we briefly review the Federal Magnuson Moss Warranty Act, to see how it changes the U.C.C. rules when a seller chooses to give a written warranty of a consumer product.

Now that you have a thumbnail description of what Chapter 6 is all about, we focus on the details. As you study this material, remember that warranties are actually "gap fillers," which together with other express contract terms (Chapter 7), and other implied terms (the Code gap fillers, which we discuss in Chapter 8), determine the parties' contract rights and obligations. The Code sections that create warranties as default terms, and that govern warranty disclaimers and remedy limitations are listed in *Figure 6-2*.

Figure 6-2: Warranty Sections and Definitions

Section	Definitions
2-312	Title
2-401	Void Title
2-402	Voidable Title
2-403	Good Faith Purchaser (See 1-201)
	Entrusting
	Value (See 1-204)
2-313	Express Warranty
	Affirmation of fact or promise
	Basis of the Bargain
	Puffing
	Sample
	Model
2-314	*Merchant with respect to goods of that kind*
	Fungible
	Fit for the ordinary purpose
2-315	Fitness for particular purpose
2-316	Warranty Disclaimer
	Conspicuous
	"as is", "with all faults", etc.
2-317	
2-318	Third Party Beneficiary
2-719	Remedy Limitation
	Failure of essential purpose

Exercise 6-1: Creating a Structure for the Study of Warranties

As you study the material in this chapter, your goal should be to be able to explain for each warranty, how it is created, how it is disclaimed, and what types of facts typically raise problems.

You can try to organize your thoughts by completing the following table:

Warranty	How Created	How Disclaimed	Problem Areas
Title § 2-312			
Express § 2-313			
Merchantability § 2-314			
Fitness for Particular Purpose § 2-315			

3. Creation of Warranties

3.1 Warranty of Title

The warranty of title guarantees a buyer that the seller has the right to transfer the goods, and that the buyer is receiving good title. It automatically arises when there is a contract of sale. To understand claims based on this warranty, you must also understand the concepts of "void" and "voidable" title, and the concept of a "chain of title." You may have already studied these concepts in your Property class. Essentially, a person who has "void" title does not have title at all. A person with void title does not have the power to transfer title to another person. A person who has "voidable" title does have title, but may lose it. Nevertheless, a person who has voidable title has the power to transfer good title to another person, who purchases in good faith and gives value.

To analyze a title problem, you may find it helpful to draw a chain of title to show how title passed from one owner to another. *Figure 6-3* is an example of a chain of title based on the following facts: Olivia Owner was the owner of a diamond necklace. She sold the necklace to Betty Buyer, who paid cash.

Under section 2-403, a purchaser of goods acquires all title which his transferor had or had power to transfer. Accordingly, after the sale, Betty is the legal owner of the diamond necklace.

If Olivia sells the necklace to Betty in exchange for a check, Betty receives "voidable" title until the check clears. This means that if the check is dishonored, Olivia has the right to get the necklace back from Betty, due to the lack of payment. If, however, Betty transfers

Figure 6-3: Basic Chain of Title in Sales Transaction

the ownership of the necklace to a third party (Theresa Thirdparty) before Olivia finds out about the problem, the third party may be able to defeat Olivia's claim to the necklace. *Figure 6-4* shows the new chain of title.

Figure 6-4: Expanded Chain of Title in Sales Transaction

```
                ┌─────────────────────┐
                │    Olivia Owner     │
                └─────────────────────┘
                          │
                          │   (Sale paid by check)
                          ▼   Warranty of Title
                ┌─────────────────────┐
                │    Betty Buyer      │
                │   (voidable title)  │
                └─────────────────────┘
                          │
                          │   (Sale)
                          ▼   Warranty of Title
                ┌─────────────────────┐
                │  Theresa Thirdparty │
                └─────────────────────┘
```

If Olivia refuses to sell her necklace to Betty and Betty steals it, Betty does not acquire title to the necklace even though she has acquired possession. Even if Betty subsequently transfers the necklace to Theresa, Theresa cannot get title to the necklace. As illustrated in *Figure 6-5*, there is no "chain of title" that runs from Olivia to Betty. Betty's title is void. Accordingly, she cannot pass good title to a third party.

Figure 6-5: Broken Chain of Title in Sales Transaction

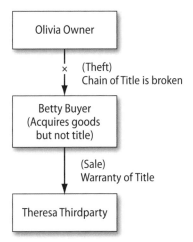

```
                ┌─────────────────────┐
                │    Olivia Owner     │
                └─────────────────────┘
                          │
                        × │   (Theft)
                          ▼   Chain of Title is broken
                ┌─────────────────────┐
                │    Betty Buyer      │
                │  (Acquires goods    │
                │    but not title)   │
                └─────────────────────┘
                          │
                          │   (Sale)
                          ▼   Warranty of Title
                ┌─────────────────────┐
                │  Theresa Thirdparty │
                └─────────────────────┘
```

The last example illustrates the importance of the warranty of title. In each of the first two examples, Olivia Owner transferred title to Betty Buyer. As part of the contract of sale, she gave a warranty of title to Betty. In each of the next two examples, when Betty Buyer transferred the diamond necklace to Theresa, as part of the contract of sale she gave a warranty of title to Theresa. In the last example (*Figure 6-5*), Betty breached that warranty. If Olivia pursues Theresa and gets her necklace back, Theresa will have recourse against Betty because of the warranty of title.

Exercise 6-2: The Warranty of Title and Good Faith Purchasers

Buyer, in California, purchased a camper shell from a local dealer, for $3000 using a bad check. (A camper shell is mounted on the top of a pickup truck's rear bed, and used to turn a normal truck into a camper that can serve as a sleeping space or a place for storing camping supplies.) He drove across country, stopping at campgrounds along the way. When he arrived in Maine, his destination, he resold the camper shell to a dealer for $750.

1. Does the original seller have any rights against the Maine dealer?

2. Does the Maine dealer have any rights against Buyer?

Exercise 6-3: The Warranty of Title and Entrustment

Owner took a watch to Jewelry Store for a cleaning and an appraisal. Jewelry Store sold the watch to Betty Buyer.

1. Does Owner have any rights to get the watch back from Betty?

2. Does Betty have any rights against Jewelry Store?

3. Would Betty's rights against Jewelry Store be different if Jewelry Store told her the sale was "AS IS"?

3.2 Express Warranties

Figure 6-6 illustrates the three ways express warranties are created by sellers. Sellers create express warranties by statements or actions that relate to the goods being sold.

Figure 6-6: How Sellers Make Express Warranties

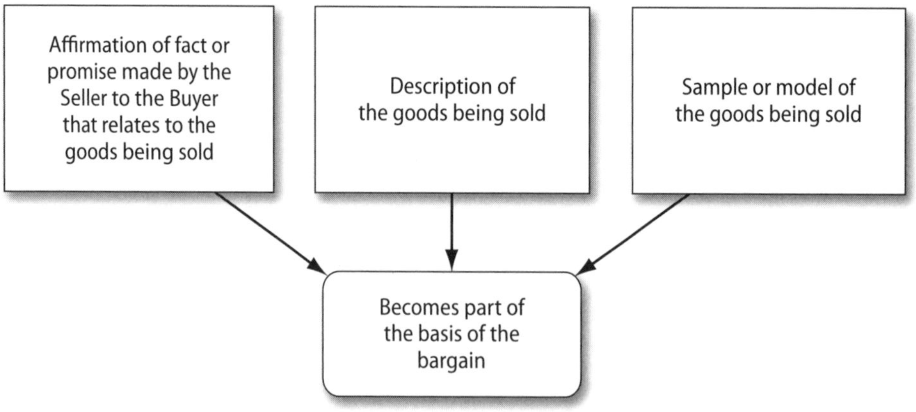

Figure 6-7: What Express Warranties Are Made

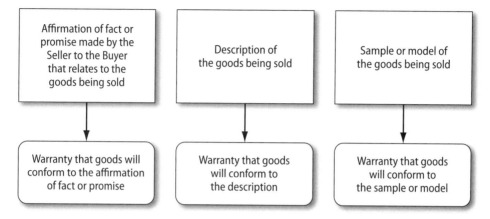

They are not required to warrant their products. No "magic words" are required to create an express warranty. To be an express warranty, however, the seller's representations must become "part of the basis of the bargain."

It is not enough to state that an express warranty arises. You must also know what the express warranty is. In each case, the express warranty is that the goods will conform to what the seller made part of the basis of the bargain. See *Figure 6-7*.

One of the most difficult issues in express warranty analysis is deciding whether a seller has made an "affirmation of fact or promise" or whether the statement was "puffing" (the seller's commendation or opinion referred to in section 2-313(2)). Puffing does not create an express warranty. *Figure 6-8* on the next page lists some of the factors courts consider to determine if a seller's statement is an affirmation of fact or promise, or "mere puffing."

Exercise 6-4: Puffing v. Affirmations of Fact

For each of the following statements, made in a contract for the sale of goods, determine whether the statement would be considered "puffing" or "an affirmation of fact."

1. Manufacturer's brochure described its irrigation system as (a) portable, (b) providing fall pasture, (c) dependable, (d) safe, (e) required little or no land preparation, (f) trouble free and (g) long lived.

2. Manufacturer of an acrylic finish states: "the finish will last for 20 years."

3. Statements by Honda that its mini trail bike was a good one for children and that "you meet the nicest people on a Honda."

4. Words on hair bleach box that product "does not run, or creep, swell or puff."

5. Statement in rental company's brochure that a particular bike trail was a "safe and enjoyable cycling area."

6. Statement in sales contract that car was a 2010 Toyota Camry.

7. Statements by the private seller of used car that the car was "in good shape" and that the noises in the rear end were "just something the car does."

8. Statement by car seller "to the best of my knowledge, the mileage stated on the odometer reflects the actual mileage of the vehicle."

9. Car seller's statement that car was mechanically in "A-1" condition.

10. Statement by server in nightclub, when asked about "watermelon shots" being promoted at the club, who said "they're good."

11. Statement by seller in connection with sale of used laundry dryer. "This dryer will work properly for 90 days."

12. Statement by seller of "Vapam," a soil fumigant, that the product, if applied in the manner recommended and instructed by seller, would control nematodes on the potato crop grown in the following year and would increase the yield and quantity of the potatoes.

The next part of an express warranty analysis is to determine whether the affirmation, description, sample or model became "part of the basis of the bargain." The Code does not define "basis of the bargain." However, the Official Comments to section 2-313 and the scholarly literature suggest that the phrase was selected to negate a pre-code requirement that the buyer must prove reliance on the seller's statement. Official Comment 3 explains the difference between a reliance requirement and the Code's "basis of the bargain" language: "[A]ffirmations of fact made by the seller about the goods during a bargain are

Figure 6-8: Factors Courts Consider to Classify Seller's Statement as Puffing or Affirmation of Fact

Affirmation of Fact	Puffing
Seller's statement is plain and unambiguous	Seller's statement is vague or ambiguous
Attribute or quality involved is not something buyer could easily ascertain on its own	Buyer could easily ascertain attribute or quality without seller's input
Seller is more of an expert with respect to the product than buyer	Buyer is sophisticated and knowledgeable about the product
It would be reasonable for the buyer to rely on the seller's statements	Buyer relies on something other than seller (for example, buyer may hire a consultant to advise him with respect to the purchase)
Nothing in the facts indicates that the seller should not be taken seriously	Facts indicate that seller is not serious or is inflating claims
Seller says nothing to the buyer that would put buyer "on guard"	Seller warns buyer not to rely on statements, or to make buyer's own investigation
The price tends to support the buyer's claim	The price tends to negate the buyer's claim
Specificity/detail	Lack of specificity/detail
Statement emphasizing years of experience with product	Statement reveals that goods are experimental in nature
Written in contract	Written in advertisement
Written	Oral

regarded as part of the description of those goods; hence no particular reliance on such statements need be shown....”

Any discussion of “basis of the bargain” must consider Official Comment 7, which states: “The precise time when words of description or affirmation are made or samples are shown is not material. The sole question is whether the language, samples or models are fairly to be regarded as part of the contract.” Litigants and courts sometimes have relied on this language to find that statements made by a seller after a contract is formed can nevertheless give rise to express warranties.

3.3 Implied Warranty of Merchantability

Unless disclaimed, the implied warranty of merchantability arises in sales when the seller is a merchant with respect to goods of the kind being sold. Not every party who is a “merchant” under section 2-104 is a merchant “with respect to goods of that kind” under section 2-314. For example, if Samantha Seller is in the business of selling cosmetics, she will be a merchant with respect to goods of that kind when she sells her cosmetics, and people who buy cosmetics from her will receive an implied warranty of merchantability. If, however, Samantha decides to sell some of her store furniture, such as chairs and tables, even though she is a merchant, she is not a merchant with respect to the furniture because she does not regularly deal in furniture. Therefore, there is no implied warranty of merchantability with respect to any of Samantha’s furniture sales.

Merchantability is not fully defined in the Code. Instead, sections 2-314(2) (a)-(f) state minimum characteristics goods must have to be merchantable. Official Comment 6 to 2-314 emphasizes that “Subsection 2 does not purport to exhaust the meaning of “merchantable” nor to negate any attributes of merchantability not mentioned in the text of the statute....” Perhaps the most common standard is that goods are “fit for ordinary purposes for which goods the type are used.” Note that merchantable does not necessarily mean perfect, or even perfectly safe. It has been suggested that by “merchantable” the Code means that the goods “will work.”

Exercise 6-5: The Implied Warranty of Merchantability

Discuss whether any of the following scenarios give rise to an implied warranty of merchantability, assuming that a contract for sale of goods was formed. If so, explain what the warranty means in that scenario.

1. Molly Merchant sells a cup of coffee to Betty Consumer.

2. Betty Consumer gives a cup of coffee to her neighbor, Louis.

3. Wally’s Warehouse Store sells a coffee grinder to Gertie, who plans to use it to make coffee at her workplace.

4. Gertie sells the coffee grinder at a garage seller to Nelly Neighbor.

5. Frank Farmer sells strawberries to Connie Consumer from a roadside fruit stand.

6. Frank Farmer sells his entire corn crop to Giant Agribusinesscorp.

7. Hattie Hairdresser uses Reddy Or Not Hairdye on Barbie’s hair at the salon.

8. Dr. S. surgically implants an artificial knee in Patient W.

3.4 Implied Warranty of Fitness for a Particular Purpose

The Implied Warranty of Fitness for a Particular Purpose arises only when: (1) the seller, at the time of contracting, was aware of the buyer's particular purpose for purchasing the goods and (2) the seller knew the buyer was relying on the seller's skill or judgment in selecting suitable goods (and the buyer did so rely). Official Comment 2 to section 2-315 emphasizes the distinction between the "ordinary purpose" of goods (covered by the implied warranty of merchantability) and a buyer's "particular purpose," as follows:

> A "particular purpose" differs from the ordinary purpose for which the goods are used in that it envisages a specific use by the buyer which is peculiar to the nature of his business whereas the ordinary purposes for which goods are used are those envisaged in the concept of merchantability and go to uses which are customarily made of the goods in question.

For example, Sky Walker goes to a shoe store and selects a pair of shoes to wear. Unless disclaimed, the seller gives an implied warranty of merchantability—the shoes are warranted to be fit for the ordinary purpose for which shoes are used. If, however, Sky consults with the shoe salesman and ask for advice with respect to a pair of shoes that she can use for light hiking in the Sierra, she has disclosed a "particular purpose" for the shoes. If the salesperson then makes a recommendation, knowing that Sky is relying on his skill or judgment to help her pick appropriate shoes, there will be an implied warranty of fitness for a particular purpose and those shoes will now be warranted to be suitable for Sky's use for light hiking in the Sierra.

Exercise 6-6: The Implied Warranty of Fitness for a Particular Purpose

Discuss whether any of the following scenarios give rise to an implied warranty of fitness for a particular purpose, assuming that a contract for sale of goods was formed. If so, explain what the warranty means in that scenario.

1. Hilary Hiker purchases Brand X Walker Model 1223 hiking sticks at the Hikers Haven Coop. Before purchasing the sticks, she advises the salesperson that she needs very sturdy sticks for her trip in the snow on Mt. Everest. She also specifies that she wants a collapsible walking stick, which includes an adjustable wrist strap. The salesperson recommends the Brand X Walker Model 1223.

2. Hilary Hiker purchases Wanderfreund Model 23X sticks hiking sticks at the Hikers Haven Coop. Before purchasing the sticks, she tells the salesperson that she is buying the Wanderfreund Model 23X sticks for an upcoming trip in the snow on Mt. Everest.

3. Farmer Joan asks the pesticide salesperson what she should buy to control nematodes on her potatoes. The salesperson recommends "Nematodes Be Gone," which he explains is designed to control nematodes on potatoes.

4. Amy brings a sample of the paint she has been using on her living room wall, and asks Paint Store to match the paint. Paint Store sells her a gallon of paint, which it has matched to the paint Amy brought in.

---

4. Warranty Disclaimers

The purpose of a warranty disclaimer is to negate the existence of a warranty. Depending on the type of warranty, the rules vary with respect to how the warranty is disclaimed.

4.1 Warranty of Title Disclaimers

Disclaimers of the warranty of title are governed by section 2-312, the same section that governs how those warranties arise. Subsection (2) provides:

> A warranty [of title] will be excluded or modified only by specific language or by circumstances which give the buyer reason to know that the person selling does not claim title in himself or that he is purporting to sell only such right or title as he or a third person may have.

There is little case law dealing with this section. However, the reported cases do suggest that courts are very strict in interpreting the disclaimer requirements. Indeed, a recent case held that the words "there are no warranties" did not suffice to disclaim the warranty of title. The court reasoned that most buyers would not anticipate a seller denying the right to pass good title to the goods being sold, so the buyers would not understand that language to extend to a warranty of title. On the other hand, most legal commentators would agree that a buyer who purchases a Rolex watch in a New York City alley should be put on notice by those circumstances that the seller may not have the ability to transfer good title to the watch. Note that the phrase "AS IS," which is effective to disclaim implied warranties, does *not* disclaim the warranty of title.

4.2 Express Warranty Disclaimers

Express Warranty disclaimers are governed by section 2-316(1). The basic concept behind an express warranty disclaimer is that a seller is not free to "give" a warranty with one hand and "take it away" with the other. At first glance, section 2-316(1) appears to be straightforward and easy to apply. It states that words that create an express warranty and words that tend to negate a warranty should be construed as consistent if possible; however, if such construction is not possible, the warranty prevails. In other words, if a seller gives an express warranty, he cannot take it away. In many cases, it is possible to construe words of warranty as consistent with words of disclaimer. See, for example, the sample warranty in *Figure 6-9*. Identify the words that create a warranty. Next identify the words that negate warranty. Explain how they are consistent.

Figure 6-9: Words creating an express warranty and consistent words disclaiming warranties

---

WARRANTY

Seller warrants that this shirt will not shrink and its color will not fade.

Except as expressly set forth herein, Seller makes no warranties, express or implied, including, without limitation, the implied warranty of merchantability.

Section 2-316(1)'s reference to the parol evidence rule causes interpretative difficulty with section 2-316(1). A common situation is where a salesman makes representations to a buyer before the buyer enters into a written sales document. The sales document contains an integration clause and a clause that disclaims all express warranties. This fact pattern is illustrated in *Figure 6-10*.

Section 2-316(1) says the words that create a warranty (here, the salesperson's statements) and the words negating warranties (here, the disclaimer in the sales document) must be construed as consistent, if possible. However, there is no way to make an express warranty consistent with an explicit statement that says "there are no express warranties." Section 2-316(1) then provides that if the words of warranty cannot be construed as consistent, *subject to the parol evidence rule*, negation is inoperative.

Accordingly, the key to whether an express warranty disclaimer contained in a written agreement will negate an oral express warranty made before the parties entered into the writing, is whether a court can be persuaded to admit the evidence of the oral express warranty, notwithstanding the parol evidence rule. If the evidence is admitted (and the trier of fact believes it), there will then be words of warranty and words of disclaimer that cannot be construed as consistent—and the disclaimer (words of negation) is inoperative. If, however, the parol evidence analysis dictates that the evidence not be admitted, all that remains is the disclaimer in the written agreement, and the warranty claim does not survive.

Figure 6-10: Common Express Warranty Disclaimer/ Parol Evidence Rule Fact Pattern

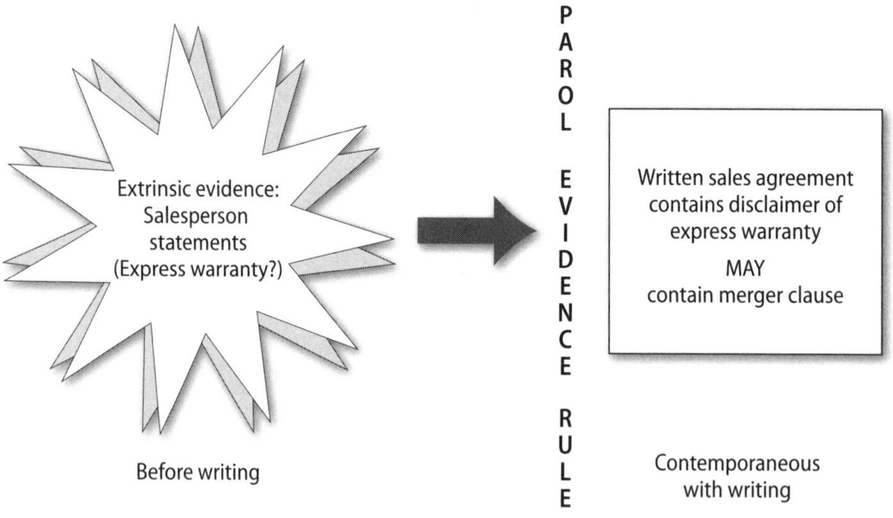

Extrinsic evidence: Salesperson statements (Express warranty?)

PAROL EVIDENCE RULE

Written sales agreement contains disclaimer of express warranty

MAY contain merger clause

Before writing

Contemporaneous with writing

Exercise 6-7: Killion v. Buran Equipment Co.

We will return to examine the efficacy of written warranty disclaimers after we study the parol evidence rule, in Chapter 7. First, however, read the following decision of the California Court of Appeal, which grappled with the application of section 2-316 to just this type of fact pattern. As you read the case, consider the following questions:

1. What is the alleged evidence of an oral express warranty?

2. Was there a dispute regarding whether a particular statement or statements constituted an express warranty?

3. What is the alleged warranty disclaimer?

4. Did the court conclude that the written agreement was fully or partially integrated? How important was its conclusion to the resolution of the warranty issue?

5. Are you satisfied by the court's explanation of how it reached its conclusion?

Killion v. Buran Equipment Co.

27 U.C.C. Rep.Serv. 970 (Cal. App. 4th Dist. 1979)

[Note: This is an unpublished opinion. Under Rule 977 of the California Rules of Court, an unpublished opinion may not be cited in any other action or proceeding except under certain limited conditions.]

PER CURIAM.

Plaintiff appeals from a judgment of dismissal entered after demurrer to his second amended complaint was sustained without leave to amend. We conclude that the complaint alleged facts sufficient to constitute a cause of action, and accordingly we reverse the judgment.

The complaint alleged that defendants misrepresented to plaintiff that the diesel engine in the subject vehicle "was the original equipment engine as installed by the manufacturer of the vehicle," and that the engine "had been given a major overhaul." We agree with defendants' concession that these statements, if made, constituted express warranties within the meaning of the California Uniform Commercial Code § 2313. Defendants urge, however, that the demurrer was properly sustained because the complaint, though it went on to allege the other elements of the causes of action in question, had appended to it the written agreement of the parties (the Used Truck Purchase Order) which contains an effective disclaimer of warranties. They argue that because the writing constituted an integrated agreement its terms cannot be contradicted by evidence of the purported oral warranties.

We note at the outset that we are here concerned with express, not implied, warranties, and that therefore some of the statutory and decisional authority upon which the parties rely is inapposite. Attempts to disclaim, exclude or modify express warranties are governed by the California Uniform Commercial Code § 2316 , subdivision (1): "Words or conduct relevant to the creation of an express warranty and words or conduct tending to negate or limit warranty shall be construed wherever reasonable as consistent with each other; but subject to the provisions of this division on parol or extrinsic evidence (Section 2202) negation or limitation is inoperative to the extent that such construction is unreasonable."

The essence of defendants' position is that the parol evidence rule bars any consideration of the alleged warranties and that without these the written disclaimer of warranties clearly governs. However, parol evidence which contradicts terms of a written agreement is only excluded where the writing was "intended by the parties as a final expression of their agreement with respect to such terms as are included therein ..." And even such written terms may be explained or supplemented by evidence of consistent additional terms "unless the court finds the writing to have been intended also as a complete and exclusive statement of the terms of the agreement." Thus, it is no longer the law in this state that absent ambiguity, the writing must be construed as having been intended to be a complete integrated agreement. On the contrary, § 2202 "assumes that a written contract does not express the full agreement of the parties unless the court expressly so finds." ... Furthermore, § 2202 definitely rejects both the notion that because an agreement is in writing "it is to be taken as including all the matters agreed upon", and the rule that before accepting parol evidence the court must find that the writing is ambiguous ... A reading of the complaint (which incorporated a copy of the written agreement) reveals both "[w]ords ... relevant to the creation of an express warranty and words ... tending to negate or limit warranty ..." within the meaning of § 2316 (1). The words relevant to creation of express warranties were quoted above, and all parties agree that they may properly be so characterized. The purchase order, on the other hand, states that the sale is "on an 'as is' basis without warranty of any character expressed or implied ..." These are obviously words tending to negate or limit warranty, which raise an ambiguity in the agreement taken as a whole. Furthermore there are portions of the written agreement itself which create express warranties or may reasonably be read as so doing. For example under the printed word "Warranty" is handwritten "Eng. & Work Performed by BAK Guaranted [sic] for 60 days" (arguably affirming the oral warranty that the engine had been overhauled); and under the printed word "Year" is handwritten "1968", arguably reducing to writing the alleged oral warranty regarding the origin and vintage of the engine.

Section 2-316 mandates that the courts attempt to construe such statements as consistent wherever possible. In so doing the purpose of the section must be kept in mind which, in essence, is that disclaimers of warranty are to be inoperative in the face of an agreement creating an express warranty. (See Hauter v. Zogarts (1975) 14 Cal3d 104, 119, fn 18 [16 U.C.C. Rep 938]).

Because a disclaimer or modification is inconsistent with an express warranty, words of disclaimer or modification give way to words of warranty unless some clear agreement between the parties dictates the contrary relationship. [Citations.] At the very least, § 2316 allows limitation of warranties only by means of words that clearly communicate that a particular risk falls on the buyer.... Moreover, any disclaimer or modification must be strictly construed against the seller....

Thus, a reasonable construction of the parties' agreement is that the purported disclaimers were conditional and that the truck was being sold "as is" and with no warranties other than those to which the parties expressly agreed.

While § 2316 has understandably been criticized as vague ... it is clear that when settled principles of law are applied to the facts of this case plaintiff stated one or more of the following causes of action in his second amended complaint: fraud (fraudulent inducement and misrepresentation), negligent misrepresentation, breach of contract, breach of warranty.

The judgment of dismissal is reversed.

4.3 Implied Warranty Disclaimers

Implied Warranty Disclaimers are governed by sections 2-316(2) and (3). Subsection (2) states a very specific rule for disclaiming implied warranties. (Note that its rules are not applicable to an attempt to disclaim the warranty of title.) To disclaim the implied warranty of merchantability, the language must use the word "merchantability" and, in case of a writing must be conspicuous. To exclude or modify the implied warranty of fitness the exclusion must be in a writing and conspicuous. The subsection provides safe harbor language that, if used, is deemed to be sufficient to disclaim the implied warranty of fitness.

The primary issue under section 2-316(2) is whether a disclaimer is "conspicuous." The meaning of "conspicuous" in a written document or record is defined in detail in section 1-201(10). However, courts have also stricken purported disclaimers for failing to be conspicuous when the disclaimer was not called to the buyer's attention at the time of the sale.[1]

Subsection (3) begins with the words "[n]otwithstanding subsection 2." It then continues with a basis for determining the validity of a disclaimer that does not satisfy the rule stated in subsection (2). One of the most discussed provisions of subsection (3) is that of (3)(a) that allows all implied warranties to be disclaimed by using words like "as is" and "with all faults." The Official Comments to section 2-316 suggest that the drafters believed that buyers would understand language like that to mean that there are no implied warranties. Nothing in subsection (3) even requires that the language of disclaimer be conspicuous. Numerous courts have nevertheless read a "conspicuousness" requirement into subsection 3.[2]

5. Remedy Limitations

Although the Code may appear to be somewhat tilted in favor of buyers of goods, particularly because of the warranty and warranty disclaimer provisions, its attitude towards remedy limitations easily outweighs that apparent favoritism. Section 2-719 specifically validates the notion that a seller can limit its liability not by excluding its warranty liability but by changing the remedy to which the buyer is entitled in the event of breach.

Section 2-719(1) specifically references and validates two of the most common types of remedy limitations employed by sellers: (1) limiting a buyer's remedies to return of the goods and repayment of the price and (2) limiting a buyer's remedies to repair or replacement of non-conforming goods or parts.

The only limits on a seller's ability to limit remedies (other than unconscionability) are stated in sections 2-719(1)(b) and 2-719(2). First, section 2-719(1)(b) provides that

---

1. *See, e.g., Hill v. BASF Wyandotte Corp.,* 696 F.2d 287, 290-91 (4th Cir. 1982); *see also Bowdoin v. Showell Growers, Inc.,* 817 F.2d 1543, 1545 (11th Cir. 1987).
2. *See, e.g., Gindy Mfg. Corp. v. Cardinale Trucking Corp.,* 111 N.J. Super. 383, 268 A.2d 345 (1970).

resort to a remedy as provided is optional unless the remedy is expressly agreed to be exclusive. Since the adoption of Article 2, most sellers have written their form sales contracts so that the agreements provide that whatever remedy the seller provides is agreed to be the exclusive remedy. Second, section 2-719(2) provides that "Where circumstances cause an exclusive or limited remedy to fail of its essential purpose, remedy may be had as provided in this Act." A determination regarding "failure of essential purpose" cannot be made at the contract formation stage because you will not know whether a remedy limitation served its purpose or not until the buyer seeks a remedy based on the contract's remedy limitation provision. Accordingly, when you first are analyzing a contract and its terms you will only be able to determine that the seller has included a remedy limitation provision that may or may not make that remedy exclusive. You will not, however, be able to determine whether the remedy limitation will be effective to restrict the buyer's remedies until you have completed your analysis of performance, which is the only stage when you will be able to determine whether the remedy limitation "failed of its essential purpose."

Official Comment 1 to section 2-719 is frequently cited by courts and legal scholars as expressing the meaning of "failure of essential purpose" when it says "it is of the very essence of a sales contract that at least minimum adequate remedies be available." Thus, as a practical matter, if a seller's remedy limitation provides for the repair and replacement of defective parts, and after the buyer requests such a repair the seller refuses to do so or is unsuccessful after many attempts, most courts would agree that the remedy limitation had failed of its essential purpose.

The last part of section 2-719 deals specifically with the limitation or exclusion of liability for consequential damages. The statute provides that such an exclusion is valid unless unconscionable, and further provides that a limitation of consequential damages for injury to the person in the case of consumer goods is prima facie unconscionable.

As in section 2-316(3), there is no express statutory requirement that a remedy limitation be "conspicuous." However, for policy reasons, some courts have imputed such a requirement.[3]

The relationship between section 2-719(2) and section 2-719(3) has been the subject of considerable litigation. The question raised is, when a contract contains both (1) a remedy limitation, such as repair and replacement of defective parts, and (2) a limitation on consequential damages, if it is determined that the first remedy limitation fails of its essential purpose, does the limitation on consequential damages also fail, or does section 2-719(3) require a separate analysis of the validity of that provision? The Illinois Supreme Court reviewed the current state of the law on that issue in *Razor v Hyundai Motor America*.[4] Its discussion of the issue in that case follows:

Razor v. Hyundai Motor America
854 N.E.2d 607 (Ill. 2006)

* * *

There are two main schools of thought on the issue. Some courts and commentators conclude that a limited remedy failing of its essential purpose operates to destroy any

---

3. *See, e.g., Avenell v. Westinghouse Electric Corp.*, 41 Ohio App 2d 150, 324 N.E.2d 483 (1975).
4. *Razor v Hyundai Motor America*, 854 N.E.2d 607 (Ill. 2006).

limitation or exclusion of consequential damages in the same contract. This approach is known as the "dependent" approach, because the enforceability of the consequential damages exclusion depends on the survival of the limitation of remedy.

Our appellate court issued one of the seminal cases for the dependent approach, *Adams v. J.I. Case Co.*, 125 Ill.App.2d 388, 261 N.E.2d 1 (1970). There, the plaintiff purchased a tractor, pursuant to a purchase agreement which limited his remedy to repair and replacement and also disclaimed consequential damages. The tractor had severe mechanical problems and was in a repair shop for over a year. Plaintiff filed suit, seeking consequential damages for the business he claimed to have lost because defendants were "willfully dilatory or careless and negligent in making good their warranty." The court concluded:

> "The limitations of remedy and of liability are not separable from the obligations of the warranty. Repudiation of the obligations of the warranty destroys its benefits. The complaint alleges facts that would constitute a repudiation by the defendants of their obligations under the warranty, that repudiation consisting of their willful failure or their careless and negligent compliance. It should be obvious that they cannot at once repudiate their obligation under their warranty and assert its provisions beneficial to them." *Adams*, 125 Ill.App.2d at 402-03, 261 N.E.2d 1.

In defense of the dependent approach, the United States District Court for the Northern District of Illinois has reasoned:

> "[P]laintiff also was entitled to assume that defendants would not be unreasonable or willfully dilatory in making good their warranty in the event of defects in the machinery and equipment. It is the specific breach of the warranty to repair that plaintiff alleges caused the bulk of its damages. This Court would be in an untenable position if it allowed the defendant to shelter itself behind one segment of the warranty when it has allegedly repudiated and ignored its very limited obligations under another segment of the same warranty, which alleged repudiation has caused the very need for relief which the defendant is attempting to avoid." (Citations omitted)

Plaintiff suggests that the dependent approach is followed by a majority of jurisdictions to consider the issue. While this may have been true 15 to 20 years ago (citations omitted) it is no longer the case. Rather, the majority of jurisdictions now follow the other of the two main approaches, the "independent" approach. [C]ourts have gone so far as to hold that if U.C.C. 2-719(2) applies, related limitations on remedies should all fall like a house of cards, so that a provision barring recovery of consequential damages would also be invalidated. However, most courts have rejected this view); (citations omitted). This school of thought holds that a limitation of consequential damages must be judged on its own merits and enforced unless unconscionable, regardless of whether the contract also contains a limitation of remedy which has failed of its essential purpose.

A representative case adopting the independent approach is *Chatlos Systems v. National Cash Register Corp.*, 635 F.2d 1081 (3d Cir.1980) (applying New Jersey law). There, the court rejected the dependent approach, holding:

> "[T]he better reasoned approach (footnote omitted) is to treat the consequential damage disclaimer as an independent provision, valid unless unconscionable. This poses no logical difficulties. A contract may well contain no limitation on breach of warranty damages but specifically exclude consequential damages. Conversely, it is quite conceivable that some limitation might be placed on a breach of warranty award, but consequential damages would expressly be permitted.

The limited remedy of repair and a consequential damages exclusion are two discrete ways of attempting to limit recovery for breach of warranty. [citations omitted.] The [U.C.C.], moreover, tests each by a different standard. The former survives unless it fails of its essential purpose, while the latter is valid unless it is unconscionable. We therefore see no reason to hold, as a general proposition, that the failure of the limited remedy provided in the contract, without more, invalidates a wholly distinct term in the agreement excluding consequential damages. The two are not mutually exclusive. (citations omitted)"

... [W]e agree with the reasoning in *Chatlos Systems*, and adopt the independent approach. The independent approach is more in line with the U.C.C. and with contract law in general. Nothing in the text or the official comments to section 2-719 indicates that where a contract contains both a limitation of remedy and an exclusion of consequential damages, the latter shares the fate of the former. See J. Eddy, *On the "Essential" Purposes of Limited Remedies: The Metaphysics of U.C.C. 2-719(2),* 65 Cal. L.Rev. 28, 92 (1977) (failure of essential purpose is separate and independent from validity of consequential damage disclaimer); E. Eissenstat, Note, *Commercial Transactions: U.C.C. § 2-719: Remedy Limitations and Consequential Damage Exclusions,* 36 Okla. L.Rev. 669, 677 (1983) ("a consequential damages disclaimer should be governed by its own [U.C.C.] standard of unconscionability, independent of whether a limited remedy has failed"). To the contrary, as noted in *Chatlos Systems,* the different standards for evaluating the two provisions-"failure of essential purpose" versus "unconscionability"-strongly suggest their independence. See also 1 White and Summers' Uniform Commercial Code § 12-10(c), at 668 (4th ed.1995) (endorsing the independent approach as most in accord with considerations of freedom of contract).

When a contract contains a limitation of remedy but that remedy fails of its essential purpose, it is as if that limitation of remedy does not exist for purposes of the damages to which a plaintiff is entitled for breach of warranty. See 810 ILCS 5/2-719(2) (West 2000) ("remedy may be had as provided in this Act"). When a contract contains a consequential damages exclusion but no limitation of remedy, it is incontrovertible that the exclusion is to be enforced unless unconscionable. 810 ILCS 5/2-719(3) (West 2000). Why, then, would a limitation of remedy failing of its essential purpose destroy a consequential damages exclusion in the same contract? We see no valid reason to so hold.

Indeed, the dependent approach operates to nullify all consequential damage exclusions in contracts which also contain limitations of remedy. For if the limited remedy fails of its essential purpose, the consequential damages exclusion would also automatically fall-regardless of whether it is unconscionable-and if the limitation of remedy does not fail of its essential purpose, the buyer would not be entitled to consequential damages in any event; he would be entitled only to the specified limited remedy.

The two provisions-limitation of remedy and exclusion of consequential damages-can be visualized as two concentric layers of protection for a seller. What a seller would most prefer, if something goes wrong with a product, is simply to repair or replace it, nothing more. This "repair or replacement" remedy is an outer wall, a first defense. If that wall is breached, because the limited remedy has failed of its essential purpose, the seller still would prefer at least not to be liable for potentially unlimited consequential damages, and so he builds a second inner rampart as a fallback position. That inner wall is higher, and more difficult to scale-it falls only if unconscionable.

The independent approach has not been immune to criticism, of course. The Eighth Circuit has rejected the independent approach under Minnesota law, based on the concern that "a buyer when entering into a contract does not anticipate that the sole remedy available will be rendered a nullity, thus causing additional damages." *Soo Line R.R. Co. v. Fruehauf Corp.*, 547 F.2d 1365, 1373 (8th Cir.1977) (applying Minnesota law). Additionally, one commentator has chastised the independent approach for "rel[ying] on imprecise assumptions about the parties' intent and an unpersuasive interpretation of section 2-719." K. Murtagh, Note, *U.C.C. Section 2-719: Limited Remedies and Consequential Damage Exclusions*, 74 Cornell L.Rev. 359, 362 (1989) (concluding that independent approach is "inherently weak"). This article suggests that by engaging in "literal construction of the parties' contract," the independent approach "encourages overly formalistic drafting," which "unfairly favors the party who can afford sophisticated bargaining techniques to ensure the use of his contract terms." 74 Cornell L.Rev. at 363. The article also contends that it is erroneous to conclude that the parties intend to shift the risk of consequential loss to the buyer, because "[t]he language structure itself does not indicate that the parties even considered the possibility of the ineffective limited remedy." 74 Cornell L.Rev. at 364. *Adams* and *Jones & McKnight,* two of the earliest cases adopting the dependent approach, implicitly concluded that the independent approach was simply unfair to the buyer. See *Adams*, 125 Ill.App.2d at 402-03, 261 N.E.2d 1; *Jones & McKnight,* 320 F.Supp. at 43-44.

We recognize these objections to the independent approach, but do not find them compelling. The reasoning in *Adams* and *Jones & McKnight,* for example, is based on the seller's failure to perform being willful. This incorporates considerations of bad faith on the part of the seller. As we discuss below, the seller's bad faith is a possible basis for finding enforcement of a limitation of consequential damages to be unconscionable. However, the dependent approach strips away limitations of consequential damages whenever a limited remedy fails of its essential purpose, without regard to the good or bad faith of the seller, which we believe goes too far.

The objections to the independent approach in *Soo Line* and the law review article noted above are similarly unpersuasive. Both argue that the independent approach is unfair because the buyer may not intend to renounce consequential damages when the limited remedy has failed of its essential purpose. *Soo Line,* 547 F.2d at 1373; 74 Cornell L.Rev. at 364. But this seems to ignore the plain language of the contract in a fundamental way- for if the buyer does not intend to renounce consequential damages when the limited remedy has failed, in what context *could* the disclaimer of consequential damages operate? As noted above, we believe this is a fundamental defect in the dependent approach, that it renders the disclaimer of consequential damages an utter nullity. If a limited remedy has *not* failed of its essential purpose, that is of course the buyer's only remedy, by definition-this is what it means to have a limited remedy. So in this circumstance a disclaimer of limited damages would be of no effect because it would be redundant. If, as the above critics argue, the disclaimer of limited damages ought not to be enforced when the limited remedy *has* failed of its essential purpose, the language would never have any effect. Moreover, to the extent that the independent approach encourages parties to pay attention in the drafting process (see 74 Cornell L.Rev. at 363), we see this as a point in favor of the independent approach, rather than the contrary ...

We conclude that the independent approach is the better-reasoned and more in accordance with the plain language of the U.C.C..This conclusion is buttressed by the fact that a majority of jurisdictions to consider the issue have adopted the independent approach. Illinois generally follows the majority interpretation of U.C.C. provisions, in order to serve the underlying U.C.C. policy of "'mak[ing] uniform the law among the various jurisdictions.'" *Connick v. Suzuki Motor Co.*, 174 Ill.2d 482, 491, 221 Ill. Dec. 389, 675 N.E.2d 584 (1996), quoting 810 ILCS 5/1-102(2)(c) (West 1994). Contractual limitations

or exclusions of consequential damages will be upheld unless to do so would be unconscionable, regardless of whether the contract also contains a limited remedy which fails
of its essential purpose.

———————

6. Warranty Litigation; Defenses in Warranty Actions

6.1 Cause of Action for Breach of Warranty

The plaintiff's prima facie case in an action for breach of warranty is outlined in *Figure
6-11*.[5] Possible defenses in an action for breach of warranty are outlined in *Figure 6-12*.

As illustrated in *Figures 6-11 and 6-12*, the basic issues we studied in connection with
warranties relate directly to the context of warranty litigation. Three additional topics
arise in the context of litigation, however. These are the requirement of notice; in some
jurisdictions, the requirement that the buyer and seller be in privity of contract; and the
statute of limitations.

Figure 6-11: Plaintiff's Prima Facie Case for Breach of Warranty

1. Existence of Warranty
   A. Contract of Sale (Warranty of title, 2-312)
   B. Seller's affirmations, etc. (Express Warranty, 2-313)
   C. Merchant with respect to goods of the kind sold goods (2-314)
   D. Seller sold goods; buyer had particular purpose (2-315)
2. Goods sold were not as warranted.
3. Injury and damages to plaintiff and his property.
4. Proximately caused by failure of goods to be as warranted.
5. Notice to Seller (Some jurisdictions).
6. Privity (Some jurisdictions).

Figure 6-12: Defenses in Warranty Action

1. Article 2 N/A to transaction; therefore alleged warranties do not exist.
2. Deny facts based on which plaintiff alleges existence of warranty; for example:
   puffing v. affirmation of fact, or representations not part of basis of bargain.
3. Goods were sold with effective warranty disclaimer; therefore, alleged warranties
   do not exist.
4. Goods sold were as warranted (scope of warranty).
5. Break in chain of causation.
6. Untimely/inadequate notice to seller.
7. Lack of Privity (Some jurisdictions).

———————

5. *See, e.g., Divis v. Clarklift of Nebraska, Inc.*, 256 Neb. 384, 590 N.W.2d 696 (1999).

6.2 Notice

Article 2 requires a buyer to give notice to a seller in at least four circumstances involving breach: section 2-607(3) requires notice of breach when a tender has been accepted; section 2-607(5) requires notice of litigation when the buyer is sued for breach of warranty; section 2-602(1) requires notice when the buyer rejects goods; and section 2-608(2) requires buyer to notify seller of revocation of acceptance. Most courts have held that notice of breach is too late if given for the first time in the complaint. Because warranty litigation arises in connection with goods that a buyer has accepted, litigants must satisfy the notice requirement of section 2-607(3)(a), which requires a buyer to "notify the seller of breach" within a reasonable time after he discovers or should have discovered any breach. The penalty for late notification is that the buyer is "barred from any remedy." Litigators suggest that the notice be detailed, and a copy be attached to the complaint as an exhibit, so that the plaintiff's case is set forth in detail. However, the Code requires only that "the content of the notification need merely be sufficient to let the seller know that the transaction is troublesome and must be watched." (Official Comment 4 to section 2-607).

6.3 Privity

Because each of the warranty sections refers to contracts for sale or sellers, in many jurisdictions a plaintiff must be in privity of contract with the warrantor to recover. In general, privity of contract is of two types: "vertical" privity, shown in *Figure 6-13*, and "horizontal" privity shown in *Figures 6-14 and 6-15*.[6]

The U.C.C. is silent with respect to vertical privity. Official Comment 3 to section 9-318 states that such issues are left to individual state law. Section 9-318 addresses horizontal privity, but instead of taking one approach, the drafters offered three alternatives. The first alternative, Alternative A, is the most restrictive, and the third, Alternative C, is the most liberal.

Figure 6-13: Vertical Privity

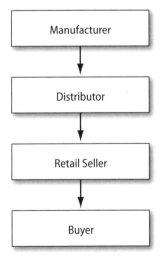

---

6. *See, e.g., Flory v. Silvercrest Industries Inc.*, 129 Ariz. 574, 633 P.2d 383 (1981).

Figure 6-14: Horizontal Privity: Buyer's Household

Figure 6-15: Horizontal Privity: Buyer's Business

6.4 The Statute of Limitations[7]

Article 2's statute of limitations, section 2-725, applies to all actions under Article 2. However, because of special provisions that affect only warranty litigation, we consider it here. Section 2-725 states that the statute of limitations is four years "after the cause of action has accrued," provided that the parties may by agreement reduce the period of limitation to not less than one year. Subsection (2) states that a cause of action accrues when the breach occurs, regardless of the aggrieved party's lack of knowledge of the breach. It then states that a breach of warranty occurs when tender of delivery is made. *The only exception is where a warranty "explicitly extends to future performance of the goods and discovery of the breach must await the time of such performance." In such a case, the cause of action accrues when the breach is or should have been discovered.*

Exercise 6-8: Poli v. DaimlerChrysler Corp.

The most litigated statute of limitations issue is whether a particular warranty "explicitly extends to future performance." In the following case, which I have edited to focus on the U.C.C. statute of limitations issue, the court examines the meaning of that phrase. As you read the case, consider the following questions:

1. What is the meaning of a warranty 'that explicitly extends to future performance'?

2. What express language is the court interpreting?

3. The court suggests that other courts have interpreted similar language in two ways. What are those two ways? Which do you think is a more correct way of applying the statute?

4. As a practical matter, will the outcome of the case be affected by the interpretation that the court adopts?

---

7. The statute of limitations is an affirmative defense; if it is not pleaded and proved, it is waived. *See Mysel v. Gross*, 70 Cal. App. 3d 10, 138 Cal. Rptr. 873, 21 U.C.C. Rep. Serv. 1338 (1977).

Poli v. DaimlerChrysler Corp.

793 A.2d 104 (N.J. Super. 2002)

SKILLMAN, P.J.A.D.

The primary issue presented by this appeal is whether a cause of action for breach of a seller's agreement to repair any product defect that occurs during a warranty period accrues upon delivery of the product or only after the seller fails to perform the agreed repairs. We conclude that such a cause of action does not accrue until the seller fails to perform the required repair within a reasonable period of time....

On March 23, 1993, plaintiff purchased a new 1992 Dodge Spirit manufactured by defendant DaimlerChrysler Corporation. When he made this purchase, plaintiff elected to obtain a seven-year, seventy-thousand-mile "powertrain" warranty from defendant.

Plaintiff's claims arise out of a series of repairs and replacements of the "engine timing belt," which was one of the parts covered by the powertrain warranty. On December 16, 1993, after the car had been driven 16,408 miles, plaintiff had the timing belt replaced. More than three years later, on March 21, 1997, after the car had been driven 36,149 miles, plaintiff had the belt repaired. Plaintiff then had to have the belt replaced on May 16, 1997, January 5, 1998 and July 6, 1998. According to plaintiff, the timing belt again failed on July 31, 1998, causing the destruction of the "short block" of the engine, which the dealer took six months to repair. All of these timing belt repairs and replacements were purportedly performed by defendant in accordance with the seven-year, seventy-thousand-mile powertrain warranty obtained by plaintiff when he purchased the car.

On December 15, 1998, plaintiff brought this action against defendant for breach of the seven-year, seventy-thousand-mile powertrain warranty....

Defendant moved for summary judgment on the ground that plaintiff's complaint [was] barred by the statute of limitations ...

The trial court granted defendant's motion ... and dismissed the complaint. The court dismissed plaintiff's warranty ... claims as untimely because they were not brought within four years after delivery of the car. The court rejected plaintiff's argument that his warranty ... claims were timely because the seven-year, seventy-thousand-mile powertrain warranty was "a guarantee of performance" which defendant breached by failing to properly repair the timing belt.

Plaintiff appeals. We ... reverse the dismissal of his warranty ... claims.

II

We turn next to the trial court's conclusion that plaintiff's claim for breach of defendant's seven-year, seventy-thousand-mile powertrain warranty was not filed within the four-year limitation period established by the Uniform Commercial Code (U.C.C.) for breach of warranty claims.

The powertrain warranty applies to all "parts, assemblies and components that together provide the power to [the] car." During the term of this warranty, which is "7 years or 70,000 miles, whichever occurs first, counted from the vehicle's Warranty Start Date," ... defendant is obligated to "cover [ ] the cost of all parts and labor needed to repair or adjust any Chrysler supplied item ... that proves defective in material, workmanship or factory preparation." ... Defendant acknowledges that the engine timing belt is covered by this warranty.

The limitations period under the U.C.C. for an action for breach of a sales contract is "four years after the cause of action has accrued." N.J.S.A. 12A:2-725(1). The U.C.C. further provides that "[a] cause of action accrues when the breach occurs, regardless of the aggrieved party's lack of knowledge of the breach[,]" and that "[a] breach of warranty occurs when tender of delivery is made[.]" N.J.S.A. 12A:2-725(2). However, the U.C.C. provides an exception to this general rule if "a warranty explicitly extends to future performance of the goods and discovery of the breach must await the time of such performance[.]" Ibid. If a seller has provided this form of warranty, "the cause of action accrues when the breach is or should have been discovered." Ibid.

Defendant contends that the powertrain warranty given to plaintiff was an ordinary sales warranty, and that plaintiff therefore had only four years after the delivery of the car on March 23, 1993, to bring an action for any breach of the warranty. If this view of the powertrain warranty were correct, plaintiff's claim for breach of the warranty would be time barred because he did not file this action until December 15, 1998, which was more than four years after delivery of the car. On the other hand, plaintiff contends that the powertrain warranty was a warranty of future performance, which defendant did not breach until 1998, when it failed to properly repair the timing belt, thus causing plaintiff recurrent problems with the operation of the car. Under this view of the warranty, plaintiff's action was filed well within the four-year period allowed under N.J.S.A. 2A:2-725(1).

In Docteroff v. Barra Corp. of Am., Inc., 282 N.J.Super. 230, 241-43, 659 A.2d 948 (App.Div.1995), we held that a "guarantee" by a seller of roofing materials that it would "maintain the roof ... [i]n a watertight condition ... for (5) five years[,]" and would repair or replace any defects that arose during that period, constituted a promise of future performance, and that the four-year U.C.C. statute of limitations did not begin to run until the seller's breach was or should have been discovered. In reaching this conclusion, we noted that a seller's agreement to repair or replace defects in parts that become evident during a specified period "fit[s] within the modern concept of warranty." Id. at 242, 659 A.2d 948 (quoting Nationwide Ins. Co. v. General Motors Corp., 533 Pa. 423, 625 A.2d 1172, 1177 (1993)). [Compare Spring Motors Distribs., Inc. v. Ford Motor Co., 191 N.J.Super. 22, 47, 465 A.2d 530 (App.Div.1983) (holding that "the words 'your vehicle has been designed to give long reliable service with the simplest and least costly maintenance requirements possible' do not make any explicit guarantee as to the vehicle's performance over or after a stated period of time"), rev'd on unrelated grounds, 98 N.J. 555, 489 A.2d 660 (1985).] We also noted that "[s]uch a warranty ...'cannot be characterized as a mere representation of the product's condition at the time of delivery rather than its performance at a future time.' " Ibid. (quoting Commissioners of Fire Dist. No. 9 v. American La France, 176 N.J.Super. 566, 573, 424 A.2d 441 (App.Div.1980)).

The seven-year, seventy-thousand-mile warranty that defendant gave plaintiff was similar to the warranty involved in Docteroff. Although defendant did not describe the warranty as a "guarantee" of future performance, it was not "a mere representation of the [car's] condition at the time of delivery" but rather a promise relating to "its performance at a future time [,]" 282 N.J.Super. at 242, 659 A.2d 948, that is, as in Docteroff, an enforceable agreement that if a covered defect arose at any time during the period of the warranty, defendant would repair that condition. Therefore, we conclude that a claim for breach of this warranty did not accrue at the time of delivery of the car but rather when defendant allegedly breached its duty to repair the defect.

The correctness of this conclusion is clearest in a case such as this, where the term of the warranty is longer than the four-year limitations period provided in N.J.S.A. 12A:2-

725(1). If we adopted defendant's view that its powertrain warranty is an ordinary sales warranty, and consequently that a buyer must bring an action for breach of that warranty within four years of delivery, this would mean that the buyer would be unable to enforce defendant's warranty obligations for any breach that occurred beyond or even near the end of that four-year period, even though by its terms the warranty extends for as long as seven years. We are unwilling to construe N.J.S.A. 12A:2- 725(2) in a way that could lead to such an unreasonable result. See State v. Gill, 47 N.J. 441, 444, 221 A.2d 521 (1966).

This conclusion is also supported by decisions in other jurisdictions. In Nationwide Ins. Co. v. General Motors Corp., supra, the Pennsylvania Supreme Court held that a "12 month/12,000 mile 'New Car Limited Warranty' promising 'repairs and needed adjustments' to correct manufacturing defects is a warranty that 'explicitly extends to future performance of the goods' for purposes of determining when a cause of action for breach of that warranty accrues" under section 2-725(2) of the U.C.C.:

> [W]e do not read the words "explicitly extends to future performance of the vehicle" to require that the warranty make an explicit promise regarding how the goods will perform in the future. We believe that the focus of § 2725 is not on what is promised, but on the duration of the promise-i.e., the period to which the promise extends.... Therefore, we agree with Appellant that the phrase "explicitly extends to future performance" can be interpreted to include a promise that, by its terms, comes into play upon, or is contingent upon, the future performance of the goods.... Logically, a promise to repair or adjust defective parts within the first 12 months or 12,000 miles after delivery cannot be breached until the vehicle requires repair or adjustment, and "discovery of the breach must await the time of [future] performance." ...
>
> Furthermore, we will not permit [General Motors] and other sellers who draft similar documents to escape the consequences of presenting them to the consumer as "extended warranties." There can be little question that the consumer will consider the length of any warranty offered in determining whether to purchase a particular vehicle: The consumer naturally would believe that the longer the warranty, the greater the protection, and hence, the better the value, he or she is receiving. If [General Motors] position were to prevail, the protection afforded the buyer during the latter part of a warranty approaching four years would be largely illusory, as the buyer would have a very short period of time in which to bring a cause of action for breach. Moreover, the longer-term protection afforded by a warranty extending beyond four years would be completely illusory ...

* * *

There are other jurisdictions which hold that the kind of repair warranty involved in this case is not "a warranty [that] explicitly extends to future performance of the goods," N.J.S.A. 12A:2-7252179731;00048; LQ; NJST12A:2-725;1000045; but that a cause of action for breach of such a warranty does not accrue upon delivery because "the promise to repair is an independent obligation that is not breached until the seller fails to repair." Cosman v. Ford Motor Co., 285 Ill.App.3d 250, 220 Ill.Dec. 790, 674 N.E.2d 61, 68 (1996), appeal denied, 172 Ill.2d 549, 223 Ill.Dec. 194, 679 N.E.2d 379 (1997); see also Versico, Inc. v. Engineered Fabrics Corp., 238 Ga.App. 837, 520 S.E.2d 505, 509-10, cert. denied (Ga.1999); Nationwide Ins. Co. v. General Motors Corp., supra, 625 A.2d at 1179-81 (Zappala, J., dissenting). The rationale for this view is that [such a] warranty does not promise a level of performance. It warrants only that the dealer will repair, replace, or adjust defects if parts of the powertrain in fact do malfunction. It does not warrant the quality of the powertrain or its performance.... A promise to repair parts of the powertrain for six years is a promise that the manufacturer will behave in a certain way, not a warranty that the vehicle will behave in a certain way....

It does not fit within the definition of warranty under the Commercial Code. Although it is a warranty made as part of the sale of the goods in the sense that it promises something associated with the sale, it does not "warrant" the quality of the vehicle or its performance. [citation omitted]

This is also the view taken of some scholarly commentaries. For example, Anderson on the Uniform Commercial Code states:

A warranty of future performance differs from a covenant to repair or replace. The future performance warranty expressly provides some form of guaranty that the product will perform as required during the specified time. The obligation to repair or replace merely imposes a duty to repair or replace when a defect exists within the required period of time....

Although ... courts [that treat a covenant to repair or replace as a warranty of future performance] are sound in their conclusion that the statute of limitations should not commence until the seller has breached its promise to repair or replace the goods or any defective parts, it makes more sense to view the seller's failure to do so as a breach of contract, rather than as a breach of warranty. By so doing, the buyer's cause of action does not arise until the seller has refused to repair or replace the goods rather than upon the tender of delivery.

[Lary Lawrence, Lawrence's Anderson on the Uniform Commercial Code § 2-725:129 at 332-33 (3d ed.2001).]

Moreover, this is the view the National Conference of Commissioners on Uniform State Laws has taken in a draft revision of the U.C.C., which treats a "promise by the seller to repair or replace the goods or to refund all or part of the purchase price upon the happening of a specified event" as a "remedial promise." Amendments to Uniform Commercial Code, Article 2- Sales (Annual Meeting 2001 Draft) § 2-103(1)(m). Under this proposed revision, a promise by a seller to repair or replace a defective part during a specified warranty period "is not a warranty at all and therefore is not subject to either the time of tender [rule of 725(1)] or [the] discovery rule [of 725(2)]." Amendments to Uniform Commercial Code, supra, preliminary comment to § 2-103(1)(m). Instead, a cause of action for breach of a remedial promise would accrue "when the remedial promise is not performed when due." Amendments to Uniform Commercial Code, supra, § 2-725(2)(c).

We have no need to decide whether defendant's seven-year/seventy-thousand-mile powertrain warranty constituted a warranty of future performance within the intent of N.J.S.A. 12A:2-725(2) or an independent promise to repair defects in the powertrain that appear during the term of the warranty because, under either view, plaintiff's cause of action would not have accrued when the car was delivered in 1993 but rather when persistent problems in the engine timing belt appeared in 1997 or when defendant was allegedly unable to repair this defect in a timely manner in July 1998, and thus plaintiff's complaint was timely filed in December 1998....

Accordingly, we ... reverse the dismissal of his breach of warranty claims.

———————

6.5 Federal Magnuson-Moss Consumer Warranty Act

Although this course focuses on U.C.C. Article 2, we cannot conclude our study of warranties without a quick look at the federal law of warranties.[8] The Federal Magnuson-Moss Warranty Federal Trade Commission Improvement Act was enacted by Congress in 1975; it works in concert with the U.C.C. and other state laws to give some protection to buyers of consumer products.[9] It applies to all consumer products covered by a written warranty, manufactured after July 4, 1975. The stated purposes of the Act are to improve the adequacy of information available to consumers, to prevent deception and to improve competition in the marketing of consumer products.

Like the other warranty law we have studied, the Magnuson-Moss Warranty Act does *not* require that a seller warrant its products. If, however, the seller *chooses* to give a *written warranty* of a *consumer product,* the warranty must meet certain minimum federal standards.

Exercise 6-9 will help you understand the scope and key provisions of the Magnuson Moss Act.

Exercise 6-9: Exploring the Magnuson-Moss Act

1. Look up the definitions of the following key terms:

   1.1 Consumer Product

   1.2 Consumer

   1.3 Supplier

   1.4 Warrantor

   1.5 Written warranty

2. Compare those definitions to the treatment of like terms in the U.C.C.

3. Now answer the following questions:

   3.1 Which statute has the greater scope, the U.C.C. or the Magnuson Moss Act?

   3.2 Are all written warranties subject to both acts? If not, which one applies?

   3.3 Are all oral warranties subject to both acts? If not, which one applies?

   3.4 Is a warranty under the U.C.C. always a warranty under Magnuson Moss?

   3.5 Is a warranty under Magnuson Moss always a warranty under the U.C.C.?

   3.6 What are the minimum requirements under Magnuson Moss for a written warranty?

   3.7 What is the difference between a "full" and a "limited" warranty? Why do you think the Magnuson Moss Act permits a seller to choose between such warranties?

---

8. Of course, in practice, lawyers must also consult other state law. Because of consumer protection policies, many states have additional warranty law affecting consumers. See, for example, California's Song-Beverly Consumer Warranty Act (Civil Code § 1790, et. seq.), which protects consumers who lease or buy new motor vehicles. These types of laws are popularly known as "lemon laws."

9. Magnuson-Moss Warranty Act, 15 U.S.C. § 2302.

Exercise 6-10: Applying the Magnuson-Moss Act

Review the following Warranty. Then write a memorandum, discussing whether the warranty complies with the requirements of the Magnuson-Moss Warranty Act.

FULL LIFE TIME WARRANTY

FOR AS LONG AS YOU OWN AND RESIDE IN YOUR HOME
ON MILGARD PRODUCTS INSTALLED IN THE UNITED STATES AFTER 12/01/09

Milgard Manufacturing, Incorporated ("Milgard") guarantees to the original consumer purchaser ("Original Purchaser") of Milgard windows, doors or skylights (hereafter referred to as "Products") installed in a single family home or a multi-family home unit ("Home") by the builder as new construction or by the Original Purchaser as replacements that are defective in materials or workmanship and will pay the costs of all parts and labor. If repair is not commercially practical or cannot timely be made, then Milgard will, at the Original Purchaser's option, either replace any defective Milgard Products or refund the purchase price.

PERSONS COVERED
This Warranty extends to the Original Purchaser of Milgard Products. The Warranty starts on the date of purchase of the Home as new construction or the installation of Milgard windows, doors or skylights in the Home as replacements ("Start Date") and remains effective as long as the Original Purchaser owns and resides in the Home. In addition, if the Original Purchaser sells the Home before ten (10) years has elapsed after the Start Date, Milgard will automatically extend full coverage under this Warranty to the new owner(s) of the Home and any subsequent owner, until the tenth (10th) anniversary of the Start Date.

EXCLUSIONS FROM COVERAGE
This Warranty does not cover damage or defects relating to misuse, abuse, the use of applied tints or films, alterations including but not limited to customer-applied finishes, normal wear and tear, bowing glass**, natural weathering of exterior finishes, acts of nature (e.g. fire, hurricane, etc.), building settling, structural failures of walls or foundations or improper installation, storage, or handling or failure to properly care for and maintain the Milgard Products*** Normal wear including discoloration or hardware component finishes is not a defect and is not covered by this Warranty. Loss of functionality of hardware (except as provided below for stainless steel hardware****) in highly corrosive environments, which includes any Home located within two miles of salt water and any Home located in the State of Hawaii, is also excluded from coverage. For Milgard Products with argon or krypton gas-filled insulating glass, Milgard injects the gas at the time of manufacture. The gradual dissipation of inert gas may occur naturally over time and is not a defect. Other than gas loss due to seal failure, this warranty does not cover the gradual dissipation of inert gas or the amount of inert gas remaining in the Milgard Products at any time after manufacture. This Warranty does not apply to any Milgard Products that are installed in a Home that has a non-drainable EIFS or DEFS siding product.

Milgard reserves the right to modify or discontinue any of its Products. For the repair or replacement of modified or discontinued Products, Milgard will have the right to substitute current Products and components of equal quality and as similar in appearance as possible. Milgard will not be obligated to replace discontinued Products and components for which no similar alternatives are available.

Milgard WoodClad™ fiberglass windows and doors may, as an option, be purchased with unfinished wood interior surfaces that must be finished prior to, or immediately after installation for maximum protection. Unfinished wood surfaces that experience water damage at the jobsite or are left unfinished after installation and become stained or damaged will not be considered as defective in materials and workmanship under the terms of this Warranty.

LIMITATIONS ON REMEDIES
In no event will Milgard be liable for incidental or consequential damages (other than labor to repair or replace Products, screens or stainless steel hardware under this Warranty), whether based on breach of express or implied warranty, breach of contract, negligence, strict liability, or any other legal theory. Some states do not allow the exclusion or limitation of incidental or consequential damages, so the above limitation or exclusion may not apply to you.

STATE REMEDIES
This Warranty gives you specific legal rights, and you may have other rights which vary from state to state.

CONTACT US
To obtain service under this Warranty, contact us at 1-800-Milgard or access Milgard's website at www.milgard.com. Please keep this certificate for your files.

*SCREENS, INTEGRATED BLINDS AND SKYLIGHT COMPONENTS
Milgard will replace any window or door screen frame and mesh that is defective in materials or workmanship at no charge to the Original Purchaser (including parts and labor) for a period of one (1) year after Start Date. Milgard will replace any integrated blind that is defective in materials or workmanship at no charge to the Original Purchaser (including parts and labor) for a period of five (5) years after Start Date. Milgard will replace the electric motor or basic drive unit of Milgard's operable skylights that are defective in materials or workmanship at no charge to the Original Purchaser (including parts and labor) for a period of one (1) year after Start Date.

**COVERAGE FOR GLASS BREAKAGE
On Tuscany® Ultra™ and WoodClad™ product series only, the Full Lifetime Warranty will extend to glass breakage including tempered glass, unless attributable to acts of nature (e.g. fire, hurricane, etc.), civil disorder, building settling, structural failures of walls or foundations or improper installation, storage, or handling. Specialty glass (e.g. V-Groove, laminated glass) is not covered by this glass breakage warranty.

***PROPER CARE AND MAINTENANCE
Please see the Care and Maintenance Instructions on the back side of this certificate or go to Milgard's website at www.milgard.com.

****HARDWARE
Milgard will replace at no charge (parts and/or labor) stainless steel hardware that loses functionality in highly corrosive environments within one (1) year after the date of installation of the windows, doors or skylights as replacements.

PURCHASE DATE _____

SALES ORDER No. _____

FLW1209

6.6 Non-U.C.C. Warranty Litigation

When a defective product causes personal injuries, an action for breach of a U.C.C. warranty is not the only basis for recovery. As you learned in Torts, there are several legal theories that may provide a basis for recovery. These legal theories include negligence and strict liability. In addition, some jurisdictions have enacted a statutory products liability cause of action.

A detailed comparison of these various alternate causes of action is beyond the scope of this book. *Figure 6-16* on pages 114 and 115 summarizes the major differences between each of the identified causes of action.

Exercise 6-11: Virgil v. Kash N' Karry Service Corp.

The following case involves litigation resulting from a defective thermos bottle, and the different legal theories upon which the plaintiffs based their claims. As you read the case, consider the following questions:

1. How many legal theories did the plaintiffs advance?
2. Upon which legal theories did the court rely for its decision?

Virgil v. "Kash N' Karry" Service Corp.
484 A. 2d 652 (Md.App. 1984)

BLOOM, Judge.

In this products liability case, the appellants, Irma Virgil and her husband, Donald Virgil, plaintiffs below, appeal from a judgment of the Circuit Court for Howard County, entered upon a directed verdict in favor of the defendants-appellees, "Kash N' Karry" Service Corporation (Kash N' Karry) and Aladdin Industries, Incorporated (Aladdin).

The suit was for personal injuries sustained by Mrs. Virgil when a thermos bottle manufactured by Aladdin and sold by Kash N' Karry imploded while Mrs. Virgil was pouring milk into it. The declaration asserted claims by Mrs. Virgil, alleging (count 1) various negligent acts and omissions including negligent failure to warn of the dangerous propensities of the product; (count 2) breach of express warranty; (counts 3 and 5) breach of implied warranty of merchantability; (counts 4 and 6) strict liability in tort. A seventh count, incorporating the allegations of count 1, asserted a claim by Mr. and Mrs. Virgil, jointly, for loss of consortium as a result of the alleged negligence of the defendants.

Mrs. Virgil testified that she purchased the pint-size thermos while shopping at Kash N' Karry two or three months prior to the implosion. Every weekday morning she filled it with coffee and a little milk and took it to work, carrying it either by its handle or in a bag with her shoes. On Saturday mornings, she filled it with coffee and milk and carried it downstairs to the den, where she spent most of the day studying. Although the thermos bottle bore a label, "Easy To Keep Clean," there were no instructions as to how to clean the thermos and no indication that any normal manner of cleaning it might damage it. Mrs. Virgil described how she washed it, filling it at night with a mild solution of baking soda in warm water, then washing it the following morning with a bottle brush. She denied dropping the thermos or misusing, abusing or damaging it in any way. One morning, after pouring coffee into the thermos, she started to pour milk into it when it imploded, throwing hot coffee and glass into her face and injuring her eye. Appellants presented no expert testimony to give any scientific explanation for the implosion.

At the conclusion of the plaintiffs' case, the trial judge granted the defendants' motion for directed verdict as to all claims, holding that the Virgils had presented no evidence that the bottle was defective when purchased.

Appellants contend that the trial judge erred in directing the verdict because they had produced sufficient evidence to warrant submission of the case to the jury on the issue of negligence in failing to warn of inherent danger, on the issue of breach of implied warranty, and on the issue of strict liability. They also contend that the judge erred "in ruling as a matter of law that a period of three months from purchase to the accident increases the plaintiffs' burden of proof." There is no contention of error in the granting of the motion as to the claim for breach of express warranty.

We find ourselves in agreement with appellants as to the claims for breach of implied warranty and strict liability (counts 3, 4, 5 and 6); we disagree with appellants as to the negligence claims (counts 1 and 7). It will not be necessary to address appellants' final contention, but we will refer to it in our discussion of the other issues....

Implied Warranty and Strict Liability

To support their claim that appellees breached an implied warranty of merchantability, appellants had to establish that a warranty existed, that the warranty was breached, and that the breach was the proximate cause of the injury.... If the seller of goods is a merchant with respect to goods of that kind ... a warranty of merchantability is implied in the contract of sale. To be merchantable, the goods must at least be fit for the ordinary purposes for which they are sold and conform to any promises or affirmations of fact made on the container or label....

Strict liability in tort, on the other hand, is described in the Restatement (Second) of Torts § 402 A, as follows:

(1) One who sells any product in a defective condition unreasonably dangerous *656 to the user or consumer or to his property is subject to liability for physical harm thereby caused to the ultimate user or consumer, or to his property, if

(a) the seller is engaged in the business of selling such a product, and

(b) it is expected to and does reach the user or consumer without substantial change in the condition in which it is sold.

(2) The rule stated in Subsection (1) applies although

(a) the seller has exercised all possible care in the preparation and sale of his product, and

(b) the user or consumer has not bought the product from or entered into any contractual relation with the seller.

To recover on either theory — implied warranty or strict liability — the plaintiff in a products liability case must satisfy three basics from an evidentiary standpoint: (1) the existence of a defect, (2) the attribution of the defect to the seller, and (3) a causal relation between the defect and the injury ... [Court's discussion of whether expert testimony was needed to establish the existence of a defect is omitted.]

In granting appellees' motion for directed verdict, the trial judge stated that he was "unable to discern that the thermos was not fit for the ordinary purposes for which it was intended ...," ...

Failure to Warn

Products liability law imposes on a manufacturer a duty to warn if the item produced has an inherent and hidden danger that the producer knows or should know could be a substantial factor in causing injury ... This duty to warn of latent dangers inherent in the use of the product extends beyond intended uses to include uses that are reasonably foreseeable ... In the case sub judice, the claim that appellees negligently failed to warn of the "dangerous propensities of the product" fails simply because there was no evidence that either of the appellees knew or should have known that the thermos bottle presented a danger. Assuming that the thermos had a latent defect that caused it to implode, there is nothing in the evidence to suggest that either the manufacturer or the retailer were or should have been aware of that defect.

Appellants suggest that the thermos label, which recommended that the product not be used by children and advised potential users that the product contained glass, permits an inference that the manufacturer had reason to know that the thermos would be inherently dangerous for a reasonably foreseeable use. Recognizing that a product partially composed of glass is breakable, however, hardly constitutes awareness that the product is defective. We hold, therefore, that although the court erred in granting a directed verdict as to those counts asserting claims for breach of implied warranty and strict liability, it did not err in granting a directed verdict as to those counts based on assertions of negligence.

JUDGMENT AFFIRMED AS TO THE FIRST, SECOND AND SEVENTH COUNTS OF THE DECLARATION BUT REVERSED AND REMANDED FOR NEW TRIAL AS TO THE THIRD, FOURTH, FIFTH AND SIXTH COUNTS.

Exercise 6-12

John Gable owns Gable Farming, Inc. (GF). GF currently owns 10,000 acres of farmland used to grow corn, soybeans, and wheat. At the end of the 2009 harvest, three of GF's KAT tractors broke down. John personally went to a KAT dealership near his home to order three new KAT tractors. The KAT tractors John had used in the past planted 5 seeds per second. When John was there, a sales agent for KAT showed John the brand new X100 tractor. The agent told John that the tractor could plant 10 seeds per second. John was so impressed that he bought three X100 tractors.

The tractors arrived on time, and the GF farmworkers put the tractors to use, but the X100 tractors only planted three seeds per second. As a result, John was unable to get his crop planted in a timely manner, and his ultimate yield was reduced. John is furious.

What rights, if any, does GF have against KAT?

Exercise 6-13

Same facts as Exercise 6-12. Now assume that the X100 tractors just threw seeds onto the ground without mixing the seeds into the ground. However, the tractors did spew out 10 seeds per second.

What rights, if any, does GF have against KAT?

Exercise 6-14

Farmer purchased Wonder Seeds from Supplier. The written contract between Supplier and Farmer provided in pertinent part:

SUPPLIER WARRANTS THAT WONDER SEEDS ARE AS DESCRIBED ON THE TAG ATTACHED TO THE BAG. IT MAKES NO OTHER WARRANTIES, EXPRESS OR IMPLIED, OF MERCHANTABILITY, FITNESS FOR PURPOSE, OR OTHERWISE, AND IN ANY EVENT ITS LIABILITY FOR BREACH OF ANY WARRANTY OR CONTRACT WITH RESPECT TO SUCH SEEDS IS LIMITED TO THE PURCHASE PRICE OF SUCH SEEDS. IN NO EVENT SHALL SUPPLIER BE LIABLE FOR ANY INCIDENTAL OR CONSEQUENTIAL DAMAGES, INCLUDING LOSS OF PROFITS.

The tag attached to each bag of seed read "Corn seed." When Farmer planted the seed, over 60% of the seed planted yielded no corn at all; that which was produced was of poor quality.

1. Can Farmer prevail in an action against Supplier for breach of warranty? Why or why not? What additional *facts*, if any, do you need to know to make this determination?

2. Assume that Farmer can prevail on its breach of warranty claim. Can Farmer recover for lost profits resulting from the defective seed?

Exercise 6-15

Buyer purchased a painting from Art Gallery on May 9, 2001. In 2006, Buyer attempted to sell the painting to an auction house, and discovered that the painting had been stolen by the Nazis from a well known Paris art dealer during World War II. On May 10, 2006, Buyer sued Seller for breach of the warranty of title. What result?

At this point in the course, you have learned enough that you can begin to put a considerable amount of material together. Exercise 6-16 requires you to use what you have learned from Chapters 2-6 of this book.

Exercise 6-16

Roberta Buyer, the owner of an accounting firm, called Sam Seller, a personal computer distributor, to discuss the purchase of ten new personal computers, which were advertised in Sam's direct-mail catalog. The catalog stated that the computers were "state of the art." In a short and to-the-point telephone conversation, the parties agreed that Roberta would buy ten S.A.M. personal computers, model no. 12345, for $1800 each. Before hanging up the telephone, Sam stated, "Now, you understand that when we end this call we will have a binding agreement?" Roberta replied, "Yes."

The next day, Sam shipped the computers to Roberta, together with the following packing slip:

SOLD BY SAM SELLER TO ROBERTA BUYER
TEN (10) S.A.M. personal computers, model no. 12345.

TERMS AND CONDITIONS OF SALE

All sales are made pursuant to the following conditions.

*Payment for items sold is due and payable on the 10th of the month following invoice date, unless payment terms are otherwise established in writing with an authorized agent of Seller. Buyer shall pay interest at the rate of 1-1/2% per month, which is an annual percentage rate of 18%, upon all delinquent accounts and further agrees to pay upon demand all reasonable collection costs and attorneys fees incurred in the collection of this account, or in enforcing the terms of this agreement.

*Buyer may return the items sold within thirty (30) days of the date of this agreement, and receive a refund of all amounts paid to Seller, less a reasonable restocking fee.

*Seller MAKES NO WARRANTIES, EXPRESS OR IMPLIED, AS TO THE ITEM(S).

Assume that a contract was formed during the referenced telephone conversation between Buyer and Seller. Discuss the following question ONLY: What are the terms of the contract? Be sure to explain in detail how you reached your conclusions.

Additional Resources

Russell Donaldson, Annotation, *Affirmations or representations made after the sale is closed as basis of warranty under U.C.C. §2-313(1)(a)*, 47 A.L.R.4th 200 (2009).

Daniel C. Hagen, "*Sections 2-719(2) & 2-719(3) of the Uniform Commercial Code: The Limited Warranty Package & Consequential Damages*," 31 Val. U. L. Rev. 111 (1996).

Elizabeth Tsai, Annotation, *Liability for representations and express warranties in connection with sale of used motor vehicle*, 36 A.L.R.3d 125 (2009).

Elizabeth Tsai, Annotation, *Sales: liability for warranty or representation that article, other than motor vehicle, is new*, 36 A.L.R.3d 237 (2008).

Figure 6-16: A Simplified Comparison of Products Liability/Warranty Actions

	Implied Warranty of Merchantability	Implied Warranty of Fitness for a Particular Purpose	Express Warranty	Products Liability (Restatement of Torts) "Strict Liability"	Negligence
Basis of Cause of Action:					
Sale	Seller is a merchant with respect to goods sold	Seller has reason to know buyer's particular purpose	Seller makes an affirmation of fact or promise; Description of the goods; Sample or model	Seller is engaged in the business of selling or otherwise distributing a product ("commercial seller")	Someone in distribution chain
Product	Unmerchantable (see § 2-314)	Not fit for a particular purpose	Does not conform to warranty	Defective (unreasonably dangerous) at the time of sale or distribution	Defective product (not reasonably safe)
Causation	Required	Required	Required	Required	Required
Basis of Liability	Breach of Warranty	Breach of Warranty	Breach of Warranty	Strict liability based on: manufacturing defect, design defect, or inadequate instructions/warnings	Negligence — duty, breach of duty (fault leading to product defect — can include failure to reasonably inspect, negligently introducing defect into product, etc.) causation, and injury
Recovery for:					
Personal Injury	Yes (see § 2-715)	Yes (see § 2-715)	Yes (see § 2-715)	Yes	Yes
Property Damage	Yes (see § 2-715)	Yes (see § 2-715)	Yes (see § 2-715)	Yes, for damages to other property but not the defective product itself	Yes, for damages to other property but not the defective product itself

Economic Loss	Yes (see § 2-715)	Yes (see § 2-715)	Yes (see § 2-715)	No recovery for "pure" economic loss	No recovery for "pure" economic loss
Defenses:					
Lack of Notice	Yes, under § 2-607(3)(a)	Yes, under § 2-607(3)(a)	Yes, under § 2-607(3)(a)	No	No
Lack of Privity	Maybe, § 2-318 provides alternatives to horizontal privity requirement	Remote buyer cannot recover; seller <u>must</u> know of buyer's particular purpose	Maybe, under a third party beneficiary theory	No	No
Warranty Disclaimers	Yes (see § 2-316)	Yes (see § 2-316)	Yes (see § 2-316)	No	No
Remedy Limitations	Yes, but limitation of consequential damages for personal injury in the case of consumer goods is prima facie unconscionable (see §§ 2-719, 2-302)	Yes, but limitation of consequential damages for personal injury in the case of consumer goods is prima facie unconscionable (see §§ 2-719, 2-302)	Yes, but limitation of consequential damages for personal injury in the case of consumer goods is prima facie unconscionable (see §§ 2-719, 2-302)	No	No
Misuse, Modification, and Alteration	Yes	Yes	Yes	Yes	Yes
Other Defenses				In common law states, assumption of the risk is a defense but contributory negligence is not. In comparative fault states, conduct of the plaintiff may reduce damages.	Yes, traditional defenses in negligence cause of action (including contributory or comparative negligence, assumption of the risk, etc.)

Figure 7-1: Graphic Organizer

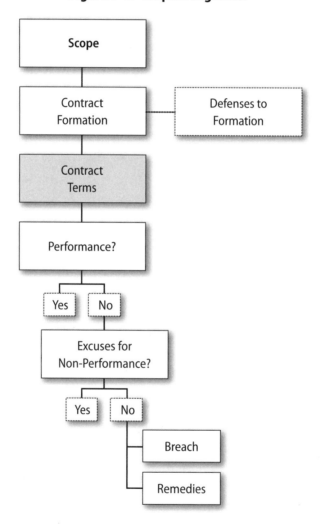

Chapter 7

Contract Terms: Express Terms, Interpretation and the Parol Evidence Rule

Chapter Problem

You are a new associate in the firm of Weno Allthelaw, LLP. You have received a memorandum from your supervising partner about a new client. Read the memorandum and prepare to conduct a client interview and to give your client legal advice. The information presented in this chapter will help you do so.

Weno Allthelaw, LLP
INTER-OFFICE MEMORANDUM

TO: Associate
FROM: Supervising Partner
RE: New Client, Printers-R-Us
DATE: October 20

Our firm has been retained by a new client, Printers-R-Us, who has requested a "legal check-up," starting with a review of the form contract the client has been using. All I know is that the client is engaged in the business of selling and repairing computer printers. Attached to this memo is a copy of the contract our client has been using. Please review it thoroughly and be prepared to discuss what, if any, changes you would suggest. As part of your review, be sure to consider whether the contract adequately protects the client against claims based on alleged oral warranties made before the signing of the contract.

CONTRACT FOR THE SALE OF GOODS

This contract is by and between _____ ("seller") and _____ ("buyer"). Seller and Buyer are collectively referred to in this contract as the "Parties."

Title

Title to the goods shall remain with the Seller until the Buyer takes physical possession and Seller has been paid in full. If multiple shipments are required, title shall be passed when the last items are paid for.

Disclaimer of Express Warranties

Seller warrants product sold will perform only within the limits of what is normally expected of the product.

Warranty of Goods

All parts, printers and repairs carry a 180 day return to depot warranty, except: stacked wire printheads which carry a 90-day return to depot warranty; and consumables which have a specified yield or life expectancy. Warranty may be altered at the time of sale by agreement of both parties and noted on the order. All modules repaired by Seller are warranted against defects in workmanship and material. If a failure unrelated to the original problem occurs within the warranty period, including neglect, abuse and acts of God, the module will not be eligible for warranty repair.

Right of Inspection & Acceptance of Goods

Buyer shall have the right to inspect the goods at the site and place of delivery. Any and all discrepancies and/or defects must be reported within 72 hours of receipt of this product.

Remedies

Buyer and Seller shall have all remedies afforded each by the Uniform Commercial Code, State of Arizona. Under no circumstances shall Seller be liable for any special incidental or consequential damages. Our responsibility is for the actual material sold.

Authority of Seller's Agents

No agent, employee or representative of the Seller has any authority to bind Seller to any affirmation, representation or warranty concerning the goods sold under this contract unless an affirmation representation or warranty made by agent, employee or representative is specifically included within this contract.

Modifications

This contract can be modified or rescinded only in writing, signed by both parties or their duly authorized agents.

Time for Bringing Action

Any action for breach of this contract must be commenced within 6 months after the cause of action occurred. This contract shall be governed by the Uniform Commercial Code as adopted in the state of Arizona as effective and in force as of the date of this contract.

DATED: (signatures)

This chapter focuses on express contract terms and how courts interpret the meaning of those terms (See *Figure 7-2*).

Figure 7-2: Express Contract Terms and Parol Evidence Rule Sections and Definitions

Section	Definitions
1-201(3)	Agreement
1-201(12)	Contract
2-202	A writing "intended by the parties as a final expression of their agreement with respect to such terms as are included therein"
	A writing "intended also as a complete and exclusive statement of the terms of the agreement"
	Consistent additional terms Course of Dealing, Usage of Trade, Course of Performance (*See* section 1-303)
2-319	F.O.B. F.A.S.
2-320	C.I.F. C. & F.
2-321	C.I.F. C. & F.
2-322	Ex Ship
2-323	Bill of Lading
2-324	"No Arrivals, No Sale"
2-325	Letter of Credit

1. Express Contract Terms

Express terms are those that the parties have stated explicitly, either orally or in writing. Such terms generally relate to a distinct element of performance or enforcement. The process of identifying express terms involves more than reading terms in a written agreement. Sometimes the parties may have reached agreements that are not reflected in the writing or writings they signed. In such cases, resort to a set of doctrinal principles called "the parol evidence rule" may be necessary to arrive at all of the terms of the parties' agreement. (Note the definitions of "agreement" and "contract" in section 1-201.)

2. Limitations on Voluntary Agreements

Although the Code broadly promises to enforce voluntary agreements made between parties, for public policy reasons, there are still limitations on what they can agree to. These limitations are expressed as the obligation of good faith (sections 1-201(20), 1-304) and the restraint imposed by section 2-302 on unconscionable bargains.

3. The Parol Evidence Rule

The "parol evidence rule" is actually a complex set of doctrines. You may recall from your Contracts class that the parol evidence rule evolved based on the assumption that when parties adopt a written document as the embodiment of their contract, it is reasonable to assume that they have incorporated all of the terms of their agreement in the writing. Accordingly, the parol evidence rule initially was developed to exclude evidence of agreements extrinsic to (outside of) the writing.[1]

Specifically, the rule first asks if the parties to a written agreement intended that writing to be the full and complete embodiment of everything they agreed to. If so, the rule bars the admission of any evidence of an agreement allegedly made before or contemporaneously with the making of the written agreement. If the parties only intended the writing to accurately represent a part of their agreement, the parol evidence rule bars the admission of any evidence that contradicts a term in the written agreement.

Figure 7-3 illustrates the key items that must be considered to apply the parol evidence rule properly. First, consider whether there is extrinsic evidence of an agreement made between the parties and, if so, whether it was made prior to or contemporaneously with the parties' written agreement. If so, you must determine whether the parol evidence rule will bar admission of the evidence of that agreement. If there is evidence of an agreement made *after* the parties' written agreement, the parol evidence rule is not implicated. (Therefore, as illustrated in *Figure 7-3*, there is no bar to the admissibility of evidence of a post-writing agreement.)

The first step of any parol evidence rule analysis is to determine if there is a written agreement and, if so, if the parties intended the written document to be the full, final

Figure 7-3: Admissibility of Extrinsic Evidence to explain or supplement a written agreement

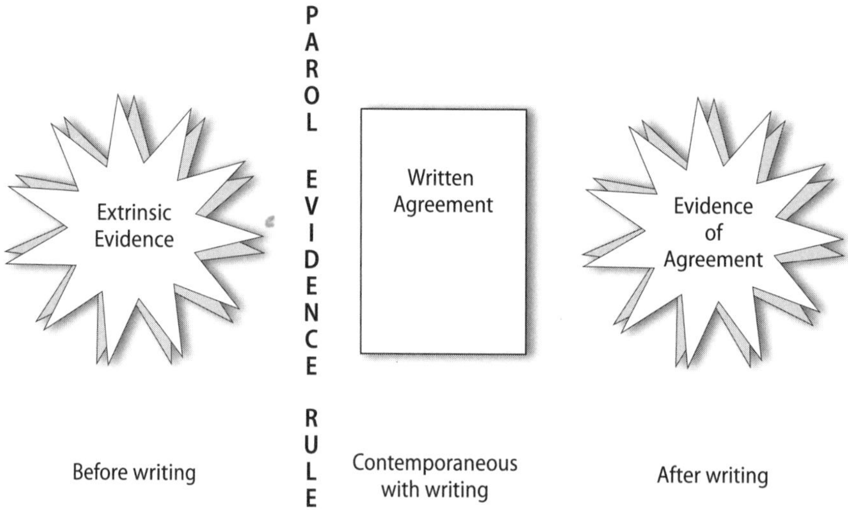

---

1. Some students mistakenly believe that the parol evidence rule applies only to alleged oral agreements. I specifically reference "extrinsic evidence" to emphasize that the parol evidence rule applies to both alleged oral and written agreements.

and complete expression of their agreement (a "full" or "complete" integration). This determination is often framed in terms of whether the writing is partially or fully "integrated." Note that the U.C.C. does not use the term "integration" at all. Instead it refers to "[a writing] intended by the parties as a final expression of their agreement with respect to such terms as are included therein" (*partial integration*) and "[a writing] ... intended also as a complete and exclusive statement of the terms of the agreement" (*complete integration*).

The next step of parol evidence rule analysis is to apply the rule: If the writing is only partially integrated, evidence of consistent additional terms can be admitted; contradictory evidence is barred. If the writing is fully integrated, evidence of any extrinsic *agreement* is barred (but evidence of course of dealing, course of performance and usage of trade is admissible to explain or supplement the written agreement.)

The most difficult part of the parol evidence rule analysis is deciding if the writing is completely or partially integrated. *Figure 7-4* lists the factors that courts cite in aid of a determination regarding integration.

Figure 7-4: Factors Used by Courts to Determine Integration

Partial Integration	Complete Integration
Absence of merger clause	Presence of merger clause
Obvious "gaps" in coverage — key terms are missing	Detailed agreement that appears to cover all issues one would expect to have covered in the type of agreement under consideration
Form of agreement — casual — handwritten, or "fill in the blanks" on a standard form	Form of agreement — negotiated over extended period of time, perhaps written by attorneys
Length of agreement — short, appears incomplete	Length of agreement — long, appears complete
Evidence that parties intended only partial integration	Evidence that parties intended complete integration

The U.C.C. continues the common law approach to analyzing parol evidence, although it continues to liberalize the common law rule. You were introduced to one common fact pattern that involves the parol evidence rule in Chapter 6, regarding warranties and warranty disclaimers. A salesperson, before a sale, makes oral representations regarding the product to a prospective buyer. When the buyer buys the product, the written sales agreement contains a disclaimer of warranties. The buyer's ability to sue for breach of warranty may turn on the court's interpretation and application of the parol evidence rule.

Like any simplistic explanation of complex doctrine, the foregoing discussion of the parol evidence rule is only the tip of an iceberg. *Figure 7-5* on the next page may help you predict when extrinsic evidence will be admissible under the U.C.C.'s parol evidence rule, section 2-202. The case that follows illustrates how a court struggles to apply the rule.

Figure 7-5: Admissibility of Extrinsic Evidence under U.C.C. § 2-202[*]

	Not Integrated Writing	Final as to Terms Contained Therein (Partially Integrated)	Final, Complete and Exclusive Statement of All Terms (Complete Integration)
Any Prior Agreement That Contradicts the Writing	Yes	No	No
Contemporaneous Oral Agreement That Contradicts the Writing	Yes	No	No
Course of Performance, Course of Dealing, Usage of Trade (1-303) to Explain or Supplement	Yes	Yes (Unless Carefully Negated, Comment 2)	Yes (Unless Carefully Negated, Comment 2)
Prior Consistent Additional Terms	Yes	Yes (Unless If Agreed upon Would Certainly Have Been Included) (Comment 3)	No
Any Subsequent Agreement, Even If Contradictory (See 2-209, Not 2-202!!!)	Yes	Yes	Yes

[*] Based on Parol Evidence Chart prepared by Prof. Corinne Cooper, UMKC School of Law.

Peter B. Sundlun v. Bruce G. Shoemaker

421 Pa. Super. 353 (Pa. Super. Ct. 1992)

BECK, Judge:

The issue is whether in interpreting a contract under the Uniform Commercial Code the trial judge properly admitted parol evidence to explain the terms of the contract. We find the judge properly admitted the parol evidence and affirm the order of the trial court.

This is an appeal from an order of the trial court denying a motion for judgment n.o.v. or a new trial. Appellant Bruce G. Shoemaker contends that the trial court erred in admitting parol evidence of additional terms to supplement or explain terms of a written contract, and that the jury's verdict in favor of appellee Peter B. Sundlun was against the weight of the evidence.

Shoemaker is an antiques dealer and Sundlun was an antiques broker. Sundlun became interested in purchasing a rare "Thomas Mendenhall Cherry Tall Case Clock, Circa 1774" which was owned by Shoemaker. The parties discussed the clock on several occasions, disassembling it and examining its condition, and Shoemaker represented to Sundlun that, inter alia, the feet on the clock case were original. Sundlun agreed to purchase the clock for $97,500.

On March 9, 1988, the parties entered into a written agreement for the sale of the clock, which provided, in pertinent part:

* * *

2. Seller [Shoemaker] represents and warrants the authenticity of the Clock through the description/authority of Lancaster Clocks prepared by Stacy B.C. Wood, Jr., attached hereto as Exhibit B and made a part hereof.

3. Seller herein personally guarantees the authenticity of the Clock and *if it is determined that the Clock is not as described, Seller shall purchase back from Buyer [Sundlun] the Clock* for the purchase price plus interest of Six Percent (6%) computed from the date of purchase until March 1, 1991. The obligation of Seller to repurchase Clock shall automatically terminate the earlier of (1) March 1, 1991; or (2) the sale of the Clock by Buyer by [sic] a third party.

* * *

(Emphasis added). Attached to the written contract was a six page report by a research horologist, which described the clock and certified that it was "made in the period 1773-1774." The only statement about the clock's feet included in this report was that "Ogee feet carry the case." ...

Shortly after the sale of the clock it was discovered that the clock's feet were not original. Both parties acknowledged that this fact substantially impaired the value of the clock. After attempting to resell the clock at various prices, Sundlun requested that Shoemaker buy back the clock in accordance with paragraph 3 of the written agreement. Sundlun's position was that the clock was *"not as described"* by the Wood report and the oral representations made by Shoemaker.

Shoemaker refused to repurchase the clock. He contends that the written agreement warranted only that the clock was "as described" in the Wood report, and that the replacement of the clock's feet did not affect the clock's "authenticity" as described in that report. Shoemaker argued that his own representation that the feet were original was not part of the "description" warranted by paragraphs 2 and 3 of the written agreement.

Sundlun then sold the clock at Christie's Auction in New York for $22,000, in order to mitigate his damages. Sundlun commenced this action against Shoemaker alleging breach of contract and breach of warranty. After trial, a jury returned a verdict in favor of Sundlun in the amount of $75,500, the difference between the clock's purchase price and its sale price at auction. Shoemaker filed a motion for judgment n.o.v. or, in the alternative, a new trial, which motion was denied. This timely appeal followed.

Shoemaker raises the following issues:

1. Did the lower court err in admitting parol evidence consisting of oral statements of the parties to the contract which contradicted, rather than explained, the contract phrases "authenticity" and "as described"?

* * *

Because we find that the trial court did not err in denying Shoemaker's motion for post-trial relief, we affirm.

We first address Shoemaker's argument that the trial court erred in admitting parol evidence of oral representations Shoemaker made about the condition of the clock's feet.... The admission or exclusion of evidence is within the sound discretion of the trial court and will not be reversed on appeal absent a clear abuse of discretion.... We find no such abuse of discretion in the trial court's admission of Shoemaker's statements about the clock's condition.

Shoemaker concedes that he told Sundlun that the feet were original and not replacements.... However, he claims that the admission of these statements improperly modified the "unambiguous language of the complete and integrated written contract," in violation of the parol evidence rule. We agree with the trial court that these oral representations simply were consistent additional terms which did not contradict but rather explained the meaning of terms in paragraphs 2 and 3 of the written agreement, and thus supplemented it, in accordance with the applicable law.

This sales transaction occurred in a commercial context, and is governed in Pennsylvania by the Uniform Commercial Code ("UCC").... Specifically, the Pennsylvania UCC includes a parol evidence rule which provides as follows ...

In this case, the parties have put forth different interpretations of the term "as described" in paragraph 3 of the written contract. Shoemaker argues that the phrase refers only to the description included in the Wood report appended to the contract. He asserts that his own statements about the original condition of the clock feet were not intended to be part of the description guaranteed by the written agreement, and that their substance contradicts the plain language of the contract in violation of the common law and UCC parol evidence rules. We disagree.

Under the UCC parol evidence rule, which governs this transaction, the oral statements about the clock feet were properly admitted as "consistent additional terms" which explained and supplemented the term "as described." ... Moreover, nothing in the parties' written agreement supports the contention that it was intended as a "complete and exclusive statement of the terms of the agreement." It did not contain an integration clause that would have made such an intention manifest.

As discussed in the Official Comment to section 2- 202, the UCC's parol evidence rule allows the fact finder to consider: 1) that a writing which is final on some matters may not include all the matters agreed upon; 2) that the language used in a written agreement has the meaning which arises out of the commercial context in which it was used; and 3) that parol evidence may be admitted even if there has been no determination by the court that the written contract language is ambiguous.... See also Campbell v. Hostetter Farms, Inc., 251 Pa.Super. 232, 380 A.2d 463 (1977) (finding that contract language is ambiguous is not prerequisite to admission of parol evidence, nor is it required that the court, rather than the jury, determine the effect of parol evidence on meaning of the contract). In other words, the UCC rule allows the jury to take into account consistent parol evidence when it attempts to discern the meaning of a written contract. In this instance, the oral statements were made by Shoemaker in the course of dealing. Unless carefully negated by the written terms of the contract, the parties' course of dealing, including any consistent oral representations, become an element of the meaning of the words used ... If Shoemaker meant to limit his personal guarantee in paragraph 3 of the written agreement to the contents of the Wood report, he could have made this intention clear by simply changing the language to read "as described in the Wood report attached hereto." Because Shoemaker's representations about the clock feet did not contradict the express written terms of the agreement, they were properly admitted to explain or supplement that agreement.

Order affirmed.

Exercises 7-1 through 7-4 ask whether a party has specific contract rights against the other party. In each case, the answer will depend on your analysis of particular contract terms, and the parol evidence rule.

Exercise 7-1: The Parol Evidence Rule and Implied Terms

Bruce, who runs an Electronics Store, enters into a written agreement for the purchase of 1000 music players from Super Music Inc. The written agreement says nothing about earphones. In the musical electronics industry, music players are customarily sold with earphones. When the music players are delivered to Bruce, he discovers that the shipment does not include earphones and he will have to purchase earphones before selling the music players to customers.

Bruce wants to sue Super Music for breach of contract, due to its failure to include earphones in its sale of the music players. What result?

Exercise 7-2: The Parol Evidence Rule and Express Terms Not Contained in a Written Agreement

Betty Bargainer and Stingy Sam enter into a written agreement for the sale of paperback text books. The agreement is silent regarding whether the books are paperbacks or hardcover books, but it does specify a price of $10 per book for 200 books. Hardcover texts generally sell for $15 per book, and paperbacks generally sell for $10 per book.

Before Betty signed the contract, Betty expressed concern about the quality of the books. Sam promised her that he would upgrade the paperback books to hardcover books at "no additional charge." Betty then signed the written agreement.

Does Betty have the right to insist on hardcover books?

Exercise 7-3: The Parol Evidence Rule: Consistent Additional Terms

Same facts as Exercise 7-2, except the written agreement specifically stated that the books would be paperback books. What result?

Exercise 7-4: Applicability of the Parol Evidence Rule

Buddy enters into a written sales agreement with Smokey on Wednesday to buy a 1929 Baseball Card. When Buddy picks up the card on Thursday, Smokey says to him "my family is the original owner of this card." Smokey had not mentioned this fact before, and neither did the sales agreement. It turns out that, unknown to Smokey, the card was in the possession of three previous owners before his family acquired it; as a result, the card is less valuable. Does

Buddy have any rights against Smokey based on the statement made on Thursday?

Exercise 7-5: The Parol Evidence Rule and Course of Performance, Course of Performance and Usage of Trade

In July, 2003, Samantha Seller ("Seller") and Barbara Buyer ("Buyer"), who were both merchants, entered into Samantha's standard form Distributorship Agreement (the "Agreement"), pursuant to which Buyer was to become a wholesale distributor of Ski-Daddlers, a type of snowmobile manufactured by Seller. As a wholesale distributor, Buyer would buy snowmobiles from Seller, and re-sell them to retailers within the designated sales territory. The Agreement defined "Buyer's Sales Territory"—the states where Buyer was authorized to sell Ski-Daddlers—as the states of Washington, Oregon, and California, but was silent as to whether Buyer had the exclusive right to distribute Ski-Daddlers in Buyer's Sales Territory.

The Agreement was all on one page, and was written in 8 point font, which looks like this: 8 point font. You may assume that all blank spaces were properly completed and the Agreement was signed by both parties. No changes were made to the standard contract provisions. (Please assume that the completed contract satisfied the Statute of Frauds in all respects.)

The Agreement contained the following paragraphs (among others, with which you need not be concerned):

1. The term of this Agreement commences on August 1, 2003, and ends on July 31, 2004.
2. This writing contains the full, final and exclusive statement of the agreement of the parties.

On July 31, 2004, the parties agreed orally to extend the term of the Agreement for an additional year. On July 31, 2005, the parties again agreed orally to extend the term of the Agreement for an additional year.

In September, 2005, Seller took a closer look at Ski-Daddler sales, and decided she could earn more money by selling directly to retail dealers. Accordingly, she immediately began making direct sales to retailers, including retailers who were located within Buyer's Sales Territory. Buyer sued Seller, alleging that Seller's direct sales to retail dealers in Buyer's Sales Territory violated her contractual right to be the exclusive distributor of Ski-Daddler snowmobiles in Buyer's Sales Territory.

At trial, should the Court admit evidence to show the matters set forth below? Analyze each separate item, determine whether or not it should be admitted, and explain your answer fully.

1. In the snowmobile trade, most distributorship agreements grant the wholesale distributor an exclusive sales area.

2. During negotiations, before the parties signed the Agreement, Seller told Buyer that Buyer's Sales Territory would be exclusive to Buyer.

3. From August 1, 2003 through September 2005, Buyer was the only Ski-Daddler distributor in Buyer's Sales Territory.

4. Seller orally agreed to an exclusivity term in the two oral extensions of the term of the Agreement.

Exercise 7-6: Applying Section 2-202

In each of the following problems, unless otherwise indicated, assume that the contract does NOT contain a "merger clause." First, determine whether a court would consider the contract to be "fully" or "partially" integrated. Then, predict whether a court would admit the described evidence.

1. On July 17, Mitchell, a farmer, discussed with Ben Franklin, Paymaster's plant manager, the prospects for fall delivery of soybeans to Paymaster. An oral agreement between the two was reached whereby Mitchell contracted to deliver 4000 bushels of soybeans at $3.11 a bushel in October and November. On July 19, a written confirmation, prepared by Paymaster, was executed by Farmer and Franklin corroborating their oral agreement. In addition to a description of the soybeans, the amount, price, and time of delivery the confirmation contained the following language: 'We confirm the purchase from you, as per our conversation Dennis Mitchell/Benny Franklin....' It did not expressly state the anticipated source of the soybeans. Should a court admit evidence that the parties had agreed that the soybeans were to be delivered from the seller's own crop?

2. Buyer purchased a car from Seller, who also arranged for financing. To evidence the sale, Buyer signed a purchase order that described the car and set forth the purchase price. In addition, Buyer signed a promissory note and security agreement in connection with the loan. None of these documents included delivery terms. Should a court permit Buyer to introduce evidence of a prior oral agreement that Seller would deliver the car to Buyer's residence in another state?

3. Where the parties signed a written contract for the rental of uniforms and the written contract was silent regarding the quality of uniforms, should a court admit evidence of an oral agreement that the seller's uniforms would be substantially as good as those formerly worn by the buyer, which had been manufactured by someone other than this seller?

4. Where the parties signed a written contract for the delivery of sprinkler systems but the contract contained no designated date for delivery, should a court admit evidence of an oral promise to deliver the systems by a certain date?

5. Where a written contract for the sale of air conditioners contained express provisions: (a) that any quoted shipping date or acknowledgement was only a "best estimate," (b) that the seller would incur no obligation or liability from untimely delivery, and (c) that the agreement was the full, final, complete and exclusive statement of the parties' agreement, should a court admit evidence of pre-contract negotiations and an alleged oral agreement as to delivery dates?

6. Buyer and Seller formed a contract through the exchange of a purchase order and responsive invoice, both of which described the subject of the contract as "paperback books." Should a court admit evidence that Seller orally promised Buyer that the books would be hardback?

4. Delivery Terms

One way the parties can agree upon risk of loss is by using express delivery terms, which have meanings defined by the Code. For example, the term "F.O.B." means "free on board" and when used in connection with the place of shipment, it means that risk of loss passes at the place of shipment. If a sales contract requires delivery to be "F.O.B. Chicago," you cannot tell whether a shipment or destination contract is intended until you know whether the seller or the buyer is located in Chicago. If the seller is in Chicago and the buyer is in New York, the contract is a shipment contract; tender occurs in Chicago, and the buyer has the risk of loss while the goods are en route from Chicago to New York. If the seller is in New York and the buyer is in Chicago, it is a destination contract; tender occurs in Chicago, and the seller has the risk of loss during the trip to Chicago. Caution: some of the same terms have different meanings in international trade.

For assistance in mastering the meaning of the various shipment terms under the U.C.C. and their relation to the risk of loss analysis under 2-509, see *Figure 7-6*.

Figure 7-6: Delivery Terms and Risk of Loss

Term	Kind of Contract	Point at Which Risk of Loss Passes	Applicable Code Sections
F.O.B. (Free on Board) point of shipment	Shipment	Possession of the carrier	2319(1)(a) 2509(1)(a) 2504
F.O.B. vessel, car or other vehicle, point of shipment	Shipment	Delivery on board carrier (Seller must load)	2319(1)(c) 2509(1)(a)
F.O.B. destination	Destination	Tender of goods in possession of carrier to Buyer at destination	2319(1)(b) 2509(1)(b) 2503
F.O.B. vessel, car or other vehicle, destination	Destination	Tender of goods on board carrier at destination	2319(1)(c) 2509(1)(b)
F.A.S. (Free alongside) vessel, named port	Shipment or Destination	Possession of the carrier (alongside vessel)	2319 (2)(a) 2509(1)(a) [2311 if Buyer fails to give instructions]
C.I.F. (Cost, insurance, freight)	Shipment	Possession of the carrier after loading	2320 (2)(a)-(e); Comment 1 2509(1)(a)
C.F. (Cost & freight)	Shipment	Possession of carrier after loading	2320(3) 2509(1)(a)
Ex ship	Destination	Upon unloading at destination	2322 (2)(b) 2509(1)(b)

Exercise 7-8: Delivery Terms

Exercise 7-8 gives you an opportunity to see the workings of the Code's delivery terms in a variety of factual settings.

1. Yacht dealer, in Florida, and Buyer, in Louisiana, entered into a contract for the sale of a yacht, F.O.B. Louisiana. Who is responsible for the costs of shipping the yacht to Louisiana?

2. Seller in Los Angeles and Buyer in San Francisco entered into a contract that quoted the cost of goods as "$15,000 C.I.F." Seller duly delivered the goods to an air carrier, who delivered the goods to a second carrier's truck, but the truck containing the goods was hijacked from the airport loading area and the goods were stolen. Who has the risk of loss?

3. What if the contract was F.O.B.?

4. What if the contract was F.O.B. Buyer's warehouse?

5. Seller, in Salinas, entered into a contract with Buyer, in San Diego, for the sale of 370 cartons of lettuce, F.O.B. Salinas. After loading the lettuce on a truck, the Seller learned that because of a local teamsters strike, the lettuce could not be delivered at buyer's place of business. Who bore the risk of any damage or delay in transit?

5. Contract Interpretation

Because we believe that contract law aims at enforcing the voluntary agreements of parties, or carrying out the intent of the parties, the process of contract interpretation is designed to ascertain exactly what the parties intended. However, because we believe that contracts are formed based on mutual expressions (outward manifestations) of the parties' intentions, we ultimately are concerned with finding what the parties objectively appeared to agree to at the time they entered into the contract, rather than what they subjectively were hoping for.

Typically, contract interpretation issues arise when the parties contest the meaning of an express term in the written contract. Such a contest generally arises due to (a) ambiguities on the face of the instrument (sometimes called "patent ambiguities"); or (b) ambiguities that come to light through parol evidence (sometimes called "latent ambiguities"). Generally, if both parties admit that words have a certain meaning, that meaning will control. If, however, the parties disagree as to the meaning of the words, the courts must ultimately determine their meaning. Corbin explains:

> In every case involving interpretation, the parties have used expressions, both words and other acts. The court is not searching for an unexpressed mental state; instead, it is searching for the meanings that each party intended to convey by his [sic] words and acts, and for the meanings that those words and acts conveyed to the other party. The meanings were in fact "expressed" in words and acts, but they may not have been successfully "conveyed." Even when a contract has been

fully "integrated" in the form of written words, those words never have a single, necessary, legally imposed meaning, unaffected by the other words and acts of the parties, whether antecedent or subsequent. Those other acts and words are admissible in evidence, to discover both the meaning that one party intended and the meaning that the other party received. If those meanings, so found, are identical, well and good; if they are substantially different, the court's problem is to determine which one of them, if either, should for reasons of policy be made legally effective.[2]

The Code has not made drastic changes to the general approach to contract interpretation that you learned in your basic Contracts class. Section 1-303 explicitly provides that the express terms of an agreement and any applicable course of performance, course of dealing or usage of trade must be construed wherever reasonable as consistent with each other. If such a construction is unreasonable, the Code establishes a hierarchy of terms, shown in *Figure 7-7*.

Figure 7-7: Hierarchy of Terms

Express Terms
Course of Performance
Course of Dealing
Usage of Trade

Official Comment 2 to section 1-303 states that the U.C.C. "rejects both the 'lay-dictionary' and the "conveyancer's" reading of a commercial agreement. Instead the meaning of the agreement of the parties is to be determined by the language used by them and by their actions, read and interpreted in the light of commercial practices and other surrounding circumstances. The measure and background for interpretation are set by the commercial context, which may explain and supplement even the language of a formal or final writing.

Section 2-202 makes it clear that no finding of ambiguity is necessary before extrinsic evidence can be introduced to assist in the interpretation of a contract.

Exercise 7-8: Frigaliment Importing Co. v. B.N.S. International Sales Corp.

The following gem of a case appears in most contracts and sales casebooks. As you read the case, consider:

1. What express terms are at the core of the lawsuit?

2. How does the court treat evidence of course of performance, course of dealing and usage of trade?

3. Is this case ultimately decided based on contract interpretation rules, or is there another basis for the court's decision?

4. The case was decided before the U.C.C. was in effect in New York. Would the outcome have been different if the Code were applied to these facts?

---

2. Arthur L. Corbin, 1 *Corbin on Contracts* § 548 (1952).

Frigaliment Importing Co. v.
B.N.S. International Sales Corp.
190 F. Supp. 116 (S.D.N.Y. 1960)

FRIENDLY, Judge. The issue is, what is chicken? Plaintiff says 'chicken' means a young chicken, suitable for broiling and frying. Defendant says 'chicken' means any bird of that genus that meets contract specifications on weight and quality, including what it calls 'stewing chicken' and plaintiff pejoratively terms 'fowl'. Dictionaries give both meanings, as well as some others not relevant here. To support its, plaintiff sends a number of volleys over the net; defendant essays to return them and adds a few serves of its own. Assuming that both parties were acting in good faith, the case nicely illustrates Holmes' remark 'that the making of a contract depends not on the agreement of two minds in one intention, but on the agreement of two sets of external signs- not on the parties' having meant the same thing but on their having said the same thing.' The Path of the Law, in Collected Legal Papers, p. 178. I have concluded that plaintiff has not sustained its burden of persuasion that the contract used 'chicken' in the narrower sense.

The action is for breach of the warranty that goods sold shall correspond to the description.... Two contracts are in suit. In the first, dated May 2, 1957, defendant, a New York sales corporation, confirmed the sale to plaintiff, a Swiss corporation, of

'US Fresh Frozen Chicken, Grade A, Government Inspected, Eviscerated 2½–3 lbs. and 1½–2 lbs. each

all chicken individually wrapped in cryovac, packed in secured fiber cartons or wooden boxes, suitable for export

75,000 lbs. 2½–3 lbs.......... @$33.00
25,000 lbs. 1½–2 lbs.......... @$36.50
per 100 lbs. FAS New York

scheduled May 10,1957 pursuant to instructions from Penson & Co., New York' (footnote omitted).

The second contract, also dated May 2, 1957, was identical save that only 50,000 lbs. of the heavier 'chicken' were called for, the price of the smaller birds was $37 per 100 lbs., and shipment was scheduled for May 30. The initial shipment under the first contract was short but the balance was shipped on May 17. When the initial shipment arrived in Switzerland, plaintiff found, on May 28, that the 2½–3 lbs. birds were not young chicken suitable for broiling and frying but stewing chicken or 'fowl'; indeed, many of the cartons and bags plainly so indicated. Protests ensued. Nevertheless, shipment under the second contract was made on May 29, the 2½–3 lbs. birds again being stewing chicken. Defendant stopped the transportation of these at Rotterdam.

This action followed....

Since the word 'chicken' standing alone is ambiguous, I turn first to see whether the contract itself offers any aid to its interpretation. Plaintiff says the 1½–2 lbs. birds necessarily had to be young chicken since the older birds do not come in that size, hence the 2½–3 lbs. birds must likewise be young. This is unpersuasive- a contract for 'apples' of two different sizes could be filled with different kinds of apples even though only one species came in both sizes. Defendant notes that the contract called not simply for chicken but for 'US Fresh Frozen Chicken, Grade A, Government Inspected.' It says the contract thereby incorporated by reference the Department of Agriculture's regulations, which favor its interpretation; I shall return to this after reviewing plaintiff's other contentions.

The first hinges on an exchange of cablegrams which preceded execution of the formal contracts. The negotiations leading up to the contracts were conducted in New York between defendant's secretary, Ernest R. Bauer, and a Mr. Stovicek, who was in New York for the Czechoslovak government at the World Trade Fair. A few days after meeting Bauer at the fair, Stovicek telephoned and inquired whether defendant would be interested in exporting poultry to Switzerland. Bauer then met with Stovicek, who showed him a cable from plaintiff dated April 26, 1957, announcing that they 'are buyer' of 25,000 lbs. of chicken 2½–3 lbs. weight, Cryovac packed, grade A Government inspected, at a price up to 33¢ per pound, for shipment on May 10, to be confirmed by the following morning, and were interested in further offerings. After testing the market for price, Bauer accepted, and Stovicek sent a confirmation that evening. Plaintiff stresses that, although these and subsequent cables between plaintiff and defendant, which laid the basis for the additional quantities under the first and for all of the second contract, were predominantly in German, they used the English word 'chicken'; it claims this was done because it understood 'chicken' meant young chicken whereas the German word, 'Huhn,' included both 'Brathuhn' (broilers) and 'Suppenhuhn' (stewing chicken), and that defendant, whose officers were thoroughly conversant with German, should have realized this. Whatever force this argument might otherwise have is largely drained away by Bauer's testimony that he asked Stovicek what kind of chickens were wanted, received the answer 'any kind of chickens,' and then, in German, asked whether the cable meant 'Huhn' and received an affirmative response. Plaintiff attacks this as contrary to what Bauer testified on his deposition in March, 1959, and also on the ground that Stovicek had no authority to interpret the meaning of the cable. The first contention would be persuasive if sustained by the record, since Bauer was free at the trial from the threat of contradiction by Stovicek as he was not at the time of the deposition; however, review of the deposition does not convince me of the claimed inconsistency. As to the second contention, it may well be that Stovicek lacked authority to commit plaintiff for prices or delivery dates other than those specified in the cable; but plaintiff cannot at the same time rely on its cable to Stovicek as its dictionary to the meaning of the contract and repudiate the interpretation given the dictionary by the man in whose hands it was put.... Plaintiff's reliance on the fact that the contract forms contain the words 'through the intermediary of: ', with the blank not filled, as negating agency, is wholly unpersuasive, the purpose of this clause was to permit filling in the name of an intermediary to whom a commission would be payable, not to blot out what had been the fact.

Plaintiff's next contention is that there was a definite trade usage that 'chicken' meant 'young chicken.' Defendant showed that it was only beginning in the poultry trade in 1957, thereby bringing itself within the principle that 'when one of the parties is not a member of the trade or other circle, his acceptance of the standard must be made to appear' by proving either that he had actual knowledge of the usage or that the usage is 'so generally known in the community that his actual individual knowledge of it may be inferred.'... Here there was no proof of actual knowledge of the alleged usage; indeed, it is quite plain that defendant's belief was to the contrary. In order to meet the alternative requirement, the law of New York demands a showing that 'the usage is of so long continuance, so well established, so notorious, so universal and so reasonable in itself, as that the presumption is violent that the parties contracted with reference to it, and made it a part of their agreement.' Walls v. Bailey, 1872, 49 N.Y. 464, 472–473.

Plaintiff endeavored to establish such a usage by the testimony of three witnesses and certain other evidence. Strasser, resident buyer in New York for a large chain of Swiss co-operatives, testified that 'on chicken I would definitely understand a broiler.' However, the force of this testimony was considerably weakened by the fact that in his own transactions the witness, a careful businessman, protected himself by using 'broiler' when that was what he wanted and 'fowl' when he wished older birds. Indeed, there are some indications, dating back to a remark of Lord Mansfield, Edie v. East India Co., 2 Burr. 1216, 1222 (1761), that no credit should be given 'witnesses to usage, who could not adduce instances in verification.' 7 Wigmore, Evidence (3d ed. 1940), § 1954; see McDonald v. Acker, Merrall & Condit Co., 2d Dept.1920, 192 App.Div. 123, 126, 182 N.Y.S. 607. While Wigmore thinks this goes too far, a witness' consistent failure to rely on the alleged usage deprives his opinion testimony of much of its effect. Niesielowski, an officer of one of the companies that had furnished the stewing chicken to defendant, testified that 'chicken' meant 'the male species of the poultry industry. That could be a broiler, a fryer or a roaster', but not a stewing chicken; however, he also testified that upon receiving defendant's inquiry for 'chickens', he asked whether the desire was for 'fowl or frying chickens' and, in fact, supplied fowl, although taking the precaution of asking defendant, a day or two after plaintiff's acceptance of the contracts in suit, to change its confirmation of its order from 'chickens,' as defendant had originally prepared it, to 'stewing chickens.' Dates, an employee of Urner-Barry Company, which publishes a daily market report on the poultry trade, gave it as his view that the trade meaning of 'chicken' was 'broilers and fryers.' In addition to this opinion testimony, plaintiff relied on the fact that the Urner-Barry service, the Journal of Commerce, and Weinberg Bros. & Co. of Chicago, a large supplier of poultry, published quotations in a manner which, in one way or another, distinguish between 'chicken,' comprising broilers, fryers and certain other categories, and 'fowl,' which, Bauer acknowledged, included stewing chickens. This material would be impressive if there were nothing to the contrary. However, there was, as will now be seen.

Defendant's witness Weininger, who operates a chicken eviscerating plant in New Jersey, testified 'Chicken is everything except a goose, a duck, and a turkey. Everything is a chicken, but then you have to say, you have to specify which category you want or that you are talking about.' Its witness Fox said that in the trade 'chicken' would encompass all the various classifications. Sadina, who conducts a food inspection service, testified that he would consider any bird coming within the classes of 'chicken' in the Department of Agriculture's regulations to be a chicken. The specifications approved by the General Services Administration include fowl as well as broilers and fryers under the classification 'chickens.' Statistics of the Institute of American Poultry Industries use the phrases 'Young chickens' and 'Mature chickens,' under the general heading 'Total chickens.' and the Department of Agriculture's daily and weekly price reports avoid use of the word 'chicken' without specification.

Defendant advances several other points which it claims affirmatively support its construction. Primary among these is the regulation of the Department of Agriculture, 7 C.F.R. § 70.300–70.370, entitled, 'Grading and Inspection of Poultry and Edible Products Thereof.' and in particular 70.301 which recited:

Chickens. The following are the various classes of chickens:
(a) Broiler or fryer ...
(b) Roaster ...
(c) Capon ...
(d) Stag ...
(e) Hen or stewing chicken or fowl..
(f) Cock or old rooster.

Defendant argues, as previously noted, that the contract incorporated these regulations by reference. Plaintiff answers that the contract provision related simply to grade and Government inspection and did not incorporate the Government definition of 'chicken,' and also that the definition in the Regulations is ignored in the trade. However, the latter contention was contradicted by Weininger and Sadina; and there is force in defendant's argument that the contract made the regulations a dictionary, particularly since the reference to Government grading was already in plaintiff's initial cable to Stovicek.

Defendant makes a further argument based on the impossibility of its obtaining broilers and fryers at the 33¢ price offered by plaintiff for the 2½–3 lbs. birds. There is no substantial dispute that, in late April, 1957, the price for 2½–3 lbs. broilers was between 35 and 37¢ per pound, and that when defendant entered into the contracts, it was well aware of this and intended to fill them by supplying fowl in these weights. It claims that plaintiff must likewise have known the market since plaintiff had reserved shipping space on April 23, three days before plaintiff's cable to Stovicek, or, at least, that Stovicek was chargeable with such knowledge. It is scarcely an answer to say, as plaintiff does in its brief, that the 33¢ price offered by the 2½–3 lbs. 'chickens' was closer to the prevailing 35¢ price for broilers than to the 30¢ at which defendant procured fowl. Plaintiff must have expected defendant to make some profit — certainly it could not have expected defendant deliberately to incur a loss.

Finally, defendant relies on conduct by the plaintiff after the first shipment had been received. On May 28 plaintiff sent two cables complaining that the larger birds in the first shipment constituted 'fowl.' Defendant answered with a cable refusing to recognize plaintiff's objection and announcing 'We have today ready for shipment 50,000 lbs. chicken 2½–3 lbs. 25,000 lbs. broilers 1½–2 lbs.,' these being the goods procured for shipment under the second contract, and asked immediate answer 'whether we are to ship this merchandise to you and whether you will accept the merchandise.' After several other cable exchanges, plaintiff replied on May 29 'Confirm again that merchandise is to be shipped since resold by us if not enough pursuant to contract chickens are shipped the missing quantity is to be shipped within ten days stop we resold to our customers pursuant to your contract chickens grade A you have to deliver us said merchandise we again state that we shall make you fully responsible for all resulting costs.' [These cables were in German; 'chicken', 'broilers' and, on some occasions, 'fowl,' were in English.] Defendant argues that if plaintiff was sincere in thinking it was entitled to young chickens, plaintiff would not have allowed the shipment under the second contract to go forward, since the distinction between broilers and chickens drawn in defendant's cablegram must have made it clear that the larger birds would not be broilers. However, plaintiff answers that the cables show plaintiff was insisting on delivery of young chickens and that defendant shipped old ones at its peril. Defendant's point would be highly relevant on another disputed issue- whether if liability were established, the measure of damages should be the difference in market value of broilers and stewing chicken in New York or the larger difference in Europe, but I cannot give it weight on the issue of interpretation. Defendant points out also that plaintiff proceeded to deliver some of the larger birds in Europe, describing them as 'poulets'; defendant argues that it was only when plaintiff's customers complained about this that plaintiff developed the idea that 'chicken' meant 'young chicken.' There is little force in this in view of plaintiff's immediate and consistent protests.

When all the evidence is reviewed, it is clear that defendant believed it could comply with the contracts by delivering stewing chicken in the 2½–3 lbs. size. Defendant's subjective intent would not be significant if this did not coincide with an objective meaning of 'chicken.' Here it did coincide with one of the dictionary meanings, with the definition in the Department of Agriculture Regulations to which the contract made at least oblique reference, with at least some usage in the trade, with the realities of the market, and with what plaintiff's spokesman had said. Plaintiff asserts it to be equally plain that plaintiff's own subjective intent was to obtain broilers and fryers; the only evidence against this is the material as to market prices and this may not have been sufficiently brought home. In any event it is unnecessary to determine that issue. For plaintiff has the burden of showing that 'chicken' was used in the narrower rather than in the broader sense, and this it has not sustained.

This opinion constitutes the Court's findings of fact and conclusions of law. Judgment shall be entered dismissing the complaint with costs.

Additional Resources

Columbia Nitrogen v. Royster, 451 F.2d 3 (4th Cir. 1971).

J.A. Indus. v. All Am. Plastics, Inc., 726 N.E.2d 1066 (Ohio App. 1999).

Margaret N. Kniffin, *Conflicting and Confusing Contract Interpretation and The Parol Evidence Rule: Is the Emperor Wearing Someone Else's Clothes?* 62 Rutgers L. Rev. 75 (2009).*Middletown Concrete Products Inc v. Black Clawson Co.*, 802 F. Supp. 1135 (D. Del. 1992).

Nanakuli Paving & Rock Co v. Shell Oil Co., 664 F.2d 772 (9th Cir. 1981).

Douglas K Newell, *Will Kindness Kill Contract?* 24 Hofstra L. Rev. 455 (1995).

Sierra Diesel Injection Services Inc. v. Burroughs Corp., 626 F. Supp. 426 (D. Nev. 1987).

Gary D. Spivey, Annotation, *Application of parol evidence rule of UCC § 2-202 where fraud or misrepresentation is claimed in sale of goods*, 71 A.L.R.3d 1059 (2008).

Ferdinand S. Tinio, Annotation, *The parol evidence rule and admissibility of extrinsic evidence to establish and clarify ambiguity in written contract*, 40 A.L.R.3d 1384 (2010).

Figure 8-1: Graphic Organizer

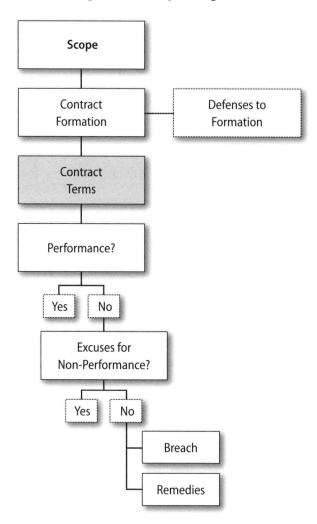

Chapter 8

Contract Terms: Gap Fillers

Chapter Problem

When Starving Student stopped making payments on his car loan, Big Bank foreclosed on the car, pursuant to its rights under U.C.C. Article 9. It then advertised the car for sale as follows:

> GREAT CAR! ONLY DRIVEN TO AND FROM CAMPUS BY STARVING STUDENT WHO COULDN'T AFFORD MUCH GAS! MINT CONDITION! $1000 BELOW LOW BLUE BOOK. FIRST COME DRIVES IT AWAY!

Betty Buyer saw the ad and went to Big Bank to see the car. She spoke with Oliver Bank Officer about the car. She explained that she needed a very reliable car that would get good gas mileage and asked whether the car met those criteria. He explained to her that Big Bank had foreclosed on the car pursuant to its rights under U.C.C. Article 9 and that he personally had no idea as to how, where, and how much Starving Student had driven the car. "Listen," he said, "We just took the car back when that flake didn't pay for it! How do you expect us to know those kinds of things??? Do you want it or not?" Betty, who had never owned a car, looked under the hood and kicked the tires. She then agreed to buy it at Big Bank's full asking price.

Oliver handed Betty the following Bill of Sale:

BILL OF SALE

SOLD TO Betty Buyer one 1987 Mint Condition Mustang, Vehicle ID # 2345500XYZ. NO WARRANTIES.

Answer the following question ONLY: WHAT ARE THE TERMS OF THE CONTRACT? (Be sure to include your ANALYSIS, explaining HOW you determined the contract terms.)

1. Introduction

The Code has a very liberal approach to contract formation; if the parties manifest an intent to be bound, and expressly agree upon a quantity of goods, the Code supplies the rest of the contract terms. (For example, price, section 2-305 and delivery, section 2-307.) Quickly read through the table of contents to Part 3 of Article 2 to see all of the topics that are covered by the gap fillers. (Note that sections 2-312 through 2-318, which govern warranties and warranty disclaimers, were discussed in Chapter 6.) *Remember that gap fillers can be used only if you first establish that the parties actually intended to be bound to a contract.* The fewer express terms the parties agree to, the more likely it is that a court will find that the parties did *not* intend to be bound.

I have included in this chapter some Code provisions outside of Part 3 that others may not commonly include in a list of "gap fillers." Specifically, I include all Code provisions not discussed elsewhere in this book that help define the rights and obligation of the parties in the absence of express contract terms, or course of performance, course of dealing or usage of trade. *Figure 8-2* shows how the gap fillers supplement the parties' express terms to constitute the parties' total legal obligation. *Figure 8-3* sets forth the code sections and definitions that we will study in this chapter.

Figure 8-2: Contract Terms, Including Warranties, Other Express Terms, and Gap Fillers

Figure 8-3: Gap Fillers Sections and Definitions

Section	Definitions
1-303	Course of Performance Course of Dealing Usage of Trade
2-303	"Unless otherwise agreed"
2-304	
2-305	Open price term
2-306	Output Contract Requirements Contract Exclusive Dealings
2-307	Single Lot Delivery Contract
2-308	Documents of Title
2-309	Termination of a contract
2-310	Shipment under reservation
2-311	
2-326	
2-327	Consignment
2-328	
2-501	Identification
2-509	Risk of Loss Bailee
2-510	

2. Course of Performance, Course of Dealing, Usage of Trade

Once a court is convinced that the parties did intend to be bound, and has identified and interpreted express contract terms, the court will turn to the Code gap fillers.[1] Unless expressly negated by the parties, course of performance, course of dealing, and usage of trade are all considered to be part of the parties' contract whether or not expressly stated in the contract documents.[2] Because these concepts are so important, we discussed them earlier in Chapter 1.

---

1. Note that the process of identifying express contract terms includes the application of the parol evidence rule previously discussed in Chapter 7. Also recall that the parol evidence rule allows the admission of evidence of any applicable trade usage or course of dealing between the parties to explain or supplement even a fully integrated writing.

2. Some trade associations make their statements of "trade usage" available to the public. *See, e.g.,* printing trade "best practices," at http://www.piasd.org/tradecustoms.html (last visited June 27, 2010); *see also* http://www.multiad.com/print/Virtual_Center_PDFs/White_Paper_PDFs/PRINTING%20CUS-TOMS-rev.6-25.pdf.

3. Price

New students are often surprised to learn that parties can conclude an enforceable contract under Article 2 without an express agreement on a price term. Contrary to the common law rule that would usually lead to a conclusion that the agreement lacked the necessary specificity to enforce, sections 2-204 and 2-305 specifically contemplate that parties can agree to be bound, without agreeing on a specific price term. In such event, the default rule is usually that the price is a "reasonable price at the time for delivery."[3] Another contrast to common law contracts is that the parties may conclude an enforceable contract that leaves the price to be fixed by the seller or the buyer.[4] A possible attack on such a promise as illusory is saved by the Code provision that requires the responsible party to fix the price in good faith.

4. Details of Delivery

Sections 2-307 through 2-310 provide default rules for parties who fail to specify certain details regarding delivery, such as the time for shipment or delivery, when payment is due, whether delivery is to be in single lots or several lots, and the delivery place.

5. Options and Cooperation Regarding Performance

As indicated by its title, section 2-311 states the default rules respecting performance for contracts (1) that leave particulars of performance to be specified by one of the parties or (2) that are silent with respect to which party specifies the assortment of goods or shipping arrangements. It also states the options of the party awaiting performance when the party obligated to state specifications fails to do so in a timely manner.

6. Identification — Insurable Interest

As you first saw in Chapter 3, the concept of identification may be important in determining whether a particular transaction is within the scope of Article 2. It is also important in defining the rights and obligations of the parties. Specifically, the Definitional Cross References that follow section 2-501 indicate that identification is important in

---

3. *Cf.* U.C.C. § 2-305(1).
4. *Cf.* U.C.C. § 2-305(2).

connection with a buyer's right to reclamation under section 2-502, risk of loss under sections 2-509 and 2-510, ascertaining a seller's remedy for breach of contract under 2-703, applying the gap filler provision on place of delivery, section 2-308, and the manner of seller's delivery under 2-503. However, the Definitional Cross-References omit several important cross-references: section 2-513 regarding a buyer's right to inspect goods, section 2-613, which we study in Chapter 10 on Excuse, and a buyer's right to replevin under section 2-716.

As you also learned in Chapter 3, the Code does not define identification. Re-read Chapter 3, Section 2.1 now. Although section 2-501 does not define identification, it does attempt to define when identification occurs. Thus, it distinguishes between goods that are "both existing and identified" at the time of the contract, and "future goods," which are not. Note that section 2-501 is a default rule.

Exercise 8-1: Identification

Using the statutory analysis skills you have been developing in this course, deconstruct section 2-501. Be sure to read the Official Comments to help you understand the statute. Use any approach that you wish. When you are done, answer the following questions:

1. How would you define identification? Is Official Comment 2 helpful? Do you agree with David Melinkoff's discussion of identification?

2. When and how does identification occur?

3. What are the consequences of identification?

4. What is the special rule regarding identification of goods in an "identified fungible bulk?"

Exercise 8-2: Applying Section 2-501

In each of the following fact patterns, **assume** that a valid enforceable contract has been formed, and determine when the goods are identified to the contract.

1. Buyer and Seller enter into a contract pursuant to which Seller is to manufacture and deliver to Buyer ten chairs, built pursuant to specifications provided by Buyer.

2. Buyer enters into a contract with Seller, a lumberyard, for the purchase and sale of two doors, which Buyer identifies by stock number based on Seller's catalog.

3. Student orders a book from Amazon.com.

4. Builder goes to Owner's warehouse, where Owner has stored 1,000 identical widgets. Builder and Owner enter into a contract pursuant to which Owner agrees to sell 300 widgets from the warehouse to Builder.

5. Builder goes to Owner's warehouse, where Owner has stored 1,000 identical widgets. Builder and Owner enter into a contract pursuant to which Owner agrees to sell 300 widgets, like the ones in the warehouse, to Builder.

6. Farmer and Buyer enter into a contract for the purchase and sale of Farmer's entire crop of corn, which is already planted in the ground.

7. Farmer and Buyer enter into a contract for the purchase and sale by Farmer to Buyer of 1,000 pounds of corn.

8. Seller owns a purebred Shih-Tzu dog named Lioness, who is very very pregnant. Since Shih-Tzu dogs usually have four-five puppies in a litter, Seller agrees to sell one of Lioness's puppies to Buyer. (You may want to know that canine pregnancies typically last 58 to 68 days.)

9. Now assume that Lioness is not yet pregnant, but Seller plans to try to breed her. She enters into a contract to sell a Shih Tzu puppy to Buyer.

---

7. Risk of Loss — in General

The Code's risk of loss provisions are another significant group of "gap fillers." Contract parties often fail to expressly address the risk that after they enter into a contract, but before the buyer receives the goods, the goods may be lost, damaged, or destroyed *without the fault of either party*.[5] *Before* performance begins, the risk of loss *is always on the seller* and *after* the contract is fully performed, *it is always on the buyer*. The question, then, is exactly when is the risk of loss transferred from seller to buyer?

The answer to this question is critical. If the goods are lost or damaged after the risk passes to the buyer, the buyer must pay the contract price for goods it does not receive.[6] If the goods are lost while the seller still bears the risk, the seller cannot recover the price and, unless the loss excuses performance, the seller also is liable to the buyer for damages for breach of contract if the seller cannot deliver substitute goods.[7]

Based on your understanding of the basic philosophy of Article 2, you should now expect that the parties may expressly agree about when the risk of loss passes.[8] One common way parties do this is by including as express contract terms the various shipment terms defined in sections 2-319 through 2-328, previously discussed in Chapter 7. If the parties do not allocate the risk of loss, two gap filler provisions (sections 2-509 and 2-510) allocate the risk of loss. Section 2-509 applies in the absence of breach and section 2-510 applies when one party is in breach.

---

5. If either party is at fault, risk will be allocated based on fault and not based on the Code's risk of loss provisions. Also, if loss is caused by a supervening event, the Code's impracticability provisions (sections 2-613-2-616) will apply rather than the risk of loss provisions. The risk of loss provisions of the Code do not address claims that either party might have against the other for losses caused by the other party's actual negligence in dealing with the goods nor do they address claims that either or both parties may have against the carrier. Thus, the party bearing the risk may have a claim against the carrier if the loss is caused by its fault. Usually, however, contracts of carriage limit liability of common carriers and first-party insurance is the most common source of indemnification to the injured buyer or seller.

6. U.C.C. § 2-709(1)(a).

7. U.C.C. § 2-711(1).

8. U.C.C. §§ 2-509(4), 2-303.

8. Risk of Loss — No Breach (Section 2-509)

Section 2-509 divides contracts into three categories, based on how the goods are to be delivered to the buyer:

(1) contracts requiring or authorizing the seller to ship the goods to the buyer by a carrier; these contracts are further divided into (a) those that require or authorize shipment but do not make the seller responsible for the actual delivery at the buyer's destination ("shipment contracts") and (b) those that make the seller responsible for the actual delivery at a particular destination ("destination contracts");[9]

(2) contracts for the sale of goods in the possession of a third-party bailee that are to be "delivered" without being moved; and

(3) all other contracts, including those in which the seller delivers the goods by its own vehicles and those in which the buyer takes delivery at the seller's place of business.

Warning: Both destination and shipment contracts may provide the seller with a "ship to" address. The language of section 2-509 (1) is somewhat misleading because it suggests that any term requiring the seller to arrange for shipment to a specified destination creates a destination contract. The important question under section 2-509 is not whether the seller must ship to a named destination but at what stage along the route the event of tender occurs and the risk of loss shifts. Use the presumption of Official Comment 5 to section 2-503 that a shipment contract is intended unless the parties use the specific destination contract terms in sections 2-319 and 2-320 so as to make risk of loss pass at the buyer's destination.

9. Risk of Loss — Breach (Section 2-510)

Section 2-510 contains three subsections. The first two apply to breach by the seller and the third applies to breach by the buyer. Essentially, these subsections state that the risk of loss is on the breaching party *but only to the extent that the non-breaching party's insurance does not cover the loss.* The Official Comments to section 2-510 make it clear that the drafters intended the result to leave the loss on insurance companies, so that the principle of subrogation does not apply.

Exercise 8-3: Applying Sections 2-509 and 2-510

1. B purchased a mobile home from S, a mobile home seller by trade. B paid for the home, but had not yet accepted delivery from S when the vehicle was stolen from S's lot. Who bears the risk of loss?

2. B purchased furniture for her home from S at S's retail store. B paid for the furniture and asked S to hold it for shipment subject to B's further instructions.

---

9. U.C.C. § 2-504 cmt. 1.

Before B gave such instructions to S, the goods were destroyed by a fire while still in S's possession. Who bears the risk of loss?

3. S, an appliance seller, was responsible for delivering goods purchased by B directly to B's home. Unfortunately, S arrived at B's home later than the time called for by the contract for delivery of the goods, and B wasn't home. S left the goods in B's unlocked garage. The goods were subsequently stolen from the garage. Who bears the risk of loss?

4. Buyer and Seller entered into a contract for gold coins to be shipped by Seller to Buyer at Buyer's home address. Seller delivered a package containing the gold coins, properly addressed, to the U.S. post office. The package was delivered, but it was stolen from the mail box before Buyer went to the mail box to take it out. Who bears the risk of loss? Is your answer the same whether or not Seller is a merchant?

5. Buyer and Seller entered into a contract for gold coins to be shipped by Seller to Buyer at Buyer's home address. Seller delivered a package containing the gold coins, properly addressed, to the U.S. post office, but the post office mis-delivered the package and Buyer never received it. Who bears the risk of loss? Is your answer the same whether or not Seller is a merchant?

6. Buyer was purchasing jewelry under a lay-away plan. The purchase contract provided that the jewelry would remain at the store until the purchase price was paid in full. While the jewelry was still at the store, the store was burglarized and the jewelry was stolen. Who bears the risk of loss?

7. Buyer purchased a mobile home from Seller, paid the price in full, and executed a "Agency Rental Agreement" which provided, inter alia, that "at the owner's request" Seller would store the vehicle at Seller's location without charge to owner and rent it to other parties on certain terms and conditions. The mobile home was registered in Buyer's name and Buyer purchased comprehensive insurance covering the mobile home. While the mobile home was sitting on Seller's lot, it caught fire and was destroyed. Who bears the risk of loss?

8. Seller stored his boat and trailer in a "Storage Yard" owned by Third Party. Seller sold the boat and trailer to Buyer, who paid for them and received a bill of sale from Seller. The parties then went together to the Storage Yard where the articles were stored, and informed Third Party that they had been sold and that Buyer would make arrangements to pick them up. When Buyer came to claim the articles the following day, however, they were discovered to be missing. Who bears the risk of loss? Is your answer the same whether or not Seller was a merchant?

9. Seller, in Florida, entered into a contract with Buyer, in New York for the purchase and sale of scrap metal. The contract provided that delivery was to be made "FAS Steamer" at Buyer's berth in New Jersey. Seller delivered the scrap metal to a barge for transport to the berth in question; unfortunately, the barge sank during the afternoon or night preceding the scheduled loading of the metal onto a steamship. Who bears the risk of loss?

10. Seller, in the United Kingdom, contracted to sell goods to Buyer in North Carolina. The contract contained no express delivery terms, nor was there any express provision governing risk of loss. Seller delivered the goods to a ship, which was subsequently lost in the North Atlantic. When news of the

loss reached Seller, it notified Buyer of the shipment and subsequent loss, and demanded payment for the goods. What result?

Additional Resources

R. Barnett, *The Sound of Silence: Default Rules and Contractual Consent*, 78 Va. L. Rev. 997 (1992).

Nellie E. Choi, *Contracts with Open or Missing Terms Under the Uniform Commercial Code and Common Law: A Proposal for Unification*, 103 Colum. L.Rev. 50 (2003).

William H. Danne, Jr., Annotation,*Who bears risk of loss of goods under UCC § 2-509, 2-510*, 66 A.L.R.3d 145 (2009).

Mark P. Gergen, *The Use of Open Terms in Contract*, 92 Colum. L. Rev. 997 (1992).

Robert Gertner, *Filling Gaps in Incomplete Contracts: An Economic Theory of Default Rules*, 99 Yale L.J. 87, 92 (1989).

Charles J. Goetz & Robert E. Scott, *The Limits of Expanded Choice: An Analysis of the Interactions Between Express and Implied Contract Terms*, 73 Cal. L. Rev. 261, 264 (1985).

Lawrence Kalevitch, *Gaps in Contracts: A Critique of Consent Theory*, 54 Mont. L. Rev. 169, 216 (1993).

Figure 9-1: Graphic Organizer

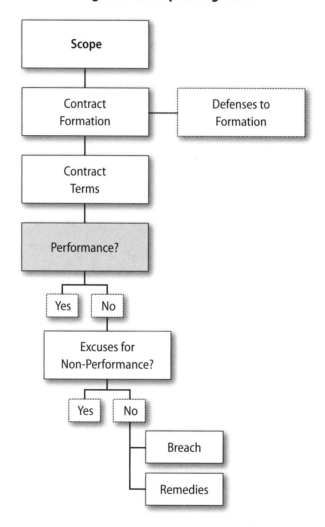

Chapter 9

Contract Performance

Chapter Problem

Patty Player makes her living as an accompanist and piano teacher. In early 2000, after substantial research, she purchased a Model B Primo Grand Piano, whose tone she loved, directly from the manufacturer. When the piano was delivered, she also received Primo's Owner's Manual, which she had not seen previously. The manual contained, among other provisions, the following:

> The Piano for Professionals! Great Tone! Primo wants you to be completely satisfied with your new Primo Grand Piano. Therefore, it will REPAIR or REPLACE your piano if you experience ANY problems during the first SIXTY days of ownership. You agree that this remedy is your SOLE and EXCLUSIVE remedy for any problems you may encounter with your new Primo Piano. Primo expressly DISCLAIMS any warranties including, without limitation, THE IMPLIED WARRANTY OF MERCHANTABILITY.

During the first month after the piano was delivered, Patty noticed deterioration in the action and tonal quality of the piano. She called Primo to request a tuning. Primo's piano technician tuned the instrument and sanded some parts. Within a few hours, the piano seemed out of tune again.

Patty lived with the problems for a while. In the next two months, Primo made three attempts to fix the piano, and concluded the piano "[h]ad some problems." By this point, the piano was deteriorating at "a geometric pace." Keys stuck, the pedals were not working properly, and the instrument developed a "twang." For two more months, Primo attempted to repair these problems, but Primo's efforts were unavailing.

Five months after the piano was delivered, Patty met with Primo's division manager. She was assured that Primo would take care of any problems. Patty left the meeting believing the problems would be resolved. By the next month, however, nothing had happened, and Patty contacted an attorney. Patty's attorney hired several technicians to inspect and report on the piano. They all agreed the piano suffered from major problems involving the key frame, strings, hammers, action and bridge. The piano was deemed to have so many deficiencies that it was "basically unplayable."

Patty's lawyer wrote to Primo, demanding a full refund of the piano's purchase price, in exchange for return of the piano. Primo responded, offering to replace the piano with another Model B Primo Grand Piano. Not surprisingly, given her previous experience with the Model B Primo Grand Piano, Patty did not find this proposal acceptable. Nevertheless, her lawyer advised her to accept Primo's offer, based on the lawyer's analysis of Patty's legal position.

Assume that you have been duly admitted to membership in your State Bar Association. Patty has consulted you for a second opinion. Based only on your

analysis of Patty's legal position under Article 2 of the U.C.C., what do you recommend? Why? (Do not address business considerations in your discussion.) Be
sure to discuss Patty's legal options if she does not accept the offer.

Both the express and implied contract terms control how the parties should conduct
themselves and their actions in relation to the contract. Sometimes the parties fail or
appear to fail to perform in accordance with their contractual obligations. This chapter
discusses the rights and obligations of the parties in the actual performance of the contract,
emphasizing the sections and definitions listed in *Figure 9-2*.

Figure 9-2: Performance Sections and Definitions

Section	Definitions
1-303	Course of Performance Course of Dealing Usage of Trade
2-106	Conforming
2-301	Constructive conditions
2-501	Identification
2-502	Insolvent Repudiation
2-503	Tender of Delivery Bailee Destination Contract
2-504	Shipment Contract
2-507	Seller's Tender
2-508	Seller's Cure Rejection Seasonably Notify
2-509, 2-510	Risk of Loss
2-513	Inspection
2-601	Single Lot Delivery Contract Commercial Unit(s) (see 2-105(b))
2-602, 2-603	Rightful (Wrongful) Rejection
2-604, 2-605	Notice of Defect
2-606	Acceptance
2-607	Effect of Acceptance
2-608	Revocation of Acceptance
2-609	Reasonable grounds for insecurity; adequate assurances of due performance
2-610	Anticipatory Repudiation
2-611	Retraction
2-612	Installment Contract

1. The Obligations of the Parties

Analysis of performance under Article 2 is heavily dependent on a firm understanding of the contract terms. Once you have mastered the approach to identifying contract terms, introduced in Chapters 6-8 you are ready to define the obligations of the parties. You will then be ready to analyze contract performance, by comparing what the parties actually did to what they were obligated to do.

As you learned in the previous chapters, the parties' total legal obligation arises from their agreement, which consists of both express and implied terms, including warranties. The Code also includes specific provisions that, unless otherwise agreed, outline the parties' respective performance obligations. The starting point is section 2-301, which states that the seller's obligation is to transfer and deliver the goods, and the buyer's obligation is to accept and pay for them, in accordance with the contract. The Official Comment to section 2-301 emphasizes that to determine what is in accordance with the contract, usage of trade, course of dealing and performance and the general background of circumstances must be given due consideration in conjunction with the lay meaning of the words used to define the scope of conditions and duties.

Usually, unless the contract provides otherwise, we expect the seller to tender goods before the buyer's obligation to pay arises. However, because section 2-301 basically makes tender and acceptance constructive concurrent conditions, unless the contract expressly provides otherwise, if a seller fails to tender, the buyer must tender performance before the seller will be in breach of contract.

2. Contract Performance

Article 2 takes an ordered approach to performance. "TIARRC," *Figure 9-3,* can help you remember how to approach contract performance analysis. However, the exact order of your analysis will not necessarily follow this list, as you will see in the discussion that follows.

Figure 9-3: "TIARRC"

Tender
Inspection
Acceptance
Rejection
Revocation of Acceptance
Cure

2.1 Tender

The performance analysis begins with the seller's tender of delivery. The Code does not define "tender," but it does prescribe the appropriate steps for a tender of delivery of the goods. Section 2-503(1) states that "[t]ender of delivery requires that the seller put and hold conforming goods at the buyer's disposition...." However, you may be somewhat confused to learn that tender occurs when the seller makes the goods available to the buyer, *even if the goods are non-conforming.*[1] Perhaps the best way to understand the meaning of "tender" is to view it as the seller's outward manifestation of willingness to deliver the goods to the buyer. When a sale takes place face-to-face, tender is accomplished when the seller makes the goods available to the buyer to take them away.[2] When the goods are to be shipped, depending on the nature of the contract, tender occurs either when the seller delivers the goods to the carrier or when the carrier delivers the goods to the buyer.[3]

Unless there is a contrary specific provision in a contract, the Code's default provisions require the seller to "transfer and deliver" the goods to the buyer in accordance with the contract.[4] Regardless of anything else the contract requires, at a minimum this means that the seller must tender conforming goods. "Conforming" is a term of art, defined in section 2-106(2): "Goods ... are 'conforming' or conform to the contract when they are in accordance with the obligations under the contract." The Seller's tender is a constructive condition to the Buyer's obligation to pay for the goods.[5] If the seller never tenders, the buyer's performance obligation does not arise.[6] If the seller tenders in accordance with the contract, the buyer's obligations to pay become due in accordance with the contract terms. If the Seller's tender conforms to the contract, the Buyer is obligated to accept and pay for the goods.[7] If the Seller's tender fails to conform to the contract, the performance analysis depends on whether the contract is an installment contract or a single lot delivery contract.

In any event, unless the contract provides otherwise, before payment, the buyer has a right to determine if the goods conform to the contract. Hence, the next step in contract performance analysis is "inspection."

2.2 Inspection

Section 2-513 describes the buyer's right to inspect goods. Inspection gives the buyer the opportunity to determine whether goods are conforming, which will determine whether the buyer is obligated to accept and pay for the goods. Whether a buyer inspects within a reasonable time is a question of fact, whose resolution may determine whether a buyer has lost the right to reject nonconforming goods.

2.3 Acceptance

Previously in this course, we discussed "acceptance" in the context of contract formation. The Code now uses the word "acceptance" again, but this time in the context of contract

---

1. Tender of non-conforming goods will give the buyer certain rights; however, it is still considered to constitute "tender." *See Ontario Hydro v. Zallea Systems Inc.*, 569 F. Supp. 1261.1267 (D. Del. 1983) (rejecting argument that there was never a proper tender of goods, so the statute of limitations never expired.)

2. U.C.C.§ 2-503(1)

3. U.C.C.§§ 2-503(2), 2-504

4. U.C.C. § 2-301.

5. U.C.C. § 2-301.

6. However, absent contrary contract provisions, because of the constructive concurrent conditions described in section 2-301, the buyer must prove tender of payment before the seller is in default.

7. U.C.C. §§ 2-301, 2-507.

performance. *Be sure that you do not get confused by the two uses of the same word.* Acceptance of an offer results in a contract. Acceptance in this chapter refers to acceptance of goods after the seller's tender of delivery, and has different legal effects.

Under section 2-606, acceptance can occur in three different ways. You can think of the first way as "active" acceptance, which occurs when the buyer, after a reasonable opportunity to inspect the goods, *signifies* to the seller that the goods are conforming or that he will take or retain them in spite of their non-conformity.[8] The second way is where the buyer fails to make an effective rejection.[9] The third way is when acceptance occurs through acts inconsistent with the seller's ownership.[10] You can think of the last two ways as "passive" acceptance.

Acceptance is a major milestone in contract performance. Its legal effects, which are listed in section 2-607, include:

- The buyer must pay at the contract rate for goods accepted
- The buyer can no longer reject the goods
- The burden is on the buyer to establish any breach with respect to accepted goods.

2.4 Rejection

A buyer's right to reject depends on whether the contract is an installment contract or a contract that calls for delivery in a single lot (a "single lot delivery contract").

2.4.1 Rejection in an Installment Contract

Section 2-612 defines installment contracts and sets forth the rules governing performance of installment contracts. Section 2-612(1) defines an "installment contract" as one that requires or authorizes the delivery of goods in separate lots to be separately accepted. Section 2-612(2) states the rule for rejection in such contracts: "The buyer may reject any installment which is non-conforming if the non-conformity substantially impairs the value of that installment and cannot be cured...." However, if the non-conformity does not fall within subsection (3) and the seller gives adequate assurance of its cure the buyer must accept that installment. *Figure 9-4* shows the steps that are followed to analyze contract performance of an installment contract when the seller's tender is non-conforming.

If you work through the language of section 2-612(2), you will quickly see that the section makes it extremely difficult for a buyer to reject an installment of non-conforming goods. Rejection is permitted only if the non-conformity "substantially impairs the value of that installment" *and* the non-conformity is *not curable*. That standard is rarely met. Although the Code does not define "substantial impairment of value," U.C.C. scholars suggest that the concept is analogous to "substantial performance" under the Restatement (Second) of Contracts.[11] Section 241 of the Restatement provides a test, balancing the following factors:

- The extent to which the injured party will be deprived of the benefit which he reasonably expected

---

8. U.C.C. § 2-606(1)(a).
9. U.C.C. § 2-606(1)(b).
10. U.C.C. § 2-606(1)(c).
11. Restatement, Second, Contracts, copyright 1981 by The American Law Institute, Reprinted with permission, All rights reserved

Figure 9-4: Performance of Installment Contract When Seller's Tender Is Non-Conforming

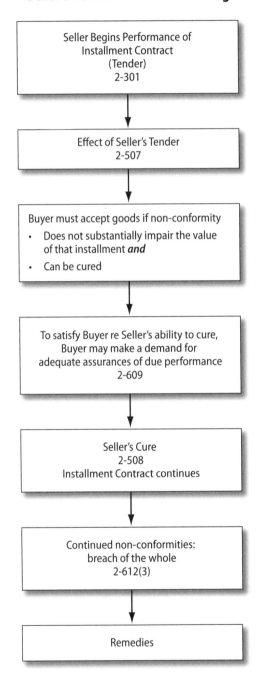

- The extent to which the injured party can be compensated for the part of that benefit of which he will be deprived
- The extent to which the party failing to perform or to offer to perform will suffer forfeiture
- The likelihood that the party failing to perform or to offer to perform will cure his failure, taking account of all the circumstances including any reasonable assurances and
- The extent to which the behavior of the party failing to perform or to offer to perform comports with standards of good faith and fair dealing.

The criteria for declaring a breach of the whole installment contract are set forth in section 2-612(3): the aggrieved party must demonstrate that non-conformity or default with respect to one or more installments substantially impairs the value of the whole contract. Official Comment 6 to section 2-612(3) explains that subsection 3 is designed to further the continuance of the contract in the absence of an overt cancellation. Accordingly, an analysis of "breach of the whole" contract under section 2-612(3) often includes a demand for adequate assurances of performance under section 2-609 (discussed in Section 2.7, below).

2.4.2 Rejection in a Single Lot Delivery Contract

Figures 9-5 and 9-6 show the complex analysis of performance of a single lot delivery contract when the seller's tender is non-conforming. As *Figure 9-5* illustrates, after you decide that you are dealing with a non-conforming tender, the next step is to see whether the contract contains a remedy limitation provision.[12] If so, the contract provisions, rather than section 2-601, will govern the buyer's options upon receipt of the non-conforming tender. In other words, if there is a valid remedy limitation provision in the contract, the buyer must seek the exclusive remedy provided in the contract, and cannot reject goods, even if they are non-conforming.

Barring such a contract provision, until a buyer accepts goods, the buyer has the right under section 2-601 to reject non-conforming goods "if the goods fail in any respect to conform to the contract." The buyer may reject the whole, or any commercial unit or units. Under section 2-602, rejection must be within a reasonable time after delivery or tender, and is ineffective unless the buyer seasonably notifies the seller. Section 2-601 is often referred to as "the perfect tender rule." However, the buyer's right to reject is tempered by the seller's right to cure (see discussion in Section 2.6, below).

Exercise 9-1: Kaspersetz v. Clarks Landing Marina, Inc.

The Kaspersetz case gives you an opportunity to see the TIARRC stages of performance in a friendly setting. As you read the case, consider the following questions:

1. How and when did the Seller tender?
2. What type of contract was involved? Was this an installment contract or a single lot delivery contract?

---

12. Remedy limitations are discussed in Chapter 6. *See* U.C.C. §2-719.

**Figure 9-5: Buyer's Response to Non Conforming Tender
When Contract Has Remedy Limitation**

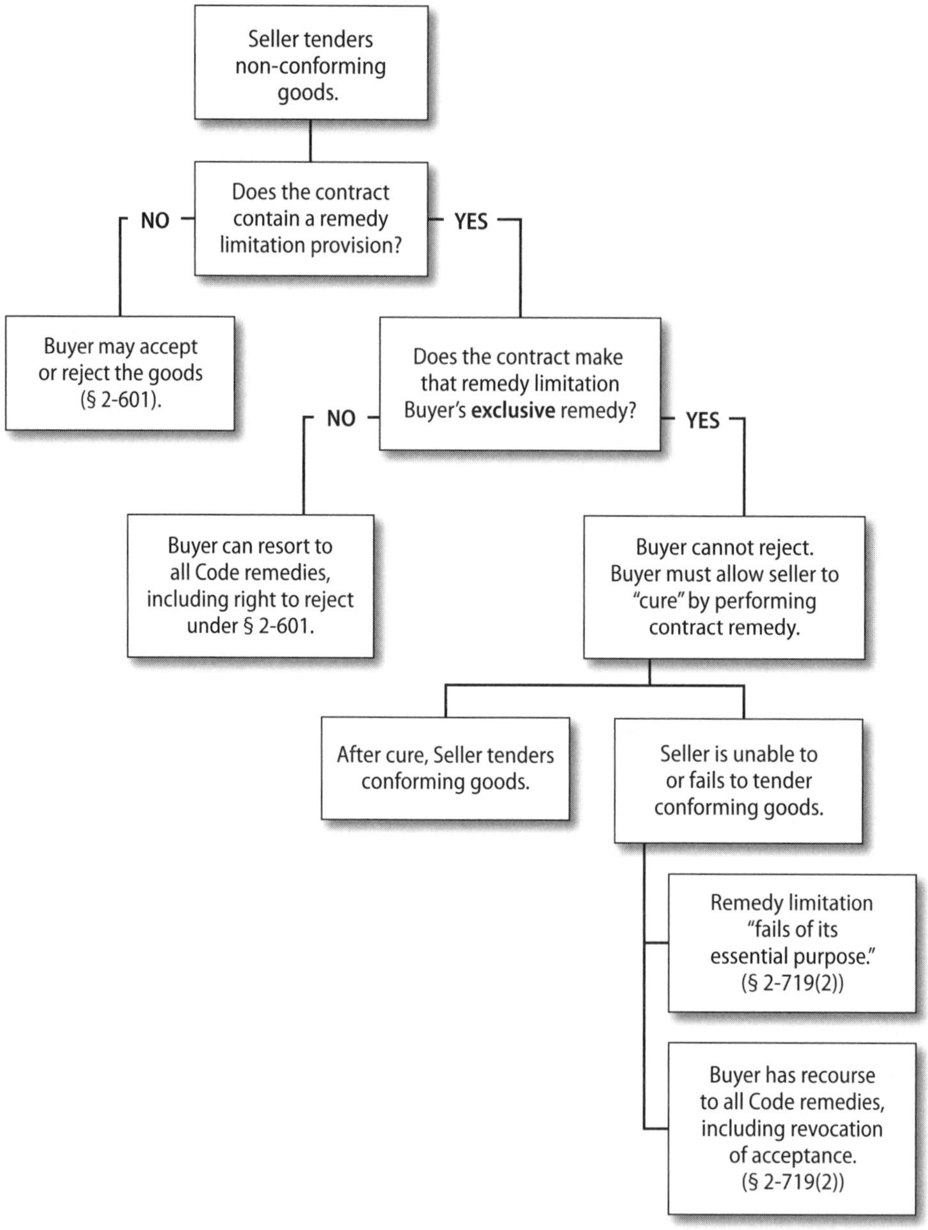

**Figure 9-6: Buyer's Response to Non Conforming Tender
When Contract Does Not Have Remedy Limitation**

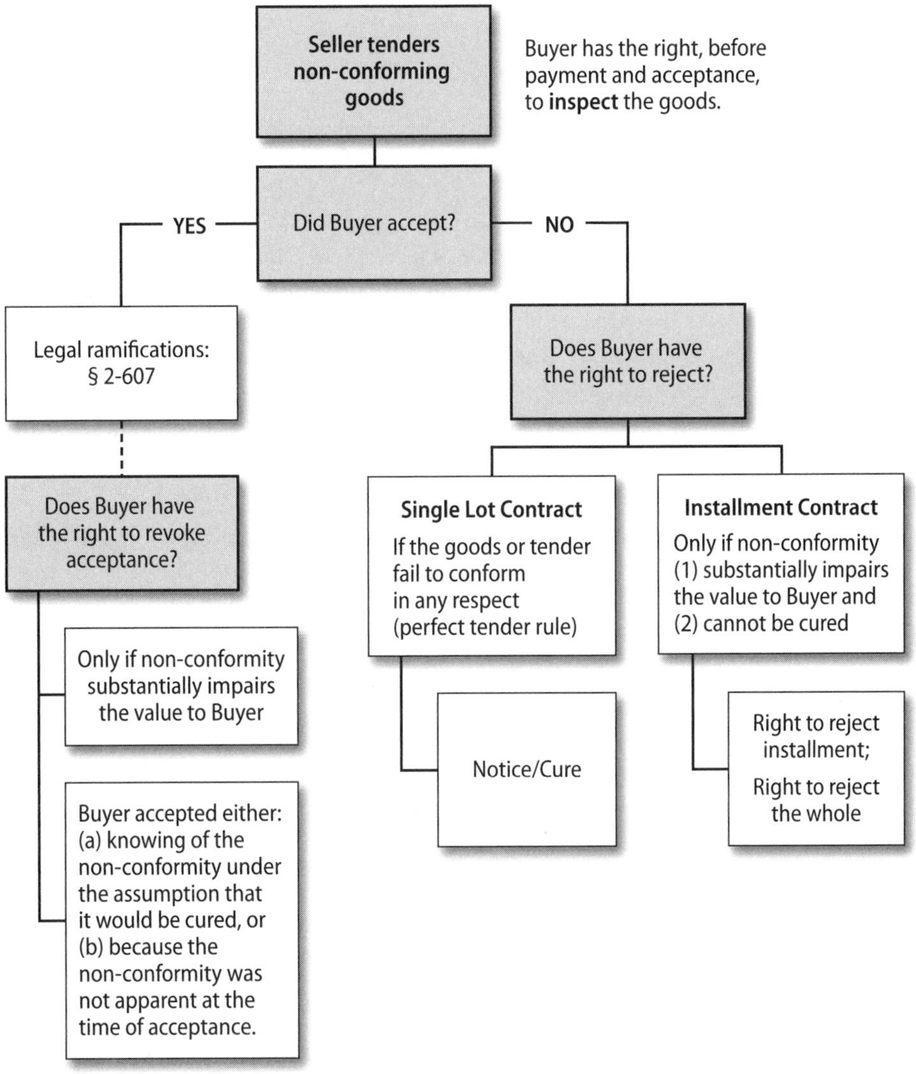

Seller tenders non-conforming goods

Buyer has the right, before payment and acceptance, to **inspect** the goods.

Did Buyer accept?

YES

NO

Legal ramifications:
§ 2-607

Does Buyer have the right to reject?

Does Buyer have the right to revoke acceptance?

Only if non-conformity substantially impairs the value to Buyer

Buyer accepted either:
(a) knowing of the non-conformity under the assumption that it would be cured, or
(b) because the non-conformity was not apparent at the time of acceptance.

Single Lot Contract

If the goods or tender fail to conform in any respect (perfect tender rule)

Notice/Cure

Installment Contract

Only if non-conformity (1) substantially impairs the value to Buyer and (2) cannot be cured

Right to reject installment;

Right to reject the whole

3. How does the Court apply the perfect tender rule? Do you agree or disagree with its application of the rule to these facts?

4. The Court concludes that the buyer could not reject the boat. Why? What rule was the Court applying? Do you agree or disagree with its application of the rule(s) to these facts?

Kaspersetz v. Clarks Landing Marina, Inc.
9 UCC Rep.Serv.2d 276 (N.J. Super. 2009)

PER CURIAM.

Plaintiff Hans J. Kaspersetz filed a seven-count complaint against defendants, including Clarks Landing Marina, Inc., alleging, among other things, breach of contract, breach of warranty, and violation of consumer protection laws. The claims arise from Clarks Landing's sale to plaintiff of a customized thirty-eight-foot Luhrs fishing boat with twin Yanmar motors for a purchase price of $386,500. The Law Division judge granted Clarks Landing's motion for summary judgment. Thereafter, plaintiff filed a motion for reconsideration, which was also denied. This appeal followed. We affirm.

On February 6, 2004, while at the Atlantic City Boat Show, plaintiff signed a conditional sales agreement with Clarks Landing. He paid a $2000 deposit in order to secure a production slot for May 2004 at the Luhrs facility. After plaintiff made custom selections, a revised contract was executed. As Clarks Landing requires on special order boats, he paid a non-refundable deposit of $15,000 by credit card on May 1, 2004.

Plaintiff's special order boat arrived at Clarks Landing on September 2, 2004, after, according to plaintiff, delivery was delayed several times. Luhrs' retail invoice to Clarks Landing was for $319,471.50, including $19,871.50 in custom options. Clarks Landing paid this amount to Luhrs by check dated September 2, 2004.

Prior to leaving the Luhrs factory, a crack had been discovered in the boat's bell housing, which is a large cone-shaped piece between the motor and the transmission. The crack was repaired by Yanmar. Clarks Landing was not informed of the crack or the repair.

Before accepting delivery, plaintiff commissioned a boat survey, which was performed on September 7, 2004. Plaintiff notified Clarks Landing of the forty-one deficiencies discovered in the survey. Clarks Landing agreed to correct the deficiencies, which were mainly cosmetic.

Plaintiff then advised Clarks Landing that he would not accept delivery on the boat until the following year because it arrived so late in the boating season. Clarks Landing refused to hold the boat in their inventory for that length of time and told plaintiff that he would forfeit his $15,000 deposit if he did not accept the boat.

Closing on the boat was conducted on September 24, 2004. Not all of the deficiencies had been corrected, but Clarks Landing assured plaintiff that the list of repairs would be completed. At closing, plaintiff signed a separate document acknowledging that limited warranties were provided solely by the boat manufacturer, not by Clarks Landing, and that Clarks Landing would perform only those repairs authorized by the manufacturer.

The sales contract included a disclaimer by Clarks Landing of any and 'all warranties, expressed or implied, including any implied warranty of merchantability or fitness for a particular purpose.' The disclaimer specified that all warranties were extended solely by the manufacturers.

The limited warranty provided by Luhrs restricted a buyer's remedies to repair or replacement of any part that Luhrs determined to be defective. Yanmar's limited warranty stated that it would 'replace or repair, at its option, without charge for the parts or labor,.... any parts of a Yanmar engine/product covered by this Warranty found to be defective in material or workmanship.'

In late May 2005, plaintiff attempted to drive the boat home from Clarks Landing for the Memorial Day weekend, when he noticed an unusual vibration. On his return, Clarks Landing assured him that nothing was wrong with the boat. Thereafter, when plaintiff drove three miles out into the ocean, he heard a 'loud pop and a rattle' upon acceleration. When he returned to Clarks Landing, smoke was pouring out of the bilge compartment. At the marina, a mechanical failure was discovered in the boat's starboard engine. About two days later, a Yanmar service representative inspected the engine and did a compression check. The following month, the faulty engine was replaced at no cost to plaintiff.

When plaintiff took the boat out in early August 2005, he was unable to turn off the starboard engine. Smoke again poured out of the bilge and from the sides of the cockpit. The engine shut off only after plaintiff disconnected the fuel line with a wrench. This time, when the Yanmar representative inspected the engine, he discovered that it had overheated as a result of a fluid leak caused by a valve that should have been tightened during the earlier repair. The leak was repaired and fluids were replaced.

Consequently, plaintiff notified Clarks Landing that he no longer wanted the boat and listed it for sale at their boatyard. Eventually, Clarks Landing requested that plaintiff remove it from their premises.On September 1, 2005, plaintiff filed the complaint. It included counts for breach of contract, breach of implied warranties, breach of express warranties, violation of the Magnuson-Moss Warranty-Federal Trade Commission Improvement Act (Magnuson-Moss), 15 U.S.C.A. §§ 2301 to 2312, violation of the Consumer Fraud Act (CFA), N.J.S.A. 56:8-1 to -20, rescission, and compensatory damages.

In October 2005, plaintiff drove the boat to another marina for storage. Upon arrival, he noted that the bilge was full of smoke, water and fluid, as the engine had overheated again. Plaintiff dry-stored the boat and abandoned any attempt to sell it, anticipating that no one would buy a boat with a faulty engine.

Plaintiff retained an expert, who issued a report on November 14, 2006. The expert indicated that he participated in two court-ordered sea trials, one on August 25, 2006, and the other on November 1, 2006, along with Yanmar and Luhrs representatives and counsel for all parties.

At the August 25 sea trial, noises were heard emanating from the marine gear area while the starboard engine was idling. Plaintiff informed everyone that he wanted no repairs to be made absent a specific directive from the court.

On October 30, 2006, everyone convened in order to determine the cause for the noise in the marine gear and discovered a small metal object under the engine in a drip pan. The object had apparently fallen out of the flywheel cavity during disassembly. It was not a part of the original assembly and was not intended to be a part of the engine or gear train. It could have been a stray part in the assembly process or could have been introduced at a later date. On November 1, when the starboard engine was started, the boat was run at full throttle for a sustained amount of time without incident.

Plaintiff's expert believed that the two instances of overheating may have caused internal damage in the starboard engine, but the extent of any damage could not be determined in a single test run. Plaintiff did not want the engine to be dismantled for inspection, although this approach was in line with industry standards and there was no other way to assess the potential damage. Plaintiff indicated to his expert that he no longer wanted the boat and was 'disgusted.' The expert acknowledged during deposition that the engines ran well during the sea trials, and that he never noted them failing to operate. Plaintiff's expert had previously opined in a July 1, 2006 report that the nine deficiencies remaining on plaintiff's punch list were 'annoyances rather than structural or serious issues; however, when all added up, it shows a pattern of poor service and response to the vessel buyer.'

On June 8, 2007, Clarks Landing moved for summary judgment. On June 26, 2007, plaintiff filed a cross-motion seeking partial summary judgment regarding the rescission count of the complaint. On July 6, 2007, the Law Division judge entered summary judgment in favor of Clarks Landing as to all counts except for the breach of contract and rescission counts. On July 20, 2007, the judge issued his decision as to those counts, dismissing them as well. Plaintiff's motion for reconsideration was also denied. Plaintiff has amicably resolved his dispute with Luhrs and Yanmar.

BREACH OF CONTRACT AND RESCISSION

Plaintiff contends that pursuant to the Perfect Tender Rule of the Uniform Commercial Code (U.C.C.), N.J.S.A. 12A:2-601, he was 'fully justified in requesting that the closing be delayed until the [forty-one] deficiencies had been corrected.' He also asserts that he would have been equally justified in canceling the contract with Clarks Landing altogether if they did not correct the deficiencies within a reasonable amount of time. We do not agree. The items on plaintiff's punch list were minor and cosmetic in nature, and Clarks Landing never disputed its obligation to repair them. Those items in and of themselves would not have warranted rescission as they cannot be said to have resulted in a nonconformity that would substantially impair the value of the boat to the buyer. [The listed deficiencies included gelcoat cracks, a small tear in the salon headliner, and the lack of interior door catches.]

In addition, the manufacturers' limited warranties restricted the remedies available to plaintiff to the replacement of defective parts. N.J.S.A. 12A:2-719 permits a warranty contract to limit the remedies available to a buyer to repairs as opposed to revocation of the transaction within the scope of N.J.S.A. 12A:2-608.

In reaching his conclusion, the Law Division judge relied upon Palmucci v. Brunswick Corp., 311 N.J.Super. 607 (App.Div.1998). In Palmucci, the plaintiff accepted delivery of a boat that he had previously owned, which had a new engine installed by the defendant. Id. at 611. The engine warranty book limited the defendant's obligation to repair or replacement of any defective parts or, at the defendant's option, refund of the purchase price. Ibid.

The plaintiff argued that N.J.S.A. 12A:2-608 allowed him to revoke his acceptance of the engine because the defect substantially impaired the product's value to him. ... We held that '[a]lthough revocation of acceptance is available to the purchaser of a defective product pursuant to N.J.S.A. 12A:2-608, that right does not accrue where, as here, the product is sold with a limitation of remedy.' Id. at 612. N.J.S.A. 12A:2-608 only affords a consumer relief where the limited remedy fails its essential purpose. Ibid. Because the plaintiff in Palmucci did not allow the manufacturer to extend the remedy as per the terms of the warranty, he was not entitled to recover under his breach of warranty claim....

In this case, the punch list defects were unrelated to the boat's essential purpose. As to the boat engine, which is obviously necessary to the boat's essential purpose, plaintiff refused to allow the engine to be taken apart, even under the supervision of his own expert, which prevented any defendant from making whatever repairs may have been necessary. This plaintiff, like the plaintiff in Palmucci, did not comply with the terms of the warranty. He refused to allow defendants to proceed as provided in the warranty.

The evidence demonstrated that Clarks Landing was willing to comply with its contractual agreements. Plaintiff was not entitled to rescission under N.J.S.A. 12A:2-608 because of the punch list. Therefore, the Law Division judge properly granted summary judgment to Clarks Landing.

Affirmed

Exercise 9-2: Buyer's Right to Inspect Goods

Seller offered an airplane for sale on E-Bay. The E-Bay listing stated that the plane was "a dream to fly" and "ready for anything." Through a series of e-mails, Seller agreed to sell the airplane to Buyer for $30,000, with a $1,000 earnest money deposit. Buyer paid the earnest money deposit through Paypal, and arranged to pick up the plane.

When Buyer arrived to pick up the plane, she asked Seller to see the plane fly. Seller refused, and stated that Buyer first had to pay the full purchase price. Buyer then refused to pay the full purchase price for the plane without being able to see it fly, and left without paying any more money. Buyer lodged a complaint with E-Bay that the plane was misrepresented, and asked for the refund of her deposit.

Did Buyer have a right to reject the plane and cancel the contract? Why or why not?

2.5 Revocation of Acceptance

Revocation of acceptance is a new name introduced by Article 2 to cover a situation where a buyer of goods has accepted the goods, and subsequently wants to "undo" the contract and return the goods to the seller, without liability for breach. Official Comment 1 to section 2-608 explains that the section purposely does not use the term "rescission," because of possible ambiguous or confusing meanings. The standard for revoking acceptance of non-conforming goods is higher than that required for rejection. Whereas a buyer can reject goods in a single lot delivery contract if the goods "fail in any respect" to conform to the contract, a buyer can revoke acceptance only if the non-conformity of the goods substantially impairs the value of the goods to the buyer in two situations: (1) Where the buyer knowingly has accepted non-conforming goods, on the reasonable assumption that the seller would cure the non-conformity, and the seller has failed to do so, and (2) Where the buyer has unknowingly accepted non-conforming goods either because the non-conformity was not readily ascertainable when the goods were first delivered (latent defects) or because of the seller's assurances (often in the form of remedy limitation provisions, such as a promise to repair or replace defective parts). The buyer's right to revoke is further limited because it must occur within a reasonable time after the buyer discovers or should have discovered the ground for it *and* before any substantial change in the condition of the goods, not caused by the defect.[13]

To be effective, a buyer must notify the seller of the revocation. Thereafter, the revoking buyer has "the same rights and duties with regard to the goods involved as if he had rejected them."[14] There is an issue regarding whether that means the seller will have a right to cure after a buyer revokes acceptance. Since a buyer who rejects goods must give the seller an opportunity to cure (see Section 2.6, below), arguably a buyer who revokes acceptance has that same obligation. However, since one of the bases for revoking acceptance is that buyer accepted non-conforming goods based on a reasonable assumption that there would be a cure, and the defect has not been seasonably cured, it seems inefficient to again force a revoking buyer to give a seller yet another opportunity to cure. One possible interpretative solution to this problem is to provide that if a buyer revokes under section 2-608(1)(a) the seller does not have an opportunity to cure, but if the buyer revokes under section 2-608(1)(b), the seller does have such an opportunity.

2.6 Cure

Section 2-508 gives a seller who has made a non-conforming tender an opportunity to replace that tender with a conforming tender in two situations: (1) Where the non-conforming tender is made before the time for performance has expired; and (2) Where the non-conforming tender is made after the time for performance has expired, but the seller had "reasonable grounds to believe" that the non-conforming tender would be acceptable. In the latter case, the seller has a "further reasonable time" to substitute a conforming tender.

Exercise 9-3: Analyzing Performance

John Gable, CEO of Gable Farms Inc., ordered the new X100 tractor from KAT Tractors, Inc. KAT confirmed Gable's order with an invoice sent directly to Gable Farms signed by KAT's CEO, Derek Camp. Gable paid the invoice in full, and KAT promptly sent the X100 to Gable. Within days, Gable put the tractor to use only to discover that the tractor could not drive in a straight line. Gable was so furious that Gable left the tractor in the field and went to the gym. Two weeks and many rains later, Gable sent KAT a letter notifying KAT of the tractor's inability to drive straight and demanding his money back. The next day, KAT called Gable and faxed Gable a signed letter, stating that a field mechanic would be over within days to fix the problem. Gable refused and again demanded his money back.

Advise Gable and KAT on how to proceed.

---

13. Because the standard for rejection in installment contracts is already the higher standard of whether a non-conformity "substantially impairs the value of that installment and cannot be cured," it is unlikely that a buyer will be able to revoke acceptance. *See* U.C.C. § 2-612.

14. U.C.C. § 2-608(3).

Figure 9-7: Performance Code Section Chart

Seller delivers conforming goods to buyer.	Seller delivers non-conforming goods to buyer.	Seller delivers non-conforming goods to buyer.	Seller delivers non-conforming goods to buyer.	Seller ships conforming goods. Goods are damaged in transit.	Seller ships conforming goods. Goods are damaged in transit.
2-301 (obligations of parties) 2-503 (Manner of Seller's Tender) 2-507 (Effect of Seller's tender) 2-513 (Buyer's right to inspect) 2-106 (conforming goods) 2-601 (Buyer's obligations) 2-606 Acceptance 2-607 (Effect of acceptance) 2-703 (Seller's remedies)	Buyer rejects.	The contract is an installment contract.	The contract contains a valid remedy limitation provision under section 2-719.	Seller had the risk of loss.	Buyer had the risk of loss.

Exercise 9-4: Linking Up Performance Code Sections

Create a "flow chart" like *Figure 9-7* that links the code sections you would need to consult, in order, to analyze each of the following scenarios. Identify the applicable Code sections and the order in which each would apply to yield a detailed analysis of the rights and obligations of the parties in each scenario. Unless otherwise indicated, assume that the contract is *not* an installment contract. I have given you an example in the first column.

Exercise 9-5: Analyzing Performance

Betty Bountiful, the owner of an art gallery, entered into a contract for the purchase of nine Lady Googoo sculptures. The Seller assured Betty that although controversial, the Lady Googoo sculptures were pleasing to the eye and brought pleasure to all who viewed them. The contract called for the delivery of one sculpture at a time, over a nine week period.

The first delivery arrived on time, and Betty put it on display. Her customers complained that the statue was so disturbing that they couldn't bear to look at it. The second sculpture arrived on time, and was even more disturbing. Customers complained until Betty had to remove it from the floor. The third sculpture was even more controversial, and Betty was afraid to even put it on show. She now wants to cancel the rest of the deliveries. Please advise her how to proceed.

Exercise 9-6: Analyzing Performance

TI agreed to sell and deliver 49 head of cattle in sound healthy condition to Allday in Texas. When the cattle arrived, Allday determined that 27 conformed to the contract but the others had various minor and major problems. Allday sought to accept the 27 healthy cattle and reject the rest. TI refused to deliver a bill of sale and sued Allday for breach of K.

What result?

Exercise 9-7: Revocation

Buyer purchased a Panoramic copying machine and subsequently revoked its acceptance and sought to return the machine. After mailing notice of revocation, it continued to use the copier and processed a further 60,000 copies post-revocation.

Assume that Buyer can prove that it accepted the machine without discovery of a non-conformity due to the difficulty of discovery, and that the non-conformity substantially impaired its value to him. Can Buyer revoke its acceptance and return the copier?

Exercise 9-8: Rejection

On discovery of defects, the Buyer, as it had done in the past, set the goods aside for inspection and adjustment by the Seller's salesman. When the salesman refused to make the requested adjustments, Buyer sought to reject the goods. The contract required that all returns be made within five days after receipt. The Buyer's rejection was attempted three months after receipt. The Seller argued that the Buyer had accepted the goods by failing effectively to reject within the stipulated time. The Buyer argued that a course of dealing between the parties justified his reliance on a method of doing business that had developed between the parties.

What result?

Additional Resources

Annotation, *Acceptance of some "commercial units" of goods purchased under UCC § 2-601(c)*, 41 A.L.R.4th 396 (2009).

William H. Danne, Annotation, *Use of goods by buyer as constituting acceptance under UCC § 2-606(1)(c)*, 67 A.L.R.3d 363 (2009).

Theresa Ludwig Kruk Annotation, *Time, place and manner of buyer's inspection of goods under UCC § 2-513*, 36 A.L.R.4th 726 (2009).

Andrea G. Nadel, Annotation, *Seller's cure of improper tender or delivery under UCC § 2-508*, 36 A.L.R.4th 544 (2009).

Lee R. Russ, Annotation, *What constitutes "substantial impairment" entitling buyer to revoke his acceptance of goods under UCC § 2-608(1)*, 38 A.L.R.5th 191 (2009).

Gary D. Spivey, Annotation, *Time for revocation of acceptance of goods under UCC § 2-608(2)*, 65 A.L.R.3d 354 (2009).

Figure 10-1: Graphic Organizer

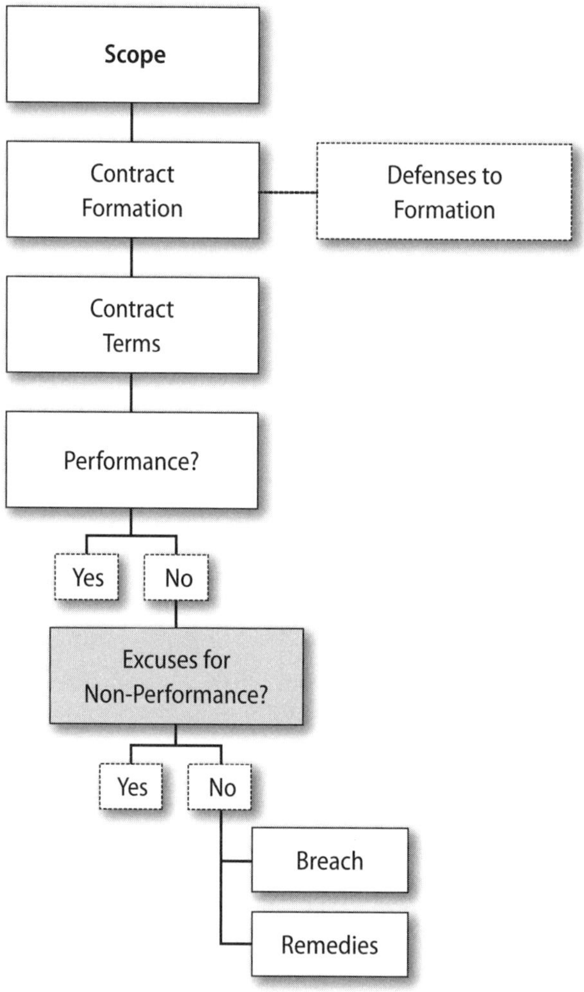

```
┌─────────────────────────┐
│          Scope          │
└─────────────────────────┘
              │
┌─────────────────────────┐        ┌─────────────────────────┐
│        Contract         │┄┄┄┄┄┄┄┄│      Defenses to         │
│        Formation        │        │      Formation           │
└─────────────────────────┘        └─────────────────────────┘
              │
┌─────────────────────────┐
│        Contract         │
│         Terms           │
└─────────────────────────┘
              │
┌─────────────────────────┐
│       Performance?      │
└─────────────────────────┘
           ┌──┴──┐
        ┌─────┐┌─────┐
        │ Yes ││ No  │
        └─────┘└─────┘
              │
┌─────────────────────────┐
│       Excuses for       │
│    Non-Performance?     │
└─────────────────────────┘
           ┌──┴──┐
        ┌─────┐┌─────┐
        │ Yes ││ No  │
        └─────┘└─────┘
                 │
              ┌─────────────────┐
              │     Breach      │
              └─────────────────┘
                 │
              ┌─────────────────┐
              │    Remedies     │
              └─────────────────┘
```

Chapter 10

Excuses for Non-Performance

Chapter Problem

You are the clerk for the Judge in the U.S. District Court for the Eastern District of New York. The Judge has asked you to review the file of Buyer v. Seller for breach of contract.

The facts are stipulated: Buyer is a New Jersey corporation that sells military supplies internationally. Seller is a New York Corporation that sells camping equipment and military supplies. Buyer had a contract to supply the Government of Ghana with 10,000 pairs of combat boots. Under the terms of the contract, delivery was to be "immediate" or "as soon as possible." Buyer and Seller entered into a fully enforceable contract pursuant to which Seller agreed to manufacture the boots in Korea and to deliver them to Buyer in New Jersey. The shipment was "F.O.B. New Jersey."

The boots were manufactured in Korea, placed in containers and then shipped by boat from Korea to the United States. They were loaded on railroad cars for shipment to the East Coast. Unfortunately, the train transporting the boots derailed and the boots were destroyed in the area of Omaha, Nebraska. Seller offered to re-order the 10,000 pairs of boots from Korea and to have them delivered within 60 days, but it was too late. As a result of Seller's failure to deliver the boots on time, Buyer suffered $44,685 in damages when the Government of Ghana cancelled its resale contract.

Seller's core defense is that the train derailment excused its performance under the contract. It invokes two provisions of the U.C.C. to support this contention, section 2-613 or, in the alternative, section 2-615.

Please write a memo to the Judge, suggesting the appropriate ruling.

The sections and definitions that apply to this chapter are shown in *Figure 10-2*.

Figure 10-2: Excuses: Sections and Definitions

Section	Definitions
2-613	When the contract "requires for its performance goods identified when the contract is made"
2-614	Commercially Impracticable
2-615	"Basic assumption on which contract was made"
2-616	Substantial Impairment of the value of the whole contract (Installment Contracts)

When one party simply cannot perform as the contract requires, that party's non performance is sometimes excused, and the other party is limited or prevented from obtaining remedies for breach of contract. This chapter discusses when a party is excused from performing. If there is no valid excuse for non-performance, the party who fails to perform is in breach of contract (See *Figure 10-3*).

Figure 10-3: Effect of Excuse

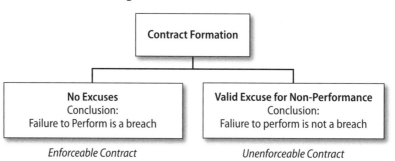

In general, the contract for sale, at least between experienced buyers and sellers, puts on the seller the risk of price rises in the market and on the buyer the risk of price falls in the market. However, such contracts presuppose that the general business climate will continue in a fashion that makes the contract performable by reasonable business effort. In a long-term relationship, unforeseen circumstances can change the value that each party originally expected to extract from the contract relationship. The parties may try to provide for such contingencies in their original contract document. Alternatively, they may try to work together to adjust to the changed circumstances. Finally, if the parties cannot agree, Article 2 "fills the gap." This chapter explores each of those possible reactions to changed circumstances.

1. Contract Provisions: Force Majeure Clauses

Sometimes, at the time of contracting, the parties negotiate for a contract provision that determines their respective rights and obligations when certain events, beyond the control of either party, occur. Such contract provisions are commonly known as force majeure clauses. There is no such thing as a "standard" force majeure clause. However, there are certain natural events that are frequently included, such as earthquakes, floods, fire, and other natural disasters. Some contracts also will reference political acts, such as terrorism, riots, and war. Because a force majeure clause can relieve a party of liability for non-performance, the contract's list of the events that excuse performance is often the subject of intense negotiation. Force majeure clauses vary depending on the type of contract involved and the types of risks that the parties wish to address. If insurance is available to insure against the risk of a particular loss, the parties may agree to omit that event from the force majeure clause and instead rely on insurance to cover the potential loss. *Figure 10-4* contains two sample force majeure clauses.

Figure 10-4: Sample Force Majeure Clauses

Example 1

Upon the occurrence of an event beyond the control of the parties, which prevents a party from complying with the terms of this contract, including but not limited to:
- Acts of God (such as earthquakes, floods, fires and tidal waves)
- Terrorism, riots, war or strikes
- Rebellion or revolution

Consequences of force majeure event:
- Neither party shall be considered in breach of this contract to the extent that performance is prevented by an event of force majeure

Example 2

Neither party shall be liable in damages or have the right to terminate this Agreement for failure to perform the terms of this Agreement when performance is hindered or prevented by strikes, lockouts, riots, war (declared or undeclared), acts of God, insurrection, fire, storm, interference of any governmental authority, or other cause beyond the reasonable control of such party, whether or not similar to the causes herein specified.

---

2. Contract Modifications to Accommodate Unforeseen Circumstances

Even if the contract initially makes no provision for excuse due to unforeseen circumstances, at the time such circumstances actually occur, the parties always can enter into negotiations and agree upon a contract modification to adjust to the changed circumstances. Section 2-209[1] encourages such agreed-upon modifications by providing that no consideration is necessary to make the modifications enforceable, as long as the modifications are made in good faith.[2]

---

1. Discussed in Chapter 5, *supra*.
2. This rule is the opposite of common law, which provides that to be enforceable, any change to an existing contract must have new consideration. *See Schwartzreich v. Bauman-Basch, Inc.*, 231 N.Y. 196, 203 (1921).

3. Code Provisions

Finally, if the contract contains no provisions that would govern the changed circumstances, and the parties are unable or unwilling to voluntarily modify their agreement at that time, three sections of Article 2 "fill the gap" and define the circumstances that partially or wholly relieve a party of contract obligations, without liability, or with only reduced liability to the other party.

3.1 Excuse by Reason of Improper Performance by Other Party

Sometimes performance by one party will be excused because of the other contracting party's improper performance or breach. For example, you have already seen how section 2-601 requires both the tender of delivery and the condition of the goods to be exactly as promised in the contract.[3] If the delivery or goods fail to conform to the contract when the time for performance is due, there is a present breach and the party receiving the delivery or goods may be excused from his or her own performance under the contract.

3.2 Excuse Due to Impossibility

Section 2-613 comes closest to the codification of the common law doctrine of excuse due to impossibility of performance. Law students usually recall the famous Contracts case of *Taylor v. Caldwell*,[4] where a landowner was excused from performing a contract to "let" a music hall because the hall burned down, without the landowner's fault, before the performance was scheduled. In that case, the court reasoned:

> [W]here, from the nature of the contract it appears that the parties must from the beginning have known that it could not be fulfilled unless when the time for the fulfilment [sic] of the contract arrived some particular specified thing continued to exist, so that, when entering into the contract, they must have contemplated such continuing existence as the foundation of what was to be done; ... the contract is ... construed as ... subject to an implied condition that the parties shall be excused in case, before breach, performance becomes impossible from the perishing of the thing without default of the contractor.

This reasoning is reflected in section 2-613, which is titled "Casualty to Identified Goods." A careful reading of that section, however, makes it clear that the scope of section 2-613 is not as broad as that title suggests. Rather, the scope is limited to situations where a contract "requires for its performance goods identified when the contract is made." In such cases, section 2-613 excuses performance if those goods suffer casualty without fault

---

3. Note this is a more stringent standard than the common law rule, applicable to non-sales contracts, which allows for substantial performance.

4. *Taylor v. Caldwell* (1863), 3 B. & S. 826, 122 Eng. Rep. 309.

of either party before the risk of loss passes to the buyer. It follows, as it did in *Taylor v. Caldwell*, that if particular goods are required for the performance of the contract, and those goods are damaged or destroyed, performance should be excused. If the destruction is not total, section 2-613 gives the *buyer* the right to choose between requiring partial performance (with due allowance for the incomplete performance) or treating the contract as avoided *but in any event without further rights against the seller.* In other words, the seller will be excused from full performance.

The only difficulty in applying section 2-613 is the need to determine whether a contract "requires for its performance goods identified when the contract was made." Note the distinction between goods identified when the contract was made and a contract that *requires* particular goods for its performance. For example, if Fancy enters into a contract to buy the Mona Lisa, the subject of that contract—the painting of the Mona Lisa—is identified when the contract is made, because it is both identified and existing.[5] The Mona Lisa is unique—there is no other painting that is the same (copies are not originals.) Hence, not only is the Mona Lisa identified at the time the contract is made, but in this case the contract also *requires* the Mona Lisa for its performance. In contrast, assume that Fancy enters into a contract to buy three GoGO watches from an identified fungible bulk of thirty GoGO watches. Based on our previous discussion of identification[6] the watches would be identified at the time of the contract because they are both existing and identified as part of an identified fungible bulk. However, if 27 of the watches were destroyed before the date set for performance, section 2-613 would not govern the excuse analysis because even though the watches were identified, no particular watches were *required* for the performance of the contract—any of the original 30 would do. That excuse analysis will be performed under section 2-615, discussed in Section 3.4, below.

3.3 Excuse of Substituted Performance Due to Changed Circumstances

Section 2-614 deals with a very narrow set of changed circumstances. It requires substitute performance to be provided and accepted under the limited circumstances outlined in that section (the agreed berthing, loading or unloading facilities fail or an agreed type of carrier becomes unavailable or the agreed manner of delivery otherwise becomes commercially impracticable.) Official Comment 1 to section 2-614 emphasizes the distinction between that section and sections 2-613 and 2-615, both of which deal with excuse and complete avoidance of the contract where the totality of the expected performance is affected, suggesting that this section deals with an "incidental matter."

3.4 Excuse Due to Commercial Impracticability

Section 2-615 introduces the Code concept of "impracticability." Under the specific language of that section, the *seller* may be excused from performance if performance has been made impracticable "by the occurrence of a contingency the non-occurrence of

---

5. *See* U.C.C. § 2-501.
6. *See* discussion in Chapters 3 and 8.

which was a basic assumption on which the contract was made." This section can be broken down into four elements:

1. Performance as agreed has been made impracticable.

The Code does not define "impracticable," but the Official Comments and relevant case law give some guidance. First, Official Comment 4 emphasizes that "increased cost alone does not excuse performance unless the rise in cost is due to some unforeseen contingency *which alters the essential nature of the performance*."[7] Similarly, some courts have referred to performance that is made *vitally different*.[8]

2. Impracticability was caused by the occurrence of a contingency, the non-occurrence of which was a basic assumption on which the contract was made.

Again the Official Comments elaborate on the meaning of this element. Official Comment 1 refers broadly to "unforeseen supervening circumstances not within the contemplation of the parties at the time of contracting." Official Comment 4 cites a severe shortage of raw materials or supplies due to contingencies, such as war, embargo, local crop failure, and unforeseen shutdown of major sources of supply. Official Comment 5 speaks directly to the failure of a particular source of supply.

Courts and commentators have sometimes used a "foreseeability" test to determine if this element has been met. Official Comment 8 specifically states that the exemptions of this section do not apply "when the contingency is sufficiently foreshadowed at the time of the contracting to be included among the business risks which are fairly to be regarded as part of the dickered terms." However, the mere fact that a contingency could have been foreseen at the time of contracting does not lead directly to the conclusion that the parties allocated the risk of its occurrence so that section 2-615 should not apply. The distinction is discussed in some detail by the court in the *Specialty Tires* case, set forth below.

3. The impracticability was not the fault of the party seeking excuse.

The meaning of this requirement is self-evident. The doctrine of excuse has never operated to relieve a party of contract obligations when the party's inability to perform was his own fault.

---

7. *See, e.g., Iowa Electric Light and Power Co. v. Atlas Corp.*, 467 F. Supp. 129 (N.D. Iowa 1978), *rev'd on other grounds*, 603 F.2d 1301(8th Cir. 1979) (noting increases of 50-58% were generally not considered sufficient to constitute impracticability), *and Publicker Ind., Inc. v. Union Carbide Corp.*, 17 U.C.C. Rep. Serv. 989, 992 (E.D. Pa. 1975) (where the court stated it was unaware of any cases where something less than a 100% cost increase was held to render performance impracticable), *but see Aluminum Co. of Am. V. Essex Group, Inc.*, 499 F. Supp. 53, 88-89 (W.D. Pa. 1980) (where the court held seller's performance was impracticable because it stood to lose over $75 million and the buyer stood to gain a windfall profit).

8. *See Eastern Airlines, Inc. v. McDonnell Douglas Corp.*, 532 F.2d 957, 997 (5th Cir. 1976), *and cf. Transatlantic Fin. Corp. v. U.S.*, 363 F.2d 312, 314-320 (D.C. Cir. 1966) (finding performance was not impracticable, when a carrier could no longer use the Suez Canal during an international crisis, because: 1) previous courts held even though the Canal was the customary route, the Cape of Good Hope was also a generally accepted means of performance, 2) there was no indication in the contract or by the parties' actions that the continued availability of the Canal was a condition of performance, 3) the parties should have been aware closure of the Canal was a possibility and could have allocated the risk, 4) the route around the Cape would not damage the goods, 5) the carrier was well-equipped to travel around the Cape, and 6) the added expense of the trip around the Cape alone was insufficient to render performance impracticable).

4. The seller did not assume a greater obligation and cannot substitute performance under 2-614.

Official Comment 8 elaborates on this point. It emphasizes that express agreements as to exemptions designed to enlarge upon or supplant the provisions of this section are to be read in the light of mercantile sense and reason.

Exercise 10-1: Specialty Tires of America, Inc. v. The CIT Group/Equipment Financing, Inc.

In the following case, the district court applied the doctrine of impracticability to a sales contract where the seller was unable to deliver the goods to the buyer because they were in the possession of a bankrupt corporation, who refused the seller access to the goods notwithstanding a bankruptcy court order granting the seller the right to possession. As you read the case, consider the following questions:

1. Was this case appropriate for the application of section 2-613 or section 2-615? Which section did the court apply?

2. According to the court, what role does "foreseeability" play in an impracticability analysis?

3. What does the court say is the legal effect of temporary impracticability?

Specialty Tires of America, Inc., v. The CIT Group/Equipment Financing, Inc.

82 F. Supp. 2d 434 (W.D. Penn. 2000)

D. BROOKS SMITH, District Judge.

In this case, Specialty Tires, Inc. ("Specialty") has sued The CIT Group/ Equipment Financing, Inc. ("CIT") for breach of contract arising out CIT's failure to deliver eleven tire presses that it had previously contracted to sell to Specialty. CIT, in turn, has filed a third-party complaint against Condere Corporation, Titan Tire Corporation and Titan International, Inc. (collectively "Condere") arising out of the latter's alleged wrongful refusal to permit those presses to be removed from its factory. Specialty has moved for partial summary judgment ... arguing that CIT's defenses are without merit, while CIT has moved for full summary judgment on the ground that its performance was excused under the doctrine of impossibility or commercial impracticability. CIT has also moved, in the alternative, to dismiss the stay I previously entered in the third-party action. For the following reasons, I will grant CIT's motion based on impossibility and deny the other two motions as moot.

I.

The material facts of this case are simple and undisputed. In December 1993, CIT, a major equipment leasing company, entered into a sale/leaseback with Condere for eleven tire presses located at Condere's tire plant in Natchez, Mississippi, under which CIT purchased the presses from Condere and leased them back to it for a term of years. CIT retained title to the presses, as well as the right to possession in the event of a default by Condere. In May 1997, Condere ceased making the required lease payments and filed for Chapter 11 bankruptcy in the Southern District of Mississippi. In September 1997, Condere rejected the executory portion of the lease agreement, and the bankruptcy court lifted the automatic stay as to CIT's claim involving the presses.

CIT thus found itself, unexpectedly, with eleven tire presses it needed to sell. Maurice "Maury" Taylor, a former minor candidate for President of the United States and the CEO of Condere and Titan International, stated his desire that the presses be removed quickly and advised CIT on how they might be sold. Later, CIT brought two potential buyers to Condere's Natchez plant, where representatives of Condere conducted them on a tour of the facility. Subsequently, Taylor and CIT negotiated concerning Condere's purchase of the presses, but negotiations fell through, after which Taylor again offered his assistance in locating another buyer.

When no buyer was found, CIT decided to advertise the presses. Specialty, a manufacturer of tires which sought to expand its plant in Tennessee, responded, and in early December 1997, representatives of Specialty, CIT and Condere met to conduct an on-site inspection of the equipment. Condere's representative discussed with CIT's personnel and in the presence of Specialty's agents the logistics concerning the removal of the presses. At that meeting, Condere's representative told CIT and Specialty that CIT had an immediate right to possession of the tire presses, and the right to sell them. At no time did any representative of Condere, whether by words or conduct, express any intent to oppose the removal of this equipment. The negotiations proved fruitful, and, in late December 1997, CIT and Specialty entered into a contract for the sale of the presses for $250,000. CIT warranted its title to and right to sell the presses.

Events then took a turn which led to this lawsuit. When CIT attempted to gain access to the presses to have them rigged and shipped to Specialty, Condere refused to allow this equipment to be removed from the plant ... This unexpected change in position was rejected by CIT, which promptly filed a complaint in replevin in the Southern District of Mississippi to obtain possession.... It became clear at that juncture that Specialty was not going to obtain its tire presses expeditiously.

CIT then advised Specialty that the presses were subject to the jurisdiction of the bankruptcy court and suggested that Specialty either withdraw its claim to the equipment and negotiate with CIT for a sum of liquidated damages or make a bid for the presses at any auction that might be held by that court. Specialty, as was its right, rejected both suggestions and affirmed the existing contract, demanding performance. To date, Condere has refused to surrender to CIT, and CIT has failed to deliver to Specialty, the tire presses.

Subsequent to the briefing of these motions, the replevin court has issued findings of fact and conclusions of law to the effect that Condere wrongfully retained possession of the presses and that CIT is entitled to remove them immediately.... Although Condere may appeal this ruling, CIT has informed Specialty that it is still willing to deliver the presses as soon as it gains possession, and Specialty has indicated its interest in accepting them, in "partial" settlement of its claims....

III.

In the overwhelming majority of circumstances, contractual promises are to be performed, not avoided: *pacta sunt servanda,* or, as the Seventh Circuit loosely translated it, "a deal's a deal." *Waukesha Foundry, Inc. v. Industrial Engineering, Inc.*, 91 F.3d 1002, 1010 (7th Cir.1996) (citation omitted …) This is an eminently sound doctrine, because typically a court cannot improve matters by intervention after the fact. It can only destabilize the institution of contract, increase risk, and make parties worse off.… Parties to contracts are entitled to seek, and retain, personal advantage; striving for that advantage is the source of much economic progress. Contract law does not require parties to be fair, or kind, or reasonable, or to share gains or losses equally. *Industrial Representatives, Inc. v. CP Clare Corp.*, 74 F.3d 128, 131-32 (7th Cir.1996) (Easterbrook, J.). Promisors are free to assume risks, even huge ones, and promisees are entitled to rely on those voluntary assumptions.…

Even so, courts have recognized, in an evolving line of cases from the common law down to the present, that there are limited instances in which unexpectedly and radically changed conditions render the judicial enforcement of certain promises of little or no utility. This has come to be known, for our purposes, as the doctrines of impossibility and impracticability. [The reported cases on this topic, unfortunately, are not characterized by either consistency or clarity of expression. As one respected treatise puts it, "Students who have concluded a first year contracts course in confusion about the doctrine of impossibility and have since … found that the cases somehow slip through their fingers when they try to apply them to new situations[ ] may take some comfort in knowing that they are in good company." 1 White & Summers, *supra* § 3-10, at 164.]

Because of the unexpected nature of such occurrences, litigated cases usually involve, not interpretation of a contractual term, but the judicial filling of a lacuna in the parties agreement. *See* 2 E. Allan Farnsworth, *Farnsworth on Contracts* § 9.5, at 603 (2d ed.1998); 1 James J. White & Robert S. Summers, *Uniform Commercial Code* § 3-10, at 169 (4th ed.1995). Such "gap-filling," however, must be understood for what it is: a court-ordered, as opposed to bargained-for, allocation of risk between the parties. *Albert M. Greenfield & Co. v. Kolea*, 475 Pa. 351, 380 A.2d 758, 760 (1977); John E. Murray, Jr., *Murray on Contracts* § 112, at 635-36 (3d ed.1990). As such, it must be applied sparingly. *Dorn v. Stanhope Steel, Inc.*, 368 Pa.Super. 557, 534 A.2d 798, 812 (1987).

Traditionally, there were three kinds of supervening events that would provide a legally cognizable excuse for failing to perform: death of the promisor (if the performance was personal), illegality of the performance, and destruction of the subject matter; beyond that the doctrine has grown to recognize that relief is most justified if unexpected events inflict a loss on one party and provide a windfall gain for the other or where the excuse would save one party from an unexpected loss while leaving the other party in a position no worse than it would have without the contract.

… [T]he Second Restatement of Contracts expresses the doctrine of impracticability this way: Where, after a contract is made, a party's performance is made impracticable without his fault by the occurrence of an event the non-occurrence of which was a basic assumption on which the contract was made, his duty to render that performance is discharged, unless the language or the circumstances indicate the contrary.

Restatement (Second) of Contracts § 261 (1981). Article 2 of the U.C.C., which applies to the sale of goods presented by the case *sub judice,* puts it similarly:

> Delay in delivery or non-delivery in whole or in part by a seller … is not a breach of his duty under a contract for sale if performance as agreed has been made impracticable by the occurrence of a contingency the non-occurrence of which was a basic assumption on which the contract was made.… U.C.C. § 2-615(1) (codified at 13 Pa.C.S. 2615(1)).

The principal inquiry in an impracticability analysis, then, is whether there was a contingency the non-occurrence of which was a basic assumption underlying the contract. It is often said that this question turns on whether the contingency was "foreseeable," 2 Farnsworth, *supra* § 9.6, at 616, on the rationale that if it was, the promisor could have sought to negotiate explicit contractual protection. *See Waldinger Corp. v. CRS Group Eng'rs, Inc.,* 775 F.2d 781, 786 (7th Cir.1985); *Yoffe v. Keller Indus., Inc.,* 297 Pa.Super. 178, 443 A.2d 358, 362 (1982); *Luria Engineering Co. v. Aetna Cas. & Sur. Co.,* 206 Pa.Super. 333, 213 A.2d 151, 153-54 (1965). This, however, is an incomplete and sometimes misleading test. Anyone can foresee, in some general sense, a whole variety of potential calamities, but that does not mean that he or she will deem them worth bargaining over. *See* Calamari & Perillo, *supra* § 13.18, at 526; Murray, *supra,* § 112, at 641 ("If 'foreseeable' is equated with 'conceivable', nothing is unforeseeable"). The risk may be too remote, the party may not have sufficient bargaining power, or neither party may have any superior ability to avoid the harm. 2 Farnsworth, *supra,* § 9.6, at 617. As my late colleague Judge Teitelbaum recited two decades ago in a famous case of impracticability:

Foreseeability or even recognition of a risk does not necessarily prove its allocation. Parties to a contract are not always able to provide for all the possibilities of which they are aware, sometimes because they cannot agree, often because they are too busy. Moreover, that some abnormal risk was contemplated is probative but does not necessarily establish an allocation of the risk of the contingency which actually occurs. *Aluminum Co. of Am. v. Essex Group, Inc.,* 499 F.Supp. 53, 76 (W.D.Pa.1980) (applying Indiana law) (quoting *Transatlantic Financing Corp. v. United States,* 363 F.2d 312 (D.C.Cir.1966) (Skelly Wright, J.)) (internal ellipses omitted); *accord Opera Co. v. Wolf Trap Found.,* 817 F.2d 1094, 1101 (4th Cir.1987) (also quoting *Transatlantic*). So, while the risk of an un-foreseeable event can safely be deemed not to have been assumed by the promisor, the converse is not necessarily true. *See* Restatement (Second) of Contracts § 261 cmt. c. Properly seen, then, foreseeability, while perhaps the most important factor, is at best one fact to be considered in resolving first how likely the occurrence of the event in question was and, second, whether its occurrence, based on past experience, was of such reasonable likelihood that the obligor should not merely foresee the risk but, because of the degree of its likelihood, the obligor should have guarded against it or provided for non-liability against the risk. *Wolf Trap,* 817 F.2d at 1102-03 (quoted in Farnsworth, *supra* § 9.6, at 617-18). [Another respected text defines the unforeseeable as "an event so unlikely to occur that reasonable parties see no need explicitly to allocate the risk of its occurrence, although the impact it might have would be of such magnitude that the parties would have negotiated over it, had the event been more likely." Calamari & Perillo, *supra,* § 13.18, at 526.]

It is also commonly said that the standard of impossibility is objective rather than subjective-that the question is whether the thing can be done, not whether the promisor can do it. 2 Farnsworth, *supra* § 9.6, at 619. This too is more truism than test, although Pennsylvania courts have couched their decisions in this rhetoric. *See Luber v. Luber,* 418 Pa.Super. 542, 614 A.2d 771, 774 (1992); *Craig Coal Mining Co. v. Romani,* 355 Pa.Super. 296, 513 A.2d 437, 439 (1986). [I do not mean to suggest that these courts in any way reached the wrong result or engaged in faulty analysis. Rather, in those cases the traditional formulation of the test yielded the unmistakably correct conclusion that the promisor had assumed the risk of his own inability to perform.] Indeed, the First Restatement took such an approach, *see* Calamari & Perillo, *supra* § 13.15, at 521, but the Second simply applies "the rationale ... that a party generally assumes the risk of his own inability to perform his duty." *Craig Coal,* 513 A.2d at 439 (quoting Restatement (Second) of Contracts § 261 cmt. e). This holds particularly when the duty is merely to pay money. *See Luber,* 614 A.2d at 774. It is therefore "preferable to say that such ['subjective'] risks as these are generally considered to be sufficiently within the control of one party that they are assumed by that party." 2 Farnsworth, *supra* § 9.6, at 619-20. It is, of course, essential that the impossibility asserted by the promisor as a defense not have been caused by the promisor. *Id.* § 9.6, at 613-14; *Dorn,* 534 A.2d at 812; *Craig,* 513 A.2d at 440.

Generally speaking, while loss, destruction or a major price increase of fungible goods will not excuse the seller's duty to perform, the rule is different when the goods are unique, have been identified to the contract or are to be produced from a specific, agreed-upon source. In such a case, the nonexistence or unavailability of a specific thing will establish a defense of impracticability. Murray, *supra,* § 113, at 649, 650; *accord Olbum v. Old Home Manor, Inc.,* 313 Pa.Super. 99, 459 A.2d 757, 761 (1983); *Lichtenfels v. Bridgeview Coal Co.,* 366 Pa.Super. 304, 531 A.2d 22, 26 (1987); *Selland Pontiac-GMC, Inc. v. King,* 384 N.W.2d 490, 492-93 (Minn.App.Ct.1986); Restatement (Second) of Contracts § 263 (1981); White & Summers, *supra* § 3-10, at 175-76. Thus, § 263 of the Second Restatement recites:

> If the existence of a specific thing is necessary for the performance of a duty, its failure to come into existence, destruction, or such deterioration as makes performance impracticable is an event the non-occurrence of which was a basic assumption on which the contract was made.

Moreover, the Supreme Court of Pennsylvania has interpreted this section's predecessor in the First Restatement to apply to, in addition to physical destruction and deterioration, interference by third parties with a specific chattel necessary to the carrying out of the agreement. *Greenfield,* 380 A.2d at 759 (quoting *West v. Peoples First Nat'l Bank & Trust Co.,* 378 Pa. 275, 106 A.2d 427 (1954)); *accord Yoffe,* 443 A.2d at 362 (acts of third parties sufficient if not foreseeable); *Luria,* 213 A.2d at 153 (same).

Thus, in *Olbum,* the plaintiffs leased the mineral rights of specific portions of their land to a coal mining concern, in exchange for minimum royalty payments extending over four years. After successfully mining the land for a little over a year, defendant ceased its mining operations because the remaining coal had become unmineable and unmerchantable. 459 A.2d at 759. Plaintiffs then sued to recover the remaining royalty payments, but the court held that because the contract depended upon the "continued existence of a particular thing," *id.* at 761, specifically mineable coal, the contract was discharged for supervening impracticability. *Id., passim.*

In *Yoffe,* the promisor owed a contractual duty to file a securities registration statement with the SEC and effect registration within a set time. The SEC, however, unforeseeably undertook an investigation of its accounting practices, delaying the approval and causing damage to the promisee. The court held that, because the third party (SEC)'s actions were unforeseeable, the promisor was discharged. 443 A.2d at 363.

Likewise, in *Selland,* the promisor contracted to sell school bus bodies produced by a particular company, Superior. After the contract was entered into, and without the knowledge of any party, Superior became insolvent and the bodies were never delivered. The promisee then sued the promisor for breach of contract, but the court, applying § 2-615 of the U.C.C., held that the contract was discharged as impracticable. 384 N.W.2d at 492-93.

In *Litman v. Peoples Natural Gas Co.,* 303 Pa.Super. 345, 449 A.2d 720 (1982), the promisee contracted with defendant gas company to install gas service to an apartment building. Defendant-promisor was unable to perform, however, because the state utility commission subsequently forbade defendant from making any new connections. Plaintiff sued for breach, but the court held that performance was discharged as impossible, owing to the interference of the third-party regulatory body. *Id.* 449 A.2d at 724-25.

Finally, in *Waldinger,* the court applied impracticability to a situation in which a third party engineer unforeseeably required, contrary to industry custom, strict compliance with a standard, making the promisor-defendant's delivery of a compliant machine, as required by contract, impossible. 775 F.2d at 787-89.

The situation presented here is in accord with these cases. To recapitulate, CIT contracted to supply specific tire presses to Specialty. This was not a case of fungible goods; Specialty inspected, and bid for, certain identified, used presses located at the Natchez plant operated by Condere. All parties believed that CIT was the owner of the presses and was entitled to their immediate possession; Condere's representatives stated as much during the inspection visit. Neither Specialty nor CIT had any reason to believe that Condere would subsequently turn an about-face and assert a possessory interest in the presses. The most that can be said is that CIT had a course of dealings with Condere, but nowhere is it argued that there was any history of tortious or opportunistic conduct that would have alerted CIT that Condere would attempt to convert the presses to its own use.

Thus, whether analyzed traditionally in terms of foreseeability, as courts apply that term, or by the risk-exposure methodology outlined *supra,* it is clear that this is not the sort of risk that CIT should have expected to either bear or contract against. In economic terms, which I apply as a "check" rather than as substantive law, it cannot be said with any reliability that either Specialty or CIT was able to avoid the risk of what Condere did at a lower cost. It was "a bolt out of the blue" for both parties. On the other hand, Specialty was in a better position to know what consequences and damages would likely flow from nondelivery or delayed delivery of the presses. This suggests that Specialty is the appropriate party on which to impose the risk, *See* Posner, *supra* § 4.5, at 118; Calamari & Perillo, *supra* § 13.2, at 498. Moreover, judicial discharge of CIT's promise under these circumstances leaves Specialty in no worse a position than it would have occupied without the contract; either way, it would not have these presses, and it has only been able to locate and purchase three similar used presses on the open market since CIT's failure to deliver. On the other hand, CIT is relieved of the obligation to pay damages. Accordingly, excuse for impracticability would appear to be a Pareto-optimal move, note 8, *supra,* increasing CIT's welfare while not harming Specialty. This too is a valid policy reason for imposing the risk of loss on Specialty. *See* Calamari & Perillo, *supra* § 13.1, at 496. Thus, economic analysis confirms as sound policy the result suggested by the caselaw discussed *supra.*

Plaintiff makes much of the argument that there was no "basic assumption" created by Condere upon which Specialty and CIT based their contract, stating that it relied upon CIT's representations alone.... This is specious. As a matter of both law and logic, a basic assumption of any contract for the sale of specific, identified goods is that they are, in fact, available for sale. Accordingly, I reject this contention and conclude that the actions of Condere in detaining the presses presents sufficient grounds on which to base an impracticability defense.

Plaintiff also argues that this is a case only of subjective impossibility, presumably because Condere-which has been holding the presses essentially hostage-could deliver them up to Specialty. Thus, plaintiff contends that only CIT is incapable of performing and therefore should not be excused. This proves too much; in theory, at least, any hold-out party can be brought to the table if the price is high enough, including the parties in the cases discussed *supra*. Certainly, if CIT offered Condere $3 million to surrender the presses, there is little doubt that they would comply, but the law of impracticability does not require such outlandish measures.

In *Lichtenfels,* the promisor was unable to obtain a mining permit because one of ten owners held out for more money, yet the contract to mine was still discharged as impracticable. 531 A.2d at 24-26. Under Pennsylvania law, "impossibility" also encompasses "impracticability because of extreme and unreasonable difficulty, expense or loss involved." *Greenfield,* 380 A.2d at 759. This is simply not a case in which CIT became insolvent and could not perform, or in which the market price of tire presses spiked upward due to a shortage, making the contract unprofitable to CIT. While CIT did assume the risk of its own inability to perform, it did not assume the risk of Condere making it unable to perform by detaining the presses, any more than CIT assumed the risk that thieves would steal the presses from Condere before the latter could deliver them. [In that hypothetical, the thieves could no doubt be induced to hand over the presses for a ransom, and thus someone is "capable" of performing. This shows in stark relief the absurdity of plaintiff's argument.] In sum, this risk was not "sufficiently within the control of [CIT] that [it should be inferred that it was] assumed by that party." 2 Farnsworth, *supra* §9.6, at 619-20. It was completely within the control of Condere. [This fact pattern points up the conceptual weakness of the "I cannot do it versus it cannot be done" rendition of the objective/subjective test. Technically, someone could perform, but that someone is in all likelihood a tortfeasor that CIT has had to resort to judicial intervention to bring to heel. Thus, while this case may be seen as one of "I cannot do it," it is still not appropriate to treat as one in which a promisor merely underestimates the financial or technical resources it will need in order to perform.]

Accordingly, I conclude on this record that CIT has made out its defense of impracticability. The ruling of the replevin court, however, indicates that CIT's performance is impracticable only in the temporary sense. Temporary impracticability only relieves the promisor of the obligation to perform as long as the impracticability lasts and for a reasonable time thereafter. *Moudy v. West Va. Pulp & Paper Co.,* 385 Pa. 39, 121 A.2d 881, 883 (1956); *accord In re 222 Liberty Assocs.,* 101 B.R. 856, 862 (Bankr.E.D.Pa.1989); Calamari & Perillo, *supra* §13.13, at 519. Once it receives possession of the presses, CIT asserts that it stands ready and willing to perform its contract with Specialty.... That issue is not ripe for adjudication and must await a separate lawsuit if CIT should fail to perform after obtaining possession. Suffice it to say that, to the extent Specialty seeks damages for nondelivery of the presses to date, CIT is excused by the doctrine of impracticability and is entitled to full summary judgment.

An appropriate order follows....

Exercise 10-2: Applying Sections 2-613 and 2-615

1. Due to the earthquakes that are destroying countries all over the world, the demand for heavy equipment (large tractors, bulldozers, cranes, etc.) to clear and rebuild these devastated nations has increased dramatically. However, the supply of steel to make these machines has dropped severely due in large part to demand and also because 98% of steel mines are located in the currently war-

torn country of Mexico. Before these earthquakes and Mexico's war with Canada, KAT entered into a contract with the United States government to deliver 1000 pieces of heavy duty machinery at a cost of $10,000,000. Currently, the market rate for these items is valued at $100,000,000. KAT wants out of the contract.

Please advise KAT of its rights.

2. Buyer entered into a contract to buy 5,000 bushels of Arkansas Certified Bragg soybeans, F.O.B. Parkin, Arkansas (Seller's place of business). The contract provided, in pertinent part, that "sale is subject to final certification." Ultimately, Seller was unable to get his soybeans certified, and Seller claimed excuse under sections 2-613 and 2-615. What result?

3. A Seller of grain whose crop was partially damaged by weather conditions claimed excuse under sections 2-613 and 2-615 from delivering the contracted-for amount of grain to the grain elevator (Buyer). The contract did not identify a specified tract of land on which the grain was to be grown. What result?

4. Buyer and Seller entered into a contract for the sale of Seller's personal automobile. The contract described the motor vehicle by serial number. Before the Buyer arrived to pay for and pick up the vehicle, it was stolen through no fault of either party. The seller claimed excuse under sections 2-613 and 2-615. What result?

5. In *Corono-Oro, Inc. v. Harry Thompson*[9], the broker argued, based on section 2-615, that if there was a contract "the owner's election not to sell the goods made performance impossible and precluded a breach." The basis of his argument was that the contract was for Radius' cubicles, and Radius decided to sell to a higher bidder. Discuss the merits of the broker's argument. What *facts* might affect your analysis?

---

4. Common Law Grounds for Excuse

As previously noted, the common law supplements the U.C.C. where it has not been displaced. Thus, common law excuses for performance, such as the death of a contracting party, or failure of a condition, supplement the other excuse provisions of Article 2.

Additional Resources

Sheldon W. Halpern, *Application of the Doctrine of Commercial Impracticability: Searching for the Wisdom of Solomon*, 135 U.Pa. L. Rev. 1123 (1987).

---

9. The facts of this case are set forth in Chapter 4.

Eliot J. Katz, Annotation, *Construction and effect of UCC § 2-613 governing casualty to goods identified to a contract, without fault of buyer or seller*, 51 A.L.R.4th 537 (2009).

Lee Russ, Annotation, *Impracticability of performance of sales contract under UCC § 2-615*, 55 A.L.R.5th 563 (2009).

John D. Wladis, *Impracticability as Risk Allocation: The Effect of Changed Circumstances Upon Contract Obligations for the Sale of Goods*, 22 Ga. L. Rev. 503 (1988).

Figure 11-1: Graphic Organizer

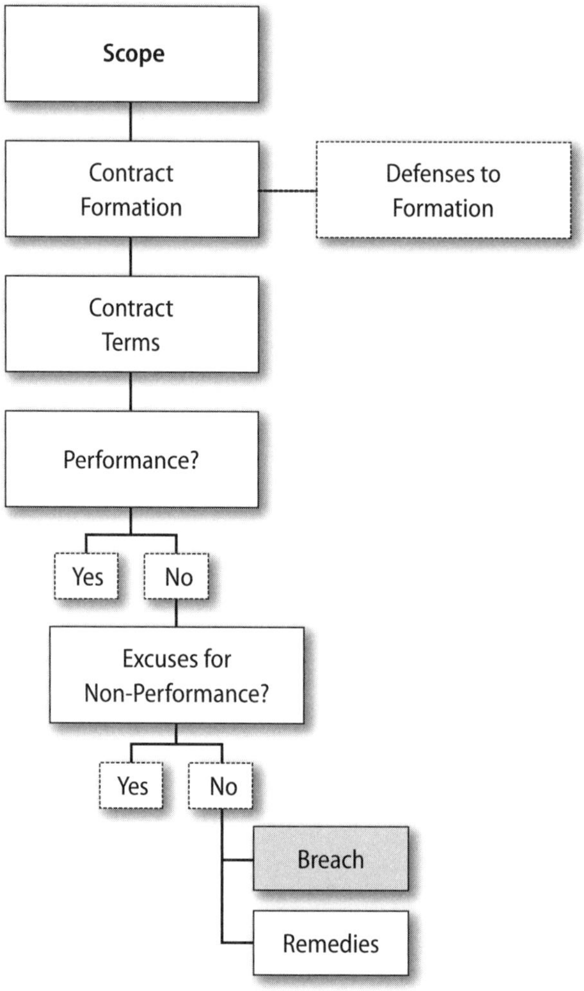

```
                  ┌─────────────────┐
                  │      Scope      │
                  └────────┬────────┘
                           │
                  ┌────────┴────────┐        ┌ ─ ─ ─ ─ ─ ─ ─ ─ ┐
                  │    Contract     │          Defenses to
                  │    Formation    │─ ─ ─ ─ │   Formation      │
                  └────────┬────────┘        └ ─ ─ ─ ─ ─ ─ ─ ─ ┘
                           │
                  ┌────────┴────────┐
                  │    Contract     │
                  │     Terms       │
                  └────────┬────────┘
                           │
                  ┌────────┴────────┐
                  │  Performance?   │
                  └────────┬────────┘
                    ┌──────┴──────┐
                  ┌ ─ ─ ┐     ┌ ─ ─ ┐
                  │ Yes │     │ No  │
                  └ ─ ─ ┘     └──┬──┘
                  ┌──────────────┴──────────┐
                  │      Excuses for        │
                  │    Non-Performance?     │
                  └──────────┬──────────────┘
                      ┌──────┴──────┐
                    ┌ ─ ─ ┐     ┌ ─ ─ ┐
                    │ Yes │     │ No  │
                    └ ─ ─ ┘     └──┬──┘
                                   │   ┌─────────────────┐
                                   ├───│     Breach      │
                                   │   └─────────────────┘
                                   │   ┌─────────────────┐
                                   └───│    Remedies     │
                                       └─────────────────┘
```

Chapter 11

Breach of Contract

Chapter Problem

On March 1, 2004, Power Co ("P") entered into a valid enforceable contract with Supplier ("S") pursuant to which S would supply condenser tubing to P for use at P's nuclear power plant. P was a large multinational corporation, and S was a family-owned local company. S was anxious to get P's business, so S readily agreed to enter into P's standard form contract. The contract provided, in pertinent part:

> S shall furnish, fabricate and deliver to P stainless steel condenser tubing in accordance with P's specifications, which are attached hereto and by this reference made a part hereof. Equal shipments of tubing shall be made on June 1, 2006, June 15, 2006, and July 1, 2006, for a total price of $990,000; provided, however, P may, upon written notice to S, delay tubing shipments. If P delays shipment beyond August 31, 2006, but not later than January 31, 2007, the contract price shall be increased by three percent (3%). If P delays shipment beyond January 31, 2007, but not later than January 31, 2008, the contract price shall be increased by an additional ten percent (10%).

On May 19, 2005, S wrote to P seeking "additional compensation" for performance under the contract. S informed P that subsequent to the formulation of the contract, S's "costs have risen at such a high rate that escalators built into our contracts have in no way adequately compensated for them. For example, the prices of various components of the tubing have increased by 21% and 24%." S requested a meeting with P to discuss possible solutions to these problems, including the renegotiation of the contract price. P refused to meet and advised S that the price increases were business risks which S must absorb.

On November 4, 2005, S wrote P, repeating its concerns about the increased price of tubing components, and stating "a current review of this matter suggests that we might be well advised not to perform under the contract." On November 19, 2005, P wrote in reply, "This is a demand for adequate assurances within thirty days, pursuant to section 2-609 of the U.C.C. that you will fully and properly perform under the contract."

S did not reply to P's letter, and on January 30, 2006, P wrote S "We consider you to have repudiated the contract." Thereafter, on February 17, 2006, S wrote P "We are willing to make delivery under the subject purchase order at our full cost of producing the material." S's full cost was higher than that specified in the contract. P rejected that offer, and solicited bids from other vendors for the supply of the tubing. Eventually, it contracted with T for the tubing at a price of $1,800,000.

P sued S for breach of contract. S defended on three principal bases: commercial impracticability, unconscionability, and alleged bad faith conduct by P.

Assume

(1) Between March of 2004 and May of 2005, S's costs for three components of the tubing had risen as follows: electrolytic nickel had risen by 24%, low carbon ferrochrome had risen by 185%, and its labor costs had risen by 21%. If S had performed under the contract as written, it would have sustained a loss of $ 428,500 on the contract; the anticipated profitability of the specific plant where the tubing would be produced would have been reduced to an overall profit of $ 589,500 for the year of performance. S would not have been unprofitable during 2006 in either its overall corporate structure or in the division responsible for the contract had it performed under the contract as written.

(2) S's unconscionability claim is based on the following contract provision, which S claims tainted the contract in its entirety, resulting in an unenforceable contract:

Provision for Cancellation

At any time after the acceptance of this Order the Purchaser ["P"] shall have the absolute right to cancel the entire Order upon the payment to the Seller ["S"] for all disbursements and expenses which the Seller has incurred or become obligated for prior to date of notice of cancellation, less the reasonable resale value of equipment which shall have been obtained or ordered to become an integral part of the Equipment plus a sum as profit bearing the same ratio to the profit that the Seller would have received upon completing the Work as that portion of Work done bears to the entire amount of Work to be done by the Seller under this Order.

(3) S's bad faith claim is based on the fact that P was unwilling to meet and renegotiate the contract price.
   Discuss the merits of P's suit against S, and each of S's defenses.

Figure 11-2: Breach: Sections and Definitions

Section	Definitions
2-106(3)	Termination
2-106(4)	Cancellation
2-609	Reasonable grounds for insecurity Adequate assurances
2-610	Anticipatory Repudiation
2-611	Retraction of Anticipatory Repudiation

---

1. Breach of Contract

Historically, at common law, most breaches of contract were analyzed based on the doctrines of "material breach" and "substantial performance." However, contracts for the sale of goods were analyzed based on the "perfect tender rule," which provided in essence that a seller breached a contract for the sale of goods if the seller failed to make a perfect tender of the goods.[1] As you saw in Chapter 10, the Code contains the perfect tender rule in section 2-601, but notwithstanding its apparent requirement of a "perfect tender," the seller is not in breach of contract until the seller's opportunity for cure has passed. In the case of an installment contract, the analysis of a seller's breach is similar to a substantial performance analysis.[2] Thus, the performance analysis we studied in Chapter 10 is actually an analysis of breach of contract as well.

1.1 Present Breach

When a contract party fails to perform when performance is due, and the failure to perform is not excused, that party has breached the contract. We have already studied some of the ways a seller can breach a contract: by failing to deliver at all, by failing to deliver the proper quantity of goods, by failing to deliver in a timely manner, or by failing to deliver conforming goods. As you have seen, the buyer can respond differently to a seller's breach, depending on the nature of the breach. The buyer does not always have the power to cancel the contract in the face of a non-conforming tender. For example, notwithstanding the so-called perfect tender rule, a seller who fails to make a perfect tender and has therefore breached the contract is entitled to attempt to cure if the time for performance has not arrived, and sometimes even after the time for performance has passed.[3]

1.2 Breach by Anticipatory Repudiation

Sometimes, in advance of the date set for performance, a contract party signifies to the other party that he or she does not intend to perform. *Repudiation* occurs before the time for performance is due, and is defined in Comment 1 to section 2-610 as "an overt communication of intention or an action which renders performance impossible or demonstrates a clear determination not to continue with performance." In the face of a breach by anticipatory repudiation, an aggrieved party has the options listed in section 2-610: (a) await performance by the repudiating party for a commercially reasonable time; (b) resort to any remedy for breach; and (c) in either case suspend his own performance. If the aggrieved party has not cancelled or materially changed his position in reliance on the repudiation, the repudiating party can retract his repudiation until performance is due.[4]

To fully understand 2-610, be sure to read its Official Comments carefully. Not only will you find a definition of repudiation, but also you will see a test for determining whether an anticipatory repudiation has occurred.

When a lawsuit is based on an alleged anticipatory repudiation, special issues arise with respect to the applicable statute of limitations and appropriate remedies. A cause of action

---

1. In this respect, the Code follows the common law that did not apply the doctrine of substantial performance to contracts for the sale of goods. *Mitsubishi Goshi Kaisha v. J. Aron & Co., Inc.* 16 F.2d 185, 186 (2d. Cir. 1926) (declaring "[t]here is no room in commercial contracts for the doctrine of substantial performance").

2. *See* discussion in Chapter 10, *supra.*

3. *See* discussion of seller's right to cure under section 2-508 in Chapter 9, *supra.*

4. *See* U.C.C. §2-611.

accrues and the statute of limitations begins to run upon the date when a right to institute and maintain a suit first arises. Since 2-610 provides that the aggrieved party may resort to any remedy for breach upon an anticipatory repudiation, it follows that the statute of limitations begins to run at the time the non-breaching party learns of the anticipatory repudiation.[5] The more complex remedies issues are discussed in Chapter 12.

1.3 Demand for Adequate Assurances of Due Performance

It is sometimes difficult to determine whether an apparent repudiation is actually a breach of contract, or whether the possible repudiator is simply equivocating or trying to open negotiations with the other party. The Code provides a mechanism to enable a seller or a buyer, after the contract formation stage, but before the tender of goods, to remove uncertainty or insecurity regarding whether performance will actually take place. Section 2-609 provides that when a party has "reasonable grounds for insecurity" with respect to performance by the other party, the insecure party may make a "demand for adequate assurances of due performance," and suspend his own performance until he receives such assurance. If the recipient of a justified demand for adequate assurances fails to respond in a timely manner, the Code states that he has repudiated the contract.[6]

As you can see, there are, then, two key decisions to be in connection with an application of section 2-609: (a) when does a party have "reasonable grounds for insecurity" (in other words, when is a party justified to make a demand for adequate assurances of due performance?) and (b) what is an appropriate demand for adequate assurances of due performance?

With respect to the first question, what constitutes "reasonable grounds for insecurity" is a question of fact. An ALR annotation collecting cases on point summarizes the case law as follows:

> Reasonable grounds for insecurity have been found on the part of the buyer where the goods were defective or nonconforming ... or were delivered late or not at all.... although claims of insecurity on these grounds have also failed.... In the two reported cases on point, the court found no grounds for insecurity based on the buyer's fears the seller would be unable to supply the goods.... Sellers have successfully asserted reasonable grounds for insecurity where the buyer failed to pay or pay timely, or failed to keep its purchases on credit below contractual or customary limits, including certain cases where the buyer claimed a right of setoff.... For a variety of reasons, such claims of insecurity have also proved unsuccessful.... The seller has also been found to be reasonably insecure because of the buyer's nonpayment under a prior or separate contract, information going to the bad character of the buyer or its operation, and the failure of the buyer to take delivery of the goods. A buyer's failure to secure project financing, however, did not give the seller reasonable grounds for insecurity under the circumstances of the one case on point.... [7]

---

5. See *American Cyanamid Co. v. Mississippi Chemical Corp.*, 817 F.2d 91 (11th Cir. 1987).

6. See U.C.C. §2-609(4).

7. Matthew C. Brenneman, Annotation, *Sales: What constitutes "reasonable grounds for insecurity justifying demand for adequate assurance of performance under U.C.C. §2-609*, 37 A.L.R. 5th 459 (2009).

With respect to the second question, if the transaction is between merchants, section 2-609(2) provides that the adequate assurances must be determined according to "commercial standards." The Code rejects the purely personal "good faith" test of *Corn Products Refining Co. v. Fasola.*[8] The Code envisions an objective test for determining whether an assurance is adequate.

If a demand for adequate assurances is not justified, either because the demanding party lacked reasonable grounds for insecurity or because it made unjustified demands, that party may be in breach of contract.

The following case contains a helpful discussion of anticipatory repudiation and demands for adequate assurance of due performance.

AMF, Incorporated, Plaintiff-Appellant, v. McDonald's Corporation, Defendant-Appellee

536 F.2d 1167 (7th Cir. 1976)

CUMMINGS, Circuit Judge.

AMF, Incorporated, filed this case in the Southern District of New York in April 1972. It was transferred to the Northern District of Illinois in May 1973. AMF seeks damages for the alleged wrongful cancellation and repudiation of McDonald's Corporation's ("McDonald's") orders for sixteen computerized cash registers for installation in restaurants owned by wholly-owned subsidiaries of McDonald's and for seven such registers ordered by licensees of McDonald's for their restaurants. In July 1972, McDonald's of Elk Grove, Inc. sued AMF to recover the $20,385.28 purchase price paid for a prototype computerized cash register and losses sustained as a result of failure of the equipment to function satisfactorily. Both cases were tried together during a fortnight in December 1974. A few months after the completion of the bench trial, the district court rendered a memorandum opinion and order in both cases in favor of each defendant. The only appeal is from the eight judgment orders dismissing AMF's complaints against McDonald's and the seven licensees. We affirm ...

In 1966, AMF began to market individual components of a completely automated restaurant system, including its model 72C computerized cash register involved here. The 72C cash register then consisted of a central computer, one to four input stations, each with a keyboard and cathode ray tube display, plus the necessary cables and controls.

In 1967, McDonald's representatives visited AMF's plant in Springdale, Connecticut, to view a working "breadboard" model 72C to decide whether to use it in McDonald's restaurant system. Later that year, it was agreed that a 72C should be placed in a McDonald's restaurant for evaluation purposes.

In April 1968, a 72C unit accommodating six input stations was installed in McDonald's restaurant in Elk Grove, Illinois. This restaurant was a wholly-owned subsidiary of McDonald's and was its busiest restaurant. Besides functioning as a cash register, the 72C was intended to enable counter personnel to work faster and to assist in providing data for accounting reports and bookkeeping. McDonald's of Elk Grove paid some $20,000

---

8. *See* U.C.C. §2-609 cmt. 4, para. 3 (citing 94 N.J.L. 181 (1920)).

for this prototype register on January 3, 1969. AMF never gave McDonald's warranties governing reliability or performance standards for the prototype.

At a meeting in Chicago on August 29, 1968, McDonald's concluded to order sixteen 72C's for its company-owned restaurants and to cooperate with AMF to obtain additional orders from its licensees. In December 1968, AMF accepted McDonald's purchase orders for those sixteen 72C's. In late January 1969, AMF accepted seven additional orders for 72C's from McDonald's licensees for their restaurants. Under the contract for the sale of all the units, there was a warranty for parts and service. AMF proposed to deliver the first unit in February 1969, with installation of the remaining twenty-two units in the first half of 1969. However, AMF established a new delivery schedule in February 1969, providing for deliveries to commence at the end of July 1969 and to be completed in January 1970, assuming that the first test unit being built at AMF's Vandalia, Ohio, plant was built and satisfactorily tested by the end of July 1969. This was never accomplished.

During the operation of the prototype 72C at McDonald's Elk Grove restaurant, many problems resulted, requiring frequent service calls by AMF and others. Because of its poor performance, McDonald's had AMF remove the prototype unit from its Elk Grove restaurant in late April 1969.

At a March 18, 1969, meeting, McDonald's and AMF personnel met to discuss the performance of the Elk Grove prototype. AMF agreed to formulate a set of performance and reliability standards for the future 72C's, including "the number of failures permitted at various degrees of seriousness, total permitted downtime, maximum service hours and cost." Pending mutual agreement on such standards, McDonald's personnel asked that production of the twenty-three units be held up and AMF agreed.

On May 1, 1969, AMF met with McDonald's personnel to provide them with performance and reliability standards. However, the parties never agreed upon such standards. At that time, AMF did not have a working machine and could not produce one within a reasonable time because its Vandalia, Ohio, personnel were too inexperienced. After the May 1st meeting, AMF concluded that McDonald's had cancelled all 72C orders. The reasons for the cancellation were the poor performance of the prototype, the lack of assurances that a workable machine was available and the unsatisfactory conditions at AMF's Vandalia, Ohio, plant where the twenty-three 72C's were to be built.

On July 29, 1969, McDonald's and AMF representatives met in New York. At this meeting it was mutually understood that the 72C orders were cancelled and that none would be delivered.

In its conclusions of law, the district court held that McDonald's and its licensees had entered into contracts for twenty-three 72C cash registers but that AMF was not able to perform its obligations under the contracts (see note 1, supra). Citing Section 2-610 of the Uniform Commercial Code (Ill. Rev. Stats. (1975) ch. 26, § 2-610) 3 and Comment 1 thereunder, the court concluded that on July 29, McDonald's justifiably repudiated the contracts to purchase all twenty-three 72C's.

Relying on Section 2-609 and 2-610 of the Uniform Commercial Code (Ill. Rev. Stats. (1975) ch. 26, §§ 2-609 and 2-610), the court decided that McDonald's was warranted in repudiating the contracts and therefore had a right to cancel the orders by virtue of Section 2-711 of the Uniform Commercial Code (Ill. Rev. Stats. (1975) ch. 26, § 2-711). Accordingly, judgment was entered for McDonald's....

Whether in a specific case a buyer has reasonable grounds for insecurity is a question of fact. Comment 3 to U.C.C. § 2-609; Anderson, Uniform Commercial Code, § 2-609

(2d Ed. 1971). On this record, McDonald's clearly had "reasonable grounds for insecurity" with respect to AMF's performance. At the time of the March 18, 1969, meeting, the prototype unit had performed unsatisfactorily ever since its April 1968 installation. Although AMF had projected delivery of all twenty-three units by the first half of 1969, AMF later scheduled delivery from the end of July 1969 until January 1970. When McDonald's personnel visited AMF's Vandalia, Ohio, plant on March 4, 1969, they saw that none of the 72C systems was being assembled and learned that a pilot unit would not be ready until the end of July of that year. They were informed that the engineer assigned to the project was not to commence work until March 17th. AMF's own personnel were also troubled about the design of the 72C, causing them to attempt to reduce McDonald's order to five units. Therefore, under Section 2-609 McDonald's was entitled to demand adequate assurance of performance by AMF.[9]

However, AMF urges that Section 2-609 of the U.C.C. (note 5 supra) is inapplicable because McDonald's did not make a written demand of adequate assurance of due performance. In Pittsburgh-Des Moines Steel Co. v. Brookhaven Manor Water Co., 532 F.2d 572, 581 (7th Cir. 1976), we noted that the Code should be liberally construed and therefore rejected such "a formalistic approach" to Section 2-609. McDonald's failure to make a written demand was excusable because AMF's Mr. Dubosque's testimony and his April 2 and 18, 1969, memoranda about the March 18th meeting showed AMF's clear understanding that McDonald's had suspended performance until it should receive adequate assurance of due performance from AMF ...

After the March 18th demand, AMF never repaired the Elk Grove unit satisfactorily nor replaced it. Similarly, it was unable to satisfy McDonald's that the twenty-three machines on order would work. At the May 1st meeting, AMF offered unsatisfactory assurances for only five units instead of twenty-three. The performance standards AMF tendered to McDonald's were unacceptable because they would have permitted the 72C's not to function properly for 90 hours per year, permitting as much as one failure in every fifteen days in a busy McDonald's restaurant. Also, as the district court found, AMF's Vandalia, Ohio, personnel were too inexperienced to produce a proper machine. Since AMF did not provide adequate assurance of performance after McDonald's March 18th demand, U.C.C. Section 2-609(1) permitted McDonald's to suspend performance. When AMF did not furnish adequate assurance of due performance at the May 1st meeting, it thereby repudiated the contract under Section 2-609(4). At that point, Section 2-610(b) (note 3 supra) permitted McDonald's to cancel the orders pursuant to Section 2-711 (note 6, supra), as it finally did on July 29, 1969.

In seeking reversal, AMF relies on Pittsburgh-Des Moines Steel Co. v. Brookhaven Manor Water Co., supra, 532 F.2d at 581. There we held a party to a contract could not resort to U.C.C. Section 2-609 since there was no demonstration that reasonable grounds

---

9. McDonald's was justified in seeking assurances about performance standards at the March 18th meeting. The parts and service warranty in the contracts for the twenty-three 72C's was essentially a limitation of remedy provision. Under U.C.C. §2-719(2) (Ill. Rev. Stats. 1975) ch. 26, §2-719(2)) if the 72C cash registers failed to work or could not be repaired within a reasonable time, the limitation of remedy provision would be invalid, and McDonald's would be entitled to pursue all other remedies provided in Article 2. See Riley v. Ford Motor Co., 442 F.2d 670, 673 (5th Cir. 1971); Earl M. Jorgensen Co. v. Mark Construction Co., 56 Haw. 466, 540 P.2d 978, 985-987 (Hawaii 1975). Because McDonald's would have a right to reject the machines if they proved faulty after delivery and then to cancel the contract, it was consistent with the purposes of Section 2-609 for McDonald's to require assurances that such eventuality would not occur. See Comment 1 to U.C.C. §2-719.

for insecurity were present. That case is inapt where, as here, McDonald's submitted sufficient proof in that respect. But that case does teach that McDonald's could cancel the orders under Sections 2-610 and 2-711 because of AMF's failure to give adequate assurance of due performance under Section 2-609....

JUDGEMENT AFFIRMED.

Exercise 11-1: Reasonable Grounds for Insecurity

Owners of a British vessel sought to refuel in Florida. They contacted an oil company, that indicated it could supply the fuel required, which would meet British standards. It was agreed the vessel owners would pay $120,000 for 500 metric tons of this particular fuel, with payment due thirty days after refueling. On July 1, the vessel was refueled. On July 15, while the vessel was still docked in Florida, the vessel owners notified the oil company that the fuel had been tested and it did not meet British standards. Fearing the British vessel would depart and leave American waters, thus rendering the vessel out of the jurisdiction of American courts, the oil company requested adequate assurance that the vessel owners would make payment, notwithstanding the non-conforming fuel type. No such assurance was provided. On July 22 and after failed attempts at negotiations, the oil company sent a second request for assurance, but this time demanded immediate payment. On July 24, after receiving no assurance and no payment, the oil company treated the contract with the vessel owners as anticipatorily repudiated and had the vessel arrested under maritime law.

Did the oil company have reasonable grounds for insecurity, thus entitling it under U.C.C. section 2-609 to request adequate assurance of the vessel owner's payment?

Exercise 11-2: Breach by Anticipatory Repudiation

Buyer contracted with Seller to purchase phosphate rock to be used in the production of fertilizer. Their contract contained the following key provisions: 1) the contract would run from January 1, 2002 until December 31, 2002, 2) the rock would be shipped in 12 equal monthly installments, 3) a one-year statute of limitations would govern all actions for breach of the contract, and 4) the contract could only be modified by express written agreement between the parties.

Seller began making the monthly shipments in January of 2002. Later in the year there was a downturn in the farming industry and the Buyer did not need as much phosphate rock as it originally agreed to buy. On September 3, 2002, Buyer sent a letter to Seller, indicating it would only need about 45% of the quantity of rock it originally estimated. It further stated that it just would not be able to purchase any more rock. Assume a court will find that Buyer anticipatorily repudiated the contract in its September 3, 2002 letter:

1. When can Seller bring its claim for breach of contact against the Buyer?

2. When must Seller file its breach of contract claim against Buyer to avoid expiration of the statute of limitations?

Additional Resources

Matthew C. Brenneman, Annotation, *Sales: what constitutes "reasonable grounds for insecurity" justifying demand for adequate assurance of performance under UCC §2-609*, 37 A.L.R.5th 459 (2010).

Milton Roberts, Annotation, *What constitutes anticipatory repudiation of sales contract under UCC §2-610,* 1 ALR 4th 527 (2010).

Figure 12-1: Graphic Organizer

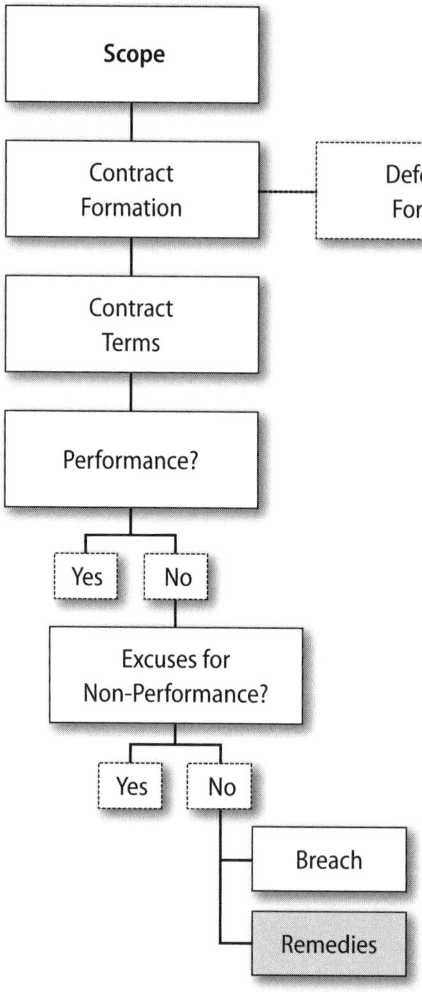

Chapter 12

Remedies

Chapter Problem

Producer is an experienced grape grower. In January 2008, he had approximately 1,000 acres planted in grape vines, and anticipated a bumper crop. He entered into a valid enforceable contract with Distributor, pursuant to which Producer promised to sell to Distributor 400,000 pounds of grapes at .30/lb. to be delivered in 100,000 pound increments, on July 1, August 1, September 1 and October 1, 2008. Producer and Distributor had known each other for 20 years and had contracted for the sale of grapes in this manner on several prior occasions. None of the contracts between Producer and Distributor had ever expressly required Producer to grow the grapes himself or to grow them in any particular location; however, Producer had always sold Distributor his own grapes. Producer knew that Distributor had already entered into a contract to resell the grapes to Third Party. Distributor expected to make a .10/lb. profit on the resale transaction.

In May, 2008, unseasonal, unexpected heavy rains severely damaged the region's grape crop, including Producer's. Producer notified Distributor that, as a result of the weather conditions, he was going to be short of grapes. Distributor responded that he would expect full performance when due. Producer delivered 75,000 pounds of grapes to Distributor on July 1, which Distributor resold as planned for .40/lb, making a $7,500 profit. At the same time, Producer notified Distributor that due to the unexpected rains Producer was unable to fulfill the balance of the contract. Distributor was able to negotiate the termination of its resale contract, at no cost to Distributor. On July 1, due to the severe crop damage in the region, the market price of grapes was .60/lb.

Producer sues Distributor for $22,500 (75,000 × .30), the contract price of the 75,000 pounds of grapes delivered.

Distributor counter-claims for $75,000, representing the difference between the Distributor's claimed damages for breach based on the volume of undelivered grapes at the market price (325,000 pounds × .60 = $195,000) less the contract price [400,000 × .30 = $120,000].

Producer objects, noting that (1) Producer's performance was excused due to the unseasonal unexpected heavy rains; and (2) even if Distributor were entitled to damages, its maximum recovery should be the $40,000 profit Distributor would have made under its resale contract with Third Party.

Who should prevail? Why?

Remedies for breach of contract are covered in the basic Contracts course and even more extensively in the upper-division course on Remedies. Accordingly, at this point in the course, we look at only selected remedies topics under Article 2. The sections and definitions we study in this chapter are shown in *Figure 12-2*.

Figure 12-2: Remedies Sections and Definitions

Section	Definitions
2-106(3)	Termination
1-305	Expectation Interest
2-701	Collateral; Ancillary
2-702	Insolvent; Reclaim; Solvency
2-703	Bailee (See § 7-102(a)(1)
2-704	Salvage
2-705	
2-706	Public Sale; Private Sale
2-707	Person in the Position of a Seller
2-708	Profit (including reasonable overhead)
2-709	Action for the Price
2-710	Incidental Damages
2-711	Security Interest
2-712	Cover
2-713	Market Price
2-714	
2-715	Consequential Damages
2-716	Specific Performance; Replevin
2-717	
2-718	Liquidated Damages
2-719	Remedy Limitations

1. The Goal of Remedies Under Article 2

Article 2 contains a wide assortment of remedial provisions. However, the starting point for any remedies analysis is section 1-305, which expresses the fundamental goal of putting the non-breaching party as nearly as possible in the financial position he or she would have enjoyed had the contract been fully performed on both sides.[1] This section further provides that *no* consequential, special or penal damages are recoverable unless specified in the Code or other rule of law.

Article 2 divides most of its remedial provisions into specific sections addressing separately the remedies available to aggrieved buyers and aggrieved sellers. Accordingly, this chapter follows that same organization.

---

1. Fuller and Perdue characterized this policy as the "expectation interest." L.L. Fuller & William R. Perdue, Jr., *The Reliance Interest in Contract Damages: 1*, 46 Yale L.J. 52, 54 (1936).

2. Buyer's Remedies for Unaccepted Goods

2.1 In General

Section 2-711 is an incomplete index to buyers' remedies. It identifies the possible reasons why buyers may be entitled to relief, and points the reader to the code sections that follow, which deal with the individual remedies in more detail. Available remedies differ, depending on whether the buyer has accepted the goods. That organization is followed below.

2.2 Cover

In the absence of specific performance, the most direct way to satisfy section 1-305 is for the non-breaching party to arrange a substitute transaction. If the seller cannot or will not deliver conforming goods, the aggrieved buyer can go to the marketplace and buy the goods from someone else. In this manner, the buyer substitutes for the performance required under the original contract. After cover, the buyer has the goods contracted for (or a reasonable substitute) and has paid for them. It should be possible to quantify the difference between the cost of the original contract performance and the substitute contract performance, and award the aggrieved buyer an amount of money damages to make up the difference. That is exactly what the Code tries to do in section 2-712 (buyer's cover). After cover, the buyer can recover the difference between the original contract price and the substitute contract price, plus consequential and incidental damages, thus preserving the benefit of the original bargain.[2]

Because the goal of cover is to put the buyer in the bargained-for position, the Code requires any cover to be "reasonable, made in good faith and without reasonable delay." The penalty for failing to make a proper cover is that damages may be calculated based on the market price, under section 2-713.

Note that cover is optional. If the aggrieved buyer covers, then damages are determined under the corresponding code sections. If the aggrieved buyer chooses not to cover, damages are calculated according to market price. However, as Official Comment 2 to section 2-712 points out, the "cover" provisions must be read in conjunction with the section that limits the recovery of consequential damages to such as could not have been avoided by cover.

Exercise 12-1: Corono-Oro, Inc. v. Harry Thompson

The following case first appeared in Chapter 4. There we focused on the portion of the opinion speaking to contract formation. The following portion of the opinion relates to damages for breach of contract. As you read the case, consider the following questions:

1. The original contract was for used goods. The buyer "covered" with new goods. Was that a "reasonable substitute"?

---

2. *See* U.C.C.§2-715.

2. What alleged damages are incidental? What alleged damages are consequential?

Corono-Oro, Inc. v. Harry Thompson

2002 Cal. App. Unpub. LEXIS 2501

[The facts regarding contract formation are set forth in Chapter 4, *supra.*]

SVC told Hollenback that if he could not find an equivalent product, SVC would find it, buy it, and bill him.

Hollenback and Dalton both looked hard and unsuccessfully for good used product before they decided to order new product that Hollenback had located. Dalton called every used furniture broker that he knew. He also looked on the Internet. Hollenback spent "numerous hours" visiting locations with an SVC representative, finding "nothing was of the same quality or near the same quality of the product that we initially were purchasing." On March 12, 1998, reseller issued a purchase order for 64 cubicles at a price of $1,562.50 per cubicle totaling $100,000.00. Hollenback explained that he would have been able to sell the extra cubicles over 64 that he wanted from Radius.

On March 12, 1998, broker called Hollenback and said he may be able to get the product for fifteen cents to the dollar. Hollenback did not trust broker and told him to talk to his lawyer.

It took Hollenback 26½ hours to locate the new product. When he charges for his time he bills out at $100 per hour.

The delivery charge was $1,350 for the new product coming from southern California. It would have been $500 for the local Radius workstations. There was a $1,000 installation charge that reseller had to pay because they were in a time crunch. Reseller completed all of these additional expenditures by April 1, 1998.

2. PROPRIETY OF DAMAGES

A. *Cover damages*

On appeal broker makes several challenges to the cover damages awarded reseller. The trial court awarded reseller $36,000 in cover damages, the difference between the cost of 64 new cubicles that reseller purchased at $1,562.50 apiece and the contract price of $1,000 apiece for the used Radius cubicles.

Section 2712 states in part: "(1) After a breach within the preceding section the buyer may 'cover' by making in good faith and without unreasonable delay any reasonable purchase of or contract to purchase goods in substitution for those due from the seller.

"(2) The buyer may recover from the seller as damages the difference between the cost of cover and the contract price together with any incidental or consequential damages as hereinafter defined (section 2715), but less expenses saved in consequence of the seller's breach."

As this court recognized in *KGM Harvesting Co. v. Fresh Network* (1995) 36 Cal.App.4th 376, 385, footnote 4, the Uniform Code comment on section 2712 states that "cover" includes "goods not identical with those involved but commercially usable as reasonable substitutes under the circumstances of the particular case." "The test of proper cover is whether at the time and place the buyer acted in good faith and in a reasonable manner, and it is immaterial that hindsight may later prove that the method of cover used was not the cheapest or most effective." (*Ibid.*)

Broker essentially contends that it was unreasonable to cover used office furniture with new because the goods differed significantly.

It is ordinarily a factual question for the fact-finder whether a buyer has made a reasonable, good faith purchase of substitute goods. (*Dangerfield v. Markel* (N.D. 1979) 278 N.W.2d 364, 368; *Dickson v. Delhi Seed Co.* (1988) 26 Ark.App. 83 [760 S.W.2d 382, 389]; see *Kanzmeier v. McCoppin* (Iowa 1987) 398 N.W.2d 826, 832.) Reseller presented evidence that the Radius work stations, though used, were of high quality. After broker was unable to deliver the Radius work stations, reseller was unable through diligent efforts to locate similar high quality used product. This amounts to substantial evidence that the Radius work stations were essentially as good as new and that it was reasonable under these circumstances for reseller to cover with new work stations.

Broker also contends that he "twice offered to provide alternates." As we pointed out earlier, the trial court was not required to accept broker's testimony on this point, which was contradicted by Dalton. Hollenback did acknowledge that broker offered a possible alternative a week after he was unable to deliver the Radius work stations. By that time, reseller had already located substitute goods. This offer by broker does not undermine the evidence that reseller made reasonable efforts to obtain cover.

Broker contends that the cover damages were calculated incorrectly because the "contract price" under his invoice was $81,700 for work stations and chairs, leaving a difference from the "cost of cover" of only $18,300. Broker is mixing apples and oranges. Reseller spent $100,000, the cost of cover, for 64 work stations at $1,562.50 apiece. The contract price of $81,700 included 76 chairs and 76 work stations, more than what reseller ultimately provided to its customer. The contract price per work station was $1,000. The trial court correctly concluded that for the 64 work stations that reseller provided, it had to pay $36,000 more than the contract price.

B. Incidental and consequential damages

On appeal broker contends that the trial court awarded improper consequential damages. The trial court awarded $2,650 for the extra 26 1/2 hours that Hollenback spent locating cover goods, $1,000 for additional installation charges, and $850 for additional delivery charges.

Section 2715 states in part: "(1) Incidental damages resulting from the seller's breach include expenses reasonably incurred in inspection, receipt, transportation and care and custody of goods rightfully rejected, any commercially reasonable charges, expenses or commissions in connection with effecting cover and any other reasonable expense incident to the delay or other breach.

"(2) Consequential damages resulting from the seller's breach include

"(a) Any loss resulting from general or particular requirements and needs of which the seller at the time of contracting had reason to know and which could not reasonably be prevented by cover or otherwise."

Broker questions the award of $1,000 for installation on the basis there is no evidence that reseller had to pay more to install the new work stations than it would have to install the Radius work stations. Broker overlooks that the trial court asked Hollenback this very question. "Why would you have not had that expense, the installation expense, if you bought it from Radius?" Hollenback answered, "I would still have it but not as much expense because of the time factor that was involved and we had to put in a lot of overtime hours." "There was a time crunch that we had to be in."

It is ordinarily a factual question for the fact-finder whether an expense was reasonably incident to effecting cover after breach of a contract. Overtime wages can qualify as incidental to a contract breach. (*Ohline Corp. v. Granite Mill* (Utah 1993) 849 P.2d 602, 605.) The quoted testimony constitutes substantial evidence supporting the trial court's implicit finding that reseller was required to pay overtime wages as a result of broker's breach of contract that it would not otherwise have had to pay.

Broker also questions the award of $2,650 for Hollenback's extra time in locating a substitute product. He contends that there was no evidence that reseller "actually paid its manager-owner $100 per hour."

Like overtime wages, a corporate officer's salary may be part of the cost of effecting cover, but it must be shown that the salary was a loss to the buyer attributable to the cover efforts. (*Cives Corp. v. Callier Steel Pipe & Tube, Inc.* (Me. 1984) 482 A.2d 852, 859-860.) Reseller responds, "The corporate Plaintiff was obviously damaged when its valued employee must divert his attention from productive work to dealing with an emergency created by" broker. While there was evidence that Hollenback spent a number of hours continuing to help a customer locate office furniture, there was no evidence whether he was working for salary or a commission. There was no evidence that he billed the customer $100 an hour for his time. Reseller produced no evidence that effecting cover was not part of Hollenback's job or that his efforts diverted him from other productive work. (*Cives Corp. v. Callier Steel Pipe & Tube, Inc., supra*, 482 A.2d 852, 860.) We conclude that the trial court erred in including the award of $2,650.00 as part of the damages.

[The Court discussed a claim for prejudgment interest and reversed to permit the trial court to recalculate those damages.]

2.3 Damages Based on the Market Price

Article 2 does not require the non-breaching party to enter a substitute transaction. If the aggrieved buyer chooses not to or is unable to enter a substitute transaction, Article 2 supplies a market-formula remedy that is intended to duplicate the price he or she would have been likely to have to pay if he or she had found another trading partner on the open market. Buyers' market formula remedies are described in section 2-713. The calculation is based on the market price of the goods determined as of the place for tender, or in case of rejection after arrival or revocation of acceptance, as of the place of arrival, plus consequential and incidental damages, thus preserving the benefit of the original bargain. An interpretative issue exists regarding the *time* for measuring the market price under section 2-713. Section 2-713(1) provides that in case of repudiation by the seller, the market price is to be measured "at the time when the buyer learned of the breach." Scholarly commentators and courts have observed that this phrase may be interpreted to refer to three different possible times. First, it may be argued that the buyer "learned of the breach" when the buyer first learned of the seller's repudiation. The problem with this interpretation is that section 2-723 specifically provides that when an action based on anticipatory repudiation comes to trial before the time for performance, damages based on market price shall be determined according to the price of such goods prevailing "at the time when the aggrieved party learned of the repudiation." If the time the buyer "learned of the breach" under section 2-713 already refers to the time the buyer "learned of the repudiation," there would be no need for section 2-723. Second, because section

2-610 provides that if a party repudiates the contract the aggrieved party may "for a commercially reasonable time await performance by the repudiating party," it is possible that the time the buyer "learned of the breach" should be construed to mean the time of repudiation *plus* "a commercially reasonable time." This interpretation seems to be favored by the majority of courts to consider the issue. Finally, because section 2-611 provides that the repudiating party can retract an anticipatory repudiation until the next performance is due, some commentators suggest that the buyer does not "learn of the breach" until the time performance is actually due.

2.4 Specific Performance and Replevin

The most obvious way to put the buyer in its bargained-for position is to require the breaching party to perform, and the Code contains a liberalized remedy of specific performance. Section 2-716 gives the buyer the right to specific performance "where goods are unique or in other proper circumstances." The history of section 2-716 suggests that the drafters wanted to make the remedy of specific performance[3] more readily available; however, case law suggests that courts grounded in the common law tradition are still somewhat hesitant to award the remedy. Official Comment 3 explains that the legal remedy of replevin is given to the buyer in cases in which cover is reasonably unavailable and goods have been identified to the contract. Unlike the equitable remedy of specific performance, which is granted at the successful conclusion of the plaintiff's case, replevin is a legal remedy pursuant to which a court may require a defendant to return specific goods to the plaintiff by means of a pre-judgment hearing. This cause of action is sometimes also known as an action for "claim and delivery."

3. Buyers' Remedies for Accepted Goods

3.1 Breach of Warranty

If the aggrieved buyer retains non-conforming goods, and gives the appropriate notice under section 2-607(3)(a), the buyer can recover damages based on the difference in the value of the goods if they were conforming and the goods that were actually received.

3.2 Additional Damages Recoverable

The foregoing substitutional remedies can be considered to compensate only for the "direct" or "general" damages caused by the breach: the lost benefit of the bargain, or the loss of the advantageous price of the original deal. But a breach can cause other forms of harm and these are classified as either consequential or incidental damages. In theory, direct damages would affect any non-breaching party equally, while consequential and incidental damages depend on the individual circumstances of each party. Especially in

---

3. U.C.C.§2-716, cmt. 1.

the case of consequential damages, the issues of causation and foreseeability also arise as possible limitations on recovery. Consequential damages are defined in section 2-715(2) as any loss (injury to person or property) resulting from requirements and needs of which the Seller, at the time of contracting had reason to know, which could not reasonably be prevented by cover or otherwise and any injury to person or property resulting from any breach of warranty. Incidental damages are defined in section 2-715(1) as including expenses reasonably incurred in inspection, receipt and transportation, and care and custody of rightfully rejected goods, any commercially reasonable charges, expenses or commission in connection with effecting cover, and any other reasonable expense incident to the delay or other breach.

3.3 Right of Offset

Under section 2-717, the buyer, upon notifying the seller, may deduct all or any part of damages resulting from breach of contract from any part of the price still due under the contract. Note that this right of offset does not extend to offsetting alleged damages for breach of one contract against monies due under a different contract.

4. Seller's Remedies

4.1 In General

Section 2-703 is an index to sellers' remedies. It identifies the possible reasons why sellers may be entitled to relief, and points the reader to the code sections that follow, which deal with the individual remedies in more detail. Available remedies differ, depending on whether the buyer has accepted the goods. That organization is followed below.

4.2 Action for the Price (Accepted Goods)

Although the Code does not contain a provision that states that a seller may have specific performance of a contract, section 2-709 allows the seller to recover the price under particular circumstances. This solution is very close to specific performance of the contract. If the seller sues for price, he must hold goods for buyer if they have been identified to the contract and are still in the seller's control. If a resale becomes possible, the seller can resell the goods at any time prior to judgment. In such a case, the net proceeds of resale must be credited to the buyer and payment of judgment entitles the buyer to any goods not resold.

4.3 Resale (Unaccepted Goods)

In the absence of specific performance, the most direct way to satisfy section 1-305 is for the non-breaching party to arrange a substitute transaction. If the buyer fails or refuses to accept the goods, the aggrieved seller can go to the marketplace and sell the goods to someone else. In this manner, the seller substitutes for the performance required under the original contract. After resale, the seller has approximately the price for the goods contracted for. It should be possible to quantify the difference between the original contract price and the substitute contract performance, and to award the aggrieved seller an amount of money damages to make up the difference. That is exactly what the Code tries to do in section 2-706 (seller's resale). After resale, the seller can recover the difference between the original contract price and the substitute contract price, plus incidental damages, thus preserving the benefit of the original bargain. There is an interpretative issue regarding whether a seller can recover consequential damages, and courts have split on the issue. Some courts take the position that the definition of incidental damages is broad enough to include consequential damages. Others believe that consequential damages are recoverable under section 1-103 because sellers could recover consequential damages at common law. Still others disagree and maintain that the absence of a specific section on sellers' consequential damages such as the section on buyers' consequential damages means that sellers cannot recover consequential damages.

Because the goal of resale is to put the seller in the bargained-for position, the Code sets forth specific rules governing any resale. A seller may elect between a "public" sale and a "private" sale (defined in the Official Comments). The penalty for failing to make a proper resale is that damages may be calculated based on the market price, under section 2-708.[4]

Note that resale is optional. If the aggrieved seller resells the goods that are the subject of the contract, then damages are determined under the corresponding code sections. If the aggrieved seller chooses not to resell, damages are calculated according to market price. To fully understand the seller's resale remedy, students should also consult section 2-704, which permits an aggrieved seller, upon the buyer's breach, to identify to the contract conforming goods not already identified if the goods are in the seller's possession or control. In addition, section 2-704 gives the seller the option to elect between completing unfinished goods before resale, or cease manufacturing and resell the unfinished goods for scrap or salvage value "or proceed in any other reasonable manner."

4.4 Damages Based on the Market Price

Article 2 does not require the non-breaching party to enter into a substitute transaction. If the aggrieved seller chooses not to or is unable to enter a substitute transaction, Article 2 supplies a market-formula remedy that is intended to duplicate the price he or she would have been likely to have received if he or she had found another trading partner on the open market. Sellers' market formula remedies are described in section 2-708(1). The calculation is based on the market price of the goods determined as of the time and place for tender, plus incidental damages, thus preserving the benefit of the original bargain.

If the seller's action is based on anticipatory repudiation, the measure of damages may change depending on when the action goes to trial. If an action based on anticipatory repudiation goes to trial before the time for performance with respect to some or all of the goods, any damages based on market price are determined according to the price of such

---

4. U.C.C. §2-706, cmt. 2.

goods at the time when the aggrieved party learned of the repudiation.[5] When the case does *not* come to trial before the performance date, damages are *not* measured as of the time when the aggrieved party learned of the repudiation, but rather are measured at the time for performance under the contract.[6]

As you learned in Contracts, in some cases, notably the lost volume seller cases, neither of these two approaches will make the non-breaching party whole. Stated simply, a "lost volume" seller is one who is able to sell such a great volume of a particular type of good that the loss of one sale will always result in a monetary loss. Contrast a lost volume seller to a seller who has a limited quantity of goods to sell. Following is a simplistic example: Larry Law Student has one car to sell. If he enters into a contract to sell that car to Linda Lovey and Linda breaches, Larry will be able to resell that car to someone else, thus avoiding some or all of the loss caused by Linda's breach. The "resale" remedy will make Larry whole. Alternatively, if Larry chooses not to sell the car, his damages can be established by reference to the market price under section 2-708(1). In sharp contrast, Carla Car Dealer theoretically has access to an unending supply of cars for sale. If she enters into a contract to sell a car to Linda Lovey and Linda breaches, when Carla next sells a car, it cannot be said that she is "reselling" the car that Linda was to have purchased. Instead, theoretically, Carla is selling a different car—one that she would always have been able to come up with to sell to the new purchaser. What Carla has lost (forever) is the profit on the sale she would have made to Linda.

For such situations, section 2-708(2) Article 2 gives the seller a remedy equal to the lost profit on the breached contract. The applicability of section 2-708(2) was discussed by the United States Court of Appeal for the Seventh Circuit in R.E. Davis Chemical Corp. v. Diasonics, Inc., as follows:

> Article 2 contains four provisions that concern the recovery of a seller's general damages (as opposed to its incidental or consequential damages): 2-706 (contract price less resale price); 2-708(1) (contract price less market price); 2-708(2) (profit); and 2-709 (price) ...
>
> The Code does not provide a great deal of guidance as to when a particular damage remedy is appropriate. The damage remedies provided under the Code are catalogued in section 2-703, but this section does not indicate that there is any hierarchy among the remedies. One method of approaching the damage sections is to conclude that 2-708 is relegated to a role inferior to that of 2-706 and 2-709 and that one can turn to 2-708 only after one has concluded that neither 2-706 nor 2-709 is applicable. Under this interpretation of the relationship between 2-706 and 2-708, if the goods have been resold, the seller can sue to recover damages measured by the difference between the contract price and the resale price under 2-706. The seller can turn to 2-708 only if it resells in a commercially unreasonable manner or if it cannot resell but an action for the price is inappropriate under 2-709 ...
>
> Two different measures of damages are provided in 2-708. Subsection 2-708(1) provides for a measure of damages calculated by subtracting the market price at the time and place for tender from the contract price. The profit measure of damages ... is contained in 2-708(2). However, one applies 2-708(2) only if "the

---

5. U.C.C. §2-723(1).
6. *Hess Energy v. Lightning Oil Co., Ltd*, 338 F.3d 357, 363 (4th Cir. 2003).

measure of damages provided in subsection (1) is inadequate to put the seller in as good a position as performance would have done....." Diasonics [the seller in this case] claims that 2-708(1) does not provide an adequate measure of damages when the seller is a lost volume seller. To understand Diasonics' argument, we need to define the concept of the lost volume seller. Those cases that have addressed this issue have defined a lost volume seller as one that has a predictable and finite number of customers and that has the capacity either to sell to all new buyers or to make the one additional sale represented by the resale after the breach. According to a number of courts and commentators, if the seller would have made the sale represented by the resale whether or not the breach occurred, damages measured by the difference between the contract price and market price cannot put the lost volume seller in as good a position as it would have been in had the buyer performed. The breach effectively cost the seller a "profit," and the seller can only be made whole by awarding it damages in the amount of its "lost profit" under Section 2-708(2).

However, we disagree with the definition of "lost volume seller" adopted by other courts. Courts awarding lost profits to a lost volume seller have focused on whether the seller had the capacity to supply the breached units in addition to what it actually sold. In reality, however, the relevant questions include not only whether the seller could have produced the breached units in addition to its actual volume, but also whether it would have been profitable for the seller to produce both units. Goetz & Scott, *Measuring Sellers' Damages: The Lost-Profits Puzzle*, 31 Stan. L. Rev. 323, 332-33, 346-47 (1979). As one commentator has noted, under the economic law of diminishing returns or increasing marginal costs[,] ... as a seller's volume increases, then a point will inevitably be reached where the cost of selling each additional item diminishes the incremental return to the seller and eventually makes it entirely unprofitable to conclude the next sale....

Thus, under some conditions, awarding a lost volume seller its presumed lost profit will result in over-compensating the seller, and 2-708(2) would not take effect because the damage formula provided in 2-708(1) does place the seller in as good a position as if the buyer had performed. Therefore, on remand, Diasonics must establish, not only that it had the capacity to produce the breached unit in addition to the unit resold, but also that it would have been profitable for it to have produced and sold both.... [7]

5. Other Remedies

It is important to remember that buyers have other remedies for breach of contract, which we discussed earlier in connection with Performance (Chapter 9). These remedies include rejection or revocation of acceptance of non-conforming goods, cancellation of the contract, withholding of payment, and the security interest where the purchase price

---

7. *R.E. Davis Chemical Corp. v. Diasonics, Inc.*, 826 F.2d 678 (7th Cir. 1987).

has been paid. Buyers may also recover payments made in an action for restitution. Sellers are empowered to stop delivery of goods or to recover them from the buyer in limited circumstances when the buyer is insolvent.

5.1 Liquidated Damages

Section 2-718 provides that a liquidated damages clause will only be enforced if it is in an amount which is reasonable in light of the anticipated and actual harm caused by the breach. The first sentence of section 2-718(1) requires an examination of the position of the parties both at the time of contracting and at the time of the breach. Accordingly, a liquidated damage provision will only be valid if reasonable with respect to either (1) the harm which the parties anticipate will result from the breach at the time of contracting or (2) the actual damages suffered by the non-defaulting party at the time of breach.[8]

Although section 2-718 is primarily thought of as addressing liquidated damage provisions, it has other topics as well. By this point of the course, your statute-reading skills have been honed. Here is a quick exercise to see what you have learned.

Exercise 12-2: Deconstructing Section 2-718

Write a description of the legal significance of all parts of section 2-718.

5.2 Contractual Remedies

Finally, the Code validates the parties' creation of their own remedial schemes, either by liquidated damages provisions (section 2-718) or by establishing limited or exclusive remedies (section 2-719). Any contractual remedies are optional, unless the contract provides they are exclusive. Thus, if the contract does not state that the remedy is the exclusive remedy, all remedies under Article 2 are still available.

However, an exclusive or limited remedy will not be enforced if it: 1) fails of its essential purpose or 2) is unconscionable.[9] If the limited remedy is unenforceable, all remedies under Article 2 will be available. These concepts were discussed in more detail in Chapter 6.

Figures 12-3 and 12-4 illustrate the remedies available to aggrieved buyers and sellers. Thereafter, *Figure 12-5* provides a quick summary of the similarities and differences between buyers' and sellers' remedies under Article 2.

---

8. *Stock Shop, Inc. v. Bozell & Jacobs, Inc.* 481 N.Y.S.2d 269 (N.Y. 1984).

9. For example, a consequential damages limitation for personal injury in consumer goods cases is prima facie unconscionable. U.C.C. §2-719(3).

Figure 12-3: Buyer's Remedies

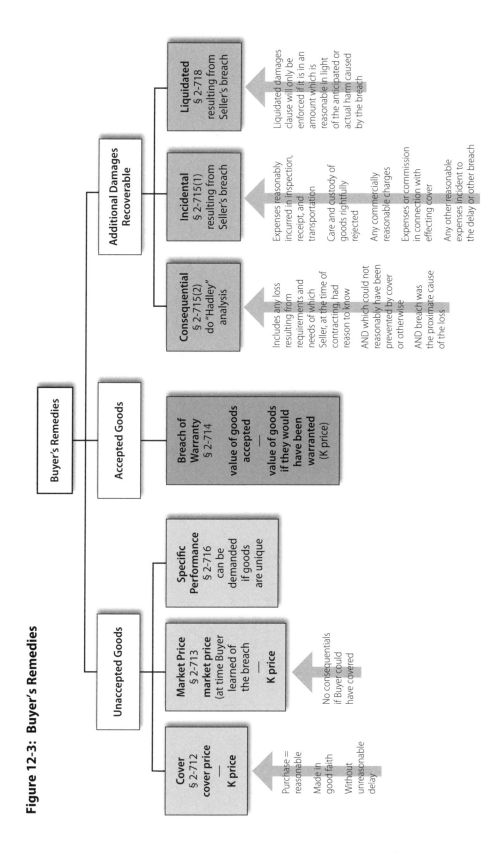

Figure 12-4: Seller's Remedies

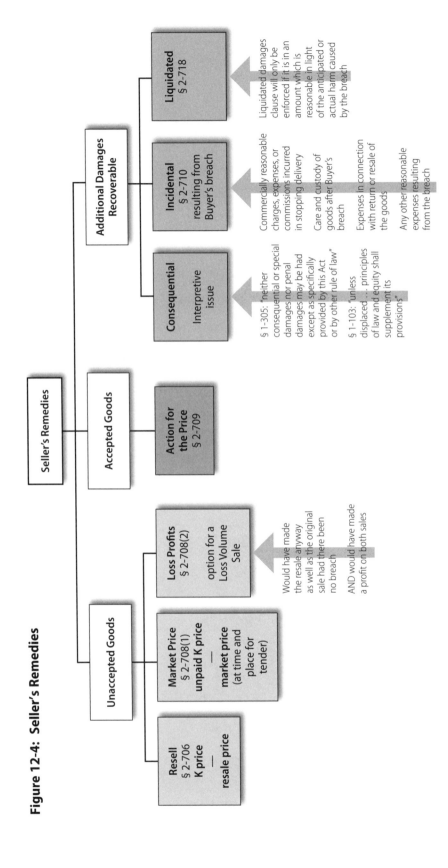

Figure 12-5: A Simplified Comparison of Buyers' and Seller's Remedies Under U.C.C. Article 2

	Buyers	Sellers
Goals	1-305: Remedies should be liberally adminis-trated to put the aggrieved party in "as good a position as if the other party had fully per-formed."	1-305: Remedies should be liberally adminis-trated to put the aggrieved party in "as good a position as if the other party had fully per-formed."
Index	2-711: If seller is in breach of the contract, the buyer may cancel AND may: (a) cover and re-ceive damages, or (b) recovery damages for non-delivery. If seller fails to delivery or repudi-ates, buyer may also: (a) recover the goods if they have been identified, or (b) obtain spe-cific performance or replevin.	2-703: If the buyer is in breach of the contract, the seller may: (a) withhold delivery of goods, (b) stop delivery, (c) proceed under 2-704, (d) resell and recover damages, (e) cancel the con-tract.
Substitute Contract	COVER 2-712: Buyer may cover by purchasing or con-tracting to purchase substitute. Calculation: Diff between Cover Price & K Price (+/-)	RESALE 2-706: "[S]eller may resell the goods." Calculation: Diff between Resale Price & K Price (+/-)
Damages: Market Price	2-713(1): Provides measure of damages for seller's breach. Calculation: Diff between Market Price at time buyer learned of breach & K Price (+/-)	2-708(1): Provides measure of damages for buyer's breach. Calculation: Diff between Market Price at time & place for tender & Unpaid K Price (+/-)
Specific Performance	SPECIFIC PERFORMANCE or REPLEVIN 2-716: Usually decreed where goods are unique; Buyer has right of replevin for goods identified to K if buyer can't cover, circum-stances indicate attempts to cover would fail, or goods shipped under reservation and satis-faction of security interest is made.	ACTION FOR THE PRICE 2-709: If buyer fails to pay, seller may recover: (a) price of goods accepted or conforming goods lost or damaged when risk of loss was on buyer, and (b) price of goods identified to K if seller cannot resell or circumstances indicate re-sell attempts would fail.
Incidental Damages	2-715(1): "[E]xpenses reasonably incurred in in-spection, receipt, transportation and care and custody of goods rightfully rejected, any com-mercially reasonable charges, expenses or commissions in connection with effecting cover and any other reasonable expense inci-dent to the delay or other breach."	2-710: "[C]ommercially reasonable charges, ex-penses or commissions incurred by stopping delivery, in the transportation, care and custody of goods after buyer's breach, in connection of return or resale of goods or otherwise resulting from the breach."
Consequential Damages	2-715(2): (a) Any loss resulting from general or special requirements and needs, of which the seller had reason to know and could not be reasonably prevented otherwise, and (b) injury to person or property that is the proximate re-sult of a breach of warranty.	INTERPRETATIVE ISSUE: SEE 1-305 ("neither consequential, or special nor penal damages may be had except as specifi-cally provided in this Act or by other rule of law") SEE ALSO 1-103 ("Unless displaced ... principles of law and equity shall supplement its provi-sions")
Liquidated Damages	2-718: Limited to amounts reasonable in light of anticipated or actual harm, difficulties of proof of loss and inconvenience or nonfeasibil-ity of obtaining an alternative remedy.	2-718: Limited to amounts reasonable in light of anticipated or actual harm, difficulties of proof of loss and inconvenience or nonfeasibility of obtaining an alternative remedy.

Exercise 12-3: Buyer's Remedies

On January 5, 2010, John Gable ordered 3 BLACKKAT tractors at a price of $100,000 per tractor from KAT. Delivery was scheduled for March 15, 2010. The price of steel went up, so the market price of these tractors went up as well. On March 14, 2010, KAT sent John a letter stating it would not send John the tractors. On March 15, the market price of BLACKKAT tractors in Kansas, where John lives and works, was $140,000. John had trouble finding a new source of tractors, so he was unable to plant his crops, as planned, by April 1. On April 1, he rented three tractors for thirty days at the market rate of $400 per day per tractor, and began planting his crop. On May 1, after diligent efforts, he finally located and bought three WHITEKAT tractors at the market price of $150,000 per tractor. The WHITEKAT is very similar in appearance to the BLACKKAT and has approximately the same performance capabilities. However, historically the WHITEKAT costs approximately $10,000 more than the comparable BLACKKAT tractor.

Based on his experience in previous years, John estimates that he will lose approximately $100,000 because of the delay in planting and the resulting delay in getting his crops to market.

Assume that KAT breached the contract. John consults an attorney (you). You wish to calculate John's potential recovery of damages. Answer the following questions:

1. Can John recover the difference in value between the BLACKKAT and WHITEKAT tractors, since they were not identical? If so, how will such damages be calculated?

2. Can John recover the cost of renting the tractors? What is the basis of such recovery, if any?

3. Can John recover his estimated lost profits resulting from the delay in planting?

4. Can John recover attorneys' fees?

Exercise 12-4: Buyer's Remedies[10]

Clara, a resident of the State of Columbia, owns a dress factory. Clara has a national reputation for producing some of the finest silk wedding dresses. She uses a very expensive Japanese silk known as "Kobe silk" in the manufacturing process. Kobe silk is highly valued because of its exquisite luster and texture. Each fall, Clara orders bolts of the fabric from Dave, a silk importer and wholesaler. Because most weddings are scheduled for June, Clara must have delivery of the silk by mid-March to make the dresses and fill her orders, which number in the hundreds.

In October 2009, Clara entered into a written contract with Dave for the purchase of 500 bolts of Kobe silk at $1,000 per bolt. The contract requires that Dave deliver the fabric no later than March 15, 2010, and time is of the essence.

---

10. My colleague, Professor Philip Merkel, was kind enough to share this exercise with me. Used with permission.

In December 2009, Kobe silk farmers suffered serious losses when a rare disease wiped out much of the silkworm population. Fortunately for Dave, his supplier in Japan was not affected. Because Dave did regular business with the supplier, he was able to purchase the 500 bolts of Kobe silk at the price he negotiated before the outbreak of the disease. A number of dressmakers who use Kobe silk in their products learned that Dave received the shipment. Some offered to give Dave substantially more than $1,000 per bolt for the silk. The highest offer came from a dressmaker in New Jersey who offered to buy the 500 bolts at $1,500 per bolt. Dave decided to sell the silk to her.

On February 25, 2010, Dave informed Clara that he would not fill her order because he was selling the silk to someone else. He mentioned that he would be shipping the silk to the New Jersey dressmaker the following afternoon.

Clara immediately contacted a number of other silk suppliers around the country to see if they had stocks of Kobe silk, but her efforts were fruitless. She says that her business will be ruined if she cannot fill her dress orders for weddings scheduled in June. She does not want to use an inferior grade of silk, as her customers will cancel their orders. She fears that her reputation as one of the nation's top dressmakers will be ruined.

Assume that the contract between Clara and Dave is valid in all respects and that Dave breached it. Clara still wishes to buy the Kobe silk and keep Dave from selling it to anyone else. She is not interested in suing for damages. Objectively discuss her equitable remedies and whether she is likely to prevail.

Additional Resources

Prof. Robert J. Harris & Kenneth Graham, *A Radical Restatement of the Law of Seller's Damages: Sales Act and Commercial Code Results Compared*, 18 Stan. L. Rev. 66, 101 n.174 (1965).

John S. Herbrand, Annotation, *Buyer's incidental and consequential damages from seller's breach under UCC § 2-715*, 96 A.L.R.3d 299 (2009).

Kristine Cordier Karnezis, Annotation, *Contractual liquidated damages provisions under UCC Article 2*, 98 A.L.R.3d 586 (2009).

Carolyn Kelly MacWilliam, Annotation, *Resale of Goods Under UCC § 2–706*, 101 A.L.R.5th 563 (2009).

Gary D. Spivey, Annotation, *Measure and elements of buyer's recovery upon revocation of acceptance of goods under UCC § 2-608(1)*, 65 A.L.R.3d 388 (2009).

Chapter 13

Advanced Issues: Clickwrap, Shrinkwrap, and Electronic Contracting

Chapter Problem

Connie Consumer received an e-mail from Giant Computer Seller, which stated:

> Be the first on your block to get the Giant Netbook 5000. Light weight and A workhorse! $399 to the first 50 callers. 1-800-123-4567.

Connie promptly called Giant's toll-free telephone number and when a sales representative finally answered, she stated "I want the Giant Netbook 5000 as described in your e-mail." "You're in luck," the sales representative replied. "You are among the first 50 callers. Give me your credit card number, and we will ship it out tonight."

Connie gave the representative her credit card number and her shipping address.

A week later, the Netbook 5000 was delivered to Connie's house. She couldn't wait to see it, so she grabbed a knife, and cut through all of the tape on the box, tossing aside everything except the netbook itself. She booted it up and began to surf the internet. Eventually, she cleaned up the room, and threw out all of the shipping materials.

Two weeks later, the Netbook 5000 died. Connie called Giant's toll-free number to complain and demand a replacement. "No way," the sales representative replied. "I'll sue you in small claims court!" Connie declared. "No, you won't," the sales representative replied. Our contract contains a mandatory arbitration provision, requiring you to arbitrate any disputes with us in the State of Montana."

Connie knows that you have just completed a course in Sales. She asks you whether Giant can insist on arbitration.

What is your advice?

Would your analysis change if Connie was Connie C.E.O. instead of Connie Consumer, and she was purchasing 50 netbooks for her entire staff in her business?

New means of entering into contracts, such as contracting over the Internet, led to new approaches to contract formation analysis. One of the more recent approaches is known as a "rolling contract" analysis.[1] The United States Court of Appeals for the Seventh Circuit introduced the idea that contract formation can take place over time, with terms "rolling" into the contract by virtue of inaction, in *ProCD v. Zeidenberg* and expanded on it in *Hill v. Gateway 2000 Inc.*

Exercise 13-1: Rolling Contracts

As you read the following cases, consider the following questions:

1. At what point in time did the court conclude a contract was formed?

2. Does that conclusion follow "traditional" contract formation analysis, or is it different?

3. If it is different, how does the court justify and explain this difference?

4. Are you persuaded?

5. How does the Court analyze section 2-207?

Pro CD Inc v Zeidenberg
86 F.3d 1447 (7th Cir 1996)

EASTERBROOK, Circuit Judge.

Must buyers of computer software obey the terms of shrinkwrap licenses? The district court held not, for two reasons: first, they are not contracts because the licenses are inside the box rather than printed on the outside; second, federal law forbids enforcement even if the licenses are contracts.... The parties and numerous amici curiae have briefed many other issues, but these are the only two that matter-and we disagree with the district judge's conclusion on each. Shrinkwrap licenses are enforceable unless their terms are objectionable on grounds applicable to contracts in general (for example, if they violate a rule of positive law, or if they are unconscionable). Because no one argues that the terms of the license at issue here are troublesome, we remand with instructions to enter judgment for the plaintiff.

ProCD, the plaintiff, has compiled information from more than 3,000 telephone directories into a computer database. We may assume that this database cannot be copyrighted, although it is more complex, contains more information (nine-digit zip codes and census industrial codes), is organized differently, and therefore is more original than the single alphabetical directory at issue in *Feist Publications, Inc. v. Rural Telephone Service Co.*, 499 U.S. 340, 111 S.Ct. 1282, 113 L.Ed.2d 358 (1991). See Paul J. Heald, The Vices of Originality, 1991 Sup.Ct. Rev. 143, 160-68. ProCD sells a version of the database, called SelectPhone (trademark), on CD-ROM discs. (CD-ROM means "compact disc-

---

1. This approach is also sometimes referred to as a "layered" contract analysis, "terms in a box," or "pay now—terms later." An entire symposium was devoted to the idea of a "common sense" approach, as suggested in *Gateway. See Sy*mposium, *Common Sense and Contract Law*, 16 Touro L. Rev. 1037 (2000).

read only memory." The "shrinkwrap license" gets its name from the fact that retail software packages are covered in plastic or cellophane "shrinkwrap," and some vendors, though not ProCD, have written licenses that become effective as soon as the customer tears the wrapping from the package. Vendors prefer "end user license," but we use the more common term.) A proprietary method of compressing the data serves as effective encryption too. Customers decrypt and use the data with the aid of an application program that ProCD has written. This program, which is copyrighted, searches the database in response to users' criteria (such as "find all people named Tatum in Tennessee, plus all firms with 'Door Systems' in the corporate name"). The resulting lists (or, as ProCD prefers, "listings") can be read and manipulated by other software, such as word processing programs.

The database in SelectPhone (trademark) cost more than $10 million to compile and is expensive to keep current. It is much more valuable to some users than to others. The combination of names, addresses, and SIC codes enables manufacturers to compile lists of potential customers. Manufacturers and retailers pay high prices to specialized information intermediaries for such mailing lists; ProCD offers a potentially cheaper alternative. People with nothing to sell could use the database as a substitute for calling long distance information, or as a way to look up old friends who have moved to unknown towns, or just as an electronic substitute for the local phone book. ProCD decided to engage in price discrimination, selling its database to the general public for personal use at a low price (approximately $150 for the set of five discs) while selling information to the trade for a higher price. It has adopted some intermediate strategies too: access to the SelectPhone (trademark) database is available via the America Online service for the price America Online charges to its clients (approximately $3 per hour), but this service has been tailored to be useful only to the general public.

If ProCD had to recover all of its costs and make a profit by charging a single price-that is, if it could not charge more to commercial users than to the general public-it would have to raise the price substantially over $150. The ensuing reduction in sales would harm consumers who value the information at, say, $200. They get consumer surplus of $50 under the current arrangement but would cease to buy if the price rose substantially. If because of high elasticity of demand in the consumer segment of the market the only way to make a profit turned out to be a price attractive to commercial users alone, then all consumers would lose out-and so would the commercial clients, who would have to pay more for the listings because ProCD could not obtain any contribution toward costs from the consumer market.

To make price discrimination work, however, the seller must be able to control arbitrage. An air carrier sells tickets for less to vacationers than to business travelers, using advance purchase and Saturday-night-stay requirements to distinguish the categories. A producer of movies segments the market by time, releasing first to theaters, then to pay-per-view services, next to the videotape and laserdisc market, and finally to cable and commercial tv. Vendors of computer software have a harder task. Anyone can walk into a retail store and buy a box. Customers do not wear tags saying "commercial user" or "consumer user." Anyway, even a commercial-user-detector at the door would not work, because a consumer could buy the software and resell to a commercial user. That arbitrage would break down the price discrimination and drive up the minimum price at which ProCD would sell to anyone.

Instead of tinkering with the product and letting users sort themselves-for example, furnishing current data at a high price that would be attractive only to commercial customers, and two-year-old data at a low price-ProCD turned to the institution of contract. Every box containing its consumer product declares that the software comes with restrictions stated in an enclosed license. This license, which is encoded on the CD-ROM disks as well as printed in the manual, and which appears on a user's screen every time the software runs, limits use of the application program and listings to non-commercial purposes.

Matthew Zeidenberg bought a consumer package of SelectPhone (trademark) in 1994 from a retail outlet in Madison, Wisconsin, but decided to ignore the license. He formed Silken Mountain Web Services, Inc., to resell the information in the SelectPhone (trademark) database. The corporation makes the database available on the Internet to anyone willing to pay its price-which, needless to say, is less than ProCD charges its commercial customers. Zeidenberg has purchased two additional SelectPhone (trademark) packages, each with an updated version of the database, and made the latest information available over the World Wide Web, for a price, through his corporation. ProCD filed this suit seeking an injunction against further dissemination that exceeds the rights specified in the licenses (identical in each of the three packages Zeidenberg purchased). The district court held the licenses ineffectual because their terms do not appear on the outside of the packages. The court added that the second and third licenses stand no different from the first, even though they are identical, because they *might* have been different, and a purchaser does not agree to-and cannot be bound by-terms that were secret at the time of purchase....

II

Following the district court, we treat the licenses as ordinary contracts accompanying the sale of products, and therefore as governed by the common law of contracts and the Uniform Commercial Code. Whether there are legal differences between "contracts" and "licenses" (which may matter under the copyright doctrine of first sale) is a subject for another day. See *Microsoft Corp. v. Harmony Computers & Electronics, Inc.,* 846 F.Supp. 208 (E.D.N.Y.1994). Zeidenberg does not argue that Silken Mountain Web Services is free of any restrictions that apply to Zeidenberg himself, because any effort to treat the two parties as distinct would put Silken Mountain behind the eight ball on ProCD's argument that copying the application program onto its hard disk violates the copyright laws. Zeidenberg does argue, and the district court held, that placing the package of software on the shelf is an "offer," which the customer "accepts" by paying the asking price and leaving the store with the goods. *Peeters v. State,* 154 Wis. 111, 142 N.W. 181 (1913). In Wisconsin, as elsewhere, a contract includes only the terms on which the parties have agreed. One cannot agree to hidden terms, the judge concluded. So far, so good-but one of the terms to which Zeidenberg agreed by purchasing the software is that the transaction was subject to a license. Zeidenberg's position therefore must be that the printed terms on the outside of a box are the parties' contract-except for printed terms that refer to or incorporate other terms. But why would Wisconsin fetter the parties' choice in this way? Vendors can put the entire terms of a contract on the outside of a box only by using microscopic type, removing other information that buyers might find more useful (such as what the software does, and on which computers it works), or both. The "Read Me" file included with most software, describing system requirements and potential incompatibilities, may be equivalent to ten pages of type; warranties and license restrictions take still more space. Notice on the outside, terms on the inside, and a right to return the software for a refund if the terms are unacceptable (a right that the license expressly extends), may be a means of doing business valuable to buyers and sellers alike. See E. Allan Farnsworth, 1 *Farnsworth on Contracts* § 4.26 (1990); *Restatement (2d) of Contracts* § 211 comment a (1981) ("Standardization of agreements serves many of the same functions as standardization of goods and services; both are essential to a system of mass production and distribution. Scarce and costly time and skill can be devoted to a class of transactions rather than the details of individual transactions."). Doubtless a state could forbid the use of standard contracts in the software business, but we do not think that Wisconsin has done so.

Transactions in which the exchange of money precedes the communication of detailed terms are common. Consider the purchase of insurance. The buyer goes to an agent, who explains the essentials (amount of coverage, number of years) and remits the premium to the home office, which sends back a policy. On the district judge's understanding, the terms of the policy are irrelevant because the insured paid before receiving them. Yet the device of payment, often with a "binder" (so that the insurance takes effect immediately even though the home office reserves the right to withdraw coverage later), in advance of the policy, serves buyers' interests by accelerating effectiveness and reducing transactions costs. Or consider the purchase of an airline ticket. The traveler calls the carrier or an agent, is quoted a price, reserves a seat, pays, and gets a ticket, in that order. The ticket contains elaborate terms, which the traveler can reject by canceling the reservation. To use the ticket is to accept the terms, even terms that in retrospect are disadvantageous. See *Carnival Cruise Lines, Inc. v. Shute*, 499 U.S. 585, 111 S.Ct. 1522, 113 L.Ed.2d 622 (1991); see also *Vimar Seguros y Reaseguros, S.A. v. M/V Sky Reefer*, 515 U.S. 528, 115 S.Ct. 2322, 132 L.Ed.2d 462 (1995) (bills of lading). Just so with a ticket to a concert. The back of the ticket states that the patron promises not to record the concert; to attend is to agree. A theater that detects a violation will confiscate the tape and escort the violator to the exit. One *could* arrange things so that every concertgoer signs this promise before forking over the money, but that cumbersome way of doing things not only would lengthen queues and raise prices but also would scotch the sale of tickets by phone or electronic data service.

Consumer goods work the same way. Someone who wants to buy a radio set visits a store, pays, and walks out with a box. Inside the box is a leaflet containing some terms, the most important of which usually is the warranty, read for the first time in the comfort of home. By Zeidenberg's lights, the warranty in the box is irrelevant; every consumer gets the standard warranty implied by the UCC in the event the contract is silent; yet so far as we are aware no state disregards warranties furnished with consumer products. Drugs come with a list of ingredients on the outside and an elaborate package insert on the inside. The package insert describes drug interactions, contraindications, and other vital information-but, if Zeidenberg is right, the purchaser need not read the package insert, because it is not part of the contract.

Next consider the software industry itself. Only a minority of sales take place over the counter, where there are boxes to peruse. A customer may place an order by phone in response to a line item in a catalog or a review in a magazine. Much software is ordered over the Internet by purchasers who have never seen a box. Increasingly software arrives by wire. There is no box; there is only a stream of electrons, a collection of information that includes data, an application program, instructions, many limitations ("MegaPixel 3.14159 cannot be used with BytePusher 2.718"), and the terms of sale. The user purchases a serial number, which activates the software's features. On Zeidenberg's arguments, these unboxed sales are unfettered by terms-so the seller has made a broad warranty and must pay consequential damages for any shortfalls in performance, two "promises" that if taken seriously would drive prices through the ceiling or return transactions to the horse-and-buggy age.

According to the district court, the UCC does not countenance the sequence of money now, terms later. (Wisconsin's version of the UCC does not differ from the Official Version in any material respect, so we use the regular numbering system. Wis. Stat. §402.201 corresponds to UCC §2-201, and other citations are easy to derive.) One of the court's reasons-that by proposing as part of the draft Article 2B a new UCC §2-2203 that would explicitly validate standard-form user licenses, the American Law Institute and the National Conference of Commissioners on Uniform Laws have conceded the invalidity of shrinkwrap licenses under current law, ... -depends on a faulty inference. To propose a change in a law's *text* is not necessarily to propose a change in the law's *effect*. New words may be designed to fortify the current rule with a more precise text that curtails uncertainty. To judge by the flux of law review articles discussing shrinkwrap licenses, uncertainty is much in need of reduction-although businesses seem to feel less uncertainty than do scholars, for only three cases (other than ours) touch on the subject, and none directly addresses it. See *Step-Saver Data Systems, Inc. v. Wyse Technology*, 939 F.2d 91 (3d Cir.1991); *Vault Corp. v. Quaid Software Ltd.*, 847 F.2d 255, 268-70 (5th Cir.1988); *Arizona Retail Systems, Inc. v. Software Link, Inc.*, 831 F.Supp. 759 (D.Ariz.1993). As their titles suggest, these are not consumer transactions. Step-Saver is a battle-of-the-forms case, in which the parties exchange incompatible forms and a court must decide which prevails. See *Northrop Corp. v. Litronic Industries*, 29 F.3d 1173 (7th Cir.1994) (Illinois law); Douglas G. Baird & Robert Weisberg, *Rules, Standards, and the Battle of the Forms: A Reassessment of* §2-207, 68 Va. L.Rev. 1217, 1227-31 (1982). Our case has only one form; UCC §2-207 is irrelevant. *Vault* holds that Louisiana's special shrinkwrap-license statute is preempted by federal law, a question to which we return. And *Arizona Retail Systems* did not reach the question, because the court found that the buyer knew the terms of the license before purchasing the software.

What then does the current version of the UCC have to say? We think that the place to start is §2-204(1): "A contract for sale of goods may be made in any manner sufficient to show agreement, including conduct by both parties which recognizes the existence of such a contract." A vendor, as master of the offer, may invite acceptance by conduct, and may propose limitations on the kind of conduct that constitutes acceptance. A buyer may accept by performing the acts the vendor proposes to treat as acceptance. And that is what happened. ProCD proposed a contract that a buyer would accept by *using* the software after having an opportunity to read the license at leisure. This Zeidenberg did. He had no choice, because the software splashed the license on the screen and would not let him proceed without indicating acceptance. So although the district judge was right to say that a contract can be, and often is, formed simply by paying the price and walking out of the store, the UCC permits contracts to be formed in other ways. ProCD proposed such a different way, and without protest Zeidenberg agreed. Ours is not a case in which a consumer opens a package to find an insert saying "you owe us an extra $10,000" and the seller files suit to collect. Any buyer finding such a demand can prevent formation of the contract by returning the package, as can any consumer who concludes that the terms of the license make the software worth less than the purchase price. Nothing in the UCC requires a seller to maximize the buyer's net gains.

Section 2-606, which defines "acceptance of goods", reinforces this understanding. A buyer accepts goods under §2-606(1)(b) when, after an opportunity to inspect, he fails to make an effective rejection under §2-602(1). ProCD extended an opportunity to reject if a buyer should find the license terms *1453 unsatisfactory; Zeidenberg inspected the package, tried out the software, learned of the license, and did not reject the goods. We refer to §2-606 only to show that the opportunity to return goods can be important; acceptance of an offer differs from acceptance of goods after delivery, see *Gillen v. Atalanta Systems, Inc.*, 997 F.2d 280, 284 n. 1 (7th Cir.1993); but the UCC consistently permits the parties to structure their relations so that the buyer has a chance to make a final decision after a detailed review.

Some portions of the UCC impose additional requirements on the way parties agree on terms. A disclaimer of the implied warranty of merchantability must be "conspicuous." UCC §2-316(2), incorporating UCC §1-201(10). Promises to make firm offers, or to negate oral modifications, must be "separately signed." UCC §§2-205, 2-209(2). These special provisos reinforce the impression that, so far as the UCC is concerned, other terms may be as inconspicuous as the forum-selection clause on the back of the cruise ship ticket in *Carnival Lines*. Zeidenberg has not located any Wisconsin case-for that matter, any case in any state-holding that under the UCC the ordinary terms found in shrinkwrap licenses require any special prominence, or otherwise are to be undercut rather than enforced. In the end, the terms of the license are conceptually identical to the contents of the package. Just as no court would dream of saying that SelectPhone (trademark) must contain 3,100 phone books rather than 3,000, or must have data no more than 30 days old, or must sell for $100 rather than $150-although any of these changes would be welcomed by the customer, if all other things were held constant-so, we believe, Wisconsin would not let the buyer pick and choose among terms. Terms of use are no less a part of "the product" than are the size of the database and the speed with which the software compiles listings. Competition among vendors, not judicial revision of a package's contents, is how consumers are protected in a market economy. *Digital Equipment Corp. v. Uniq Digital Technologies, Inc.*, 73 F.3d 756 (7th Cir.1996). ProCD has rivals, which may elect to compete by offering superior software, monthly updates, improved terms of use, lower price, or a better compromise among these elements. As we stressed above, adjusting terms in buyers' favor might help Matthew Zeidenberg today (he already has the software) but would lead to a response, such as a higher price, that might make consumers as a whole worse off....

REVERSED AND REMANDED.

Hill v. Gateway 2000

105 F3d 1147, 1150 (7th Cir 1997)

EASTERBROOK, Circuit Judge.

A customer picks up the phone, orders a computer, and gives a credit card number. Presently a box arrives, containing the computer and a list of terms, said to govern unless the customer returns the computer within 30 days. Are these terms effective as the parties' contract, or is the contract term-free because the order-taker did not read any terms over the phone and elicit the customer's assent?

One of the terms in the box containing a Gateway 2000 system was an arbitration clause. Rich and Enza Hill, the customers, kept the computer more than 30 days before complaining about its components and performance. They filed suit in federal court arguing, among other things, that the product's shortcomings make Gateway a racketeer (mail and wire fraud are said to be the predicate offenses), leading to treble damages under RICO for the Hills and a class of all other purchasers. Gateway asked the district court to enforce the arbitration clause; the judge refused, writing that "[t]he present record is insufficient to support a finding of a valid arbitration agreement between the parties or that the plaintiffs were given adequate notice of the arbitration clause." Gateway took an immediate appeal, as is its right ...

The Hills say that the arbitration clause did not stand out: they concede noticing the statement of terms but deny reading it closely enough to discover the agreement to arbitrate, and they ask us to conclude that they therefore may go to court. Yet an agreement to arbitrate must be enforced "save upon such grounds as exist at law or in equity for the revocation of any contract." 9 U.S.C. §2. *Doctor's Associates, Inc. v. Casarotto*, 517U.S. 681, 116 S.Ct. 1652, 134 L.Ed.2d 902 (1996), holds that this provision of the Federal Arbitration Act is inconsistent with any requirement that an arbitration clause be prominent. A contract need not be read to be effective; people who accept take the risk that the unread terms may in retrospect prove unwelcome. *Carr v. CIGNA Securities, Inc.*, 95 F.3d 544, 547 (7th Cir.1996); *Chicago Pacific Corp. v. Canada Life Assurance Co.*, 850 F.2d 334 (7th Cir.1988). Terms inside Gateway's box stand or fall together. If they constitute the parties' contract because the Hills had an opportunity to return the computer after reading them, then all must be enforced.

ProCD, Inc. v. Zeidenberg, 86 F.3d 1447 (7th Cir.1996), holds that terms inside a box of software bind consumers who use the software after an opportunity to read the terms and to reject them by returning the product. Likewise, *Carnival Cruise Lines, Inc. v. Shute*, 499 U.S. 585, 111 S.Ct. 1522, 113 L.Ed.2d 622 (1991), enforces a forum-selection clause that was included among three pages of terms attached to a cruise ship ticket. *ProCD* and *Carnival Cruise Lines* exemplify the many commercial transactions in which people pay for products with terms to follow; *ProCD* discusses others. 86 F.3d at 1451-52. The district court concluded in *ProCD* that the contract is formed when the consumer pays for the software; as a result, the court held, only terms known to the consumer at that moment are part of the contract, and provisos inside the box do not count. Although this is one way a contract could be formed, it is not the only way: "A vendor, as master of the offer, may invite acceptance by conduct, and may propose limitations on the kind of conduct that constitutes acceptance. A buyer may accept by performing the acts the vendor proposes to treat as acceptance." *Id.* at 1452. Gateway shipped computers with the same sort of accept-or-return offer ProCD made to users of its software. *ProCD* relied on the Uniform Commercial Code rather than any peculiarities of Wisconsin law; both Illinois and South Dakota, the two states whose law might govern relations between Gateway and the Hills, have adopted the UCC; neither side has pointed us to any atypical doctrines in those states that might be pertinent; *ProCD* therefore applies to this dispute.

Plaintiffs ask us to limit *ProCD* to software, but where's the sense in that? *ProCD* is about the law of contract, not the law of software. Payment preceding the revelation of full terms is common for air transportation, insurance, and many other endeavors. Practical considerations support allowing vendors to enclose the full legal terms with their products. Cashiers cannot be expected to read legal documents to customers before ringing up sales. If the staff at the other end of the phone for direct-sales operations such as Gateway's had to read the four-page statement of terms before taking the buyer's credit card number, the droning voice would anesthetize rather than enlighten many potential buyers. Others would hang up in a rage over the waste of their time. And oral recitation would not avoid customers' assertions (whether true or feigned) that the clerk did not read term X to them, or that they did not remember or understand it. Writing provides benefits for both sides of commercial transactions. Customers as a group are better off when vendors skip costly and ineffectual steps such as telephonic recitation, and use instead a simple approve-or-return device. Competent adults are bound by such documents, read or unread. For what little it is worth, we add that the box from Gateway was crammed with software. The computer came with an operating system, without which it was useful only as a boat anchor. See *Digital Equipment Corp. v. Uniq Digital Technologies, Inc.*, 73 F.3d 756, 761 (7th Cir.1996). Gateway also included many application programs. So the Hills' effort to limit *ProCD* to software would not avail them factually, even if it were sound legally-which it is not.

For their second sally, the Hills contend that ProCD should be limited to executory contracts (to licenses in particular), and therefore does not apply because both parties' performance of this contract was complete when the box arrived at their home. This is legally and factually wrong: legally because the question at hand concerns the *formation* of the contract rather than its *performance*, and factually because both contracts were incompletely performed. *ProCD* did not depend on the fact that the seller characterized the transaction as a license rather than as a contract; we treated it as a contract for the sale of goods and reserved the question whether for other purposes a "license" characterization might be preferable.... All debates about characterization to one side, the transaction in *ProCD* was no more executory than the one here: Zeidenberg paid for the software and walked out of the store with a box under his arm, so if arrival of the box with the product ends the time for revelation of contractual terms, then the time ended in *ProCD* before Zeidenberg opened the box. But of course ProCD had not completed performance with delivery of the box, and neither had Gateway. One element of the transaction was the warranty, which obliges sellers to fix defects in their products. The Hills have invoked Gateway's warranty and are not satisfied with its response, so they are not well positioned to say that Gateway's obligations were fulfilled when the motor carrier unloaded the box. What is more, both ProCD and Gateway promised to help customers to use their products. Long-term service and information obligations are common in the computer business, on both hardware and software sides. Gateway offers "lifetime service" and has a round-the-clock telephone hotline to fulfil this promise. Some vendors spend more money helping customers use their products than on developing and manufacturing them. The document in Gateway's box includes promises of future performance that some consumers value highly; these promises bind Gateway just as the arbitration clause binds the Hills.

Next the Hills insist that *ProCD* is irrelevant because Zeidenberg was a "merchant" and they are not. Section 2-207(2) of the UCC, the infamous battle-of-the-forms section, states that "additional terms [following acceptance of an offer] are to be construed as proposals for addition to a contract. Between merchants such terms become part of the contract unless...." Plaintiffs tell us that *ProCD* came out as it did only because Zeidenberg was a "merchant" and the terms inside ProCD's box were not excluded by the "unless" clause. This argument pays scant attention to the opinion in *ProCD*, which concluded that, when there is only one form, "sec. 2-207 is irrelevant." 86 F.3d at 1452. The question in *ProCD* was not whether terms were added to a contract after its formation, but how and when the contract was formed-in particular, whether a vendor may propose that a contract of sale be formed, not in the store (or over the phone) with the payment of money or a general "send me the product," but after the customer has had a chance to inspect both the item and the terms. *ProCD* answers "yes," for merchants and consumers alike. Yet again, for what little it is worth we observe that the Hills misunderstand the setting of *ProCD*. A "merchant" under the UCC "means a person who deals in goods of the kind or otherwise by his occupation holds himself out as having knowledge or skill peculiar to the practices or goods involved in the transaction", §2-104(1). Zeidenberg bought the product at a retail store, an uncommon place for merchants to acquire inventory. His corporation put ProCD's database on the Internet for anyone to browse, which led to the litigation but did not make Zeidenberg a software merchant.

At oral argument the Hills propounded still another distinction: the box containing ProCD's software displayed a notice that additional terms were within, while the box containing Gateway's computer did not. The difference is functional, not legal. Consumers browsing the aisles of a store can look at the box, and if they are unwilling to deal with the prospect of additional terms can leave the box alone, avoiding the transactions costs of returning the package after reviewing its contents. Gateway's box, by contrast, is just a shipping carton; it is not on display anywhere. Its function is to protect the product during transit, and the information on its sides is for the use of handlers rather than would-be purchasers.

Perhaps the Hills would have had a better argument if they were first alerted to the bundling of hardware and legal-ware after opening the box and wanted to return the computer in order to avoid disagreeable terms, but were dissuaded by the expense of shipping. What the remedy would be in such a case-could it exceed the shipping charges?- is an interesting question, but one that need not detain us because the Hills knew before they ordered the computer that the carton would include *some* important terms, and they did not seek to discover these in advance. Gateway's ads state that their products come with limited warranties and lifetime support. How limited was the warranty—30 days, with service contingent on shipping the computer back, or five years, with free onsite service? What sort of support was offered? Shoppers have three principal ways to discover these things. First, they can ask the vendor to send a copy before deciding whether to buy. The Magnuson-Moss Warranty Act requires firms to distribute their warranty terms on request, 15 U.S.C. § 2302(b)(1)(A); the Hills do not contend that Gateway would have refused to enclose the remaining terms too. Concealment would be bad for business, scaring some customers away and leading to excess returns from others. Second, shoppers can consult public sources (computer magazines, the Web sites of vendors) that may contain this information. Third, they may inspect the documents after the product's delivery. Like Zeidenberg, the Hills took the third option. By keeping the computer beyond 30 days, the Hills accepted Gateway's offer, including the arbitration clause.

The decision of the district court is vacated, and this case is remanded with instructions to compel the Hills to submit their dispute to arbitration.

Exercise 3-2: Step-Saver Data Systems, Inc. v. Wyse Technology and Klocek v. Gateway

Not all courts agree with Judge Easterbrook's approach. For a contrasting approach, read the next two cases, and consider the following questions:

1. At what point in time did the court conclude a contract was formed?

2. Does that conclusion follow "traditional" contract formation analysis, or is it different?

3. If it is different, how does the court justify and explain this difference?

4. Are you persuaded?

5. How does the Court analyze section 2-207?

6. How did you think Judge Easterbrook would have decided this case?

Step Saver Data Systems Inc. v. Wyse Technology
939 F.2d 91 (3d Cir. 1991)

WISDOM, Circuit Judge:

The "Limited Use License Agreement" printed on a package containing a copy of a computer program raises the central issue in this appeal. The trial judge held that the terms of the Limited Use License Agreement governed the purchase of the package, and, therefore, granted the software producer, The Software Link, Inc. ("TSL"), a directed verdict on claims of breach of warranty brought by a disgruntled purchaser, Step-Saver Data Systems, Inc. We disagree with the district court's determination of the legal effect of the license, and reverse and remand the warranty claims for further consideration.

Step-Saver raises several other issues, but we do not find these issues warrant reversal. We, therefore, affirm in all other respects.

I. FACTUAL AND PROCEDURAL BACKGROUND

The growth in the variety of computer hardware and software has created a strong market for these products. It has also created a difficult choice for consumers, as they must somehow decide which of the many available products will best suit their needs. To assist consumers in this decision process, some companies will evaluate the needs of particular groups of potential computer users, compare those needs with the available technology, and develop a package of hardware and software to satisfy those needs. Beginning in 1981, Step-Saver performed this function as a value added retailer for International Business Machine (IBM) products. It would combine hardware and software to satisfy the word processing, data management, and communications needs for offices of physicians and lawyers. It originally marketed single computer systems, based primarily on the IBM personal computer.

As a result of advances in micro-computer technology, Step-Saver developed and marketed a multi-user system. With a multi-user system, only one computer is required. Terminals are attached, by cable, to the main computer. From these terminals, a user can access the programs available on the main computer....

After evaluating the available technology, Step-Saver selected a program by TSL, entitled Multilink Advanced, as the operating system for the multi-user system. Step-Saver selected WY-60 terminals manufactured by Wyse, and used an IBM AT as the main computer. For applications software, Step-Saver included in the package several off-the-shelf programs, designed to run under Microsoft's Disk Operating System ("MS-DOS") ... as well as several programs written by Step-Saver. Step-Saver began marketing the system in November of 1986, and sold one hundred forty-two systems mostly to law and medical offices before terminating sales of the system in March of 1987. Almost immediately upon installation of the system, Step-Saver began to receive complaints from some of its customers....

Step-Saver, in addition to conducting its own investigation of the problems, referred these complaints to Wyse and TSL, and requested technical assistance in resolving the problems. After several preliminary attempts to address the problems, the three companies were unable to reach a satisfactory solution, and disputes developed among the three concerning responsibility for the problems. As a result, the problems were never solved. At least twelve of Step-Saver's customers filed suit against Step-Saver because of the problems with the multi-user system.

Once it became apparent that the three companies would not be able to resolve their dispute amicably, Step-Saver filed suit for declaratory judgment, seeking indemnity from either Wyse or TSL, or both, for any costs incurred by Step-Saver in defending and resolving the customers' law suits. The district court dismissed this complaint, finding that the issue was not ripe for judicial resolution. We affirmed the dismissal on appeal.... Step-Saver then filed a second complaint alleging breach of warranties by both TSL and Wyse and intentional misrepresentations by TSL.... The district court's actions during the resolution of this second complaint provide the foundation for this appeal.

On the first day of trial, the district court specifically agreed with the basic contention of TSL that the form language printed on each package containing the Multilink Advanced program ("the box-top license") was the complete and exclusive agreement between Step-Saver and TSL under § 2-202 of the Uniform Commercial Code (UCC). [All three parties agree that the terminals and the program are "goods" within the meaning of UCC § 2-102 & § 2-105....) Based on § 2-316 of the UCC, the district court held that the box-top license disclaimed all express and implied warranties otherwise made by TSL. The court therefore granted TSL's motion in limine to exclude all evidence of the earlier oral and written express warranties allegedly made by TSL. After Step-Saver presented its case, the district court granted a directed verdict in favor of TSL on the intentional misrepresentation claim, holding the evidence insufficient as a matter of law to establish two of the five elements of a prima facie case: (1) fraudulent intent on the part of TSL in making the representations; and (2) reasonable reliance by Step-Saver. The trial judge requested briefing on several issues related to Step-Saver's remaining express warranty claim against TSL. While TSL and Step-Saver prepared briefs on these issues, the trial court permitted Wyse to proceed with its defense. On the third day of Wyse's defense, the trial judge, after considering the additional briefing by Step-Saver and TSL, directed a verdict in favor of TSL on Step-Saver's remaining warranty claims, and dismissed TSL from the case.

The trial proceeded on Step-Saver's breach of warranties claims against Wyse. At the conclusion of Wyse's evidence, the district judge denied Step-Saver's request for rebuttal testimony on the issue of the ordinary uses of the WY-60 terminal. The district court instructed the jury on the issues of express warranty and implied warranty of fitness for a particular purpose. Over Step-Saver's objection, the district court found insufficient evidence to support a finding that Wyse had breached its implied warranty of merchantability, and refused to instruct the jury on such warranty. The jury returned a verdict in favor of Wyse on the two warranty issues submitted.

Step-Saver appeals on four points. (1) Step-Saver and TSL did not intend the box-top license to be a complete and final expression of the terms of their agreement. (2) There was sufficient evidence to support each element of Step-Saver's contention that TSL was guilty of intentional misrepresentation. (3) There was sufficient evidence to submit Step-Saver's implied warranty of merchantability claim against Wyse to the jury. (4) The trial court abused its discretion by excluding from the evidence a letter addressed to Step-Saver from Wyse, and by refusing to permit Step-Saver to introduce rebuttal testimony on the ordinary uses of the WY-60 terminal.

II. THE EFFECT OF THE BOX-TOP LICENSE

The relationship between Step-Saver and TSL began in the fall of 1984 when Step-Saver asked TSL for information on an early version of the Multilink program. TSL provided Step-Saver with a copy of the early program, known simply as Multilink, without charge to permit Step-Saver to test the program to see what it could accomplish. Step-Saver performed some tests with the early program, but did not market a system based on it.

In the summer of 1985, Step-Saver noticed some advertisements in Byte magazine for a more powerful version of the Multilink program, known as Multilink Advanced. Step-Saver requested information from TSL concerning this new version of the program, and allegedly was assured by sales representatives that the new version was compatible with ninety percent of the programs available "off-the-shelf" for computers using MS-DOS. The sales representatives allegedly made a number of additional specific representations of fact concerning the capabilities of the Multilink Advanced program.

Based on these representations, Step-Saver obtained several copies of the Multilink Advanced program in the spring of 1986, and conducted tests with the program. After these tests, Step-Saver decided to market a multi-user system which used the Multilink Advanced program. From August of 1986 through March of 1987, Step-Saver purchased and resold 142 copies of the Multilink Advanced program. Step-Saver would typically purchase copies of the program in the following manner. First, Step-Saver would telephone TSL and place an order. (Step-Saver would typically order twenty copies of the program at a time.) TSL would accept the order and promise, while on the telephone, to ship the goods promptly. After the telephone order, Step-Saver would send a purchase order, detailing the items to be purchased, their price, and shipping and payment terms. TSL would ship the order promptly, along with an invoice. The invoice would contain terms essentially identical with those on Step-Saver's purchase order: price, quantity, and shipping and payment terms. No reference was made during the telephone calls, or on either the purchase orders or the invoices with regard to a disclaimer of any warranties.

Printed on the package of each copy of the program, however, would be a copy of the box-top license. The box-top license contains five terms relevant to this action:

(1) The box-top license provides that the customer has not purchased the software itself, but has merely obtained a personal, non-transferable license to use the program.

(2) The box-top license, in detail and at some length, disclaims all express and implied warranties except for a warranty that the disks contained in the box are free from defects.

(3) The box-top license provides that the sole remedy available to a purchaser of the program is to return a defective disk for replacement; the license excludes any liability for damages, direct or consequential, caused by the use of the program.

(4) The box-top license contains an integration clause, which provides that the box-top license is the final and complete expression of the terms of the parties's *(sic)* agreement.

(5) The box-top license states: "Opening this package indicates your acceptance of these terms and conditions. If you do not agree with them, you should promptly return the package unopened to the person from whom you purchased it within fifteen days from date of purchase and your money will be refunded to you by that person."

The district court, without much discussion, held, as a matter of law, that the box-top license was the final and complete expression of the terms of the parties's agreement. Because the district court decided the questions of contract formation and interpretation as issues of law, we review the district court's resolution of these questions *de novo*....

Step Saver contends that the contract for each copy of the program was formed when TSL agreed, on the telephone, to ship the copy at the agreed price.... The box-top license, argues Step-Saver, was a material alteration to the parties's contract which did not become a part of the contract under UCC § 2-207.... Alternatively, Step-Saver argues that the undisputed evidence establishes that the parties did not intend the box-top license as a final and complete expression of the terms of their agreement, and, therefore, the parol evidence rule of UCC § 2-202 would not apply. [Two other issues were raised by Step-Saver. First, Step-Saver argued that the box-top disclaimer is either unconscionable or not in good faith. Second, Step-Saver argued that the warranty disclaimer was inconsistent with the express warranties made by TSL in the product specifications. Step-Saver argues that interpreting the form language of the license agreement to override the specific warranties contained in the product specification is unreasonable, citing *Consolidated*

Data Terminals v. Applied Digital Data Sys., 708 F.2d 385 (9th Cir.1983). *See also Northern States Power Co. v. ITT Meyer Indus.*, 777 F.2d 405 (8th Cir.1985). Because of our holding that the terms of the box-top license were not incorporated into the contract, we do not address these issues.]

TSL argues that the contract between TSL and Step-Saver did not come into existence until Step-Saver received the program, saw the terms of the license, and opened the program packaging. TSL contends that too many material terms were omitted from the telephone discussion for that discussion to establish a contract for the software. Second, TSL contends that its acceptance of Step-Saver's telephone offer was conditioned on Step-Saver's acceptance of the terms of the box-top license. Therefore, TSL argues, it did not accept Step-Saver's telephone offer, but made a counteroffer represented by the terms of the box-top license, which was accepted when Step-Saver opened each package. Third, TSL argues that, however the contract was formed, Step-Saver was aware of the warranty disclaimer, and that Step-Saver, by continuing to order and accept the product with knowledge of the disclaimer, assented to the disclaimer.

In analyzing these competing arguments, we first consider whether the license should be treated as an integrated writing under UCC § 2-202, as a proposed modification under UCC § 2-209, or as a written confirmation under UCC § 2-207. Finding that UCC § 2-207 best governs our resolution of the effect of the box-top license, we then consider whether, under UCC § 2-207, the terms of the box-top license were incorporated into the parties's agreement.

A. Does UCC § 2-207 Govern the Analysis?

As a basic principle, we agree with Step-Saver that UCC § 2-207 governs our analysis. We see no need to parse the parties's various actions to decide exactly when the parties formed a contract. TSL has shipped the product, and Step-Saver has accepted and paid for each copy of the program. The parties's performance demonstrates the existence of a contract. The dispute is, therefore, not over the existence of a contract, but the nature of its terms.... When the parties's conduct establishes a contract, but the parties have failed to adopt expressly a particular writing as the terms of their agreement, and the writings exchanged by the parties do not agree, UCC § 2-207 determines the terms of the contract.

As stated by the official comment to § 2-207:

1. This section is intended to deal with two typical situations. The one is the written confirmation, where an agreement has been reached either orally or by informal correspondence between the parties and is followed by one or more of the parties sending formal memoranda embodying the terms so far as agreed upon and adding terms not discussed....

2. Under this Article a proposed deal which in commercial understanding has in fact been closed is recognized as a contract. Therefore, any additional matter contained in the confirmation or in the acceptance falls within subsection (2) and must be regarded as a proposal for an added term unless the acceptance is made conditional on the acceptance of the additional or different terms.

Although UCC § 2-202 permits the parties to reduce an oral agreement to writing, and UCC § 2-209 permits the parties to modify an existing contract without additional consideration, a writing will be a final expression of, or a binding modification to, an earlier agreement only if the parties so intend.... It is undisputed that Step-Saver never expressly agreed to the terms of the box-top license, either as a final expression of, or a modification to, the parties's agreement. In fact, Barry Greebel, the President of Step-Saver, testified without dispute that he objected to the terms of the box-top license as applied to Step-Saver. In the absence of evidence demonstrating an express intent to adopt a writing as a final expression of, or a modification to, an earlier agreement, we find UCC § 2-207 to provide the appropriate legal rules for determining whether such an intent can be inferred from continuing with the contract after receiving a writing containing additional or different terms....

To understand why the terms of the license should be considered under § 2-207 in this case, we review briefly the reasons behind § 2-207. Under the common law of sales, and to some extent still for contracts outside the UCC ... an acceptance that varied any term of the offer operated as a rejection of the offer, and simultaneously made a counteroffer.... This common law formality was known as the mirror image rule, because the terms of the acceptance had to mirror the terms of the offer to be effective.... If the offeror proceeded with the contract despite the differing terms of the supposed acceptance, he would, by his performance, constructively accept the terms of the "counteroffer", and be bound by its terms. As a result of these rules, the terms of the party who sent the last form, typically the seller, would become the terms of the parties's contract. This result was known as the "last shot rule".

The UCC, in § 2-207, rejected this approach. Instead, it recognized that, while a party may desire the terms detailed in its form if a dispute, in fact, arises, most parties do not expect a dispute to arise when they first enter into a contract. As a result, most parties will proceed with the transaction even if they know that the terms of their form would not be enforced ... The insight behind the rejection of the last shot rule is that it would be unfair to bind the buyer of goods to the standard terms of the seller, when neither party cared sufficiently to establish expressly the terms of their agreement, simply because the seller sent the last form. Thus, UCC § 2-207 establishes a legal rule that proceeding with a contract after receiving a writing that purports to define the terms of the parties's contract is not sufficient to establish the party's consent to the terms of the writing to the extent that the terms of the writing either add to, or differ from, the terms detailed in the parties's earlier writings or discussions.... In the absence of a party's express assent to the additional or different terms of the writing, section 2-207 provides a default rule that the parties intended, as the terms of their agreement, those terms to which both parties have agreed, ... along with any terms implied by the provisions of the UCC.

The reasons that led to the rejection of the last shot rule, and the adoption of section 2-207, apply fully in this case. TSL never mentioned during the parties's negotiations leading to the purchase of the programs, nor did it, at any time, obtain Step-Saver's express assent to, the terms of the box-top license. Instead, TSL contented itself with attaching the terms to the packaging of the software, even though those terms differed substantially from those previously discussed by the parties. Thus, the box-top license, in this case, is best seen as one more form in a battle of forms, and the question of whether Step-Saver has agreed to be bound by the terms of the box-top license is best resolved by applying the legal principles detailed in section 2-207.

B. Application of § 2-207

TSL advances several reasons why the terms of the box-top license should be incorporated into the parties's agreement under a § 2-207 analysis. First, TSL argues that the parties's contract was not formed until Step-Saver received the package, saw the terms of the box-top license, and opened the package, thereby consenting to the terms of the license. TSL argues that a contract defined without reference to the specific terms provided by the box-top license would necessarily fail for indefiniteness. Second, TSL argues that the box-top license was a conditional acceptance and counter-offer under §2-207(1). Third, TSL argues that Step-Saver, by continuing to order and use the product with notice of the terms of the box-top license, consented to the terms of the box-top license.

1. Was the contract sufficiently definite?

TSL argues that the parties intended to license the copies of the program, and that several critical terms could only be determined by referring to the box-top license. Pressing the point, TSL argues that it is impossible to tell, without referring to the box-top license, whether the parties intended a sale of a copy of the program or a license to use a copy. TSL cites *Bethlehem Steel Corp. v. Litton Industries* in support of its position that any contract defined without reference to the terms of the box-top license would fail for indefiniteness....

From the evidence, it appears that the following terms, at the least, were discussed and agreed to, apart from the box-top license: (1) the specific goods involved; (2) the quantity; and (3) the price. TSL argues that the following terms were only defined in the box-top license: (1) the nature of the transaction, sale or license; and (2) the warranties, if any, available. TSL argues that these two terms are essential to creating a sufficiently definite contract. We disagree.

Section 2-204(3) of the UCC provides:

> Even though one or more terms are left open a contract for sale does not fail for indefiniteness if the parties have intended to make a contract and there is a reasonably certain basis for giving an appropriate remedy.

Unlike the terms omitted by the parties in *Bethlehem Steel Corp.*, the two terms cited by TSL are not "gaping holes in a multi-million dollar contract that no one but the parties themselves could fill." ... First, the rights of the respective parties under the federal copyright law if the transaction is characterized as a sale of a copy of the program are nearly identical to the parties's respective rights under the terms of the box-top license.... Second, the UCC provides for express and implied warranties if the seller fails to disclaim expressly those warranties.... Thus, even though warranties are an important term left blank by the parties, the default rules of the UCC fill in that blank.

We hold that contract was sufficiently definite without the terms provided by the box-top license.

2. The box-top license as a counter-offer?

TSL advances two reasons why its box-top license should be considered a conditional acceptance under UCC §2-207(1). First, TSL argues that the express language of the box-top license, including the integration clause and the phrase "opening this product indicates your acceptance of these terms", made TSL's acceptance "expressly conditional on assent to the additional or different terms". Second, TSL argues that the box-top license, by permitting return of the product within fifteen days if the purchaser does not agree to the terms stated in the license (the "refund offer"), establishes that TSL's acceptance was conditioned on Step-Saver's assent to the terms of the box-top license, citing *Monsanto Agricultural Products Co. v. Edenfield* While we are not certain that a conditional acceptance analysis applies when a contract is established by performance, we assume that it does and consider TSL's arguments.

To determine whether a writing constitutes a conditional acceptance, courts have established three tests. Because neither Georgia nor Pennsylvania has expressly adopted a test to determine when a written confirmation constitutes a conditional acceptance, we consider these three tests to determine which test the state courts would most likely apply....

Under the first test, an offeree's response is a conditional acceptance to the extent it states a term "materially altering the contractual obligations solely to the disadvantage of the offeror".[*Daitom, Inc.*, 741 F.2d at 1576. *See, e.g., Roto-Lith Ltd. v. F.P. Bartlett & Co.*, 297 F.2d 497 (1st Cir.1962)] Pennsylvania, at least, has implicitly rejected this test. In *Herzog Oil Field Service, Inc.*, [391 Pa.Super. 133, 570 A.2d 549 (Pa.Super.Ct.1990).] a Pennsylvania Superior Court analyzed a term in a written confirmation under UCC § 2-207(2), rather than as a conditional acceptance even though the term materially altered the terms of the agreement to the sole disadvantage of the offeror. [The seller/offeree sent a written confirmation that contained a term that provided for attorney's fees of 25 percent of the balance due if the account was turned over for collection. 570 A.2d at 550.]

Furthermore, we note that adopting this test would conflict with the express provision of UCC § 2-207(2)(b). Under § 2-207(2)(b), additional terms in a written confirmation that "materially alter [the contract]" are construed "as proposals for addition to the contract", not as conditional acceptances.

A second approach considers an acceptance conditional when certain key words or phrases are used, such as a written confirmation stating that the terms of the confirmation are "the only ones upon which we will accept orders". [*Ralph Shrader, Inc. v. Diamond Int'l Corp.*, 833 F.2d 1210, 1214 (6th Cir.1987); *see McJunkin Corp.*, 888 F.2d at 488. Note that even though an acceptance contains the key phrase, and is conditional, these courts typically avoid finding a contract on the terms of the counteroffer by requiring the offeree/counterofferor to establish that the offeror assented to the terms of the counteroffer. Generally, acceptance of the goods, alone, is not sufficient to establish assent by the offeror to the terms of the counteroffer. *See, e.g., Ralph Shrader, Inc.*, 833 F.2d at 1215; *Diamond Fruit Growers, Inc.*, 794 F.2d at 1443-44; *Coastal Indus. v. Automatic Steam Prods. Corp.*, 654 F.2d 375, 379 (5th Cir. Unit B Aug.1981). If the sole evidence of assent to the terms of the counteroffer is from the conduct of the parties in proceeding with the transaction, then the courts generally define the terms of the parties's agreement under § 2-207(3). *See, e.g., Diamond Fruit Growers, Inc.*, 794 F.2d at 1444.]

The third approach requires the offeree to demonstrate an unwillingness to proceed with the transaction unless the additional or different terms are included in the contract.{ *Ralph Shrader, Inc. v. Diamond Int'l Corp.*, 833 F.2d 1210, 1214 (6th Cir.1987); *see McJunkin Corp.*, 888 F.2d at 488. Note that even though an acceptance contains the key phrase, and is conditional, these courts typically avoid finding a contract on the terms of the counteroffer by requiring the offeree/counterofferor to establish that the offeror assented to the terms of the counteroffer. Generally, acceptance of the goods, alone, is not sufficient to establish assent by the offeror to the terms of the counteroffer. *See, e.g., Ralph Shrader, Inc.*, 833 F.2d at 1215; *Diamond Fruit Growers, Inc.*, 794 F.2d at 1443-44; *Coastal Indus. v. Automatic Steam Prods. Corp.*, 654 F.2d 375, 379 (5th Cir. Unit B Aug.1981). If the sole evidence of assent to the terms of the counteroffer is from the conduct of the parties in proceeding with the transaction, then the courts generally define the terms of the parties's agreement under § 2-207(3). *See, e.g., Diamond Fruit Growers, Inc.*, 794 F.2d at 1444.]

Although we are not certain that these last two approaches would generate differing answers, [Under the second approach, the box-top license might be considered a conditional acceptance, but Step-Saver, by accepting the product, would not be automatically bound to the terms of the box-top license. *See Diamond Fruit Growers, Inc.*, 794 F.2d at 1444. Instead, courts have applied UCC § 2-207(3) to determine the terms of the parties's agreement. The terms of the agreement would be those "on which the writings of the parties agree, together with any supplementary terms incorporated under any other provisions of this Act." UCC § 2-207(3). Because the writings of the parties did not agree on the warranty disclaimer and limitation of remedies terms, the box-top license version of those terms would not be included in the parties's contract; rather, the default provisions of the UCC would govern.] we adopt the third approach for our analysis because it best reflects the understanding of commercial transactions developed in the UCC. Section 2-207 attempts to distinguish between: (1) those standard terms in a form confirmation, which the party would like a court to incorporate into the contract in the event of a dispute; and (2) the actual terms the parties understand to govern their agreement. The third test properly places the burden on the party asking a court to enforce its form to demonstrate that a particular term is a part of the parties's commercial bargain....

Using this test, it is apparent that the integration clause and the "consent by opening" language is not sufficient to render TSL's acceptance conditional. As other courts have recognized ... this type of language provides no real indication that the party is willing to forego the transaction if the additional language is not included in the contract.

The second provision provides a more substantial indication that TSL was willing to forego the contract if the terms of the box-top license were not accepted by Step-Saver. On its face, the box-top license states that TSL will refund the purchase price if the purchaser does not agree to the terms of the license.... Even with such a refund term, however, the offeree/counterofferor may be relying on the purchaser's investment in time and energy in reaching this point in the transaction to prevent the purchaser from returning the item. Because a purchaser has made a decision to buy a particular product and has actually obtained the product, the purchaser may use it despite the refund offer, regardless of the additional terms specified after the contract formed. But we need not decide whether such a refund offer could ever amount to a conditional acceptance; the undisputed evidence in this case demonstrates that the terms of the license were not sufficiently important that TSL would forego its sales to Step-Saver if TSL could not obtain Step-Saver's consent to those terms.

As discussed, Mr. Greebel testified that TSL assured him that the box-top license did not apply to Step-Saver, as Step-Saver was not the end user of the Multilink Advanced program. Supporting this testimony, TSL on two occasions asked Step-Saver to sign agreements that would put in formal terms the relationship between Step-Saver and TSL. Both proposed agreements contained warranty disclaimer and limitation of remedy terms similar to those contained in the box-top license. Step-Saver refused to sign the agreements; nevertheless, TSL continued to sell copies of Multilink Advanced to Step-Saver.

Additionally, TSL asks us to infer, based on the refund offer, that it was willing to forego its sales to Step-Saver unless Step-Saver agreed to the terms of the box-top license. Such an inference is inconsistent with the fact that both parties agree that the terms of the box-top license *did not represent the parties's agreement* with respect to Step-Saver's right to transfer the copies of the Multilink Advanced program. Although the box-top license prohibits the transfer, by Step-Saver, of its copies of the program, both parties agree that Step-Saver was entitled to transfer its copies to the purchasers of the Step-Saver multi-user system. Thus, TSL was willing to proceed with the transaction despite the fact that one of the terms of the box-top license was not included in the contract between TSL and Step-Saver. We see no basis in the terms of the box-top license for inferring that a reasonable offeror would understand from the refund offer that certain terms of the box-top license, such as the warranty disclaimers, were essential to TSL, while others such as the non-transferability provision were not.

Based on these facts, we conclude that TSL did not clearly express its unwillingness to proceed with the transactions unless its additional terms were incorporated into the parties's agreement. The box-top license did not, therefore, constitute a conditional acceptance under UCC § 2-207(1).

3. Did the parties's course of dealing establish that the parties had excluded any express or implied warranties associated with the software program?

TSL argues that because Step-Saver placed its orders for copies of the Multilink Advanced program with notice of the terms of the box-top license, Step-Saver is bound by the terms of the box-top license. Essentially, TSL is arguing that, even if the terms of the box-top license would not become part of the contract if the case involved only a single transaction, the repeated expression of those terms by TSL eventually incorporates them within the contract.

Ordinarily, a "course of dealing" or "course of performance" analysis focuses on the actions of the parties with respect to a particular issue.... If, for example, a supplier of asphaltic paving material on two occasions gives a paving contractor price protection, a jury may infer that the parties have incorporated such a term in their agreement by their course of performance.... Because this is the parties's first serious dispute, the parties have not previously taken any action with respect to the matters addressed by the warranty disclaimer and limitation of liability terms of the box-top license. Nevertheless, TSL seeks to extend the course of dealing analysis to this case where the only action has been the repeated sending of a particular form by TSL. While one court has concluded that terms repeated in a number of written confirmations eventually become part of the contract even though neither party ever takes any action with respect to the issue addressed by those terms, most courts have rejected such reasoning.... .Yet, the facts and result in *Barliant* do not support the reasoning in *Schulze*. In *Barliant*, the buyer had paid some twenty-four invoices, which included charges for freight and warehousing even though the agreement specified charges were F.O.B. The court found that the buyer had paid the invoices with knowledge of the additional charge for freight and warehousing. Because of this *conduct with respect to the term in question*, the buyer waived any right to complain that the charges should not have been included.... In contrast, in *Schulze*, neither party had taken any action with respect to the arbitration provision. Because no disputes had arisen, there was no conduct by either party indicating how disputes were to be resolved. Nevertheless, the *Schulze* Court held that, because the provision had been repeated in nine previous invoices, it became part of the parties's bargain.... We note that the Seventh Circuit refused to follow *Schulze* in a more recent case raising the same issue....

For two reasons, we hold that the repeated sending of a writing which contains certain standard terms, without any action with respect to the issues addressed by those terms, cannot constitute a course of dealing which would incorporate a term of the writing otherwise excluded under § 2-207. First, the repeated exchange of forms by the parties only tells Step-Saver that TSL *desires* certain terms. Given TSL's failure to obtain Step-Saver's express assent to these terms before it will ship the program, Step-Saver can reasonably believe that, while TSL desires certain terms, it has agreed to do business on other terms-those terms expressly agreed upon by the parties. Thus, even though Step-Saver would not be surprised ... to learn that TSL desires the terms of the box-top license, Step-Saver might well be surprised to learn that the terms of the box-top license have been incorporated into the parties's agreement.

Second, the seller in these multiple transaction cases will typically have the opportunity to negotiate the precise terms of the parties's agreement, as TSL sought to do in this case.

The seller's unwillingness or inability to obtain a negotiated agreement reflecting its terms strongly suggests that, while the seller would like a court to incorporate its terms if a dispute were to arise, those terms are not a part of the parties's commercial bargain. For these reasons, we are not convinced that TSL's unilateral act of repeatedly sending copies of the box-top license with its product can establish a course of dealing between TSL and Step-Saver that resulted in the adoption of the terms of the box-top license.

With regard to more specific evidence as to the parties's course of dealing or performance, it appears that the parties have not incorporated the warranty disclaimer into their agreement. First, there is the evidence that TSL tried to obtain Step-Saver's express consent to the disclaimer and limitation of damages provision of the box-top license. Step-Saver refused to sign the proposed agreements. Second, when first notified of the problems with the program, TSL spent considerable time and energy attempting to solve the problems identified by Step-Saver.

Course of conduct is ordinarily a factual issue. But we hold that the actions of TSL in repeatedly sending a writing, whose terms would otherwise be excluded under UCC § 2-207, cannot establish a course of conduct between TSL and Step-Saver that adopted the terms of the writing.

4. Public policy concerns.

TSL has raised a number of public policy arguments focusing on the effect on the software industry of an adverse holding concerning the enforceability of the box-top license. We are not persuaded that requiring software companies to stand behind representations concerning their products will inevitably destroy the software industry. We emphasize, however, that we are following the well-established distinction between conspicuous disclaimers made available before the contract is formed and disclaimers made available only after the contract is formed. [*Compare Hill v. BASF Wyandotte Corp.*, 696 F.2d 287, 290-91 (4th Cir.1982). In that case, a farmer purchased seventy-three five gallon cans of a herbicide from a retailer. Because the disclaimer was printed conspicuously on each can, the farmer had constructive knowledge of the terms of the disclaimer before the contract formed. As a result, when he selected each can of the herbicide from the shelf and purchased it, the law implies his assent to the terms of the disclaimer. *See also Bowdoin v. Showell Growers, Inc.*, 817 F.2d 1543, 1545 (11th Cir.1987) (disclaimers that were conspicuous before the contract for sale has formed are effective; post-sale disclaimers are ineffective); *Monsanto Agricultural Prods. Co. v. Edenfield*, 426 So.2d at 575-76.]

When a disclaimer is not expressed until after the contract is formed, UCC § 2-207 governs the interpretation of the contract, and, between merchants, such disclaimers, to the extent they materially alter the parties's agreement, are not incorporated into the parties's agreement.

If TSL wants relief for its business operations from this well-established rule, their arguments are better addressed to a legislature than a court. Indeed, we note that at least two states have enacted statutes that modify the applicable contract rules in this area, ... but both Georgia and Pennsylvania have retained the contract rules provided by the UCC.

C. The Terms of the Contract

Under section 2-207, an additional term detailed in the box-top license will not be incorporated into the parties's contract if the term's addition to the contract would materially alter the parties's agreement.... Step-Saver alleges that several representations made by TSL constitute express warranties, and that valid implied warranties were also a part of the parties's agreement. Because the district court considered the box-top license to exclude all of these warranties, the district court did not consider whether other factors may act to exclude these warranties. The existence and nature of the warranties is primarily a factual question that we leave for the district court, ... but assuming that these warranties were included within the parties's original agreement, we must conclude that adding the disclaimer of warranty and limitation of remedies provisions from the box-top license would, as a matter of law, substantially alter the distribution of risk between Step-Saver and TSL.... Therefore, under UCC § 2-207(2)(b), the disclaimer of warranty and limitation of remedies terms of the box-top license did not become a part of the parties's agreement. [The following recent cases reach a similar conclusion concerning indemnity or warranty disclaimers contained in writings exchanged after the contract had formed: *McJunkin Corp.*, 888 F.2d at 488-89; *Valtrol, Inc. v. General Connectors Corp.*, 884 F.2d at 155; *Trans-Aire Int'l v. Northern Adhesive Co.*, 882 F.2d at 1262-63; *Bowdoin*, 817 F.2d at 1545-46; *Diamond Fruit Growers, Inc.*, 794 F.2d at 1445; *Tuck Industries*, 542 N.Y.S.2d at 678; *South-eastern Adhesives Co.*, 366 S.E.2d at 507-08.]

Based on these considerations, we reverse the trial court's holding that the parties intended the box-top license to be a final and complete expression of the terms of their agreement. Despite the presence of an integration clause in the box-top license, the box-top license should have been treated as a written confirmation containing additional terms.... Because the warranty disclaimer and limitation of remedies terms would materially alter the parties's agreement, these terms did not become a part of the parties's agreement. We remand for further consideration the express and implied warranty claims against TSL.

[The Court's discussion of the implied warranty of merchantability claim against Wyse and evidentiary rulings has been omitted.]

We will reverse the holding of the district court that the parties intended to adopt the box-top license as the complete and final expression of the terms of their agreement. We will remand for further consideration of Step-Saver's express and implied warranty claims against TSL. Finding a sufficient basis for the other decisions of the district court, we will affirm in all other respects.

Klocek v. Gateway

104 F. Supp. 2d 1332 (D Kan 2000)

VRATIL, District Judge.

William S. Klocek brings suit against Gateway, Inc. and Hewlett-Packard, Inc. on claims arising from purchases of a Gateway computer and a Hewlett-Packard scanner. This matter comes before the Court on (two *Motions to Dismiss*) ... For reasons stated below, the Court overrules Gateway's motion to dismiss, sustains Hewlett-Packard's motion to dismiss, and overrules the motions filed by plaintiff.

A. Gateway's Motion to Dismiss

Plaintiff brings individual and class action claims against Gateway, alleging that it induced him and other consumers to purchase computers and special support packages by making false promises of technical support. Individually, plaintiff also claims breach of contract and breach of warranty, in that Gateway breached certain warranties that its computer would be compatible with standard peripherals and standard internet services.

Gateway asserts that plaintiff must arbitrate his claims under Gateway's Standard Terms and Conditions Agreement ("Standard Terms"). Whenever it sells a computer, Gateway includes a copy of the Standard Terms in the box which contains the computer battery power cables and instruction manuals. At the top of the first page, the Standard Terms include the following notice:

NOTE TO THE CUSTOMER:

This document contains Gateway 2000's Standard Terms and Conditions. By keeping your Gateway 2000 computer system beyond five (5) days after the date of delivery, you accept these Terms and Conditions.

The notice is in emphasized type and is located inside a printed box which sets it apart from other provisions of the document. The Standard Terms are four pages long and contain 16 numbered paragraphs. Paragraph 10 provides the following arbitration clause:

DISPUTE RESOLUTION. Any dispute or controversy arising out of or relating to this Agreement or its interpretation shall be settled exclusively and finally by arbitration. The arbitration shall be conducted in accordance with the Rules of Conciliation and Arbitration of the International Chamber of Commerce. The arbitration shall be conducted in Chicago, Illinois, U.S.A. before a sole arbitrator. Any award rendered in any such arbitration proceeding shall be final and binding on each of the parties, and judgment may be entered thereon in a court of competent jurisdiction.[Gateway states that after it sold plaintiff's computer, it mailed all existing customers in the United States a copy of its quarterly magazine, which contained notice of a change in the arbitration policy set forth in the Standard Terms. The new arbitration policy afforded customers the option of arbitrating before the International Chamber of Commerce ("ICC"), the American Arbitration Association ("AAA"), or the National Arbitration Forum ("NAF") in Chicago, Illinois, or any other location agreed upon by the parties. Plaintiff denies receiving notice of the amended arbitration policy. Neither party explains why-if the arbitration agreement was an enforceable contract-Gateway was entitled to unilaterally amend it by sending a magazine to computer customers.]

Gateway urges the Court to dismiss plaintiff's claims under the Federal Arbitration Act ("FAA"), 9 U.S.C. § 1 *et seq.* The FAA ensures that written arbitration agreements in maritime transactions and transactions involving interstate commerce are "valid, irrevocable, and enforceable." 9 U.S.C. § 2....

FAA Section 3 states:

If any suit or proceeding be brought in any of the courts of the United States upon any issue referable to arbitration under an agreement in writing for such arbitration, the court in which such suit is pending, upon being satisfied that the issue involved in such suit or proceeding is referable to arbitration under such agreement, shall on application of one of the parties stay the trial of the action until such arbitration has been had in accordance with the terms of the agreement, providing the applicant for the stay is not in default in proceeding with such arbitration....

Although the FAA does not expressly provide for dismissal, the Tenth Circuit has affirmed dismissal where the applicant did not request a stay.... Here, neither Gateway nor plaintiff requests a stay. Accordingly, the Court concludes that dismissal is appropriate if plaintiff's claims are arbitrable....

Gateway bears an initial summary-judgment-like burden of establishing that it is entitled to arbitration.... Thus, Gateway must present evidence sufficient to demonstrate the existence of an enforceable agreement to arbitrate.... If Gateway makes such a showing, the burden shifts to plaintiff to submit evidence demonstrating a genuine issue for trial.... In this case, Gateway fails to present evidence establishing the most basic facts regarding the transaction. The gaping holes in the evidentiary record preclude the Court from determining what state law controls the formation of the contract in this case and, consequently, prevent the Court from agreeing that Gateway's motion is well taken.

Before granting a stay or dismissing a case pending arbitration, the Court must determine that the parties have a written agreement to arbitrate.... When deciding whether the parties have agreed to arbitrate, the Court applies ordinary state law principles that govern the formation of contracts.... .The existence of an arbitration agreement "is simply a matter of contract between the parties; [arbitration] is a way to resolve those disputes-but only those disputes-that the parties have agreed to submit to arbitration...." If the parties dispute making an arbitration agreement, a jury trial on the existence of an agreement is warranted if the record reveals genuine issues of material fact regarding the parties' agreement....

The Uniform Commercial Code ("UCC") governs the parties' transaction under both Kansas and Missouri law. *See* K.S.A. § 84-2-102; V.A.M.S. § 400.2-102 (UCC applies to "transactions in goods."); Kansas Comment 1 (main thrust of Article 2 is limited to sales); K.S.A. § 84-2-105(1) V.A.M.S. § 400.2-105(1) (" 'Goods' means all things ... which are movable at the time of identification to the contract for sale...."). Regardless whether plaintiff purchased the computer in person or placed an order and received shipment of the computer, the parties agree that plaintiff paid for and received a computer from Gateway. This conduct clearly demonstrates a contract for the sale of a computer. *See, e.g., Step-Saver Data Sys., Inc. v. Wyse Techn.,* 939 F.2d 91, 98 (3d Cir.1991). Thus the issue is whether the contract of sale includes the Standard Terms as part of the agreement.

State courts in Kansas and Missouri apparently have not decided whether terms received with a product become part of the parties' agreement. Authority from other courts is split. *Compare Step-Saver,* 939 F.2d 91 (printed terms on computer software package not part of agreement); *Arizona Retail Sys., Inc. v. Software Link, Inc.,* 831 F.Supp. 759 (D.Ariz.1993) (license agreement shipped with computer software not part of agreement); *and U.S. Surgical Corp. v. Orris, Inc.,* 5 F.Supp.2d 1201 (D.Kan.1998) (single use restriction on product package not binding agreement);*with Hill v. Gateway 2000, Inc.,* 105 F.3d 1147 (7th Cir.), *cert. denied,* 522 U.S. 808, 118 S.Ct. 47, 139 L.Ed.2d 13 (1997) (arbitration provision shipped with computer binding on buyer); *ProCD, Inc. v. Zeidenberg,* 86 F.3d 1447 (7th Cir.1996) (shrinkwrap license binding on buyer); ... *and M.A. Mortenson Co., Inc. v. Timberline Software Corp.,* 140 Wash.2d 568, 998 P.2d 305 (2000) (following *Hill* and *ProCD* on license agreement supplied with software).... It appears that at least in part, the cases turn on whether the court finds that the parties formed their contract *before* or *after* the vendor communicated its terms to the purchaser. *Compare Step-Saver,* 939 F.2d at 98 (parties' conduct in shipping, receiving and paying for product demonstrates existence of contract; box top license constitutes proposal for additional terms under § 2-207 which requires express agreement by purchaser); *Arizona Retail,* 831 F.Supp. at 765 (vendor entered into contract by agreeing to ship goods, or at latest by shipping goods to buyer; license agreement constitutes proposal to modify agreement under § 2-209 which requires express assent by buyer); *and Orris,* 5 F.Supp.2d at 1206 (sales contract concluded when vendor received consumer orders; single-use language on product's label was proposed modification under § 2-209 which requires express assent by purchaser); *with ProCD,* 86 F.3d at 1452 (under § 2-204 vendor, as master of offer, may propose limitations on kind of conduct that constitutes acceptance; §2-207 does not apply in case with only one form); *Hill*, 105 F.3d at 1148-49 (same); *and Mortenson*, 998 P.2d at 311-314 (where vendor and purchaser utilized license agreement in prior course of dealing, shrinkwrap license agreement constituted issue of contract formation under §2-204, not contract alteration under §2-207).

Gateway urges the Court to follow the Seventh Circuit decision in *Hill*. That case involved the shipment of a Gateway computer with terms similar to the Standard Terms in this case, except that Gateway gave the customer 30 days-instead of 5 days-to return the computer. In enforcing the arbitration clause, the Seventh Circuit relied on its decision in *ProCD*, where it enforced a software license which was contained inside a product box. *See Hill*, 105 F.3d at 1148-50. In *ProCD*, the Seventh Circuit noted that the exchange of money frequently precedes the communication of detailed terms in a commercial transaction. *See ProCD*, 86 F.3d at 1451. Citing UCC §2-204, the court reasoned that by including the license with the software, the vendor proposed a contract that the buyer could accept by using the software after having an opportunity to read the license.... .Specifically, the court stated:

A vendor, as master of the offer, may invite acceptance by conduct, and may propose limitations on the kind of conduct that constitutes acceptance. A buyer may accept by performing the acts the vendor proposes to treat as acceptance.*ProCD*, 86 F.3d at 1452. The *Hill* court followed the *ProCD* analysis, noting that "[p]ractical considerations support allowing vendors to enclose the full legal terms with their products." *Hill*, 105 F.3d at 1149. [Legal commentators have criticized the reasoning of the Seventh Circuit in this regard. *See, e.g.*, Jean R. Sternlight, *Gateway Widens Doorway to Imposing Unfair Binding Arbitration on Consumers*, Fla. Bar J., Nov. 1997, at 8, 10-12 (outcome in *Gateway* is questionable on federal statutory, common law and constitutional grounds and as a matter of contract law and is unwise as a matter of policy because it unreasonably shifts to consumers search cost of ascertaining existence of arbitration clause and return cost to avoid such clause); Thomas J. McCarthy et al., *Survey: Uniform Commercial Code*, 53 Bus. Law. 1461, 1465-66 (Seventh Circuit finding that UCC §2-207 did not apply is inconsistent with official comment); Batya Goodman, *Honey, I Shrink-Wrapped the Consumer: the Shrinkwrap Agreement as an Adhesion Contract*, 21 Cardozo L.Rev. 319, 344-352 (Seventh Circuit failed to consider principles of adhesion contracts); Jeremy Senderowicz, *Consumer Arbitration and Freedom of Contract: A Proposal to Facilitate Consumers' Informed Consent to Arbitration Clauses in Form Contracts*, 32 Colum. J.L. & Soc. Probs. 275, 296-299 (judiciary (in multiple decisions, including *Hill*) has ignored issue of consumer consent to an arbitration clause). Nonetheless, several courts have followed the Seventh Circuit decisions in *Hill* and *ProCD*. *See, e.g.*, *M.A. Mortenson Co., Inc. v. Timberline Software Corp.*, 140 Wash.2d 568, 998 P.2d 305 (license agreement supplied with software); *Rinaldi v. Iomega Corp.*, 1999 WL 1442014, Case No. 98C-09-064-RRC (Del.Super. Sept. 3, 1999) (warranty disclaimer included inside computer Zip drive packaging); *Westendorf v. Gateway 2000, Inc.*, 2000 WL 307369, Case No. 16913 (Del. Ch. March 16, 2000) (arbitration provision shipped with computer); *Brower v. Gateway 2000, Inc.*, 246 A.D.2d 246, 676 N.Y.S.2d 569 (N.Y.App.Div.1998) (same); *Levy v. Gateway 2000, Inc.*, 1997 WL 823611, 33 UCC Rep. Serv.2d 1060 (N.Y.Sup. Oct. 31, 1997) (same).]

The Court is not persuaded that Kansas or Missouri courts would follow the Seventh Circuit reasoning in *Hill* and *ProCD*. In each case the Seventh Circuit concluded without support that UCC §2-207 was irrelevant because the cases involved only one written form. *See ProCD*, 86 F.3d at 1452 (citing no authority); *Hill*, 105 F.3d at 1150 (citing *ProCD*). This conclusion is not supported by the statute or by Kansas or Missouri law.

Disputes under § 2-207 often arise in the context of a "battle of forms," *see, e.g., Diatom, Inc. v. Pennwalt Corp.,* 741 F.2d 1569, 1574 (10th Cir.1984), but nothing in its language precludes application in a case which involves only one form. The statute provides:

> Additional terms in acceptance or confirmation.
>
> (1) A definite and seasonable expression of acceptance or a written confirmation which is sent within a reasonable time operates as an acceptance even though it states terms additional to or different from those offered or agreed upon, unless acceptance is expressly made conditional on assent to the additional or different terms.
>
> (2) The additional terms are to be construed as proposals for addition to the contract [if the contract is not between merchants]....

K.S.A. § 84-2-207; V.A.M.S. § 400.2-207. By its terms, § 2-207 applies to an acceptance or written confirmation. It states nothing which requires another form before the provision becomes effective. In fact, the official comment to the section specifically provides that §§ 2-207(1) and (2) apply "where an agreement has been reached orally ... and is followed by one or both of the parties sending formal memoranda embodying the terms so far agreed and adding terms not discussed." Official Comment 1 of UCC § 2-207. Kansas and Missouri courts have followed this analysis. *See Southwest Engineering Co. v. Martin Tractor Co.,* 205 Kan. 684, 695, 473 P.2d 18, 26 (1970) (stating in dicta that § 2-207 applies where open offer is accepted by expression of acceptance in writing or where oral agreement is later confirmed in writing); ... Thus, the Court concludes that Kansas and Missouri courts would apply § 2-207 to the facts in this case..... .

In addition, the Seventh Circuit provided no explanation for its conclusion that "the vendor is the master of the offer." *See ProCD,* 86 F.3d at 1452 (citing nothing in support of proposition); *Hill,* 105 F.3d at 1149 (citing *ProCD*). In typical consumer transactions, the purchaser is the offeror, and the vendor is the offeree. *See Brown Mach., Div. of John Brown, Inc. v. Hercules, Inc.,* 770 S.W.2d 416, 419 (Mo.App.1989) (as general rule orders are considered offers to purchase); *Rich Prods. Corp. v. Kemutec Inc.,* 66 F.Supp.2d 937, 956 (E.D.Wis.1999) (generally price quotation is invitation to make offer and purchase order is offer). While it is possible for the vendor to be the offeror, *see Brown Machine,* 770 S.W.2d at 419 (price quote can amount to offer if it reasonably appears from quote that assent to quote is all that is needed to ripen offer into contract), Gateway provides no factual evidence which would support such a finding in this case. The Court therefore assumes for purposes of the motion to dismiss that plaintiff offered to purchase the computer (either in person or through catalog order) and that Gateway accepted plaintiff's offer (either by completing the sales transaction in person or by agreeing to ship and/or shipping the computer to plaintiff)....

Under § 2-207, the Standard Terms constitute either an expression of acceptance or written confirmation. As an expression of acceptance, the Standard Terms would constitute a counter-offer only if Gateway expressly made its acceptance conditional on plaintiff's assent to the additional or different terms. K.S.A. § 84-2-207(1); V.A.M.S. § 400.2-207(1). "[T]he conditional nature of the acceptance must be clearly expressed in a manner sufficient to notify the offeror that the offeree is unwilling to proceed with the transaction unless the additional or different terms are included in the contract." *Brown Machine,* 770 S.W.2d at 420.... Gateway provides no evidence that at the time of the sales transaction, it informed plaintiff that the transaction was conditioned on plaintiff's acceptance of the Standard Terms. Moreover, the mere fact that Gateway shipped the goods with the terms attached did not communicate to plaintiff any unwillingness to proceed without plaintiff's agreement to the Standard Terms....

Because plaintiff is not a merchant, additional or different terms contained in the Standard Terms did not become part of the parties' agreement unless plaintiff expressly agreed to them. *See* K.S.A. § 84-2-207, Kansas Comment 2 (if either party is not a merchant, additional terms are proposals for addition to the contract that do not become part of the contract unless the original offeror expressly agrees). [The Court's decision would be the same if it considered the Standard Terms as a proposed modification under UCC § 2-209....]

Gateway argues that plaintiff demonstrated acceptance of the arbitration provision by keeping the computer more than five days after the date of delivery. Although the Standard Terms purport to work that result, Gateway has not presented evidence that plaintiff expressly agreed to those Standard Terms. Gateway states only that it enclosed the Standard Terms inside the computer box for plaintiff to read afterwards. It provides no evidence that it informed plaintiff of the five-day review-and-return period as a condition of the sales transaction, or that the parties contemplated additional terms to the agreement. [The Court is mindful of the practical considerations which are involved in commercial transactions, but it is not unreasonable for a vendor to clearly communicate to a buyer- at the time of sale-either the complete terms of the sale or the fact that the vendor will propose additional terms as a condition of sale, if that be the case.] *See Step-Saver*, 939 F.2d at 99 (during negotiations leading to purchase, vendor never mentioned box-top license or obtained buyer's express assent thereto). The Court finds that the act of keeping the computer past five days was not sufficient to demonstrate that plaintiff expressly agreed to the Standard Terms. *Accord Brown Machine*, 770 S.W.2d at 421 (express assent cannot be presumed by silence or mere failure to object). Thus, because Gateway has not provided evidence sufficient to support a finding under Kansas or Missouri law that plaintiff agreed to the arbitration provision contained in Gateway's Standard Terms, the Court overrules Gateway's motion to dismiss....

———————

Discussion of electronic contracting issues first began to appear in the journal of the Business Law Section of the American Bar Association in 2001. Regular annual surveys began in 2005. In the 2009-2010 survey, the authors observed that there are now fewer cases that deal with electronic issues and the cases themselves present fewer interesting issues. They conclude that there is no difference between contracts formed electronically and those formed by other means and state "The law should no longer treat electronic contracts with wonder or skepticism. Electronic contracts should no longer be a separate concern." Now that you have read the leading cases, what do you think? Do we need to change basic rules of contract law to accommodate modern technology and new means of contract formation?

Additional Resources

Christina L. Kunz, Maureen F. Del Duca, Heather Thayer, and Jennifer Debrow Click-Through Agreements: Strategies for Avoiding Dispute on Validity of Assent 57 Bus. Law. 401 (2001).

Juliet M. Moringiello and Wiliam L. Reynolds, Electronic Contracting Cases 2009–2010, 66 Bus. Law. 175 (2010).

Chapter 14

Sales Problems

Problem 14-1

You have just passed the Bar and you have been hired as a junior associate in a local law firm. The senior partner sends you the following memorandum.

WORKSALOT, INC.

Inter-Office Memorandum

TO: Junior Associate
FROM: Senior Partner
RE: New Client/Legal Audit
DATE: December 5

A new client has asked us to perform a "legal audit." Essentially, that means that we will be reviewing all of her standard business practices, along with her standard forms, and making suggestions as to how they can be improved. I have identified eight contract provisions in her standard forms that I think deserve our input. Could you please draft a memorandum that I can use to write her a letter, discussing these provisions. I have set seven provisions out below.

For each contract provision set forth below, please identify:

(a)   the TYPE of provision;
(b)   <u>BRIEFLY</u> describe the OPERATIVE LEGAL EFFECT of the provision; and
(c)   If you think it should be rewritten, take a stab at rewriting it.

I've given you an example of what I am looking for.

PLEASE ASSUME THAT ALL OF THE CONTRACT PROVISIONS ARISE IN CONNECTION WITH TRANSACTIONS THAT FALL WITHIN THE SCOPE OF ARTICLE 2.

EXAMPLE:
Provision: Seller shall not revoke this offer for a period of two months.
   (a)   If this provision is in a writing, signed by a merchant, it constitutes a firm offer.
   (b)   The operative legal effect is that the offer cannot be revoked for a period of two months, even if there is no consideration given in exchange for the offer.

PROVISIONS TO ANALYZE:

1. Buyer's acceptance is expressly conditional on Seller's assent to the terms set forth below.

2. Buyer assumes all responsibility for resale and agrees that its sole remedy for breach shall be an action for breach of warranty.

3. No verbal understanding will be recognized by either party hereto; this contract expresses all the terms and conditions of this agreement.

4. Acceptance of this Purchase Order must be made on its exact terms and if additional or different terms are proposed by Seller such response will constitute a counter-offer.

5. The price of the goods is $.50 per pound F.O.B. Portland. (Assume that Buyer's place of business is in Los Angeles and Seller's place of business is in Portland.)

6. Either party may be excused for delay or failure to perform its agreements and undertakings, in whole or in part, when and to the extent that such failure or delay is occasioned by fire, flood, wind, lightning, or other acts of the elements.

7. To the extent allowed by law, this warranty is in place of all other warranties, express or implied.

Problem 14-2

Ben Buyer ("Buyer") was engaged in the business of cutting and installing glass for use in residential construction. Buyer entered into a carefully negotiated written contract with Sandra Seller ("Seller") for her to produce a "horizontal batch tempering furnace" for Buyer's use in the glass cutting business, pursuant to Buyer's specifications, for $1.45 million. The machine's design was complex, if not experimental. Nevertheless, Seller assured Buyer that it could be made to work and would be a "state of the art" furnace.

Seller completed delivery of the furnace by November 1, 1990. Seller and Buyer then worked together through a contractual "debugging" period. Although the contract did not guarantee a specific time for completion of debugging, in the industry, a complete period for startup and debugging would usually take 6-8 weeks. Notwithstanding the Seller's substantial remedial efforts, after 2-1/2 years of effort, the Seller was unable to cause the furnace to consistently perform to the contract specifications.

The parties' contract contained the following provision:

> In the event of a breach of any warranty, express, implied or statutory, or in the event the equipment is found to be defective in workmanship or material or fails to conform to the specifications thereof, Seller's liability shall be limited to the repair or replacement of such equipment as is found to be defective or non conforming. Seller assumes no liability for consequential or incidental damages of any kind (including fire or explosion in the starting, testing or subsequent operation of the equipment) and Buyer assumes all liability for the consequences of its use or misuse. In no event will Seller be liable for damages resulting from the non operation of Buyer's plant as a result of the use, misuse or inability to use the equipment.

Buyer sued Seller, alleging breach of contract and breach of warranty. Seller counter-claimed for the balance of the purchase price. The trial court granted judgment in favor of Seller on the Buyer's breach of contract and breach of warranty claims, and awarded the Seller the balance of the purchase price. Buyer appealed.

Write the decision of the Appellate Court.

Problem 14-3

Bonnie Buyer, who was engaged in the business of producing knitted fabrics, wanted to expand her business. She contacted Sonia Seller, a knitting machine manufacturer, to discuss how automated knitting machines could help her increase her volume of business. On September 8, 2001, Bonnie toured Sonia's plant, and Sonia demonstrated the operation of her Model 12345 automated knitting machines. As Bonnie watched, Sonia used a Model 12345 to produce high quality knit fabric, in perfect condition. Sonia told Bonnie that each two of these machines would enable Bonnie to double her then-present volume of business without adding employees. During the tour, Sonia told Bonnie, "You get the customers, my machines make the fabric. I stand behind my machines; if you have any problems, I'll fix them, but don't count on any implied warranties."

After the tour, the parties signed a written sales contract. The contract provided in part:[1]

---

1. Seller shall sell and Buyer shall buy ten (10) Model 12345 Automated Knitting Machines ("Equipment") for a total price of $750,000 F.O.B. Seller's plant, to be delivered at the times requested by Buyer, between September 15, 2001 and June 30, 2002.

2. SELLER SHALL NOT BE LIABLE FOR ANY INJURY, LOSS OR DAMAGES, DIRECT OR CONSEQUENTIAL, ARISING OUT OF THE USE OR INABILITY TO USE THE EQUIPMENT. SELLER'S SOLE OBLIGATION SHALL BE TO REPAIR OR REPLACE DEFECTIVE EQUIPMENT.

3. THERE ARE NO UNDERSTANDINGS, AGREEMENTS, REPRESENTATIONS OR WARRANTIES, EXPRESS OR IMPLIED, NOT SPECIFIED HEREIN.

Bonnie requested immediate delivery of the first two machines, and Sonia delivered them on September 15, 2001. Shortly thereafter, Bonnie notified Sonia that the machines were operating slowly, leaking oil, and producing low quality and damaged fabric. Sonia worked on the machines, and, although they continued to operate slowly, the other problems disappeared.

Bonnie was able to generate new customer orders that doubled her pre-September 15 business volume. Because the first two machines were still working slowly, Bonnie hired an additional employee to keep up with the orders. She then requested and Sonia delivered two more machines, which arrived on November 17, 2001. Bonnie experienced the same problems as she had after the September 15 delivery, and so notified Sonia. Sonia fixed these machines as well, again eliminating all problems, except slow operation. Bonnie continued to generate new customer orders and she was forced to hire another employee to keep up with her growing volume of business.

---

1. The font and style of each paragraph set forth above corresponds to the font and style as they appeared in the actual agreement.

Despite continuing difficulties with the four machines, Bonnie's business was flourishing, and to keep up with the demand, she ordered four additional machines in March 2002. Sonia sent four Model 45678 machines, with a cover letter stating, "These are the 'next generation' of the Model 12345 machines. You should not experience any problems with them, so I am shipping them as an accommodation." When the carrier attempted to deliver the machines, Bonnie noticed that they were the wrong model, and refused to accept delivery. She told the carrier to take them back and to tell Sonia that the delivery of the wrong models was the last straw and she considered her contract at an end. Disgusted, she then called a competitor of Sonia's and bought ten machines from the competitor, for a total price of $1,000,000. She never asked Sonia to deliver any more machines, and refused to accept Sonia's phone calls.

Sonia attempted to deliver six more Model 12345 machines on June 30, 2002, but Bonnie would not allow the carrier to unload them. While the carrier's truck was returning to Sonia's plant, a giant fireball from an angry God came down and hit the truck, and the truck and its contents, including the six machines that had been sent to Bonnie, were destroyed.

It is now February 18, 2006. Sonia has retained your law firm to sue Bonnie for the $750,000 purchase price, none of which has been paid. Write a memo analyzing Sonia's legal position. Be sure to consider any defenses or counter claims that Bonnie might raise if suit is filed.

Problem 14-4

You represent a small parts supplier that has an opportunity to enter into a contract to supply widgets to Bowing Corporation. Your client has been given a copy of Bowing's standard form contract. It is non-negotiable. Your client has asked you to review the contract and to explain the meaning of four of the contract provisions. In particular, your client wants to know:

(a) What each provision means;

(b) The extent to which each provision reflects what the legal rights of the parties would be if there were no such provision in the contract;

(c) The extent to which each provision change the parties' legal rights; and

(d) What risks and concerns your client needs to be aware of if it decides to proceed with the contract.

Assume that the contract contains price and quantity terms and a description of the widgets. Also assume that all references in the contract provisions to "Bidder" or "Seller" are to your client and all references to "Products" are to the widgets. Write a letter to your client in which you discuss each provision in the order presented. Also advise your client of any applicable "gap filler" provisions.

Bowing Contract Provisions

1.   Bidder's proposal is a firm offer to contract for a period of 120 days from the date of Bowing's receipt of the proposal.

2.   Bowing may issue Orders to Seller from time to time. Each Order is Bowing's offer to Seller and acceptance is strictly limited to its terms. Bowing will not be bound by and specifically objects to any term or condition which is different from or in addition to the provisions of the Order, whether or not such term or condition will materially alter the Order.

3.   Products shall be subject to final inspection and acceptance by Bowing at destination, notwithstanding any payment or prior inspection. Bowing may reject any Product which does not strictly conform to the requirements of the applicable Order. Bowing shall by notice, rejection tag or other communication notify Seller of such rejection. Whenever possible, Bowing may coordinate with Seller prior to disposition of the rejected Products, however Bowing shall retain final disposition authority with respect to all rejections. At Seller's risk and expense, all such products shall be returned to Seller for immediate repair, replacement or other correction or redelivery provided however at Bowing's election and at Seller's risk and expense Bowing may (a) hold, retain or return such products without permitting any repair, replacement or other correction by Seller; or (b) hold, or retain such Products for repair by Seller or at Bowing's election for repair by Bowing with such assistance from Seller as Bowing may require; hold such products until Seller has delivered conforming replacements for such products.

4.   Bowing may revoke its acceptance of any Products and have the same rights with regard to the Products involved as if it had originally rejected them.

Problem 14-5

On April 7, 2005, Buyer, a sophisticated businessman, with years of experience as a manufacturer of dog food, agreed to buy from Seller, and Seller, the owner and operator of a family farm, agreed to sell to Buyer approximately 1400 tons of feed wheat for $200 a ton, or a total of $280,000. On April 8, Seller met with Buyer and asked Buyer to sign a two-sided form contract, prepared by Seller's attorney, which described the goods as "feed wheat,"[2] and contained, among others, the following provisions:[3]

CONFIRMATION: This document contains a contract between Buyer and Seller for the purchase and sale of feed wheat (hereinafter "goods").

12. WARRANTIES: Seller has made no warranty to the Buyer except as appearing expressly within the written terms of this contract. The goods are sold **AS IS**.

17. DAMAGE LIMITATION: IN NO EVENT SHALL SELLER BE LIABLE FOR INCIDENTAL OR CONSEQUENTIAL DAMAGES. Buyer shall within ten days after receipt examine the goods for any and all defects. If the goods fail to meet the contract description, Buyer shall give immediate notice to Seller and submit samples for Federal Inspection. If the inspection establishes the goods failed to conform to the contract Seller may at its Chip Sellertion either replace the goods with conforming goods within a reasonable time, or pay to the Buyer the difference between the contract price and fair market value of the goods delivered. **THE REMEDIES PROVIDED IN THIS PARAGRAPH ARE EXCLUSIVE**.

Buyer was in a hurry, and scribbled his name on the contract without reading the entire contract carefully. There was no discussion of particular contract terms, nor did the parties negotiate regarding the terms in the written confirmation. Paragraphs 12 and 17 were on the reverse side of the form contract.

In accordance with the terms of their agreement, Seller timely delivered the contracted-for wheat to Buyer on April 30, 2005. Buyer included the wheat in dog food he manufactured in May 2005, and paid the contract price in full. The dog food was sold to the general public through Seller's distributors, in June. However, almost immediately, customers who purchased the dog food from the distributors reported that their pets either refused to eat the food or became sick after eating it. As soon as Buyer learned of these complaints (still within the month of June), he had samples of the dog food federally inspected, and learned that it contained unacceptable levels of vomitoxin.[4] Buyer immediately recalled

---

2. Please **assume** that it is customary in the dog food manufacturing business for a product known as "feed wheat" to be incorporated into dog food; further **assume** that it is customary for the **seller** to have the feed wheat inspected to assure safe levels of vomitoxin, a mildly poisonous substance that can result in illness in animals that consume feed containing vomitoxin.

3. Please **assume** that the physical appearance of the contract was exactly as indicated (with respect to size of font, bolding, etc.)

4. Please **assume** that this could only be the result of the use of wheat that contained unacceptable vomitoxin levels for feed wheat.

all of the dog food manufactured in May. Simultaneously, he notified Seller of the complaints, but Seller denied any liability, citing the contract provisions set forth above.

Buyer sued Seller for damages for breach of contract, claiming breach of express warranty and breach of the implied warranty of merchantability. The trial court ruled in Buyer's favor, and awarded the Buyer damages in the sum of $135,000, calculated as follows: (a) $30,000 to manufacture and distribute the dog food; plus (b) $50,000 to pay the costs of recalling the dog food manufactured with the wheat purchased from Seller; plus (c) $50,000 to settle claims made by its distributors (for claims asserted by their customers), plus (d) $5,000 for the costs of the federal inspection. The court specifically ruled that the limitation of remedies provision in the Confirmation failed its essential purpose and that the consequential damages limitation was unconscionable.

Seller has appealed the trial court's decision. Write the **seller's** opening brief on appeal.

Problem 14-6

On March 8, 2004, Seller, a fruit dealer, and Buyer, a fruit distributor, contracted orally for the sale and shipment to Buyer of three mixed truckloads of produce, each truckload consisting of (1) 436 baskets of peaches, known as "fancy Belles and Thurbers" at $2.25 per basket; (2) 25 cartons of cantaloupes Jumbo size 56 at $17.75 per carton; and (3) 85 cartons of cantaloupes Jumbo size 45 at $15.25 per carton. At the contract price, each truckload cost $2721. It was agreed that shipment would start on March 8. The parties estimated that delivery would be in time for the market of Tuesday morning, March. 12.

Seller shipped the produce from Arizona at 10:00 p.m. on March 8, in three trucks operated by Arkansas Traffic Service Inc. of Redfield, Arkansas. At that time, Seller faxed the following to Buyer:

SHIPMENT CONFIRMATION

1   We have shipped per your order three (3) mixed truckloads of produce, consisting of:

    (1) 436 baskets of peaches, known as "fancy Belles and Thurbers" at $2.25 per basket;

    (2) 25 cartons of cantaloupes Jumbo size 56 at $17.75 per carton; and

    (3) 85 cartons of cantaloupes Jumbo size 45 at $15.25 per carton.

2   Estimated Delivery: March 12, 3:00 a.m.

3   Not responsible for delays in delivery caused by shipper.

4   Due to perishable nature of goods, Buyer assumes all responsibility for resale and agrees that its sole remedy for breach shall be an action for breach of warranty.

5   ***In no event shall Seller be liable for consequential damages.***

At about 12:00 a.m. March 12 the truck dispatcher called Buyer, stating that the first truck would arrive about 3:00 a.m., but the second truck had had engine trouble, and would be delayed until approximately 3:30 p.m. The dispatcher requested that Buyer's workers wait to unload the truck. Buyer checked with its workers, who said they would not wait, and then told the truck dispatcher to have the second truck arrive at 3:00 a.m. the morning of March 13. The dispatcher promised to advise Buyer of the whereabouts of the third truck as soon as possible.

The first truckload of produce arrived at Buyer's place of business at 3:30 a.m. The second truckload of produce arrived at Buyer's place of business at 5:00 a.m. March 13. The third truckload of produce never arrived.

On arrival of the first truck, Buyer paid the freight and examined the produce. Buyer immediately found that the peaches were not the varieties ordered. The varieties shipped would sell for fifty percent less than those specified. Buyer wired Seller: "Referring to our contract of March 8, we are rejecting first truckload received. Peaches fail to conform to contract." Seller wired back "Truck yours. Care not what you do with it. Gave you best colored stock possible as ordered and hold you responsible for amount of contract." Buyer put the produce in a warehouse and wired Seller, informing Seller of the location of the produce.

Before the arrival of the second truck, the market price of cantaloupe dropped sharply. When the truck arrived, although the cantaloupe conformed to the contract description, Buyer refused to pay the freight and instructed the driver to take the produce back to Seller.

Seller seeks to recover the full delivered price for all three truckloads of produce. Buyer refuses to pay the full price. It contends that the contract required the Seller to deliver the goods by 3:30 a.m. on March 12. Buyer states that Seller's failure to deliver the produce on time caused Buyer to miss a large chain store order, and further made Buyer unable to resell the second truckload at a profit.

Your research into the produce industry reveals it conducts retail sales daily, generally between the hours of 3:00 a.m. and 6:00 a.m. Most shipments between dealers and distributors are made F.O.B. the seller's place of business.

Discuss the result in an action by Seller v. Buyer, in which Buyer files a cross-complaint against Seller.

Problem 14-7. Practice Problem: Drafting a Reply to a Motion for Summary Judgment

You are still working at Worksalot. Another partner sends you the following memorandum.

WORKSALOT, INC.

Inter-Office Memorandum

TO: Junior Associate
FROM: Senior Partner
RE: Litigation Response Required
DATE: December 5

Our firm represents Packaging Corporation, a manufacturer of plastic shells that serve as packaging products.

Last year, our client was contacted by Chip Seller Corporation, who manufactures and distributes computer memory modules. It requires special packaging to package and ship its memory modules to its customers. Chip Seller had decided to change its packaging supplier, and after talking to a number of competitors, selected Packaging Corporation for its new supplier.

Our client exchanged some e-mails with Chip Seller, and eventually Chip Seller sent in a purchase order. At that time, our client realized that its earlier price quote was in error, and brought the mistake to Chip Seller's attention. Chip Seller claimed that it had a contract (based on some e-mails exchanged) at lower prices. Subsequently, our client shipped packaging material to Chip Seller, who paid at the price it claimed was originally agreed to.

Notwithstanding the receipt of invoices at higher amounts, Chip Seller refused to pay the balances due. I filed a collection action on Packaging's behalf, seeking the difference between the amounts owing and the amounts paid.

Chip Seller has now filed a motion for summary judgment, claiming that it has paid everything that was due, based on a contract that it claims arose last December. I am attaching the motion for summary judgment ("MSJ"). The exhibits to the MSJ contain all of the factual information you will need. Please draft our response, in opposition to the MSJ.

IN THE UNITED STATES DISTRICT COURT FOR
THE SOUTHERN DISTRICT OF OHIO

Packaging Corporation	)	CASE NO.: 11-UCC-12345
	)	
	)	The Honorable Judge Merry Wisdom,
	)	presiding
	)	
	)	
Plaintiff,	)	
Vs	)	
	)	
Chip Seller Corporation	)	
.	)	MOTION FOR
	)	SUMMARY JUDGMENT
.	)	
	)	Filing Date: May 14
Defendant	)	Trial Date: June 6,
	)	
	)	[Declarations of Judith LaRue,
	)	and Michael Holder,
.	)	and Statement of Undisputed
	)	Facts In Support Thereof Filed
	)	Concurrently]
	)	

MEMORANDUM OF POINTS AND AUTHORITIES

Pursuant to Federal Rule of Civil Procedure 56, and direction of this Honorable Court, Defendant Chip Seller Corporation ("Chip Seller"), by and through its attorney, submits the following Memorandum of Points and Authority in Support its Motion for Summary Judgment.

I.   INTRODUCTION

This is a simple case; one which can and should be disposed of in Chip Seller's favor at summary judgment. The following facts are undisputed. Chip Seller is a distributor of flash memory products. Plaintiff Packaging Corporation ("Packaging") is a manufacturer of plastic shells that serve as packaging products.

After several months of negotiating, in early December 2008 Packaging and Chip Seller entered into an agreement wherein Packaging was to supply its manufactured products to Chip Seller at an agreed upon price.

Packaging's National Accounts Manager, Bob Dolan, confirmed the pricing particulars in an email dated December 5, 2008 to Judith LaRue, Chip Seller's Purchasing Agent.

Chip Seller ordered goods manufactured by Packaging, who then shipped the subject goods to Chip Seller.

Two and a half months after the agreement was reached, Packaging claimed it had made a "mistake" in its pricing. Chip Seller's general manager listened to Mr. Dolan's explanation about his pricing error, however, Chip Seller demanded that Packaging honor the pricing commitment the parties previously agreed upon.

Packaging insisted that Chip Seller honor the pricing commitment it had made. Chip Seller paid Packaging for all the goods at the agreed price; Chip Seller has paid approximately one million US dollars ($1,000,000.00) to Packaging to date for the subject products.

Packaging's collection action has no basis in fact or law and should be dismissed at Summary Judgment.

II.   SUMMARY JUDGMENT STANDARD

A party is entitled to summary judgment "if the pleadings, depositions, answers to interrogatories and admissions on file, together with affidavits, if any, show there is no genuine issue as to any material fact and that the moving party is entitled to judgment as a matter of law." *Fed. R. Civ. P. 56(c)*. The moving party bears the initial responsibility of "informing the district court of the basis for its motion, and identifying those portions of 'the pleadings, depositions, answers to interrogatories, and admissions on file, together with affidavits, if any,' which it believes demonstrate the absence of a genuine issue of material fact." *Celotex Corp. v. Catret*, 477 U.S. 317, 323 (1986). If the moving party meets this burden, the nonmoving party "must set forth specific facts showing that there is a genuine issue for trial." *Anderson v. Liberty Lobby, Inc.*, 477 U.S. 242, 250 (1986) (quoting Fed R. Civ. P. 56(e)). "In considering a motion for summary judgment, the Court must view the facts and draw all reasonable inferences there from in a light most favorable to the non-moving party." *Williams v. Belknap*, 154 F. Supp. 2d 1069, 1071 (E.D.Mich.2001) (citing, 60 *Ivy Street Corp. v. Alexander*, 822 F.2d 1432, 1435 (6th Cir. 1987)). If, after reviewing the record as a whole, a rational fact finder could not find for the nonmoving party, summary judgment is appropriate since there is no genuine issue for trial. <u>See</u> <u>LaPointe v. United Autoworkers Local 600</u>, 8 F.3d 376, 378 (6th Cir. 1993).

III.   STATEMENT OF FACTS

In October, November and December of 2008, Packaging negotiated with Chip Seller via electronic mail and telephone conversation for the sale of two different card packaging sizes and blisters (collectively, the "Goods"). The price, quantity, quality, and shipping of the Goods were discussed during said negotiations. After about two months, Packaging and Chip Seller (collectively, the "Parties") reached an agreement as to quantity and price of the Goods. Chip Seller confirmed verbally and in writing that the pricing was correct. As a result, on December 5, 2008, Packaging sent Chip Seller a confirmation, via electronic mail, confirming the Parties' agreement, more specifically, the price and quantity of the Agreement. A true and correct copy of the aforementioned written electronic communication is attached hereto as Exhibit-A to the Declaration of Judith LaRue. A minimum quantity of six to ten million products was agreed. The final price expressly agreed upon by the Parties was 09.50 *cents* for the 5 x 7 size and 06.73 *cents* for the 3.5 x 6 size.

In January 2009, Chip Seller submitted written Purchase Orders to Packaging denoting the agreed upon price and quantity. Packaging responded with written Confirmation Orders to Chip Seller's Purchase Orders and subsequently shipped the Goods to Chip Seller.

On or about February 2009, Packaging notified Chip Seller that Packaging had made a mistake in its pricing. Packaging offered Chip Seller a new price to modify the agreement. Chip Seller never agree to Packaging's proposed new price.

IV.   ARGUMENT

A.   PACKAGING'S OFFER TO SELL GOODS COUPLED WITH CHIP SELLER'S ACCEPTANCE CONSTITUTES A VALID, ENFORCEABLE AND BINDING CONTRACT ACCORDING TO THE OHIO REVISED CODE

1.   PACKAGING'S OFFER

The only offer that was accepted and thereby formed the basis of the contract was Packaging's offer to sell its manufactured products to Chip Seller for 09.50 *cents* for the

5 x 7 size packages and 06.73 *cents* for the 3.5 x 6 packages, which is exemplified in Exhibit—A. In Ohio, a contract is defined as a " … description of an agreement or obligation, whether verbal or written, in which one party becomes bound to another to pay a sum of money, perform and act, or omit to perform an act." *Hocking Valley Community Hospital v. Community Health Plan of Ohio*, 2003 Ohio 4243, P13 (2003). The Supreme Court of Ohio has determined that, "[t]he law is clear that to constitute a valid contract, there must be a meeting of the minds of the parties, and there must be an offer on the one side and an acceptance on the other." *Noroski v. Fallet, 2 Ohio St.*, 3d 77, 79 (1982).

Notwithstanding the common law definition of offer, Ohio's version of the Uniform Commercial Code provides that "an offer to make a contract shall be construed as inviting acceptance in any manner and by any medium reasonable in the circumstances." *American Bronze Corp. v. Streamway Products*, 8 Ohio App. 3d 223, 226 (1982), *citing Ohio Rev. Code 1302.09(A)(1)*. In the instant case, Packaging's December 5, 2008 email to Chip Seller is an offer that clearly invited acceptance from Chip Seller to purchase Packaging's products at the agreed upon price. <u>See</u> Exhibit—A.

2.   CHIP SELLER ACCEPTED PACKAGING'S OFFER

Similar to its definition of an offer, Ohio courts have stated, that " … conduct sufficient to show agreement, including performance, constitutes acceptance." *Nagle Heating and Air Conditioning Co. v. Heskett*, 66 Ohio App. 3d 547, 550 (1990). "Acceptance of an offer may be expressed by 'word, sign, writing, or act.'" *Nilavar v. Osborn*, 127 Ohio App. 3d 1, 12 (1998). Further, Ohio Rev. Code 1302.07(A) provides that conduct sufficient to show agreement, including performance, is a reasonable mode of acceptance. *American Bronze Corp. v. Streamway Products*, 8 Ohio App. 3d 223, 227 (1982). Assent is to be judged objectively, construing both acts and words as having the meaning which a reasonable person present would ascribe to them in view of the surrounding circumstances. *Nilavar*, 127 Ohio App. 3d at 12. Indeed, " … courts properly consider only objective manifestations of intent. Thus, expressions of assent are generally sufficient to show a meeting of the minds." *Id.* It is evident from the written Chip Seller communications between Packaging and Chip Seller in response to Packaging's offer, and Chip Seller's following purchase order to Packaging that Chip Seller accepted Packaging's offer exemplified in Exhibit—A. There is uncontroverted evidence that Chip Seller expressed its acceptance when Chip Seller replied assenting to the terms and further, submitted its purchase orders to Packaging denoting the agreed upon price.

3.   THE OFFER ACCEPTED BY CHIP SELLER ESTABLISHES A VALID, ENFORCEABLE, BINDING AGREEMENT ON THE TERMS OF THE AGREEMENT

A written contract is evidence of what was in the minds of the parties at the time they entered into the contract. *Nagle Heating*, 66 Ohio App. 3d at 549. The conduct of the parties can also indicate that all recognized the existence of the contract. *Hocking Valley*, 2003 Ohio 4243 at P19. Packaging sent written electronic communication to Chip Seller confirming and offering to sell Chip Seller Goods at the agreed upon price. The agreed upon price was the result of numerous telephone calls, written and verbal communication between Packaging and Chip Seller, negotiating the agreement. In response to Packaging's offer, Chip Seller responded with written electronic communication accepting Packaging's offer, followed by a purchase order to buy Goods at the agreed upon price, thereby forming a valid, enforceable, and binding contract under the Ohio Rev. Code. The binding contract included the price term of 09.50 *cents* for the 5 x 7 packages and 06.73 *cents* for the 3.5 x 6 packages, as exemplified in Exhibit—A. As a result, the documents and dealings between Packaging and -Chip Seller establish an agreement between the Parties.

4.   CHIP SELLER DID NOT AGREE TO A MODIFICATION AND THUS, THE NEW PRICE PROPOSAL SHALL NOT BE PART OF THE CONTRACT

"A contract cannot be unilaterally modified. In order to modify a contract, the parties to that contract must mutually consent to the modification." *Nagle*, 66 Ohio App. 3d, at 550. As previously established, Chip Seller accepted Packaging's offer to sell Goods at the agreed upon price. Chip Seller's purchase orders to Packaging buying the Goods only reference the agreed upon price as set forth in Packaging's offer, as exemplified in Exhibit—A. After Packaging provided a proposed new price term, Chip Seller did not agree to the new proposed price term. There is nothing in the record to support a finding that Chip Seller consented to any additional or different terms as to the proposed price and

Packaging cannot unilaterally modify the contract without the consent and agreement of Chip Seller.

In *Nagle*, the plaintiff alleged that an additional term to the original contract was added at a subsequent date. *Id.* However, the court examined the record, and found that the defendant had never consented to the addition of a term, and thus determined that there was no modification to the contract. Similarly, the record is devoid of Chip Seller discussing, negotiating or consenting to any additional price term offered by Packaging.

B.   UNDER UCC § 2-207, THE ADDITIONAL PRICE TERMS CANNOT BE-
     COME PART OF THE CONTRACT BECAUSE IT MATERIALLY ALTERS
     THE AGREEMENT

   1.   THE PARTIES ARE MERCHANTS UNDER UCC § 2-104(1) AND
        THUS, THE PROVISIONS OF UCC § 2-207(B) APPLY

Under the Uniform Commercial Code ("UCC"), Chip Seller and Packaging are merchants. Pursuant to UCC § 2-104(1), a merchant is "a person who deals in goods of the kind or otherwise by his occupation holds himself out as having knowledge or skill peculiar to the practices or goods involved in the transaction or to whom such knowledge or skill may be attributed by his employment of an agent or broker or other intermediary who by his occupation holds himself out as having such knowledge or skill." *UCC 2-104,(1); see also, Ohio Rev. Code § 1302.01(5).* Packaging deals with carded packaging and Chip Seller deals with memory modules and are both therefore merchants under the UCC with respect to the issues at bar.

   2.   THE SUBSEQUENT PRICE DID NOT BECAME PART OF THE
        PARTIES' CONTRACT BECAUSE THE ADDITIONAL TERM MA-
        TERIALLY ALTERS THE PARTIES' AGREEMENT

Under UCC § 2-207, "a proposed deal which in commercial understanding has in fact been closed is recognized as a contract. Therefore, any additional matter contained either in the writing intended to close the deal or in a latter confirmation falls within subsection (2) and must be regarded as a proposal for an added term." *UCC 2-207 cmt. 2; see also Ohio Rev. Code § 1302.10 cmt. 2.* The parties had reached an agreement and a legally binding contract was formed in December 2008, when Chip Seller replied to Packaging's offer accepting it and prepared its internal purchase order forms. Thus, the written confirmations to Chip Seller's purchase orders sent by Packaging denoting a proposed new price term, constituted written confirmations stating an additional proposed term, and an analysis would then proceed under UCC § 2-207(2). *See UCC § 2-207(2). See UCC § 2-207; Ohio Rev. Code § 1302.10.*

Where acceptance of an offer or written confirmation of an agreement is sent with additional or different terms, "[t]he additional terms are to be construed as proposals for addition to the contract." *UCC § 2-207(2); Ohio Rev. Code § 1302.10(B).* As merchants, the proposed additional terms in Packaging's written confirmation (including the new price term) became part of the parties' contract *unless* it can be demonstrated that (1) the offer expressly limited acceptance to its terms; (2) the new price term materially altered the parties' agreement; or (3) notification of objection to the new price term has already been given or is given within a reasonable time after notice of them is received. *See UCC § 2-207(2); Ohio Rev. Code § 1302.10(B). See* Dorton v. Collins & Aikman Corporation, *453 F. 2d 1161, 1169 (6th Cir. 1972).*

The new price term contained in Packaging's written confirmation materially altered the Parties agreement with respect to price, as exemplified in Exhibit—A. A material alteration is one that would "result in surprise or hardship if incorporated without express awareness by the other party." *UCC § 2-207 cmt. 4; Ohio Rev. Code § 1302.10 cmt. 4.*

"Surprise includes both a subjective element of what a party actually knew and an objective element of what a party should have known" and, the non-assenting "party must establish that, under the circumstances, it cannot be presumed that a reasonable merchant would have consented to the additional term." Aeros Prefabricados, S.A. v. TradeArbed, Inc., *282 F.3d 92, 100 (2nd Cir. 2002).* Packaging represented that the price for the Goods would be 09.50 cents for the 5 x 7 size and 06.73 cents for the 3.5 x 6 size. A reasonable merchant would not have consented to the substantial price increase, and Chip Seller never assented to the additional term of the price increase in light of the subsequent agreements entered into with third parties on reliance on Packaging's original price term. Thus, an incorporation of the new price term would result in surprise if incorporated without express awareness and consent by Chip Seller.

Further, the proposed new price term would materially alter the contract because it would result in hardship if incorporated without express awareness and consent by the other party. Chip Seller and Packaging agreed to the specified price for the Goods, as exemplified in Exhibit A. Chip Seller relied on the agreed upon price from Packaging and proceeded to enter into contracts with other corporations on reliance of the price Packaging offered and Chip Seller accepted. If the new price term were to be an addition to the contract, it would result in substantial financial hardship because Chip Seller relied on the initial price term and subsequently entered into multiple contracts on reliance of the price term. An incorporation of the new price term would result in substantial financial loss, which would have been due to a unilateral change in the contract of the new price term, which Chip Seller did not consent to.

Therefore, it can be construed that the new price term would be a material alteration pursuant to UCC § 2-207. *See UCC § 2-207 cmt. 3; Ohio Rev. Code § 1302.10 cmt. 3* ("*If [additional or different terms] are such as materially to alter the original bargain, they will not be included unless expressly agreed to by the other party.*" Inclusion of the substantial price increase into the contract would be both a surprise and a substantial hardship to Chip Seller in light of the undisputed facts and thus, is a material alteration which will **not** be included unless expressly agreed to by Chip Seller.

Chip Seller never agreed to any new price term, and thus, the proposed material alteration cannot be considered a part of the agreement.

V. CONCLUSION

Packaging and Chip Seller entered into a legally binding contract in December 2008 when Chip Seller unequivocally stated its acceptance of Packaging's offer in subsequent written electronic communications, followed by purchase orders to Packaging regarding the Goods. Packaging's offer via electronic mail and Chip Seller's acceptance via response and purchase order contained the same specified price, as exemplified in Exhibit—A. The price was negotiated for about two months verbally and in writing by the Parties prior to Packaging's offer and subsequently Chip Seller's acceptance. The price was further checked and re-checked by the Parties. The contract between Packaging and Chip Seller therefore included the price term exemplified in Exhibit—A.

Chip Seller *never* agreed to the additional term of a new price, by which Packaging attempted to modify the contract. Further, the additional price term would result in a material alteration of the contract, which also denies the inclusion of Packaging's new price term. In the absence of any dispute about the fact that the Parties entered into a legally binding contract and Chip Seller never agreed to pay the higher price, Chip Seller is entitled to judgment as a matter of law on Packaging's causes of action.

Respectfully submitted,

Dated: February 3, 2011

/s/_____

Attorneys for Chip Seller Corporation

CERTIFICATE OF SERVICE (intentionally omitted)

IN THE UNITED STATES DISTRICT COURT FOR
THE SOUTHERN DISTRICT OF OHIO

Packaging Corporation	)	CASE NO.: 11-UCC-12345
	)	
	)	The Honorable Judge Merry Wisdom,
	)	presiding
	)	
	)	
Plaintiff,	)	DECLARATION OF Judith
vs.	)	LaRue IN SUPPORT
	)	OF DEFENDANT Chip Seller's
Chip SellerCorporation	)	MOTION FOR
	)	SUMMARY JUDGMENT
	)	
	)	Filing Date: May 14
	)	Trial Date: June 6
	)	
Defendant.	)	
	)	
	)	
	)	

DECLARATION OF JUDITH LARUE

I, JUDITH LARUE, do hereby declare as follows:

1.   I am the Manager of Purchasing and Planning for Chip Seller Corporation ("Chip Seller"), the defendant in this action, and I have personal knowledge of each fact stated in this declaration, and can testify to them if called upon to do so.

2.   As Manager of Purchasing and Planning, I am very familiar with Chip Seller's purchasing procedures and I am in charge of placing written purchase orders with suppliers. I determine the quantity, pricing and delivery contained in purchase orders. I also negotiate with suppliers regarding pricing.

3.   Chip Seller is a distributor of flash memory products.

4.   In October of 2008, I began to seek out a supplier for a certain type of new packaging needed by Chip Seller for some of its products.

5.   The new packaging was more eco-friendly than Chip Seller's former packaging.

6.   The new packaging consisted of two printed cards and a clear plastic "bubble." The "bubble" and the two printed cards are collectively referred to as a "package."

7.   In the final assembly (to occur at Chip Seller's facility in Long Beach, California), Chip Seller's product would be placed into the "bubble" and then sealed between the two printed cards using specialty equipment acquired by Chip Seller.

8.   Packaging Corporation ("Packaging"), among other suppliers, responded to my initial inquiries.

9.   In November and December of 2008, I had several communications with Bob Dolan, Packaging's National Account Manager and Tori Venture, Packaging's sales agent. We discussed product pricing based on Chip Seller's 2009 minimum forecasted requirements of six to ten million packages.

10.   Initially, Packaging's pricing was higher than what Chip Seller was willing to entertain.

11.   After further discussions, Chip Seller agreed to a lower price. On December 5, 2008, Mr. Dolan sent me an email which "confirmed" Packaging's lower pricing.

12.   Mr. Dolan's December 5, 2008 email confirmed the cost per package at 06.73 *cents* for the small size packaging, and 09.50 *cents* for the larger size packaging.

13.   Shortly after receiving his email, and after meeting with my supervisors at Chip Seller, I informed Packaging that Chip Seller accepted Packaging's proposal at the prices confirmed in Mr. Dolan's December 5, 2008 email.

14.   Packaging activated Chip Seller's account and on December 10, 2008, I received an email from Jill Desert, Packaging's "Customer Service Manager." Ms. Desert provided me with a "user name" and "password" for Chip Seller to use to access Packaging's system.

15.   On December 12, 2008, I sent Mr. Dolan an email regarding the projected timeline I was working on for the "new packaging roll out".

16.   Over the course of the next several weeks, Chip Seller and Packaging attended to details identified in my "roll out" email of December 12, 2008.

17.   On February 12, 2009 I placed Chip Seller's initial written Purchase Order for certain quantities of product predicated on the agreed prices in Mr. Dolan's December

5, 2008 email. Chip Seller's written Purchase Orders contained a description of the products ordered, the quantity ordered, the price and a specific delivery date.

18.   Thereafter, I continued to place additional written Purchase Orders to Packaging for additional quantities of the product predicated on the agreed price in Mr. Dolan's December 5, 2008 email.

19.   After I placed the initial written Purchase Order, I was informed by Chip Seller's General Manager, Mike Holder, that Mr. Dolan had informed him that Mr. Dolan had made a mistake in the agreed upon pricing. Mr. Holder told me that Mr. Dolan admitted that he had made a mistake and that the prices should have been higher.

20.   Mr. Holder further informed me that he had told Mr. Dolan that Chip Seller expected Packaging to honor the prices the parties previously agreed upon.

21.   Subsequent to the initial written Purchase Order, and after placing each additional Purchase Order, I received an "Order Confirmation" document from Packaging. In Packaging's written "Order Confirmation," Packaging had inserted higher prices than the prices which had been agreed upon.

22.   Packaging's written Order Confirmations had a signature line for me to sign to "acknowledge" Packaging's higher price. I *never* signed any of these "Order Confirmation" documents as I *never* agreed to any price change from the prices which had been agreed upon and confirmed in Mr. Dolan's email of December 5, 2008.

23.   Packaging shipped the product which Chip Seller had ordered.

24.   In late February 2009, Chip Seller's accounting department informed me that Chip Seller had received invoices from Packaging. Packaging's invoices were *not* at the prices that Packaging and Chip Seller agreed upon.

25.   After discussions with Mr. Holder and Chip Seller's Chief Financial Officer, I was instructed to check Packaging's invoices as to quantities received and to make hand written notations note on Packaging's invoices with the correct pricing.

26.   I reviewed Packaging's invoices and made correction notations on the invoicing as to the pricing errors so that the agreed upon pricing would be put into Chip Seller's accounting system so that payment would be made to Packaging predicated on the correct pricing.

I declare under penalty of perjury under the laws of the State of California that the foregoing is true and correct. Executed on February 2, 2011 at Long Beach, California.

Judith LaRue

Judith LaRue

CERTIFICATE OF SERVICE intentionally omitted)

IN THE UNITED STATES DISTRICT COURT FOR
THE SOUTHERN DISTRICT OF OHIO

PACKAGING CORPORATION	)	CASE NO.: 11-UCC-12345
	)	
	)	The Honorable Judge Merry Wisdom,
	)	presiding
	)	
	)	
Plaintiff,	)	DECLARATION OF MICHAEL
vs.	)	HOLDER IN SUPPORT
	)	OF DEFENDANT CHIP SELLER
Chip Seller Corporation	)	CORPORATION'S MOTION FOR
	)	SUMMARY JUDGMENT
	)	
,	)	Filing Date: May 14
	)	Trial Date: June 6
	)	
Defendant.	)	
	)	
	)	
	)	

DECLARATION OF MICHAEL HOLDER

I, Michael Holder, do hereby declare as follows:

1.   I am the General Manager of Chip Seller Corp. USA ("Chip Seller"), the defendant in this action, and I have personal knowledge of each fact stated in this declaration, and can testify to them if called upon to do so.

2.   On or about February 13, 2009 I received a telephone call from Bob Dolan of Packaging Corporation.

3.   Mr. Dolan explained that he had recently realized that he had made a mistake in his pricing. He indicated that the error was entirely his mistake and he claimed he was in trouble with his higher management on account of his error. He said he wanted me to agree to higher prices for the particular product.

4.   After hearing him out, I told Mr. Dolan that Chip Seller had made commitments based on the agreed pricing that Mr. Dolan had confirmed in his email of December 5, 2008 and that Chip Seller expected Packaging to honor the pricing commitments that he had made on Packaging's behalf.

5.   I told Ms. LaRue about my conversation with Mr. Dolan.

6.   Later, I learned that in response to receipt of Chip Seller's Purchase Orders, Packaging had sent written "Order Confirmation" documents to Ms. LaRue seeking to obtain Ms. LaRue's signature for higher prices than had been agreed upon.

7.   I instructed Ms. LaRue _not_ to sign any "Order Confirmation" documents that contained prices higher than what had been agreed upon.

8.   Later, I was informed by Ms. LaRue that Packaging was sending invoices to Chip Seller with incorrect prices on the invoices; prices that were higher than had been agreed upon.

9.   I instructed Ms. LaRue to check the quantities received for the product in question and to approve payment for product received, but _only_ at the agreed upon price based on Mr. Dolan's email of December 6, 2008.

I declare under penalty of perjury under the laws of the State of California that the foregoing is true and correct. Executed on February 2, 2011 at Long Beach, California.

Michael Holder

Michael Holder

CERTIFICATE OF SERVICE (intentionally omitted)

Index

Note: *f* denotes figures; *n*, notes.